Second Edition

THE CHALLENGE OF THIRD WORLD DEVELOPMENT

Howard Handelman
University of Wisconsin-Milwaukee

Prentice Hall, Upper Saddle River, New Jersey 07458

Library of Congress Cataloging-in-Publication Data
HANDELMAN, HOWARD [date]
    The challenge of third world development / Howard
Handelman. — 2nd ed.
    p. cm.
    Includes bibliographical references and index.
    ISBN 0-13-083757-1
    1. Developing countries—Economic conditions.   2. Developing
countries—Economic policy.   3. Developing countries—Politics and
government.   4. Economic development.   I. Title.
    HC59.7 .H299 2000
    338.9'009172'4—dc21   99-31566

Editorial director: *Charlyce Jones Owen*
Editor in chief: *Nancy Roberts*
Senior acquisitions editor: *Beth Gillett Mejia*
Editorial/production supervision: *Joanne Riker*
Buyer: *Benjamin D. Smith*
Cover director: *Jayne Conte*
Marketing manager: *Christopher DeJohn*
Editorial assistant: *Brian Prybella*

This book was set in 10/12 Palatino by East End Publishing Services, Inc.,
and was printed and bound by Courier Companies, Inc. The cover was
printed by Phoenix Color Corp.

Printed in the United States of America

10   9   8   7   6   5   4

ISBN   0-13-083757-1

Prentice-Hall International (UK) Limited, *London*
Prentice-Hall of Australia Pty. Limited, *Sydney*
Prentice-Hall Canada Inc., *Toronto*
Prentice-Hall Hispanoamericana, S.A., *Mexico*
Prentice-Hall of India Private Limited, *New Delhi*
Prentice-Hall of Japan, Inc., *Tokyo*
Pearson Education Asia Pte. Ltd., *Singapore*
Editora Prentice-Hall do Brasil, Ltda., *Rio de Janeiro*

To Michael

CONTENTS

PREFACE

Since the end of the Cold War, Americans have increasingly focused their attentions on the nations of Africa, Asia, Latin America, and the Middle East. North-South tensions have seemingly replaced East-West conflict as the flash point of international relations. Iraq, Rwanda, the Palestinian West Bank, Indonesia, and Mexico now occupy prominent positions on the evening news previously reserved for countries such as the USSR, Japan, and Britain. Yet despite their increased importance, phenomena such as Islamic fundamentalism, ethnic warfare, and democratic transitions in less developed countries remain shrouded in mystery for most Americans.

For want of a better term, this book refers to the more than 140 disparate, developing nations as the Third World. They include desperately poor countries, such as Afghanistan and Ethiopia, and rapidly developing industrial powers such as South Korea and Taiwan. Some, such as Trinidad and Costa Rica, are stable democracies, while others, such as Myanmar and Syria, suffer under highly repressive dictatorships. All of them, however, share at least some of the aspects of political, economic, and social underdevelopment that are analyzed in this book.

No text is capable of examining fully the political and economic systems of so many highly diverse countries. Instead, we will look for common problems and issues, first exploring the nature of political and economic underdevelopment and then probing the dominant explanatory theories. The chapters on "religion and politics," "cultural pluralism and ethnic conflict," and "women and development" analyze broad social forces and gender issues that have often divided developing nations. The chapters on "rural change" and "urbanization" discuss the specific issues and challenges that many countries face in those regions. The next chapters on "revolutionary change" and "the military in politics" consider the value of these respective regime types as alternative models of political and economic development. The chapter dealing with "Third World political economies" compares alternative paths of industrial development and evaluates the relative effectiveness of each. Finally, the concluding chapter examines the recent wave of democratic change that has swept over the Third World and considers its ramifications.

It is easy to despair when considering the tremendous obstacles facing most Third World nations and the failures of political leadership that many of them have endured. Unfortunately, many people in the First World have suffered from compassion fatigue or have become cynical about cooperative efforts with the world's developing countries. Yet the recent trend toward democratization in the developing world (most notably in Latin America), the increased stability that has come to southern Africa, and the enormous economic growth that has taken place in parts of East and Southeast Asia, all provide new bases for hope. It is incumbent upon America's next generation of citizens and leaders to renew its efforts to understand the challenge of Third World development.

THE SECOND EDITION

Nearly four years have passed since the publication of the first edition of this book. During that time the most important political development in the Third World has been the region's continued transition toward (or, often, consolidation of) democratic government. This second edition features a new chapter analyzing the growth of democracy in the developing world. In addition, the new edition is updated throughout and particularly examines important developments in recent years, such as the consolidation of majority rule in South Africa, ethnic conflict in Rwanda and the Congo, and the emergence, respectively, of Hindu and Islamic fundamentalist governments in India and Turkey. New sections have also been added analyzing Third World environmental challenges as well as the recent economic crisis in East and Southeast Asia.

ACKNOWLEDGMENTS

Because of the broad geographic and conceptual scope of a book on Third World politics, I am particularly indebted to others for their kind help and advice.

First, I would like to thank St. Martin's Press for granting me permission to reproduce a portion of Chapter 1 which is incorporated from *Politics in a Changing World* by Marcus Ethridge and Howard Handelman (Copyright 1993 St. Martin's Press). Thanks also to Karen S. Horton, a past Political Science Senior Editor at Prentice Hall, who initiated the idea of doing this book and was kind enough to ask me to write it. Beth Gillett Mejia, the current Political Science Editor at Prentice Hall, as always, has been very supportive and helpful.

Much of the research and writing of the first edition took place during a sabbatical from the University of Wisconsin–Milwaukee. I am grateful to my own university for granting me that sabbatical support and to the University of Wisconsin-Madison, whose outstanding libraries, lectures, and other scholarly activities informed me during a wonderful year there. Thanks also to the University of Wisconsin's many helpful librarians, including Beverly Phillips of the Land Tenure Center Library.

Finally, my greatest debt is to the scholars who generously agreed to read portions of the manuscript. Reviewers of the first edition include: Lourdes Benería (Cornell University), Josef Gugler (University of Connecticut), Stephan Haggard (University of Californian-San Diego), Kathleen Staudt (University of Texas-El Paso), Mark Tessler (University of Wisconsin-Milwaukee and currently, the University of Arizona), William Thiesenhusen (University of Wisconsin-Madison), and M. Crawford Young (University of Wisconsin-Madison). Thanks also to Prentice Hall's readers: Jennie Purnell (Boston College) and Rudra Sil (University of Pennsylvania) who were helpful in reviewing the second edition. The quality of the book benefits greatly from all the reviewers' many insights, suggestions, and corrections. The usual caveat, of course, applies: any remaining errors of fact or interpretation, particularly the revisions for the second edition, are my own responsibility.

Howard Handelman
University of Wisconsin–Milwaukee

1

∞

UNDERSTANDING
UNDERDEVELOPMENT

From the perspective of both experts and casual observers, the problems plaguing Africa, Asia, Latin America, the Caribbean, and the Middle East appear exceedingly daunting. These regions are frequently beset by conflict, turmoil, and suffering: civil war in Liberia, poverty and revolutionary conflict in Colombia, ethnic violence in Rwanda, civil war and starvation in Sudan, and political repression in Myanmar. Of course, some of those problems exist in industrialized democracies as well, if only in more modest proportions. For example, during the 1980s and 1990s Northern Ireland, the Basque regions of Spain, and Quebec have experienced varying degrees of ethnic conflict. Portions of Washington, DC, have higher infant mortality rates than Cuba or Malaysia. But it is the scope and persistence of the developing world's economic, social, and political quandaries that ultimately draw our attention.

Understanding the nature and causes of underdevelopment is a complex task complicated by theoretical debates among scholars and a profusion of terminology. There is not even agreement on a collective name for the approximately 140 countries that constitute the developing world. At one time it was common to speak of underdeveloped nations. But some found this title objectionable, suggesting as it did that those countries' political and economic systems were backward. Because of its pejorative connotations and implied inferiority, "underdeveloped" fell into disfavor. Developing nations (or areas) has often been employed in its place. Clearly more positive, this term unfortunately suffers from a different problem, excessive optimism. At various times during the 1970s and 1980s, most African and Latin American countries suffered political and economic decay. Today, the previously thriving economies of East Asia are plummeting. Thus for extended time periods, many of these countries have shown little sign of economic or political development. To escape this problem, the United Nations and many other international organizations favor the expression "Less Developed Countries" (or LDCs), an expression that escapes the normative flaws of its competitors.

The title "Third World" countries (or simply the Third World) is preferred by many social scientists; it is the phrase most frequently employed in this book.[1] This term has both the virtue and flaw of being a bit fuzzy. Simply put, Third World countries are the nations of Africa, Asia, the Middle East, Latin America, and the Caribbean that belong neither to the First World (Japan and the Western industrialized democracies—the first countries to develop advanced industrial economies and pluralist democracies)[2] nor to the Second World (the bloc of former Communist nations that included the Soviet Union and Eastern Europe).

Thus, in large part "Third World" is a residual category. Countries fall under its banner not because of any specific quality, but simply because they are neither economically developed democracies nor former members of the Soviet bloc.[3] Like all the aforementioned terms, Third World glosses over the many political and socioeconomic differences between developing nations, throwing all of them into one big box. In fact, a few Third World countries (including Singapore, Taiwan and Kuwait)[4] are relatively affluent, while many others (such as Afghanistan, Ethiopia and Mali) are desperately poor. Some (Barbados, Costa Rica and India, for example) are fairly stable democracies. Many of the others, however, suffer either from severe political instability, government repression, or a mixture of both.

Therefore, as with any residual category, "Third World" suffers from a certain imprecision. Its virtue, however, is that unlike "underdeveloped nations" or "developing nations," it makes no value judgment or predictions. As one author writes, paraphrasing Winston Churchill's comments on democracy, "it is the worst term we have, except for all the others."[5] With more than a trace of British irony, Christopher Clapham has written, "I have chosen to use the term [Third World] . . . because of its meaninglessness. Its alternatives all carry conceptual overtones which are even more misleading, in that they imply positive elements of commonality rather than a simply negative residual category."[6] Such irony notwithstanding, I will suggest in the section that follows that there are enough commonalities between Third World countries to make the category useful and usable. Although some scholars challenge the term's value, and even though the demise of the Second World (the Soviet bloc) has made the category Third World somewhat anachronistic, the term continues to play a useful role.

In this book I often alternate the terms Less Developed Countries (or LDCs) and developing countries (developing world) with Third World, mainly for the purpose of avoiding repetition. But all of these labels will be employed without the normative baggage that Clapham objects to and should be understood by the reader as equivalent.

THIRD WORLD COMMONALITIES:
THE NATURE OF UNDERDEVELOPMENT

Despite the substantial diversity among Third World nations, most share a set of common characteristics. All of them suffer from some aspects of economic, social, and political underdevelopment. Although the economies of Kuwait, Saudi Arabia ,and some of East Asia's Newly Industrializing Countries (NICs)—South Korea, Singapore, Taiwan— are no longer underdeveloped, they share a high vulnerability to global economic forces (as evidenced by East Asia's current slide) and, to varying degrees, problems of political underdevelopment. Indeed, many countries are far more developed in some measures of development than in others. As we will see, economic, social, and political underdevelopment are closely related, but they are by no means perfectly correlated.

Economic Underdevelopment

Perhaps the most salient characteristic of many Third World countries is their poverty. This is manifested at the national level by low per capita gross domestic product (GDP),[7] unequal income distribution, poor infrastructure (including communications and transportation), limited use of modern technology, and low consumption of fossil fuels and nuclear energy. At the household level, economic underdevelopment expresses itself in widespread poverty, including substandard housing and substantial malnutrition.

Poverty can be measured by two interrelated economic phenomena: a low level of national production (per capita GDP) and an inequitable distribution of national income. In other words, less developed countries not only produce less wealth and income, but frequently what they have is poorly distributed.

Table 1.1 presents basic economic data for the United States (included for comparative purposes), two relatively affluent developing countries (Kuwait and South Korea), two "middle-income" countries (Mexico and Brazil), and three low-income countries (China, Egypt and Cameroon).[8] The first column, real GDP per capita as measured by purchasing power (called PPP or Parity Purchasing Power), is a comparatively new statistic used by international agencies to more accurately compare national production.[9] The data illustrate the tremendous variation in the productive resources of Third World nations. Though Mexico and South Korea produce only about 30 to 45 percent, respectively, of the United States' per capita GDP, they are more than 3 to 4 times as affluent as Cameroon and roughly 15 to 20 times wealthier than Ethiopia or Rwanda (not shown in the table). Average real GDP per capita for the entire developing world was $2,904 in the late 1990s, but there is enormous variation among the LDCs (even more than Table 1.1 reveals). Hong Kong and a few very small countries (including Singapore, and Kuwait) are at the top of this scale with per capita GDPs of over $22,000 (about the same as Japan and Norway). At the bottom we find a substantial number of African nations, including

Table 1.1 Measures of Economic Development

			Income Distribution	
Country	GDP/capita (PPP estimates)	Annual GNP Growth (1985–1995)	Poorest 40%	Richest 20%
United States	$28,740	1.3%	15.7	41.9
Kuwait	23,790	1.1	NA	NA
South Korea	13,500	7.7	NA	NA
Mexico	8,120	0.1	11.9[a]	60.1[a]
Brazil	6,240	-0.8	15.3	64.2
China	3,570	6.0	15.3	47.5
Egypt	2,940	1.1	21.2	41.1
Cameroon	1,980	-6.6	NA	NA

[a]While all the other income distribution data are drawn from the World Bank's 1998/99 report, Mexico's comes from the 1997 report since the Bank's more recent data are dramatically out of line with virtually all other available data (including prior World Bank data).

NA: Data Not Available

Sources: World Bank, *World Development Report, 1998/99* (New York: Oxford University Press, 1998), pp. 190–191, 198–199; *World Development Report, 1997* (New York: Oxford University Press, 1997), pp. 214–215, 222–223.

Ethiopia ($450), Sierra Leon ($580), and Mali ($550), with GDPs as little as fifty times smaller.[10]

As the second column of Table 1.1 indicates, some economies also have been growing rapidly (at least until 1997), while other LDCs have been losing ground. In East Asia, countries such as South Korea, China, Singapore, Taiwan, Thailand, Indonesia, and Malaysia (as well as Hong Kong) grew at spectacular rates from the 1970s into the mid 1990s, but most have suffered severe economic setbacks since that time (not shown in the table) due to overextended foreign borrowing. Latin America, which grew steadily, though far more modestly, in the 1960s and 1970s, experienced a sharp downturn in the 1980s from which it only began to emerge in the early 1990s (a recovery now threatened by the spreading effects of East Asia's and Russia's financial crises).[11] Although it also grew in the 1960s and 1970s, Africa began at a much lower level of economic development. Furthermore, most countries in the region have yet to rebound from their disastrous decline in the 1980s. Some such as Cameroon (Table 1.1) continued their downward spiral through the mid-1990s.

Overall, East Asia has emerged as the Third World's most economically advanced region and generally retains that position in spite of the financial crisis of the late 1990s. (Indonesia, whose corrupted economy is on the brink of collapse, is a notable exception.) Conversely, South and Southeast Asia encompass some of the world's poorest countries (including Cambodia, Laos, Afghanistan, India, and Bangladesh), though some (such as India and Vietnam) have shown signs of strengthening. Most Latin American nations fall in the United Nations' middle-income category, though there is a wide gap between the region's poorer nations, including Bolivia and Honduras, and more developed ones, such as

Chile or Mexico. Finally, sub-Saharan Africa includes most of the poorest countries in the world (with Ethiopia, Rwanda, Mali, Sierra Leon, and Burundi constituting the poorest of the poor.)

Ultimately, individual standards of living are determined not only by per capita production and income (as measured by GDP), but also by how that income is distributed. Columns 3 and 4 together (Table 1.1) indicate how equitably or how poorly income is distributed in these counties. Column 3 reveals the percentage of a country's annual national income that is earned by the poorest 40 percent of the population, while column 4 indicates the income share going to the wealthiest 20 percent. Although the World Bank does not offer data on South Korea's income distribution, other research demonstrates that it is quite equitable (with a relatively high proportion of national income going to the poorest 40 percent of the population.[12] By contrast, in Brazil, the richest 20 percent of the population earns an extraordinary 64.2 percent of the national income—the highest proportion in the world. Similarly, the wealthiest segments of the population in Mexico as well as Kenya and South Africa (not shown in Table 1.1) also receive over 60 percent of their nation's income. On the other hand, Egypt, China and South Korea, as well as Taiwan, Rwanda, Vietnam, and India, (not shown in Table 1.1) have income distributions comparable to those of most industrialized democracies.

In short, while many Third World countries suffer from wide gaps between rich and poor, some do not. The figures (in Table 1.1) for Brazil and Mexico are relatively representative of Latin America as a whole, a region with the world's widest income gaps between rich and poor. On the other hand, income (and land ownership) tends to be far more equitably distributed in Asia. Data on Africa are spottier but suggest a very mixed pattern. On average, income distribution in that region is probably better than in Latin America, but worse than in Asia.

Social Underdevelopment

Poverty and poor public policy adversely affect many social conditions in the Third World, thereby narrowing opportunities for human development. Limited education and resultant low literacy rates are among the Third World's greatest challenges. For a long time scholars have agreed that the spread of education furthers economic development. An educated work force —from peasants who can read the instructions on insecticide containers to doctors and construction engineers—contributes to higher labor productivity. Improved education also leads to political development, though not in a linear fashion. For example, a major exploration of the factors contributing to democratic government worldwide, found literacy to be perhaps the most important.[13]

Table 1.2 presents data on several important social development indicators. For purposes of comparison, data are presented for two highly developed countries, France and the United States. Column 1 lists each nation's Human Development Index (HDI), a composite measurement of educational level, life

Table 1.2 Indicators of Social Development

Country	Human Development Index (HDI)	Life Expectancy (years)	Adult Literacy	Real Income Rank (PPP) HDI Rank
France	.946	78.7	99.0%	12
United States	.943	76.4	99.0	-1
South Korea	.894	71.7	98.0	6
Mexico	.855	72.0	89.6	5
Kuwait	.848	75.4	77.6	-49
Brazil	.809	66.4	83.3	1
China	.650	68.9	81.5	1
Egypt	.612	64.3	51.4	-20
Cameroon	.481	55.1	62.1	-13

Source: United Nations Development Programme (UNDP), *Human Development Report, 1998* (New York: Oxford University Press, 1998), pp. 128–130, 148.

expectancy, per capita real GDP, and income distribution. More so than per capita income or any other single indicator, it is considered to be an accurate measure of a nation's living standard. The highest possible HDI score a country may achieve is 1.000 and the lowest is .000. Table 1.2 indicates that some Third World nations, such as South Korea and Mexico, have relatively high indices (indeed, they are comparable to poorer European nations such as Greece and Poland). On the other hand, Cameroon and Egypt score much lower (.481 and .612). And at the bottom of the ladder, impoverished nations such as Rwanda and Afghanistan (not shown) have abysmally low scores (under .200).

Life expectancy (column 2) and adult literacy (column 3) are among the best individual (nonindex) measures of mass living standards. The first statistic is greatly influenced by the availability of health care, adequate calories, and clean drinking water, while the second indicates the accessibility of education. Unlike per capita income, statistical averages for life expectancy and education are not distorted by highly skewed distribution.[14] Note the substantial gap between, say, Kuwaiti or Mexican life expectancy and Cameroon's! Similarly, while adult literacy levels in Mexico and South Korea are close to those of the United States and France, Egypt lags far behind.

While economic development usually bring about improvement in social indicators, government social policy determines what share of the country's economic resources is invested in education, sanitation and health care— hence, how much translates into social development. Column 4 compares a country's income ranking with its rank for HDI. A high positive score, such as France's, indicates that the country's social indicators are higher than its per capita income would lead us to expect, presumably because of a strong government commitment to health, education, and economic equity. Conversely, a highly negative score such as Kuwait's, Egypt's, and Cameroon's indicates the government's failure to translate its available economic resources into improved living standards. While only one LDC in the table, South Korea, has a significant positive score, other developing countries not shown there, such as Vietnam (+26), Cuba (+17), and Grenada (+17), also scored very well in the recent past. Many of the poorest performers, including Kuwait (-49), and others not shown here such as Oman (-49) and Brunei (-36), are oil-rich nations which have failed to educate their female populations adequately due to religious or other cultural values (see Chapter 4).

Fortunately, despite substantial economic declines in Africa and Latin America during the 1980s and early 1990s, and despite East Asia's recent economic crisis, developing countries as a whole have made considerable progress in these areas during recent decades. From 1965 to 1995 alone, adult illiteracy in developing countries was cut in half. Improved health care and sanitation helped reduce infant mortality rates by a remarkable 60 percent. Together with other advances in public health care, these changes raised life expectancy from 53.4 years in 1960 to 64.7 years in 1990. And, the United Nations Development Program (UNDP) estimates that Third World poverty has fallen faster in the past 50 years than in the previous 500. In 1965 an estimated 2-3 billion people (mostly in the LDCs) lived in poverty. By the start of the twenty-first century that figure will have been reduced to 1-2 billion in the face of significant increases in total Third World population.[15] These figures indicated both how much progress has been made in several critical areas and how much remains to be done.

Tables 1.3 and 1.4 reveal the remarkable strides some LDCs have made in lowering child mortality (deaths of children prior to the age of five) and adult illiteracy. Some of those countries, Oman and Saudi Arabia especially, started the period covered with very high child mortality (280 and 185 per 1,000 live births, respectively) but have since lowered those rates by up to 90 percent. Similarly, Kenya and Jordan (both over 50 percent illiterate in 1970) have lowered adult literacy by an impressive 68 to 75 percent, respectively (Table 1.4). Cuba and South Korea, on the other hand, began the period with relatively low infant mortality and adult illiteracy levels, yet still managed to reduce those figures considerably. In all, illiteracy rates throughout the entire developing world fell from 57 to 30 percent in a span of only 25 years (1970–1995).

Table 1.3 Greatest Improvements in Lowering Infant Mortality (1970–1995)

Country	Child Mortality (per 1,000 live births)		% Reduction
	1970	1995	
Oman	280	25	90%
South Korea	71	9	87
Chile	105	15	87
Saudi Arabia	185	34	82
Cuba	54	10	81
Barbados	81	10	81
Singapore	30	6	80

Source: United Nation Development Programme (UNDP), *Human Development Report, 1997* (New York: Oxford University Press, 1997), p. 4.

Table 1.4 Greatest Improvements in Reducing Adult Illiteracy (1970–1995)

Country	Adult Illiteracy Rate		Percent Reduction
	1970 (percent)	1995 (percent)	
South Korea	12%	2%	83%
Lebanon	31	8	75
Jordan	53	13	75
Thailand	21	6	75
Philippines	17	5	68
Kenya	68	22	68
Cuba	13	4	67

Source: United Nations Development Programme (UNDP), *Human Development Report*, 1997 (New York: Oxford University Press, 1997), p. 4.

Still, as an aggregate, less developed countries continue to lag considerably behind the developed world. Third World adult literacy rates trail the industrialized nations by 33 percent, while life expectancy and calorie consumption are both 20 percent below first world levels. Some 1.3 billion people (about one-third of the developing world's population) live on incomes of under $1 per day, and 800 million of them do not get a sufficient amount to eat. While impressive progress has been made in some regions, others continue to lag, most notably sub-Saharan Africa and South Asia. Furthermore, great gaps persist between urban centers (where, for example, 72 percent of the population has access to proper home sanitation) and rural areas (where that figure falls to 20 percent.)[16] And, despite overall gains in the LDCs, the absolute gap between the First and Third Worlds (and within the Third World itself) continues to widen.

Political Underdevelopment

Defining political development and underdevelopment is far more problematic than specifying the parameters of social and economic underdevelopment. Ideological and cultural lenses divide political analysts sharply. Of course, Marxist and market-oriented economists disagree on the proper path to development, but they share a common commitment to the goals of GDP growth, increased literacy, and lower infant mortality. Marxist and liberal-democratic political scientists, however, differ sharply on such fundamental issues as the desirability of competitive elections, the role of opposition parties, and the limits of free speech.

When Western political scientists first began to study the Third World seriously, they soon recognized that evaluating political systems in very different cultural and socioeconomic settings was no easy task. While many modernization theorists (discussed later) felt that Western industrialized democracies should serve as models for Third World governments, they were also mindful of important differences between the two regions that limited that prescription. For example, aware that most Western European countries did not become fully democratic until they were well along the path to industrial development, political scientists were reluctant to criticize the authoritarian systems that prevailed in much of the developing world. African social scientists added to the debate by arguing that their continent had extensive, grass-roots village- and tribal-based democracies that made competitive elections at the national level unnecessary. Indeed, many of them warned that a multiparty system would inevitably develop along tribal or regional lines, contributing to national disintegration.

Heedful of such cultural and ideological land mines, some prominent political scientists despaired of even defining political underdevelopment or development in any meaningful way.[17] Others, however, offered a set of standards that they maintained were relatively free of ideological and cultural biases. Political development, they posited, involves the creation of specialized and differentiated government institutions that effectively carry out functions such as raising tax revenue, defending the national borders, maintaining political stability, stimulating economic development, improving the quality of human life, and communicating with the citizenry.

In addition, they argued, developed governments are responsive to a broad segment of society and respect the population's fundamental freedoms and civil rights. Presumably, governments satisfying the aforementioned standards would enjoy a reasonable level of legitimacy (i.e., citizens would recognize the regime's right to govern), leading the population to pursue their political objectives peacefully, through established political institutions rather than through violent or illegal channels.

But while early definitions of political development stipulated that governments should be responsive, representative, and nonrepressive, they generally did not insist that governments be democratic. Note that democracy encompasses the following basic components: honest and competitive elections in which opposition parties have a reasonable chance of winning; universal or nearly universal suffrage; widespread opportunities for political participation; a free and open mass media; and government respect for human rights, including minority rights.[18]

As we have noted, many political scientists initially felt that it was unrealistic (and perhaps culturally biased) to expect pluralist democracy to exist in Third World countries. Others were concerned about the high levels of violence and instability that characterized the LDCs' shaky political systems. Consequently, they argued, it was imperative to achieve political stability first, even if that required military rule or other forms of authoritarianism.[19]

More recently, however, troubled by extensive government repression in the developing world, political scientists have increasingly insisted that democracy and social equity must be integral parts of political development.[20] Beyond its obvious moral attraction, democracy also has pragmatic appeal. For example, governments that are held accountable to their citizens by means of competitive elections are more likely to be efficient and honest (though the sorry records of democracy in countries such as Brazil and the Philippines demonstrate that there are no guarantees). Similarly, a free and independent mass media helps keep governments accountable.

Events in Eastern Europe and the Third World since the early 1980s demonstrate that while authoritarian regimes may be stable in the short run, they are fragile in the long term. Thus, there is not necessarily the trade-off between democracy and political stability that many had imagined. Quite the contrary, democracies are relatively immune to revolutionary insurrection and are less prone than dictatorships to other forms of mass violence.

Only a relatively restricted (but growing) number of developing countries conform closely to the standards of political development, for example, Trinidad, the Bahamas, Uruguay, and Costa Rica (all small countries). Others, such as Chile, Argentina, Venezuela, India, South Korea and Taiwan—currently satisfy most of the criteria. Even a cursory review of Third World politics, however, soon reveals that most governments fall woefully short. Thus, for example, most Central American regimes respond disproportionately to the demands of the most affluent minority; the Middle East and North Africa are still ruled by a self-perpetuating and self-serving elites; while sub-Saharan African governments frequently serve the interests of dominant ethnic groups. Corruption, inefficiency, and repression are endemic to the politics of much of the developing world. In the fairly recent past, class-based revolutionary movements have erupted in various Asian and Latin American nations, while a number of African countries have been torn apart by ethnic civil wars. Thus, until recently few Third World governments were neither democratic, nor stable, nor legitimate. During the closing decades of the twentieth century, however, democracy (and with it goverment legitimacy) advanced in much of the developing world, most notably in Latin America and East Asia (see Chapter 10); but it is still uncertain how extensive or enduring this positive trend will be.[21]

Some Relationships among the Components of Development

It seems obvious that political, economic, and social underdevelopment are interrelated. More economically advanced countries can educate more of their population and provide better health care. An educated citizenry, in turn, contributes to economic growth and participates in politics more responsibly. Responsive and legitimate governments, constrained by competitive elections, are more likely to educate their people and to make responsible economic decisions. In fact, these logical intuitions are supported by empirical evidence. Wealthier LDCs tend to have greater life expectancy, higher literacy rates, and more stable and democratic governments.

But these correlations are not absolute. For example, a country's literacy and infant mortality rates depend not only on its economic resources, but also on government policies in the areas of education, public health, and welfare. Therefore, elitist government policies in some countries have contributed to social indicators (HDIs) that are far lower than those of other nations with comparable economic resources. This is most apparent in the petroleum-rich states (Kuwait, Oman, and Brunei) but is true in countries such as Namibia and Egypt as well.[22] On the other hand, governments such as China, Costa Rica, Cuba, Grenada, and Vietnam, with strong commitments to social welfare programs, have generated much higher life expectancy rates and educational levels than their economic resources alone would lead us to predict.

Political development also tends to correlate with economic and social development. Wealthier, more educated countries such as Barbados, Chile, Costa Rica, and Taiwan tend to be more stable, responsive, and democratic than desperately poor nations such as Mozambique, Haiti, and Cambodia. Indeed, Third World countries are very unlikely to become democracies unless they have attained a minimal threshold of socioeconomic development.[23] That does not imply, however, that wealthier countries are assured of becoming democratic. That economic threshold is a relatively necessary, but not sufficient, condition for democratization.

Moreover, there is no linear relationship between economic and political development. As countries become more economically developed, there is seldom a steady movement toward greater stability, democracy, or the other components of political development. In fact, Samuel Huntington observed that while it is true that the richest countries in the world (Switzerland, Japan, and other industrialized democracies) are politically very stable and the poorest countries (Afghanistan, Congo, and others) are very unstable, many countries in the process of moving from economic underdevelopment to development actually become more unstable as they pass through the intermediate stages of economic growth.[24]

Thus, for example, some of Latin America's most industrialized and economically advanced countries (Argentina, Brazil, Chile, and Uruguay) became politically unstable in the 1960s and 1970s and eventually fell to military dictatorships (though Mexico, Venezuela, and Colombia did not). Huntington posited that as countries modernize, the spread of education, urbanization, and mass media consumption produces an increasingly politically mobilized society whose citizens make far greater demands on the government. Unless political institutions, such as political parties, can be developed quickly enough to handle the rising tide of demands, the system will become overloaded and unstable.

Guillermo O'Donnell posited another reason for the rise of extremely repressive dictatorships in South America's most economically advanced and modernized nations during the 1960s and 1970s. He suggested that as those countries reached a more advanced stage of industrial growth, they required extensive new investment that could only be secured by attracting foreign capital. That, in turn, required controlling the countries' militant labor unions and keeping down the wage levels of industrial workers. To achieve those goals, the nations' business leaders and technocrats turned to repressive military rule.[25]

In a similar vein, many analysts have noted that the Asian countries that had been enjoying the most spectacular economic growth from the 1970s to the mid-1990s—Indonesia, Malaysia, Thailand, Singapore, Taiwan, and South Korea—were almost all authoritarian during their economic takeoff. Many concluded from this that an authoritarian government was necessary in the early to middle stages of industrialization in order to control labor and reduce popular consumption so as to encourage heavy investment of capital (see Chapter 9). While these theories remain subject to debate, they do demonstrate that the relationship between economic and political development is complex.

THE CAUSES OF UNDERDEVELOPMENT

Our initial discussion suggested that the very definitions of political and socioeconomic underdevelopment are subject to some debate. But social scientists disagree far more intensely when they turn their attention to the underlying *causes* of underdevelopment and the preferred paths to change. How, for example, do we account for patterns of military intervention in Pakistan, contemporary political turmoil in Kenya, or repression in Syria? Do all these problems begin with internal causes such as nondemocratic cultural values or weak political parties? Or do many of these political and economic problems arise from these nations' contacts with the West from the colonial era to the age of multinational corporations and the IMF?

An array of similar questions on the origins of underdevelopment and on the pathways to development elicit very different responses from social scientists. Frequently, their evaluations reflect their personal ideologies or cultural origins. Thus, for example, theories that attribute Third World political unrest or economic backwardness to traditional cultural and religious values have generally emanated from the United States. Conversely, approaches such as dependency and world systems theory, which see Western exploitation as the root cause of Third World underdevelopment, are particularly popular among Latin American and African scholars. Not surprisingly, Marxist analysts are drawn to different explanations than are liberals or conservatives.

For years, two competing paradigms have shaped scholarly analysis of Third World politics and economic change. The first, modernization theory, emerged in the early 1960s as American political science's mainstream interpretation of underdevelopment. The second, dependency theory, offered a more radical perspective on development, one more sensitive to the concerns of Third World scholars. In time it came to exert tremendous influence over political research on Latin America and other parts of the developing world.[26]

MODERNIZATION THEORY AND THE IMPORTANCE OF CULTURAL VALUES

During the 1950s and 1960s, as the demise of European colonialism produced a host of newly independent nations in Africa and Asia, Western social scientists began to study Third World politics and economics. From that interest came a complex model of underdevelopment and development known as moderniza-tion theory. Its proponents included some of the most prominent figures in com-parative politics: Gabriel Almond, James Coleman, Samuel Huntington, Lucian Pye, and David Apter.[27] For perhaps a decade, the theory reigned supreme in the study of the development process. Though sharply challenged subsequently, it has continued to influence our understanding of the Third World. While there has been substantial variation and some disagreement among modernization theorists, they generally share a number of underlying assumptions and per-spectives.

Despite the tremendous array of problems facing the LDCs, modernization theory was initially relatively optimistic about their prospects for development. After all, Western industrialized democracies had also started out as underde-veloped nations. Consequently, the theory argued, most Third World countries could, and should, follow a path to economic and political modernization par-allel to the one the First World had traveled. To accomplish this, developing nations had to acquire modern cultural values and create modern economic and political institutions.

Transforming traditional cultures (including political cultures) was often seen as the opening step in the modernization process. Drawing on the theories of eminent sociologists such as Max Weber and Talcott Parsons, these analysts made a distinction between traditional and modern values.[28] Modern men and women, it was argued, are more prone to judge others by universal standards (e.g., to vote for or hire people based on their ability rather than family or eth-nic ties); to believe in the possibility and desirability of change; to think about political and other issues beyond the scope of family, neighborhood, or village; to believe that one can and should try to influence the political system.[29]

How could a traditional society make the transition to modernity? Educa-tion, urbanization, and the spread of mass media were seen as key agents of change. As peasants move to cities, as more people send their children to schools (presumably teaching modern values), and as more citizens follow the mass media, cultural change can ensue. The theory focused on the diffusion of mod-ern ideas from the developed world to the developing world and, within the Third World, from city to countryside. Western foreign aid and institutions such as the Peace Corps could also help to speed this process.

Gabriel Almond and G. Bingham Powell saw modernization as a somewhat inexorable force. "The forces of technological change and cultural diffusion are dri-ving political systems in certain directions, which seem discernible and suscepti-ble to analysis in terms of increasing levels of development."[30] More importantly, modernization was envisioned, in part, as a process of getting developing nations to think and act "more like us" (i.e., the West). "As time goes on," Marion Levy predicted, "they and we will increasingly resemble one another.... [T]he more highly modernized societies become, the more they resemble one another."[31]

Along with modern values, LDCs would have to develop more specialized and complex political and economic institutions. For example, whereas tribal cultures might have a council of elders that carried out legislative, executive, and judicial activities, a modern society needs separate institutions with more specialized functions. Trained bureaucracies have to be created where advancement is determined by merit rather than connections and decisions are based on universally applied standards. Political parties have to channel popular demands and aspirations effectively to government policymakers.

In time, however, many of the early assumptions of modernization theory had to be modified. For one thing, it had been too optimistic and simplistic in its initial view of change. Its proponents expected modernizing countries simultaneously (and even smoothly) to achieve economic growth, greater equality, democracy, stability, and greater national autonomy. As Samuel Huntington has noted, the theory erroneously assumed that "all good things go together."[32]In fact, economic growth proved to be no guarantee of either political stability or democracy. In nations such as Brazil, Mexico, South Korea, and Taiwan, industrialization and economic development were first achieved under the direction of authoritarian governments. In nations such as Iran and Nigeria, rapid socioeconomic change undermined traditional institutions and values, leading to political upheaval.

Particularly disturbing was the realization that in many Third World countries the very process of social and economic modernization itself often ushered in political instability and violence, rather than political development.[33]In Latin America some of the region's most industrialized and well-educated nations (Argentina, Brazil, Chile, and Uruguay) experienced bitter class conflict followed by the imposition of repressive military dictatorships.[34]And in much of Africa and Asia, the hopes inspired by decolonization have succumbed to ethnic conflict, military coups, and political repression.

Clearly, the development process revealed itself to be more complex and unpredictable than originally imagined. The initial optimism of modernization theorists gave way to conflict theories. Developing rations, they argued, would have to make hard choices between seemingly irreconcilable development goals. Concerned about the growing political turmoil in many developing nations, Huntington insisted on the paramount importance of political stability, even if attaining it might temporarily necessitate authoritarian rule. That is to say, democracy might have to take a back seat to stability, at least temporarily. At the same time, many economists and political scientists argued that early economic growth requires the concentration of wealth in the hands of the few so that incipient capitalists may acquire sufficient capital for investment.

Additional case studies, particularly from Latin American and East Asia, have once again produced a new perspective. While certainly less naively optimistic than the earliest modernization theories, current analysis is also less pessimistic than conflict theory. The **reconciliation approach**, currently adopted by many modernization theorists, suggests that under the right circumstances developing nations can simultaneously achieve certain goals previously thought to be incompatible.[35]Taiwan and South Korea, for example, have shown that it is possible to achieve rapid economic development with a highly equitable distribution of income. Trinidad-Tobago and Costa Rica have managed to achieve democracy and stability simultaneously. One objective of contemporary research is to isolate factors such as state policy, historical traditions, and cultural values that may explain the more successful development records of some nations.

A second, distinct modification of modernization theory relates to its initial view of cultural change. Social scientists now agree that the differences between traditional and modern culture are not always as stark or clear as originally thought. For example, while the United States is a highly modern society, many Americans retain traditional values such as judging others by the color of their skin. Nor have the peoples of the Third World been as universally attracted to modern (Western) values as some analysts had expected. In Iran and other parts of the Middle East, for example, a large portion of the population, including many individuals with high school or university educations, have rejected Westernization in favor of Islamic fundamentalism. Finally, it is now recognized that some traditional values are not only worth keeping but also contribute to political and economic development. Students of contemporary Japanese culture and religion have argued that traditional religious values contributed to that nation's work ethic. Even "magic and miracles," notes one expert on East Asian religions, "are entirely compatible with the 'rationality' of industrial society."[36]

Dependency Theory

During the 1960s and 1970s a number of social scientists in Latin America and the United States raised further fundamental objections to modernization theory. Many of them, though not all, were Marxists. Under the banner of dependency theory they challenged the modernization literature's most fundamental assumptions.

To begin with, they rejected the notion that Third World countries could follow the same path to development as did Western nations. When Britain became the world's first industrial power, they noted, it faced no external competition. Today, however, newly industrializing nations must compete against well-established industrial giants. In addition, argued Brazilian Theotonio Dos Santos, these countries have to borrow financial capital and purchase advanced technology from the developed world, thereby making them dependent on external economic forces and weakening their growth.[37]

Indeed, whereas modernization theorists generally saw Western influence in the Third World as beneficial (since it spread modern values and institutions), dependencistas (as dependency theorists are known) argued that it had been Western colonialism and economic imperialism that had turned Africa, Asia, and Latin America into sources of cheap food and raw materials for the colonial powers. And, they charged, long after Third World nations had achieved political independence, developed countries continued to use their economic power to create an international division of labor between nations. Under that division, production and export of manufactured goods—the most profitable economic activity—were concentrated in the industrialized West (and then Japan), the core. Third World nations, the periphery, were largely relegated to the production and export of food and raw materials and were left to trade for industrial imports on unfavorable terms.[38]

Finally, dependency theorists insisted that economic dependence had important political implications for the LDCs. Third World elites, backed by the economic and military power of the core nations (especially the United States), maintained a political system that benefited the few at the expense of the majority.

As one might imagine, dependency theory (whose most articulate proponents were Latin Americans) was extremely attractive to Third World scholars. It suggested that underdevelopment was not the fault of the LDCs and their traditional values but rather stemmed from foreign domination and exploitation. In the United States as well, dependency theory challenged, and often displaced, modernization theory as the major scholarly explanation of underdevelopment.

However, just as early modernization theory had been overly optimistic about the prospects for simultaneous economic and political development, early dependency theory proved to be excessively pessimistic about the prospects for economic growth. Authors such as Andre Gunder Frank had warned that Third World nations, consigned to producing nonindustrial goods and ruled by unrepresentative elites, were doomed to continued backwardness. Some dependencistas believed that radical revolution was the only solution. Other authors merely prescribed greater economic independence for developing nations; still others offered no solutions.

Despite the bleak prognosis of many dependencistas, it was clear by the mid-1960s that nations such as Brazil and Mexico were experiencing substantial industrialization. In a far more sophisticated version of dependency theory, Fernando Henrique Cardoso rejected the contention that all Third World countries were condemned to underdevelopment and precluded from industrial growth.[39] Drawing heavily from the example of his native Brazil, Cardoso noted that through the active intervention of the state and the linkage of domestic firms with multinational corporations, some LDCs could industrialize and enjoy considerable economic growth. He referred to this process as associated-dependent development.

Cardoso radically altered dependency theory by arguing that countries such as Brazil, Colombia, or Mexico could experience considerable industrialization and economic growth while remaining dependent on foreign banks and multinationals for loans, investment, and technology. Brazilian industrialization, he noted, had been stimulated, to a large extent, by a sharp rise in investment from Multinational Corporations (MNCs). For Cardoso and his colleagues, however, this kind of development was tainted in several ways. It still meant that key economic decisions were being made outside of the LDCs' borders. More important, associated-dependent development was being led by companies that were heavily mechanized (and, consequently, did not hire much local labor) and that produced relatively expensive consumer goods (that were more profitable) destined for the country's middle and upper classes. Rather than reduce poverty, dependencistas argued, such associated-dependent development had widened the income gap separating the poor from the middle and upper classes. At the same time, Peter Evans and others maintained, an alliance of the MNCs with some Latin American economic, political, and military elites helped maintain nonrepresentative regimes (including military dictatorships) in power.

Modernization and Dependency Theory Compared

The dependency approach offered useful corrections to modernization theory. Most important, it highlighted an important influence on Third World societies that modernization theory had largely neglected: international trade, finance, and investment patterns. Many political scientists argue that the principle common characteristic defining Third World countries is their peripheral economic and cultural status relative to the major core nations. Thus, even wealthy nations such as Saudi Arabia or stable democracies like Costa Rica are still considered Third World because their economic, cultural, and political outlooks and structures are largely shaped by the developed world.[40]

Regardless of how much of the dependencistas' argument they accepted, subsequent authors on underdevelopment have recognized that political and economic modernization require more than adopting new values or changing domestic political structures. Dependency theory shifted the focus of research from exclusively internal factors to international economic and cultural relations, creating new fields of research including international political economy.

Dependency theorists also helped redefine the concept of economic development. Whereas early studies of the Third World focused heavily on economic growth, dependencistas emphasized the importance of economic distribution. When rapid economic growth is accompanied by an increased concentration of wealth and income for a minority, as has frequently occurred, it offers little benefit to the impoverished majority, which may be left worse off. Influenced by dependency theory and other leftist critiques, even such pillars of the establishment as the World Bank have reoriented their focus toward "growth and redistribution."[41]

However, just as early modernization theorists tended to overemphasize the internal causes of underdevelopment, dependencistas erroneously attributed virtually all Third World problems to external economic factors. Furthermore, periphery nations (LDCs) were often portrayed as helpless pawns with no way out of their poverty. Indeed, what is striking about much of the dependency literature is its economic determinism and scant analysis of political forces within the developing nations. Its proponents frequently dismissed the governments of nonsocialist LDCs as agents of the local economic elite who, in turn, colluded with Western- or Japanese-based MNCs. Consequently, there is a disturbing sameness to many of the dependency-based studies of politics in individual nations. The details of Mexican, Colombian, or Peruvian politics might differ, but they always seemed to fit the same, broader pattern.

Cardoso refined the theory by insisting that developing nations had options within the limits of dependency. Depending on the relationships between social classes as well as government policies (both internal factors), associated-dependent development was possible. Combining Cardoso's ideas with elements of modernization theory, Argentinean political scientist Guillermo O'Donnell offered a powerful explanation for the problems of industrialization and the rise of authoritarian military governments in the more developed nations of South America.[42]

East Asia's "economic miracle" (most notably in South Korea, Taiwan, Hong Kong, and Singapore), however, confounded dependency theory. These countries tied themselves very closely to the developed world through trade, credit, investment, and technology transfer. Contrary to what even the more sophisticated dependency scholars had predicted, however, they achieved spectacular economic growth coupled with comparatively equitable economic distribution. Some may object that East Asia's current economic woes validate dependency theory since the financial crisis originated with massive external (and internal) debt and was exacerbated when foreign capital fled the region, sending Asian stock markets on a downward spiral. Still most scholars see this as a temporary setback or, at worst, a signal that the Asian growth model needs some modification. But the current East Asian crisis is unlikely to revive dependency theory to its former stature. One piece of anecdotal evidence for this is the fact that Fernando Henrique Cardoso, once dependency's most brilliant exponent (in his role as university scholar), now enthusiastically seeks foreign investment, trade, and technology for Brazil in his current capacity as that nation's president.

Developments in East Asia have forced modernization theorists to revise their ideas as well. They now recognize that some traditional values, most notably Confucian concepts of group loyalty and hard work, have contributed to economic modernization. At the same time the region's rapid economic growth has not produced either the political unrest that Huntington feared or, until recently, the democratization that early modernization theorists expected (during the past decade, however, Taiwan and South Korea have completed transitions to democracy).

CONTEMPORARY PERSPECTIVES

Today, few analysts accept either modernization or dependency theories in their entirety and particularly not in their original formulations. Subsequent approaches, such as bureaucratic-authoritarianism (which seeks to explain the rise of military dictatorships in more economically developed Third World nations) or neoliberal economics (which offers a set of conservative prescriptions for the LDCs), have generally shied away from global explanations and focused instead on more specific issues. Indeed, most contemporary scholars reject the very idea of a single theory of development.[43] First, it is now apparent that the Third World is too diverse to be encompassed by a single theory of change. Second, the processes of political and socioeconomic development themselves, even in a particular region or nation, are far too complex to be explained by any single theory.

This does not mean, however, that the insights offered by dependency and modernization theories have not been useful. Our current understanding of development draws on the strengths of both approaches, while recognizing the limitations of each. But political scientists today are less prone to advance global explanations. In addition to limiting themselves to more manageable and specific issues (such as the role of political parties or the basis of government economic planning), they generally focus more often on specific geographic regions (East Asia or Latin America, for example, or a comparison of the two).

The chapters that follow will turn from general development theory to examine important issues facing less developed countries today. Chapters 2 through 6 discuss some of the broad social forces that underlie the challenges and conflicts of contemporary Third World politics: the political impact of religion; the nature of ethnic politics and ethnic conflict; the political significance of gender; agrarian reform and rural development; and the political implications of rapid urbanization. Chapters 7 and 8 explore the politics of two types of regimes that are largely limited to the Third World—revolutionary and military—and examine the reasons for their rise and fall as well as their approach to the problems of development. Chapter 9 examines economic development strategies currently being employed in much of the Third World. And, finally, Chapter 10 analyzes the impressive spread of democracy in the closing decades of the twentieth century.

DISCUSSION QUESTIONS

1. To what extent is democracy an integral part of political development? Why were political scientists initially reluctant to include democracy in their definitions of political development?

2. To what degree do social and economic development contribute to or undermine political development?

3. What do you believe are the most important differences between modernization theory and dependency theory?

4. How have both early modernization theory and early dependency theory been modified? Why were those modifications needed?

5. What is the difference between economic and social underdevelopment?

NOTES

1. For a discussion of the strengths and many weaknesses of the term, see Allen H. Merriam, "What Does ' 'Third World' Mean?" in *The Third World: States of Mind and Being*, ed. Jim Norwine and Alfonso Gonzalez (Boston: Unwin Hyman, 1988), pp. 15–22.

2. The term "pluralist democracy" indicates that the political system not only supports contested elections and civil liberties (formal democracy) but also allows a large num-

ber of independent interest associations (business groups, labor unions, farmers associations, women's groups, environmental organizations and the like) to operate politically or otherwise, free of government controls. For more on different aspects of democracy, see Chapter 10.

3. Scholars have disagreed on whether or not to include non-European communist nations—such as China, Cuba, and Vietnam—in the Third World. I include them in this category because they resemble other developing nations on many dimensions.

4. Taiwan and, especially, Singapore were less damaged by East Asia's economic depression in the late 1990s than were countries such Indonesia, Malaysia, and South Korea.

5. Merriam, "What Does 'Third World' Mean?", p. 20.

6. Christopher Clapham, *Third World Politics: An Introduction* (Madison: University of Wisconsin Press, 1985), p. 2.

7. Gross Domestic Product (GDP) is a measure similar to Gross National Product (GNP), the indicator commonly used in the United States, but excludes "net factor income from abroad." GDP is used more often than GNP for comparing production between countries.

8. Some countries' GNP or GDP rankings vary considerably depending on what statistical method is applied to the data. There may also be considerable variation *within* particular nations. Thus, China's coastal region is quite developed, comparing well with South Korea or Mexico. Its interior, however, is generally quite impoverished, more analogous to rural India or Bangladesh.

9. Previous crossnational comparisons of GDP were based on conversion of local currencies to U.S. dollars at the official exchange rate, producing arbitrary data which painted an unrealistic picture of many nations' living standards. Real GDP, on the other hand, is based on currency purchasing power and is a more accurate measure of how people really live. For example, the new method revealed that China has an economy several times larger than previously thought and real income (what people can actually purchase) is three to four times what was previously estimated.

10. Unless otherwise indicated, all data in this section come from the same sources as Tables 1.1 and 1.2.

11. Brazil, which had the region's most dynamic economy in the late 1960s and 1970s (accounting for its relatively strong showing in Table 1.1), is now considered the weak link among Latin America's major economies. During the 1990s Chile and Argentina had some of the fastest growth rates in the Americas (though Argentina's growth was more erratic).

12. Robert Wade, *Governing the Market* (Princeton, NJ: Princeton University Press, 1990), p. 42.

13. Axel Hadenius, *Democracy and Development* (London: Cambridge University Press, 1992).

14. A simple example illustrates the problem with income averages. If one person in a generally poor village makes a million dollars a year, he or she will totally distort the town average, producing a figure that in no way reflects how the average villager really lives. But the same kind of distortions do not take place with social indicators such as life expectancy, infant mortality, and literacy.

15. All of the data in this paragraph come from the United Nation's Development Program (UNDP), *Human Development Report 1997* (New York: Oxford University Press, 1997), pp. 24–26.

16. Ibid.

17. Samuel P. Huntington, "The Goals of Development," in *Understanding Political Development*, ed. Myron Weiner and Samuel P. Huntington (Boston: Little, Brown, 1987), p. 3.

18. Hadenius, *Democracy and Development*; Robert A. Dahl, *Democracy and Its Critics* (New Haven, CT: Yale University Press, 1989); Scott Mainwaring, "Transitions to Democracy and Democratic Consolidation," in *Issues in Democratic Consolidation: The New South American Democracies in Comparative Perspective*, ed. Scott Mainwaring, Guillermo O'Donnell, and Samuel Valenzuela (Notre Dame, IN: University of Notre Dame Press, 1992); Samuel P. Huntington, *The Third Wave: Democratization in the Late Twentieth Century* (Norman: University of Oklahoma Press, 1991).

19. Samuel P. Huntington, *Political Order in Changing Societies* (New Haven, CT: Yale University Press, 1968).

20. Guillermo O'Donnell and Philippe Schmitter, *Transitions from Authoritarian Rule: Tentative Conclusions about Uncertain Democracies* (Baltimore, MD: Johns Hopkins University Press, 1986); Abraham Lowenthal, ed., *Exporting Democracy* (Baltimore, MD: Johns Hopkins University Press, 1991); Dahl, *Democracy and Its Critics*.

21. Huntington, *The Third Wave*.

22. Eighty-six members of the United Nations have been ranked on both economic resources (per capita GNPs) and socioeconomic indicators of living standards (HDIs). If we subtract each country's HDI rank from its GNP rank, a positive score indicates the country is performing better on social indicators than its economic ranking would predict while a negative score suggests the opposite.

23. Huntington, *The Third Wave*; Mitchell A. Seligson, "Democratization in Latin America: The Current Cycle" in *Authoritarians and Democrats: Regime Transition in Latin America*, ed. James M. Malloy and Mitchell A. Seligson (Pittsburgh, PA: University of Pittsburgh Press, 1987); Hadenius, *Democracy and Development*.

24. Huntington, *Political Order*.

25. Guillermo O'Donnell, *Modernization and Bureaucratic-Authoritarianism: Studies in South American Politics* (Berkeley: University of California Press, 1973).

26. For a useful summary of major theories of development see Alvin Y. So, *Social Change and Development* (Newbury Park, CA: Sage Publications, 1990); for ongoing contributions in these areas, see Weiner and Huntington, *Understanding Political Development*; Vicky Randall and Robin Theobald, *Political Change and Underdevelopment* (London: Macmillan, 1985).

27. Modernization literature is extensive. The most important works include Huntington, *Political Order*, widely considered the best work in this area; Gabriel Almond and James Coleman, eds., *The Politics of Developing Areas* (Princeton, NJ: Princeton University Press, 1960); Lucian Pye and Sidney Verba, *Political Culture and Political Development* (Princeton, NJ: Princeton University Press, 1965); and Cyril E. Black, ed., *Comparative Modernization: A Reader* (New York: Free Press, 1976). These works as well as those mentioned below regarding dependency theory are recommended for advanced undergraduates.

28. Max Weber, *The Protestant Ethic and the Spirit of Capitalism* (New York: Scribner, 1958); Talcott Parsons, *The Social System* (Glencoe, IL: Free Press, 1951).

29. For examples of such arguments see Parsons, *Social System*; Gabriel Almond and Sidney Verba, *The Civic Culture* (Princeton, NJ: Princeton University Press, 1963); Pye and Verba, *Political Culture*; Alex Inkeles and David Horton Smith, *Becoming Modern: Individual Change in Six Developing Countries* (Cambridge, MA: Harvard University Press, 1974); Daniel Lerner, *The Passing of Traditional Society* (Glencoe, IL: Free Press, 1958); David McClelland, *The Achieving Society* (Princeton, NJ: Van Nostrand, 1961).

30. Gabriel A. Almond and G. Bingham Powell, *Comparative Politics: A Developmental Approach* (Boston: Little, Brown, 1966), p. 301.

31. Marion Levy, Jr., "Social Patterns (Structures) and Problems of Modernization," in *Readings on Social Change*, ed. Wilbert Moore and Robert Cooke (Upper Saddle River, NJ: Prentice Hall, 1967), p. 207.

32. Huntington, "The Goals of Development."

33. Huntington, *Political Order in Changing Societies.*

34. See Juan Linz and Alfred Stepan, eds., *The Breakdown of Democratic Regimes: Latin America* (Baltimore, MD: Johns Hopkins University Press, 1978); David Collier, ed., *The New Authoritarianism in Latin America* (Princeton, NJ: Princeton University Press, 1979).

35. Huntington, "The Goals of Development."

36. Winston Davis, "Religion and Development: Weber and the East Asian Experience" in Weiner and Huntington, eds., *Understanding Political Development*, p. 258; see also, So, *Social Change and Development*, Chapter 4.

37. Theotonio Dos Santos, "The Structure of Dependence," *American Economic Review* (May 1970).

38. Werner Baer, "The Economics of Prebisch and ECLA," in *Latin America: Problems in Economic Development*, ed. C. T. Nisbet (New York: Free Press, 1969). Major early dependency studies include Andre Gunder Frank, *Capitalism and Underdevelopment in Latin America* (New York: Monthly Review Press, 1967); and Paul Baran, *The Political Economy of Growth* (New York: Monthly Review Press, 1957).

39. The most influential work on this sophisticated version of dependency theory is Fernando Henrique Cardoso and Enzo Faletto, *Dependency and Development in Latin America* (Berkeley: University of California Press, 1979). A more readable work on the same topic is Peter Evans, *Dependent Development: The Alliance of Multinational, State and Local Capital* (Princeton, NJ: Princeton University Press, 1979).

40. Christopher Clapham, *Third World Politics: An Introduction* (Madison: University of Wisconsin Press, 1985), p. 3.

41. Hollis Chenery et al., *Redistribution with Growth* (London: Oxford University Press with the World Bank and the University of Sussex, 1974).

42. O'Donnell, *Modernization and Bureaucratic-Authoritarianism.*

43. See, for example, two recent works that dismiss the search for a single paradigm of development: James Manor, ed., *Rethinking Third World Politics* (New York: Longman, 1991), especially the introduction by Manor and the chapter by Geoffrey Hawthorn; Paul Cammack, David Pool, and William Tordoff, *Third World Politics*, 2d ed. (Baltimore, MD: Johns Hopkins University Press, 1993).

2

❧

RELIGION AND POLITICS

The rise of urban civilization and the collapse of traditional religion are the two main hallmarks of our civilization and are closely related. . . . What is secularization? . . . It is the loosening of the world from religion. . . . The gods of traditional religions live on . . . but they play no role whatever in the public life of the secular metropolis. . . .[1]

That death knell for traditional religion was sounded in the 1960s, not by an opponent of religion, but by one of America's preeminent Protestant theologians, Harvey Cox. He was not predicting the demise of religion per se, but rather of its traditional form, including its historic role in politics and other forms of public life. Cox's influential book *The Secular City* corresponded with the observations and predictions of contemporary social scientists. And while religion obviously remained a more pervasive force in the Third World, secularization of society seemed inevitable there as well.

In Latin America the Catholic church no longer exercised nearly as much control over education as it once did. Following Indian independence, the government tried to ameliorate the injustices of the caste system, a cornerstone of Hindu religious practice. And in the Middle East, modernizing regimes in Egypt, Iraq, and Syria created more secular political systems. Accordingly, a leading authority, Donald Eugene Smith, observed, "Political development includes, as one of its basic processes, the secularization of politics, the progressive exclusion of religion from the political system."[2]

Generally speaking, early modernization theorists viewed religion as an impediment to political and economic development, while dependency theorists deemed it so unimportant as to warrant only an occasional footnote in their writings (see Chapter 1). Since Cox and Smith chronicled its decline, however, religion has been an unexpectedly resilient political force, withstanding the onslaughts of modernization, and even, at times, being stimulated by it. As David Little observed, "Modernization was supposed to mean the gradual decline and eventual disappearance of religion from public life, but, as we know, that hasn't happened. . . . Religion is very much alive as a part of politics."[3] In fact, since the 1970s much of the Third World (and the developed world too, for that matter) has experienced a religious resurgence intensifying the role of religion in the political arena.[4]

Nowhere is that more apparent than in the Middle East, where a renewal of Islamic fundamentalism (or revivalism) has had dramatic political impact in Iran, Lebanon, Algeria, and Egypt. The seizure of American hostages in Iran and Lebanon, the assassination of Egyptian President Anwar Sadat, and the bombing of New York's World Trade Center and two United States embassies in East Africa have all focused Western attention on "religion and politics." In fact, with the collapse of Soviet communism and the end of the Cold War, many politicians and journalists have labeled radical (militant) Islamic fundamentalism as the greatest threat to Western security. Prior to the Gulf War a Gallup Poll survey revealed that 37 percent of British respondents expected a war in the 1990s between Muslims and Christians.[5]

While this chapter discusses Islamic and Hindu fundamentalism at some length, and while their political import is undeniable, many scholars properly warn against obsessing over that phenomenon.[6] Important as it is in Middle Eastern, Asian, and North African politics, religious fundamentalism (particularly its more radical or militant variant) still represents a minority of Muslims and Hindus. Furthermore, any discussion of religious extremism should not obscure the positive role of mainstream religion in so many aspects of personal and public life.

THE MEETING OF CHURCH AND STATE

Many of our preconceptions about religion and politics are based on serious misunderstandings, both of our own government and of political systems elsewhere. Americans generally accept as natural a constitutional separation between church and state. Such formal barriers, however, do not exist in many other industrial democracies or in many LDCs. Moreover, even in the United States religious organizations and beliefs continue to influence political behavior. Black Baptist churches, for example, have always been in the forefront of the American civil rights movement. Recently, conflicts over issues such as school prayer and abortion have led one expert to observe that "far from rendering religion largely irrelevant to politics . . . the structure of [American] government . . . may actually encourage a high degree of interaction."[7] Most Western European nations, though more secular than the United States in most aspects of everyday life, have not tried to build a wall between religion and politics. In Britain, for example, the Anglican church (or Church of England) is the official state religion. The Catholic church was closely linked to the Italian Christian Democratic Party, until the 1990s the nation's leading party.[8]

Religious values are more firmly entrenched in most Third World cultures and the impact of religion on politics is correspondingly more pronounced.

Indeed, religion is so central to traditional values that we often identify national or regional cultures by the predominant religion: Buddhist culture in Thailand, Confucian culture in China and Korea, Hindu culture in much of India and Nepal, and Islamic culture in North Africa and the Middle East.[9]

The blending of religion and politics is most apparent in theocratic states such as Iran where, since the Ayatollah Khomeini's Islamic revolution, public policy has been shaped by the Shi'ite clergy. But it is also significant in Islamic fundamentalist states like Afghanistan and Sudan, and more moderate Muslim nations such as Pakistan. In Brazil and Nicaragua, the theology of liberation espoused by progressive members of the Catholic church has motivated priests and nuns to organize the poor against economic and political oppression. And, in India, the Bharatiya Janata Party (BJP), currently the country's largest political party and until recently head of its governing coalition, carries the torch of Hindu fundamentalism.

GREAT RELIGIONS OF THE THIRD WORLD

Four of the world's "great religions" dominate the LDCs. Catholicism, the only major religion to have penetrated extensively into both the industrial democracies and the developing world, predominates throughout Latin America and the Philippines, while also representing important portions of the population in Lebanon and parts of sub-Saharan Africa, particularly former French and Portuguese colonies. Hinduism is confined primarily to India, along with neighboring Nepal and parts of Sri Lanka. Buddhism is of major import in East and Southeast Asia, as well as parts of South Asia. Islam, the world's second largest religion, predominates across a broad span of Asia, the Middle East, and Africa, stretching from Indonesia in the east through Pakistan and Bangladesh in the Indian subcontinent, the former Soviet republics of Central Asia, the Middle East, and North Africa. It also represents close to half the populations of Malaysia and Nigeria, as well as substantial minorities in countries as far flung as Tanzania and Trinidad.[10]

To be sure, not everyone in the developing world subscribes to one of these major religions. Protestantism is the leading religion in the English-speaking islands of the Caribbean, and represents important minorities in a number of other LDCs. Confucianism still influences Chinese society, even after its Revolution. Christian Orthodox minorities are significant in Lebanon and Egypt. And a large portion of Black Africa's population believes in local tribal religions (animism). The impact of these religions on politics, however, is considerably more limited. Consequently, this chapter limits its analysis to the four global religions described earlier, with particular emphasis on Islam and Catholicism.

None of the Third World's major religions is monolithic, though the Catholic church, with its doctrine of papal infallibility and its hierarchical structure, comes closest. Buddhism has two major schools, each basing its doctrines on a different set of ancient texts. Theravada ("Way of Elders") Buddhism, practiced in

Myanmar (Burma), Sri Lanka (Ceylon), Thailand, Laos, and Cambodia, is believed to be closer to the original teachings of Buddha. Mahayana ("Great Vehicle") Buddhism emerged in China, Japan, Korea, Vietnam, and Tibet.[11]

Islam is also divided in a number of ways, the most important being the division between Sunni and Shi'ite. The split between them dates to the period following the death of the Prophet Muhammad and the issue of his spiritual successor.[12] Ninety percent of the Islamic population are Sunni, while Shi'ism, which has drawn the greatest attention in the West for its nationalistic and militant manifestations, accounts for only about 8 percent. Shi'ism is the dominant faith only in Iran, where it is centered. But it also represents 50 to 60 percent of Iraq's population, a plurality in Lebanon, and significant minorities in Afghanistan, Pakistan, Kuwait, and other Gulf states. In countries having both significant Sunni and Shi'ite populations, there are commonly sharp political and cultural tensions between the two.[13]

Even religions that have no formal divisions still experience important political differences. Latin American Catholics span the ideological spectrum from right-wing followers of opus dei to radical adherents of liberation theology. In the name of God and anticommunism, some Latin American Catholics have supported fascist movements, rightist death squads, and repressive military regimes. Conversely, in the name of God and social justice, other Catholic priests and nuns have supported the Sandinista revolution in Nicaragua, fought with Marxist guerrillas in Colombia, and politically organized the poor in the slums of Brazil.

RELIGION, MODERNITY, AND SECULARIZATION

We have already observed that modernization does not necessarily produce a decline in religious observance. What about the other side of the relationship? That is, what is the impact of religion on modernity? Here again, early theorists saw an incompatibility. "It is widely, and correctly, assumed," said Donald Smith, "that religion is in general an obstacle to modernization."[14] In the realm of politics, this suggested that the intrusion of religious institutions and values impedes the development of a modern state.

Subsequently, political scientists have developed a more nuanced understanding. Religious institutions may inhibit development in some respects, while encouraging it in others. For example, all of the great religions have legitimized the state's authority at some point in history. As nations modernize their political systems, religious authorities or groups may oppose important aspects of change (Hindu and Islamic fundamentalists, for example) or they may offer explicit or tacit support (Islamic leaders in Indonesia and Catholic clergy in Chile). No longer facilely dismissing religion's possible contribution to development, many scholars have now credited Confucianism with facilitating East Asia's rapid modernization in recent decades.[15] Specifically, they have noted that religion's work ethic and spirit of cooperation.

Depending on their theology and structure, individual religions may either bolster or impede government development initiatives. Different religions emphasize distinctive values; thus, states wishing to create welfare programs based on communal responsibility often receive strong support from Islamic leaders or the Catholic church. At the same time, modernizing political leaders who emphasize individual rights and responsibilities will find those values warmly received by Buddhist monks. Ultimately, then, organized religions can strengthen the modern nation-state by offering it legitimacy and by disseminating the government's political message. Should religious leaders oppose the state, however, they can often delegitimize the political system.[16]

The assertion that political modernization requires secularization contains two components, one empirical and the other normative. The first component posits that as societies modernize (i.e., become more literate, urban, and industrial) their political systems invariably become more secular. In effect there is a specialization of functions: Increasingly, the state controls politics while the church oversees religion, and neither interferes with the other's function. That had been the tendency in the West and political scientists anticipated the same division of responsibilities in the Third World as it modernized.

The related normative assumption holds that secularization is desirable since it increases religious freedom, reduces the likelihood of state persecution of religious minorities, and permits the state to make more rational decisions free of religious bias.

We have already indicated the weakness of the first assumption. To be sure, modernization has induced political secularization in many developing countries, such as Turkey and Argentina. Elsewhere it has not altered church-state relations; indeed, it has precipitated a religious backlash when pushed too rapidly. Saudi Arabia illustrates the first possibility. The royal family has introduced far-reaching socioeconomic changes affecting the lives of nearly every Saudi citizen. Yet modernization has been carefully controlled to preserve a very traditionalist Islamic culture and to maintain the close links between Islam and the state. India represents an intermediate case, where the modernization of politics and constitutional secularization were accepted by most citizens, but rejected by the growing number of Hindu fundamentalists. In Iran, on the other hand, the Shah's rapid imposition of Western-style socioeconomic development destabilized society and helped precipitate radical Islamic revivalism.

At an individual level, many people in Africa, Asia, and the Middle East have defied the notion that more educated and professionally trained citizens will be less religiously orthodox. For example, Hindu and Islamic fundamentalist activists in India, Afghanistan, and Egypt are frequently educated professionals, not poor, uneducated peasants.[17] Nor are traditional religious values and modern technology necessarily incompatible. In Iran, opponents of the Shah undermined his authority by distributing audiotapes of Ayatollah Ruhollah Khomeini's political message throughout the country. Once in power, the theocratic government has made extensive use of television and other modern technologies to maintain its influence.

Normative evaluations of the church-state relationship need to be more complex than early development theory had assumed. Clearly, some religious influences contradict accepted norms of modernity, such as when they induce political leaders to violate the rights of religious minorities (or majorities). Iran's Islamic government, for example, has persecuted members of the Baha'i faith.[18] In Guatemala, the government of General Efraín Rios Montt, a right-wing Evangelical, converted Catholic peasants to Protestantism at virtual gunpoint. Similarly, religiously inspired restrictions on women or racial minorities are clearly antithetical to modernization.

Can one infer from such cases, however, that there need always be a strict wall between politics and religion or between clerics and politicians? The same people who lament the political activities of Catholic priests in Nicaragua and Brazil or protest marches by Buddhist monks in Sri Lanka may cheer the political involvement of the Reverend Martin Luther King, Jr., or the presidential candidacy of Pat Robertson in the United States.

Ultimately, our normative evaluations of religion's role in politics are influenced by whether or not that interaction furthers goals and policies that we believe in. Perhaps this is as it should be. The recent histories of Iran and Tibet illustrate this point well. Iran has been a theocracy since its 1979 revolution, just as Tibet was prior to its absorption by China in the 1950s. Each has had a political system "in which the political structures are clearly subordinate to the ecclesiastical establishment."[19] Yet the world has judged them quite differently.

Under the leadership of the Ayatollah Khomeini and the Islamic mullahs (clerics) who succeeded him, Iran has become an international outcast because of its repression of civil liberties, persecution of religious minorities, interference in the affairs of neighboring countries, and support for international terrorism. Until the late 1950s, Tibetan politics was also dominated by clerics.[20] Viewed as divine by his people, the Dalai Lama had been the country's secular and spiritual leader. Buddhist monks held key posts in the government bureaucracy. Because of Tibetan Buddhism's record of pacifism and tolerance, however, theocratic rule aroused no foreign indignation. Indeed, the world was appalled when China occupied the country and secularized the state. Since that time the Dalai Lama's long struggle to free his people has won him worldwide admiration and the Nobel Peace Prize.

STRUCTURAL AND THEOLOGICAL BASES
OF CHURCH-STATE RELATIONS

The extent to which religious values influence political attitudes and behavior and the degree of political involvement by organized religions vary considerably from place to place. Just as the separation of church and state in Western Europe is usually more clearly defined in predominantly Protestant nations (Denmark,

Britain) than in Catholic ones (Italy, Spain), the Third World's great religions also vary greatly in their political impact. Two factors are particularly relevant: each religion's theological view regarding the relationship between temporal and spiritual matters, and the degree of hierarchical structure within the religion.

Donald Smith distinguishes the two different types of religio-political systems as the organic and the church. In the first case, the organic, political leaders are relatively unrestricted by religious leaders because the clergy is insufficiently organized to challenge them. Examples of organic systems include Hindu and traditional Sunni Islamic societies. Church religio-political systems, on the other hand, have a well-organized ecclesiastical structure that exercises considerable authority over society. They include Catholicism, Shi'ite Islam, and sometimes Buddhism (in countries such as Tibet and Burma). All offer more formalized relations between church and state, and greater potential for religious challenge to the political order, than found in organic systems. In some church systems the state dominates the religious order; in others the church dominates; and in yet others there is an equal partnership.[21]

Islam

From its inception in seventh-century Arabia, Islam was a "religio-political movement in which religion was integral to state and society."[22] Perhaps more than any other great religion, traditional Islam recognized no borderline between religion and politics. On the one hand, the Islamic faith and its clergy legitimized the state. At the same time, however, the political leadership recognized the supremacy of Shariah (path of God), the Islamic law. Thus, prior to the intrusion of colonialism, Muslims took it as a given that they lived in an Islamic state. Since religious Muslims still believe that God wants them to live in a community governed in accordance with the Quran (divinely revealed law, much of it temporal), the very concept of separating church and state is alien to their culture.

This should not suggest that traditional Islamic culture or theology was inhospitable to other religions. Perhaps because it accepted Jewish and Christian scriptures and drew from both religions since its inception, Islam was especially tolerant toward other faiths. During the Middle Ages, for example, Jews in Spain and in other Muslim-controlled areas experienced one of their greatest periods of freedom and influence.[23] But even under those circumstances, ultimate political authority remained Muslim.

The bond between Islam and politics remains strong in most Muslim societies today, though there is considerable variation. John Esposito distinguishes three types of Islamic regimes as follows: the secular state, the Islamic state, and the Muslim state.[24] Turkey is perhaps the most noted secular state in the Islamic world. Starting in the 1920s, Kemal Ataturk (the father of modern Turkey) ousted the sultan of the Ottoman Empire, abolished the caliphate (the basis of the sultan's religious authority), emancipated women, closed seminaries, and westernized Turkish society in many ways. Today, Turkey is not fully secularized because its constitution still endorses belief in God, but the political system offers Islam no special status.[25]

During the 1980s and 1990s, however, an Islamic political party, the Refah (Welfare) Party steadily gained strength, particularly among residents of Turkey's urban slums who had migrated from the countryside to large cities and had found modern, secular culture corrupt and oppressive. As its name indicates, the Welfare Party gained considerable support among the poor by offering them social services which the government had failed to provide. In the 1995 parliamentary elections, Refah won the largest number of seats, setting off a frantic effort by Turkey's other major parties to exclude it from power. When those parties were unable to put together a stable, governing coalition, Refah formed a new government. Despite its sometimes radical and inflammatory rhetoric, the Welfare Party's policies in office were relatively moderate when compared to those of many other Islamic parties in the region. Still, its program of religious reforms— including a proposed amendment to the constitutional ban on religious dress so as to allow female students to cover their hair with scarves at school—were unacceptable to the powerful Turkish military, which views itself as the guardian of the country's secular tradition. In 1998, the armed forces forced parliament to remove the Welfare Party from office and to dissolve it as a legal political party.

At the other end of the spectrum, Islamic states use the Quran (the holy book) and other Islamic law as their governing philosophies. Saudi Arabia and Iran are perhaps the two best known examples of Islamic states, but Afghanistan, Sudan, Pakistan, and Libya also fall in this category. Despite their superficial similarity, however, these regimes are quite distinct from each other. While Iran subscribes to Shi'ite Islam, the other countries are all Sunni. Libya, Iran, and Sudan have pursued militant, anti-Western foreign policies (and supported terrorism), while Saudi Arabia and Pakistan are quite conservative and closely allied to the West. Thus, the term Islamic state (like the notion of fundamentalism) must be used carefully to avoid creating artificial categories that hide more than they reveal.

Finally, Muslim states, such as Egypt and Morocco, occupy an intermediate status. Unlike secular states, they identify Islam as the official religion and require the head of state to be Muslim. However, the impact of religion on politics is far more limited than in Islamic states. For example, political leaders are not clerics and some are even non-Muslims. In Iraq and Egypt, Christians have served as foreign ministers or deputy foreign ministers (most notably, Egypt's Boutros-Ghali, who later held the post of Secretary General of the United Nations). Many of the founders of Syria's ruling Baath party were Christians. The hold and style of Islam also varies between Muslim states. Sometimes the religion is less influential than political leaders claim.

Catholicism

More than any major religion, Catholicism has a well-defined, hierarchical ecclesiastical structure that permits it to have a great impact on the political order.

At the Church's apex is the Pope, whose authority is unchallenged and whose pronouncements on matters of faith and morals are infallible. Consequently, papal declarations can have great political impact. For example, many of the twentieth-century Catholic-based reform movements in Latin America can be traced to Pope Leo XII's 1891 encyclical *Rerum Novarum*, an indictment of early capitalism's exploitation of workers. Within each country the Church hierarchy is headed by the bishops, who may have tremendous political influence in the Philippines and in Latin America.

Like Islam in the Middle East, Catholicism used to be the state religion in most Latin American countries. In Colombia, for example, as recently as 1953 government treaties with the Vatican gave the Church special authority in areas such as education.[26] Over the years, however, most Latin American governments either have ceased having a state religion or have rendered the title unimportant. Still, Church doctrine has generally supported the established political regime and helped legitimize it. "The ruling powers," said one encyclical, "are invested with a sacredness more than human. . . . Obedience is not the servitude of man to man, but submission to the will of God."[27]

That does not mean, however, that the Church has always supported the government. Over the years, there have been periodic clashes between the Catholic hierarchy and some governments, most notably when the state challenged Church authority in areas such as education. Church support of Corazón Aquino's reform movement in the Philippines helped topple the right-wing dictatorship of Ferdinand Marcos. And Church relationships with Marxist regimes in Cuba and Nicaragua have often been tense.[28] In countries such as Brazil and El Salvador, where there were serious government human rights violations in recent decades, Catholic bishops have spoken out forcefully against the regime. In other countries, however, the local hierarchy has been far more cautious about criticizing the government.

Hinduism and Buddhism

Asia's major religions, Hinduism and Buddhism, have generally been less directly involved in politics than have Catholicism or Islam. Of course, Hinduism's cultural and philosophical values, most notably the caste system, have affected Indian and Nepalese politics profoundly. For example, the king of Nepal is worshiped as the incarnation of the god Vishnu.[29] But the religion is so diverse, composed of a series of local religious groups, cults, and sects loosely tied together by a common set of beliefs, that there is no centralized political influence. Moreover, although there are gurus, holy men, temple priests, and even a priestly caste (Brahmans, though most of them no longer choose to be priests), there is no ecclesiastical organization.

Buddhism grew out of the Hindu religion in the sixth century B.C., emerging from the teachings of a Nepalese prince, Siddartha Gautama, who later came to be known as the Buddha (Enlightened One). Though greatly influenced by

Hinduism, Buddhism rejects one of its basic tenets, the caste system. Indeed, as Buddhism spread through Asia one of its great appeals was its egalitarian outlook. Even today, many of India's untouchables continue to leave Hindu for Buddhism, a religion far more hospitable to them.[30]

Buddhism also differs from Hinduism in having an organized ecclesiastical organization, namely the Sangha (the monastic orders). In some countries, such as Myanmar, each sangha has its own leader, providing a hierarchical structure. Still, when compared to the Roman Catholic Church or the mullahs of Shi'ite Islam, Buddhism's religious structure is less centralized and, thus, less able to impact on the political system.

To be sure, Hindu and Buddhist groups on occasion have influenced their nation's politics. During the early 1960s, Burma was even declared a Buddhist state, though that was terminated after a few years. Protests led by Buddhist monks during that decade also helped topple three successive South Vietnamese leaders in a short period of time.[31] Monks have led major protests against government human rights violations in Tibet, Myanmar, and Thailand as well. The modern liberator of India, Mahatma Gandhi, drew upon reformist Hindu theology when demanding greater equality for untouchables and the lower castes. Conversely, the Bharatiya Janata Party (BJP), recently heading the Indian government, and other contemporary fundamentalist Hindu groups call upon conservative Hinduism to support the traditional caste system.

In addition to having less hierarchically organized ecclesiastical orders, Eastern religions are less theologically oriented toward political involvement. Their otherworldly philosophy doesn't stress temporal matters such as politics. Hence, the remainder of this chapter focuses more heavily on the political impact of Islam and Catholicism in the Third World.

RELIGIOUS FUNDAMENTALISM: ISLAM AND HINDUISM

No manifestation of religious influence on Third World politics has attracted more attention, or inspired more fear and loathing, than Islamic fundamentalism. Highly influential Washington columnists such as *U.S. News and World Report's* Morton Zuckerman and the *New Republic's* Charles Krauthammer have warned of "religious Stalinism" and a fanatical international movement orchestrated from Iran.[32] Nor are such concerns limited to Westerners. They are frequently expressed by the leaders of moderate Muslim nations who find themselves under siege from militant fundamentalists. Thus, for example, Tunisia's president, Zine Abidine Ben Ali, cautioned about a "fundamentalist international" financed by Iran and Sudan.[33]

While only a small percentage of the world's Hindus and Muslims identify with radical fundamentalism, its political importance is undeniable. So too are the confusion and misinformation that often accompany discussion of the topic. Many scholars of religion object to using the word fundamentalism to describe current militant revivals. They note that it may falsely imply the existence of a unified threat to the West and, in the case of Islam, that it lumps together regimes that have little in common, such as conservative Saudi Arabia and radical Libya. Instead, these authors prefer to use such terms as revivalism, militancy, and activism.[34] Other respected authorities, however, employ the term fundamentalism in their writings.[35] This chapter uses fundamentalism because of its currency in contemporary political discourse. On occasion, however, it will employ the term revivalism interchangeably (referring to the desire to revive the true faith).

Defining and Explaining Fundamentalism

> Fundamentalism is the . . . effort to define the fundamentals of a religious system and adhere to them. One of the cardinal tenants of Islamic Fundamentalism is to protect the purity of Islamic precepts from the adulteration of speculative exercises. Related to [Islamic] fundamentalism is . . . revival or resurgence, a renewed interest in Islam. Behind all this is a drive to purify Islam in order to release all its vital force.[36]

The precise meaning of fundamentalism varies somewhat from religion to religion. For example, in Anglo-Saxon Protestantism it refers to the belief that the Bible must be interpreted and believed literally. Fundamentalist Sunni Muslims share a fairly similar orientation toward the Quran, but Shi'ite fundamentalists do not accept that doctrine.[37] Still, fundamentalists share certain points of view across religions. To begin with, they all wish to preserve their religion's traditional worldview and resist the efforts of religious liberals to reform it. They also desire to revive the role of religion in private and public life, including dress, lifestyle, and politics.

In the developing world, fundamentalism appeals particularly to people who are disgusted by the inequalities and injustices in their country's political-economic system. It reflects popular revulsion against local political and economic elites, against pervasive corruption and repression. In Lebanon, for example, the radical Hizbullah grew out of the Shi'ites' resentment against the economically powerful Christian community (as well as their indignation against Israel and the West). In India, the BJP has attracted much of its support from voters (including some non-Hindus) embittered by government corruption. And in Algeria, Egypt, and the Sudan, militant fundamentalists have expanded their support as a result of the government repression directed against them. Ironically, then, many Muslims and Hindus are attracted to radical fundamentalism for the same reasons that drew Latin Americans to Marxist movements.

Radical fundamentalists also tend to be quite nationalist or chauvinistic, rejecting "outside" influences that they feel challenge or pollute the true faith. Western culture is perceived as particularly deleterious with its immodest dress, films, and music that allegedly promote promiscuous sex, drugs, and the like. But Western values are rejected for another reason. For years government leaders such as the Shah of Iran and Egypt's President Anwar Sadat promoted

Western-style modernization as the route to national development. After decades of failed development in the Middle East, North Africa, and other parts of the Third World, however, many of those regions' citizens feel that they were deceived and must look elsewhere for answers to their problems.

Radical and Conservative Fundamentalists

Finally, a distinction must be made between radical and conservative fundamentalists. Radicals, inspired by a "sacred rage," feel that they are conducting a holy war against forces that threaten to corrupt their fundamental religious values.[38] As a Hizbullah manifesto declared, "We have risen to liberate our country, to drive the imperialists and the invaders out of it and to take our fate in our own hands."[39] Holy War was waged in Afghanistan by Islamic mujahadeen against the country's Soviet occupiers as well as the Afghan Marxist government, which Soviet troops defended;[40] Iran's Ayatollah Khomeini declared a jihad (holy war) against both the United States ("the great Satan") and Soviet communism. Elsewhere, the battle has been waged against internal enemies as well. Having been denied an almost certain electoral victory in 1992 (the military canceled the elections after the first round), Algeria's fundamentalist Islamic Salvation Front (FIS) attacked the nation's armed forces, police, and secular politicians, as well as foreigners.[41]More violent militants, most notably the Armed Islamic Group (GIA), also launched massive terrorist attacks on civilians (often mixing banditry with supposed religious warfare). From 1992 through early 1998, over 75,000 people were killed either by armed Islamic groups or by the Algerian military and its allied civilian militias which reacted with equal savagery. In India, Hindu fundamentalists periodically have directed their rage against the country's Muslim minority. (For a more detailed discussion of the earlier massive communal violence between Hindus and Muslims in the postindependence period, see Chapter 3.)

Because these are perceived to be holy wars against a grave threat, religious radicals feel justified in initiating bloody attacks against Muslim civilians in India, bombing the American embassies in Kenya and Tanzania, and pronouncing a fatwah (religious edict) sentencing author Salman Rushdie to death for having written *The Satanic Verses*.

By contrast, conservative fundamentalists, be they Hasidic Jews or Saudi Arabian princes, do not envision themselves in such a battle. They too wish to shield their flock from unwanted outside influences. But most do not view adherents of other religions or nonfundamentalist members of their own faith as enemies.[42]

In recent years, radical Islamic fundamentalists have become a political force in a number of Third World countries. In Algeria, FIS was the country's leading political party before a military coup prevented its anticipated victory in the 1992 elections. Elsewhere in northern Africa, the Sudanese military government is closely allied with the radical National Islamic Front (NIF). And Afghanistan's Taliban government is perhaps the world's most rigidly fundamentalist, prohibiting girls and women, for example, from attending school or being employed. But nowhere has the impact of radical Islamic fundamentalism had a greater impact than in Iran. In turn, the Iranian revolution has been a beacon for other revivalist movements throughout the Muslim world.

"Sacred Rage": Radical Fundamentalism and the Iranian Revolution

The origins of the Iranian revolution can be traced to the early decades of the twentieth century and the clergy's ongoing resistance to secular modernization imposed from above by the royal family.[43] Military, political, and economic intervention by a series of foreign powers—Czarist Russia, Britain, and finally, the United States—turned the country into "a virtual protectorate" and made the ruling Shahs appear to be tools of the great powers.[44] Indeed, the last Shah, Mohammad Reza Pahlavi, was placed on the throne in 1941 by a joint Soviet-British invasion and restored to power by the CIA in 1953 after he had been briefly ousted. Not surprisingly, resentment against foreign domination was later to become an important component of the Islamic revolution.

During the 1920s and 1930s, Shah Reza Khan antagonized the Muslim mullahs (clergy) with a series of reforms.[45] Seeking to reinvigorate the country's ancient (pre-Islamic) Persian traditions, he needlessly slighted Islamic cultural practices of Arabic origin (a practice that his son continued).[46] At the same time, influenced both by the West and the secularization of Turkey, he banned the veiling of women, opened all public places to women, required Western dress for both sexes, limited the mullahs' economic resources, and established state control over schools, courts, and taxes that previously had been controlled by the clergy. This secularization of society and its accompanying diminution of Islamic power inspired the quiet opposition of a popular young mullah, Ruhollah Khomeini.

In the decades after he assumed the royal throne in 1941, Mohammad Reza Pahlavi accelerated his father's development and secularization programs. The new Shah funneled Iran's massive oil wealth into one of the Third World's most ambitious modernization programs. In 1963, prodded by the United States, he launched his "White Revolution" involving land reform, expanded literacy, voting rights for women, and other socioeconomic reforms. In the United States, the Shah was hailed as a progressive modernizer. Thus, when President Jimmy Carter visited Iran in 1977 (only two years before the Islamic Revolution), he praised the monarch for establishing "an island of stability in one of the more troubled areas of the world." "This is a great tribute to you, Your Majesty," added Carter, "and to . . . the respect, admiration and love which your people give to you."[47]

To be sure, the land reform had benefited some 3 million peasants, education had expanded greatly, and oil wealth had doubled the size of the middle class.[48] By 1976, Iran had the highest GNP per capita in the Third World. At the same time, however, the gap between rich and poor had widened and the government was widely resented for its corruption and repressiveness. Indeed, the

Shah's secret police, the SAVAK, had a well-deserved international reputation for torture and brutality. At the same time, some positive changes like land reform were staunchly opposed by the Islamic religious community, which lost substantial revenues.

Even many Iranians who had become more affluent felt psychologically wounded. The Shah was widely viewed as a tool of American neocolonialism. The mullahs, supported by other religious Muslims, objected to the erosion of their political influence, the progressive secularization of society, and the decline of traditional values. Together with urban merchants, middle-class nationalists, and students, they resented the tremendous political influence of the American government and petroleum companies. In the early 1960s, as tensions between the government and the Islamic clergy intensified, Khomeini became one of the Shah's most acerbic critics. When he was briefly imprisoned in 1964, riots broke out in a number of cities, leading to the massacre of up to 10,000 demonstrators by the Shah's army.[49] Khomeini was soon sent into exile for nearly 15 years. The effect was to turn him into a martyr in a culture that especially admires martyrdom, thereby greatly enhancing his influence over the masses.

By 1978 a substantial segment of Iran's urban population was participating in strikes and demonstrations against the regime. Brutal government crackdowns only intensified popular opposition. Finally, in January 1979, the Shah went into exile amid growing popular unrest. Khomeini returned to a frenzied welcome in Iran shortly thereafter. By then he had achieved the rank of grand ayatollah, the most exalted level of religious interpreters in the Shi'ite clergy.[50]

Like many new revolutionary regimes, Iran's turned increasingly radical in its early stage.[51] Over the years, three interrelated developments set the tone for the Islamic revolution. First was the merger of the country's religious and political leadership. In a national referendum held soon after Khomeini's triumphal return, 98 percent of all voters allegedly favored the establishment of an Islamic Republic. The new regime, declared the Ayatollah, was "the government of God."[52] Nonclerical figures have continued to hold government posts since that time. Thus, Abolhassan Bani-Sadr, a French-trained economist, was elected the Islamic republic's first president. Interestingly, Khomeini had decided that the president should not be a cleric, though he had to be a fundamentalist Muslim. And from 1980 to 1988 over half the members of the Iranian parliament were not clerics. That number jumped to 73 percent in the 1988 election.[53] In actuality, however, real power lay with the Revolutionary Council (a radical body of Muslim clerics) and with Khomeini, whose control was absolute. When Bani-Sadr clashed with the council, he was overruled and eventually ousted and imprisoned. The presidency has been held by a cleric ever since. Since Khomeini's death, power has resided in the hands of the leading mullahs.

The second development has been the revival of traditional Islamic observances. Women must be veiled in public and are strongly encouraged to wear the chador, the shapeless shroud that conceals all parts of the body. Highly intrusive Revolutionary Guards have penetrated all aspects of Iranian life, policing possible violations of Islamic behavior (as defined by the mullahs). Together with local neighborhood vigilante committees, they have arrested and occasionally executed suspected enemies of the Islamic order. In the Shi'ite tradition of martyrdom, thousands of young volunteers died in the holy war against Iraq. Assuring them and their families that it is a privilege to die for the faith, the Ayatollah Khomeini proclaimed, "We should sacrifice all our loved ones for the sake of Islam. If we are killed, we have performed our duty."[54]

Finally, Iran's radical revivalism embraced an aggressive foreign policy. This encompassed support for radical kindred groups abroad, such as Lebanon's Hizbullah, and a burning hostility toward foreign powers that are perceived as enemies of Khomeini's brand of Islam. Prior to the revolution Khomeini had declared, "America is worse than Britain, Britain is worse than America. The Soviet Union is worse than both of them. They are all worse and more unclean than each other."[55] Once in power, he reserved his most bitter attacks for the United States and Israel. It is every Muslim's duty, he declared, "to prepare himself for battle against Israel."[56]

Iran's hostility toward the outside world was best illustrated by two events. On November 4, 1979, revolutionary students seized the U.S. embassy in Tehran, taking diplomats and embassy staff hostage in an extraordinary breach of diplomatic rules.[57] While the Iranian regime claimed that the students had acted independently, no one doubted that the government had the capacity to release the hostages. It was not until 444 days later that the remaining 52 hostages were released. In the West, the incident created widespread animosity toward Iran and, unfortunately, toward Islam in general.

For the Iranian people, however, a second manifestation of their country's radical foreign policy—the prolonged war against Iraq (1980–1988)—was far more tragic. The war had multiple origins, most of them unrelated to religion. The most proximate cause was a long-standing border dispute. Also at play were Iran's support for Iraq's repressed Shi'ite population as well as the two governments' shared desire to lead the Gulf region. Once the conflict began, however, "both sides . . . portrayed the war as a noble crusade: Iraq as a historic defense of Arab sovereignty . . . against the marauding Persians; Iran as a holy war against the [secular Iraqi] infidels."[58]

When Saddam Hussein's troops invaded Iran (for what he erroneously thought would be a quick victory), Khomeini became obsessed with a jihad against his secular opponent. Before the war finally ground to a halt in 1988, with no victor, it had inflicted tremendous damage on the Iranian economy and cost the country several hundred thousand lives. Even so, Khomeini, who had vowed to pursue the battle until Saddam Hussein was toppled, reluctantly agreed to the truce, which he called "more deadly than taking poison."[59]

Since the late 1980s, following Khomeini's death, the Islamic revolution has moderated somewhat. The Revolutionary Guard has relaxed its grip on daily life; in the secrecy of their homes middle-class Iranians dance to Western music at social gatherings and women shed their veils; and the country has retreated from its aggressive foreign policy. The Islamic leadership is now divided between relative moderates and radical clerics.[60]

Radical Hindu Fundamentalism

Compared to its Muslim counterpart, Hindu fundamentalism has received scant attention in the West. Perhaps this is because Hinduism is largely confined to one country, India, and the leading fundamentalist political voice there, the Bharatiya Janata Party has risen only recently from just two parliamentary seats (1984) to the largest bloc in parliament and head of the ruling coalition.[61] The BJP itself is divided into factions. Hard-liners take a militant stance and often use inflammatory language against the nation's Muslim minority. Indeed, leaders of India's Center and Left opposition parties, and many of India's 120 million Muslims, blame that faction for the destruction of a major Muslim mosque in 1992 and for anti-Muslim riots that killed 3,000 people in 1995. On the other hand, the BJP moderates and pragmatists who headed the country until recently recognize that the party has nowhere near a parliamentary majority and must cooperate with secular parties in order to govern. They preach a form of Hindu nationalism that stresses broad, Indian cultural themes and even opens its arms to Muslims (a few of whom vote for the BJP).

But the roots of Hindu revivalism lie in India's communal politics, that is, the tensions between the Hindu majority (over 80 percent of the country), the Muslim minority (12 percent of the population), and the smaller Sikh population (about 2 percent) (see Chapter 3). During the 1980s, militant Hinduism grew rapidly, partly as a response to the surge of Islamic revivalism in Pakistan and the Middle East. Indeed, Muslim, Sikh, and Hindu fundamentalists all feed on their common hostility toward each other. The rise of fundamentalism (of all kinds) was indirectly encouraged by politicians from the ruling Congress party, most notably Prime Minister Indira Gandhi, who played the dangerous game of using communal politics for their own advantage. A further factor that has troubled many Hindus and increased their militancy is the conversion of large numbers of untouchables to Buddhism or Islam. In the eyes of many middle- and higher-caste Hindus, these conversions threaten the caste system, a linchpin of Hinduism. The BJP and other Hindu nationalist groups also gained considerable support among voters disgusted with corruption within the secular parties such as the powerful Congress Party. Its strength is rooted in northern India's Hindi-speaking heartland but extends throughout the country, particularly within the urban middle class.

Since Hinduism is a less clearly defined religion than Islam and lacks a formal church structure, its fundamentalist beliefs are less clearly spelled out as well. Nationalism is certainly an important element, specifically the insistence that India should cease being officially multicultural and instead define itself as a Hindu nation. Some traditional religious practices shunned (or prohibited) by modern Indian society are occasionally endorsed by revivalist spokespersons, though they are not central to their message. Thus, some party leaders have occasionally defended the revival of sati, the brutal, traditional Hindu practice of burning a widow on her husband's funeral pyre. Ironically, the BJP has several female representatives in parliament and a number of active women's organizations.

In the absence of an organized Hindu church or clergy, fundamentalist leadership has been divided among various interest groups and parties, not all of which have the same religious or political position; moreover, some groups (including the BJP) have changed their position sharply over time. The Vishwa Hindu Parishad (VHP) and Shiv Sena have openly encouraged attacks on Muslim mosques and neighborhoods, most notably in the Hindu strongholds of Uttar Pradesh, Madhya Pradesh, and Bihar states. The political consequences of such conflicts are substantial. For example, in 1990 Prime Minister V. P. Singh's government fell when he used troops to prevent a Hindu mob from tearing down a famed Muslim mosque. The mosque, built on the site where the Hindu god Ram is believed to have been born, is bitterly resented by Hindu militants. Bloody Hindu-Muslim riots over the site in 1989 and 1992 left thousands dead each time.

The majority of India's Hindus have rejected the fundamentalist movement and for many years the BJP and its predecessor party, the Bharatiya Jana Sang (BJS) were shunned by the country's secular parties and excluded from coalition governments at the national and state level. More recently, however, the party's support has grown as voters have become increasingly disenchanted with the traditional secular parties. A 1992 BJP rally in New Delhi, demanding limits on Islamic rights, attracted 1 million demonstrators. In its platform the party called for Indian production of nuclear weapons (India has since tested such weapons underground), limits on foreign investment, greater economic self-sufficiency, and reduced imports. Party leaders also oppose birth control programs and have expressed the belief that it is not necessary for peasants and other poor Indians to be literate.[62] By moderating its rhetoric, however, the BJP emerged as the largest bloc in parliament following the 1996 national elections. When opposition parties were unable to agree upon a governing coalition, the BJP finally was asked to head the national government. Faced with the need to maintain their coalition with secular parties, the party's more pragmatic leaders avoided anti-Muslim or other extremist positions. The government, however, fulfilled a longtime BJP goal by developing and testing nuclear weapons.

THE PROGRESSIVE CATHOLIC CHURCH

At roughly the same time that many Muslims and Hindus were turning in a reactionary direction, important sectors of Latin America's Catholic church were embarking on a progressive one. From the time of Spanish colonialism through the first half of the twentieth century, the Church had supported the political and economic status quo, thereby legitimizing Latin America's elite-based governments. In a region marked by a high concentration of income and wealth, the Church was often a major land owner. Alienated by the anticlerical sentiments of European and Latin American liberals, it usually allied with conservative political factions.

In the decades after World War II, however, that pattern began to change dramatically among important portions of the clergy, particularly at the parish level. The process of change accelerated greatly in the 1960s, when Pope John XXIII moved the "Church universal" in a far more liberal direction, placing greater emphasis on social concerns. "The Second Vatican Council [convened by Pope John between 1962 and 1965] moved international Catholicism from a generally conservative and even authoritarian position to one that supported democracy, human rights and social justice."[63] Catholics were encouraged to address social issues and to enter into a political dialogue with liberals and even leftists.

In 1968, the Latin American Bishops Conference (CELAM) met in Medellín, Colombia, to apply the lessons of Vatican II to their own region. Boldly challenging the status quo, their ideas reflected the influences of the reformist and radical theologians who represented the "progressive church."[64] The themes of "dependency" and "liberation" of Latin America's oppressed poor echoed through many of CELAM's pronouncements. The clergy, said the bishops, must heed the "deafening cry . . . from the throats of millions asking their pastors for a liberation that reaches them from nowhere else." To do so, the Church must "effectively give preference to the poorest and the most needy sectors." In short, an institution historically allied with the region's power elite was now to be the Church of the poor.[65]

The Medellín conference must be understood in the broader context of political change that was shaking Latin America at the time. In 1959, the triumph of Cuba's revolutionaries spotlighted the poverty and oppression afflicting so much of Latin America. The far-reaching educational, health, and land reforms being carried out in Cuba impressed and radicalized many Catholics. In Colombia, Father Camilo Torres had left the priesthood to join a guerrilla movement three years before the conference. He was soon killed by counterinsurgency forces, thereby becoming a hero to leftists throughout Latin America.[66] Elsewhere in Latin America few priests or nuns became involved in armed struggle. Many, however, organized and politicized the urban poor while accepting important elements of Marxist political and economic analysis.

Though always a minority within the Church, leftist clergy had an important influence in Central America during the 1970s and 1980s, most notably in Nicaragua, El Salvador, and Guatemala.[67] Many Nicaraguan priests and nuns actively supported the Sandinista revolution in the 1970s. When the Sandinistas came to power, Father Miguel D'Escoto was named foreign minister, Jesuit priest Xabier Gorostiaga was appointed head of national planning, Father Ernesto Cardenal served as minister of culture, and his brother, Father Fernando Cardenal, became director of the national adult literacy campaign and was subsequently named minister of education. No government in Latin America has had nearly the number of priests in its Cabinet as did Nicaragua's Marxist revolutionary government.

For most of Latin America, however, the 1960s and 1970s were not years of revolution. Instead, much of the region was governed by right-wing military dictatorships. Reacting to a perceived radical threat, repressive military regimes replaced civilian democracies in Brazil, Argentina, Chile, and Uruguay. At the same time, armed-forces rule continued in much of Central America and the central Andes, where democratic traditions had never been strong. Ironically, right-wing repression spurred the growth of the progressive Church far more than the Cuban or Nicaraguan revolutions did.

Not surprisingly, radical clergy and laity were very outspoken in their criticisms of the military regimes and, consequently, suffered severe reprisals. Dozens of priests and nuns were murdered and many more persecuted in Brazil, El Salvador, and Guatemala. In El Salvador, for example, a far-right death squad called the White Warriors distributed handbills reading, "Be a Patriot, Kill a Priest."[68] But such repression only brought more moderate Catholic figures into the opposition. "When committed Catholics were imprisoned, tortured, and even killed, bishops in a significant number of cases then denounced the state, setting off a spiral of greater repression against the Church, followed by new Church denunciations of authoritarianism."[69]

In Chile, Brazil, El Salvador, and Peru, the Church became a leading critic of government human rights violations.[70] The most celebrated example was El Salvador's Archbishop Oscar Romero, the nation's highest-ranking cleric, who, ironically, had begun his tenure as a conservative.[71] Increasingly appalled by his government's massive human rights violations, he gradually moved to the left. In 1980, Romero wrote President Carter asking him to terminate U.S. military aid to the ruling junta until human rights violations had ended. Subsequently, he broadcast a sermon calling on Salvadorian soldiers to disobey orders to kill innocent civilians. "No soldier is obliged to obey an order against God's law," he declared. "In the name of God and in the name of this suffering people . . . I implore you, I beg you, I order you—stop the repression."[72] The following day Archbishop Romero was murdered by a right-wing hit squad as he said a Requiem Mass.

Like Romero, Latin America's progressive clergy are far more likely to be reformers than radicals. At times their political rhetoric and analysis may find some common ground with the left. Thus, they share the Marxists' indignation over the plight of the poor and many of them identify dependency and U.S. domination as root causes of Latin American underdevelopment. But they reject revolutionary violence and the Leninist state as solutions. Reform, not revolution, was also the proscription of CELAM's bishops when they suggested progressive Catholic theology as an alternative to both capitalism and Marxism.

A number of the bishops' pronouncements at Medellín originated with a radical Peruvian priest, Gustavo Gutiérrez, the father of liberation theology. In the following decades, writings by Gutiérrez and other liberation theologians greatly influenced the progressive Church in Latin America and other parts of the world. Liberation theology calls on Catholic laity and clergy to become politically active and to direct that activity toward the emancipation of the poor. Drawing on Marxist analysis, Gutiérrez accepts the notion of class struggle, but his form of struggle is nonviolent. The poor, liberation theologians argue, should organize themselves into Ecclesial (or Christian) Base Communities (CEBs) where they can raise their social and political consciousness. In that way they can recognize the need to transform society through their own mobilization.[73]

Starting in the early 1960s, CEBs spread through much of Latin America, most notably to Brazil, Chile, Peru, and Central America. While the number of communities and even their precise definition are subject to debate, a CEB is essentially "any group that meets on a regular basis to deepen its members' knowledge of the gospel, stimulate reflection and action on community needs . . . and evangelize."[74] In part, the Church has created CEBs as a response to the serious shortage of priests in Latin America, particularly among the poor.

Typically composed of 10 to 40 people, Ecclesial Communities are primarily found in poor, urban neighborhoods and, to a lesser degree, in rural villages (though there are also some middle-class CEBs). Guesses as to how many exist in Latin America vary widely, but one estimate placed the number in the 1980s at perhaps 200,000, with a total membership of several million people. Perhaps 40 percent of all communities were in Brazil, home of the world's largest Catholic population.[75] The majority of CEB members are probably not politically active and join for strictly religious purposes.[76] Still, many communities were the foundations for popular protests against oppression, most notably in Central America but also in Brazil, Chile, and Peru.[77] In other cases, CEBs helped raise political awareness and sharpen political skills among the poor.

Since the early 1980s, the influence of Latin America's progressive Church has diminished considerably.[78] One cause, ironically, has been the transition from military dictatorships to democracy in much of the region. Absent massive human rights violations and open assaults on the poor, the clergy has had less motivation to enter the political arena. Furthermore, without a common foe, moderate and radical priests no longer have a common cause. Finally, many political activists who had used the Church as a protective "umbrella" during the military dictatorships (it was, after all, respectable to be an active Catholic) are now able to participate in political activities through other, newly legal political organizations.[79]

At the same time, the Vatican, under the pontificate of John Paul II, has been unsympathetic to any type of political activism among priests and nuns, particularly when related to the CEBs and liberation theology. "Rome has called liberation theologians such as Leonardo Boff and Gustavo Gutiérrez to account, if not to recant. . . ."[80] As progressive bishops and archbishops such as Brazil's Don Helder Camara have died or retired, they have been replaced by more conservative clerics.[81] Still, though liberation theology and the progressive Church have lost much of their momentum, they have still made an important contribution to the political mobilization of Latin America's poor.

CONCLUSION

The hold of religion on the human heart and its consequent impact on the political process have been frequently misunderstood by Western scholars. As we have seen, the initial error of both modernization and dependency theorists was to underestimate its significance. Several factors account for the unanticipated resurgence of fundamentalism and other forms of religiously based politics in recent decades. In many countries rapid modernization has left people psychologically adrift, searching for their cultural identity. The breakdown of traditional village life and long-accepted customs often creates a void not filled by the material rewards of modern life. In the Middle East, the indignities of colonialism and then neocolonialism, resentment against Israel and the West, and a feeling of failed development have all contributed to that region's religious revival.[82] In Latin America, the progressive Church offered a shield against political repression and a voice for the poor. As different as they are, Islamic revivalism and the progressive Catholic Church both received much of their impetus from government repression and corruption. In short, the resurgence of Third World religion was, in part, a reaction to the deficiencies of modernization and the political-economic order.

Contemporary analysts risk miscalculating the impact of religion on Third World politics once again, this time by overstating its importance. To begin with, the political weight of the movements that have attracted the most attention, Islamic and Hindu radical fundamentalism and progressive Catholicism, must be put into perspective. Influential as they have been, they are not representative of the religions from which they have sprung. This point requires particular emphasis in relation to Islam, since a militant minority has left many Westerners with an extremely negative image of the entire Muslim religion. Islam is seen as backward and intolerant when, in fact, like all religions it encompasses a range of outlooks, some very progressive. For example, the media may suggest that Muslim women are all repressed and confined, yet there are many Islamic feminists and professional women in countries such as Egypt, Lebanon, and Malaysia. It is worth remembering that three Muslim nations—Bangladesh, Pakistan, and Turkey—have had female prime ministers in recent years. Similarly, contrary to stereotype, some Muslim countries, including fundamentalist Saudi Arabia, are on very good terms with the West. Finally, in at least some cases such as Turkey and India, when fundamentalist parties finally led national governments, their behavior in office was moderated by their need to attract coalition partners in parliament and to appeal to a wider range of voters in future elections.

When considering the broader scope of the current religious revival, again, its importance should be recognized but not exaggerated. History reveals that "religious resurgence is a cyclical phenomenon."[83] Some analysts feel that the contemporary religious surges in Islamic and Catholic activism reached their peaks in the late 1970s. Thus, Jeff Haynes argues, "There is no reason to doubt that the current wave of religion-oriented political ideas and movements will in time give way . . . to [a] partial resurrection of secular ideologies."[84] For the foreseeable future, however, religion will continue to be an important force in the politics of many developing nations.

In the chapter that follows, we will examine the various communal and ethnic divisions, including religion, that have so violently divided many developing nations.

DISCUSSION QUESTIONS

1. Discuss the various types of relationships that exist between church and state in Islamic societies.

2. What factors caused the growth of the progressive Church in Latin America and what is distinct about its followers' beliefs?

3. Discuss why the Buddhist and Hindu religions have usually been less actively involved in national politics than Islam or Catholicism.

4. What factors have led to the resurgence of Islamic fundamentalism (or revivalism) in Iran and other parts of the Middle East?

NOTES

1. Harvey Cox, *The Secular City* (New York: Macmillan, 1966).

2. Donald Eugene Smith, ed., *Religion and Modernization* (New Haven, CT: Yale University Press, 1974), p. 4.

3. Quoted in Timothy D. Sisk, *Islam and Democracy* (Washington, DC: United States Institute of Peace, 1992), p. 3.

4. Emile Sahliyeh, ed., *Religious Resurgence and Politics in the Contemporary World* (Albany, NY: SUNY Press), pp. 1–16.

5. Jeff Haynes, *Religion in Third World Politics* (Boulder, CO: Lynne Rienner Publishers, 1994), p. 3.

6. John L. Esposito, *The Islamic Threat: Myth or Reality?* (New York: Oxford University Press, 1992); Akbar S. Ahmed, *Discovering Islam* (New York: Routledge and Kegan Paul, 1988).

7. Kenneth D. Wald, "Social Change and Political Response: The Silent Religious Cleavage in North America," in *Politics and Religion in the Modern World*, ed. George Moyser (New York: Routledge and Kegan Paul, 1991), p. 240.

8. The Christian Democratic Party was the dominant party in Italian politics for decades but was destroyed in the early 1990s by scandal. It has changed its name to the Italian Popular Party.

9. Leonard Binder, a leading specialist on the Middle East, is critical of such terminology, arguing, for example, that Islam is only one part of Middle Eastern culture. See *Islamic Liberalism* (Chicago: University of Chicago Press, 1988), pp. 80–81.

10. For data on the size and percentage of the Islamic populations in the nations of the world, see John L. Esposito, ed., *Islam in Asia* (New York: Oxford University Press, 1987), pp. 262–263.

11. Donald Eugene Smith, *Religion and Political Development* (Boston: Little, Brown, 1970), p. 40.

12. Robin Wright, *Sacred Rage: The Crusade of Modern Islam* (London: Andre Deutsch, 1986), p. 63; William Montgomery Watt, *Islamic Fundamentalism and Modernity* (London:

Routledge and Kegan Paul, 1988), pp. 125–131; Dilip Hiro, *Holy Wars: The Rise of Islamic Fundamentalism* (New York: Routledge and Kegan Paul, 1989), pp. 5–26.

13. Ahmed, *Discovering Islam*, pp. 55–61; Saleem Qureshi, "The Politics of the Shia Minority in Pakistan" in *Religious and Ethnic Minority Politics in South Asia*, ed. Dhirendra Vajpey and Yogendra K. Malik (New Delhi, India: Monhar, 1989), p. 109.

14. Smith, *Religion and Political Development*, p. xi.

15. For a discussion of the strengths and weaknesses of such arguments see Winston Davis, "Religion and Development: Weber and the East Asian Experience," in *Understanding Political Development*, ed. Myron Weiner and Samuel Huntington (Boston: Little, Brown, 1987), pp. 221–280.

16. Terrance G. Carroll, "Secularization and States of Modernity," *World Politics* 36, no. 3 (April 1984): 362–382.

17. John L. Esposito, *Islamic Revivalism* (Washington, DC: American Institute of Islamic Affairs, American University, 1985), pp. 5–6; Eden Naby, "The Changing Role of Islam as a Unifying Force in Afghanistan," in *The State, Religion, and Ethnic Politics*, ed. Ali Banuazizi and Myron Weiner (Syracuse, NY: Syracuse University Press, 1986), p. 137; Yogendra K. Malik and V.B. Singh, *Hindu Nationalism in India* (Boulder, CO: Westview Press, 1994), pp. 53 and 206.

18. John L. Esposito, *Islam and Politics*, 2d ed. (Syracuse, NY: Syracuse University Press, 1987), p. 231.

19. Smith, *Religion and Political Development*, p. 70.

20. H. E. Richardson, *Tibet and Its History* (London: Oxford University Press, 1962).

21. Smith, *Religion and Political Development*, pp. 57–84.

22. Esposito, *Islam and Politics*, p. 1.

23. Contemporary hostilities between Jews and Muslims in the Middle East, as well as Islamic fundamentalist hostility toward the West, are relatively recent phenomena that are not rooted in Islam's fundamental beliefs.

24. Esposito, *The Islamic Threat*, pp. 78–79.

25. Anthony H. Johns, "Indonesia: Islam and Cultural Pluralism," in *Islam in Asia*, p. 203.

26. Donald Eugene Smith, *Religion, Politics and Social Change in the Third World* (New York: Free Press, 1971), pp. 12–22.

27. Smith, *Religion and Political Development*, p. 54.

28. At the same time, however, many parish priests and nuns supported the revolution in Nicaragua and several priests served in the Sandinista cabinet.

29. Ibid., pp. 57, 34–39; Haynes, *Religion in Third World Politics*, p. 146.

30. Janet A. Contursi, "Militant Hindus and Buddhist Dalits: Hegemony and Resistance in an Indian Slum," *American Ethnologist* 16, no. 3 (August 1989): 441–457.

31. Donald Eugene Smith, "The Limits of Religious Resurgence," in *Religious Resurgence and Politics*, pp. 36–39.

32. Morton Zuckerman, "Beware of Religious Stalinists," *U.S. News and World Report*, March 22, 1993, p. 80; Charles Krauthammer, "Iran: Orchestrator of Disorder," *Washington Post*, January 1, 1993, p. A19. Both articles are also cited in the 1993 preface to the paperback edition of John L. Esposito, *The Islamic Threat: Myth or Reality?*

33. Esposito, *The Islamic Threat*, p. vii.

34. Contursi, "Militant Hindus"; Esposito, *The Islamic Threat*, pp. 7–24; Shireen T. Hunter, ed., *The Politics of Islamic Revivalism* (Bloomington: Indiana University Press, 1988); Esposito, *Islamic Revivalism*; Sisk, *Islam and Democracy*, pp. 2–7, 73 (fn. 1, 2).

35. Among the many examples are Watt, *Islamic Fundamentalism and Modernity*; and Hiro, *Holy Wars*.

36. Hiro, *Holy Wars*, pp. 1–2.

37. Watt, *Islamic Fundamentalism and Modernity*, p. 2.

38. Wright, *Sacred Rage*.

39. Robin Wright, "Lebanon," in *The Politics of Islamic Revivalism*, p. 66.

40. Naby, "The Changing Role of Islam," pp. 124–154; Paul Overby, *Holy Blood: An Inside View of the Afghan War* (Westport, CT: Praeger, 1993).

41. For a discussion of the origins of the FIS and the nature of Algeria's violence since 1992, see Claire Spencer, "The Roots and Future of Islamism in Algeria," in *Islamic Fundamentalism*, ed. Abdel Salam Sidahmed and Anoushiravan Ehteshami (Boulder, CO: Westview Press, 1996), pp. 93–109.

42. To be sure, some Israeli "ultra-orthodox" Jews are radical fundamentalists who have carried out violent attacks against Muslims or secular Jews. The most notorious example was the attack by an ultra-orthodox Jewish gunman against worshipers in a Hebron Mosque and the assassination of Israeli Prime Minister Izhak Rabin by a Jewish fundamentalist who objected to Rabin's efforts to achieve peace with the Palestinian Liberation Organization (PLO).

43. Useful sources on the background of the revolution include Robin Wright, *In the Name of God: The Khomeini Decade* (New York: Simon & Schuster, 1989); Hiro, *Holy Wars*, Chapter 6.

44. Hiro, *Holy Wars*, p. 151.

45. Ibid., pp. 151–153.

46. Shireen T. Hunter, *Iran after Khomeini* (New York: Praeger, 1992), pp. 11–12. Hunter argues that the Shahs foolishly made their people choose between their Persian and their Islamic heritage. Faced with that option, they chose the latter.

47. Ibid., p. 57.

48. Cheryl Bernard and Zalmay Khalilzad, *The Government of God: Iran's Islamic Republic* (New York: Columbia University Press, 1984), pp. 12–13.

49. HIro, *Holy Wars*, p. 160.

50. M. M. Salehi, *Insurgency through Culture and Religion: The Islamic Revolution of Iran* (New York: Praeger, 1988), p. 54.

51. The classic study of the natural cycle of revolutions is Crane Brinton, *The Anatomy of Revolution* (New York: Vintage, 1965).

52. Wright, *In the Name of God*, p. 65.

53. A few parliamentary seats were even reserved for religious minorities including Jews, Christians, and Zoroastrians (though not the persecuted Baha'i minority). Wright, *In the Name of God*, pp. 180–181.

54. Ibid., p. 87.

55. Quoted in Bernard and Khalilzad, *The Government of God*, pp. 151–152.

56. Ibid., p. 154. Ironically, it emerged during the so-called "Irangate" Senate hearings that Iran had purchased arms from the United States by way of Israel in a deal arranged by Oliver North.

57. Wright's *In the Name of God* offers one of the better accounts, but there are many others.

58. Gary Sick, "Trial by Error: Reflections on the Iran-Iraq War," in *Iran's Revolution*, ed. R. K. Ramazani (Bloomington: Indiana University Press, 1990), p. 105.

59. Ibid., p. 104.

60. Wright, *In the Name of God*, p. 191; Hunter, *Iran after Khomeini*, pp. 32–41. (Hunter gives a more cautious view of the move toward moderation.)

61. This section draws heavily on Gail Omvelt, "Hinduism, Social Inequality and the State," in *Religion and Political Conflict in South Asia*, ed. Douglas Allen (Westport, CT: Greenwood Press, 1992), pp. 17–36. See also Ian Talbot, "Politics and Religion in Contemporary India," in *Politics and Religion in the Modern World*, pp. 135–161 and Malik and Singh, *Hindu Nationalism in India*.

62. *New York Times*, February 26, 1993.

63. Paul Sigmund, *Liberation Theology at the Crossroads* (New York: Oxford University Press, 1990), p. 19; David Lehmann, *Democracy and Development in Latin America* (Cambridge, England: Polity Press, 1990), pp. 108–110.

64. Scott Mainwaring and Alexander Wilde, eds., *The Progressive Church in Latin America* (Notre Dame, IN: University of Notre Dame Press, 1989).

65. Sigmund, *Liberation Theology at the Crossroads*, pp. 29–30.

66. Father Camilo Torres: *Revolutionary Writings* (New York: Harper and Row, 1962).

67. Philip Berryman, *Stillborn Hope: Religion, Politics and Revolution in Central America* (Maryknoll, NY: Orbis Books, 1991); Margaret E. Crahan, "Religion and Politics in Revolutionary Nicaragua," in *The Progressive Church*.

68. Jennifer Pearce, "Politics and Religion in Central America: A Case Study of El Salvador," in *Politics and Religion*, p. 234.

69. Mainwaring and Wilde, *Progressive Church*, p. 13.

70. Scott Mainwaring, *The Catholic Church and Politics in Brazil* (Stanford, CA: Stanford University Press, 1986); Brian H. Smith, *The Church and Politics in Chile* (Princeton, NJ: Princeton University Press, 1982).

71. Philip Berryman, "El Salvador: From Evangelization to Insurrection," in *Religion and Political Conflict in Latin America*, ed. Daniel H. Levine (Chapel Hill: University of North Carolina Press, 1986), pp. 58–78.

72. Ibid., p. 114.

73. Sigmund, *Liberation Theology at the Crossroads*, pp. 28–39.

74. W. E. Hewitt, *Base Christian Communities and Social Change in Brazil* (Lincoln: University of Nebraska Press, 1991), p. 6.

75. Hewitt, *Base Christian Communities*; Thomas C. Bruneau, "Brazil: The Catholic Church and Basic Christian Communities," in *Religion and Political Conflict in Latin America*, pp. 106–123.

76. John Burdick, "The Progressive Catholic Church in Latin America," *Latin American Research Review* 24, no. 1 (1994): 184–198; Hewitt, *Base Christian Communities*.

77. Daniel H. Levine and Scott Mainwaring, "Religion and Popular Protest in Latin America," in *Power and Popular Protest: Latin American Social Movements*, ed. Susan Eckstein (Berkeley: University of California Press, 1988).

78. Burdick, "The Progressive Catholic Church."

79. Thomas C. Bruneau, "The Role and Response of the Catholic Church in the Redemocratization of Brazil," in *The Politics of Religion and Social Change*, ed. Anson Shupe and Jeffrey K. Hadden (New York: Paragon House, 1986), pp. 95–98.

80. Mainwaring and Wilde, *Progressive Church*, p. 30.

81. Lehmann, *Democracy and Development*, pp. 144–145.

82. Mark Tessler and Jamal Sanad, "Women and Religion in Modern Islamic Society: The Case of Kuwait," in *Religious Resurgence*, p. 209.

83. Smith, "The Limits of Religious Resurgence," p. 34.

84. Haynes, *Religion in Third World Politics*, p. 155.

3

❦

THE POLITICS
OF CULTURAL PLURALISM
AND ETHNIC CONFLICT

Political analysts since the time of Karl Marx (1818–1883) have insisted on the primacy of class divisions in both industrialized and developing nations. Significant as those have been, however, no cleavage has more sharply, and oftentimes violently, divided countries during the past century than has ethnicity. "Cultural pluralism [i.e., ethnic diversity]," argues Crawford Young, "is a quintessentially modern phenomenon." It has been closely linked to the growth of the middle class and the emergence of intellectuals, journalists, and politicians who articulated nationalist or other ethnic aspirations while mobilizing workers and peasants behind that ideal.[1]

Since the close of World War II, the most frequent arena for violent conflict has not been wars between sovereign states, but rather internal strife tied to cultural, tribal, religious, or other ethnic animosities.[2] Any listing of the world's most brutal wars since 1980 would include ethnically based confrontations in Bosnia, Lebanon, Ethiopia, Rwanda, Sudan, Liberia, and Indonesia (East Timor).[3] More recently, the collapse of Soviet and Eastern European communism has released a torrent of pent-up ethnic hatreds in Azerbaijan, Armenia, Georgia, Chechnya, the former Yugoslavia, and other parts of Central and Eastern Europe. Indeed, with the end of the Cold War, the closing decades of the twentieth century increasingly became the era of world ethnic strife. Perhaps 12–15 million people have died in ethnic violence since World War II.[4]

Warfare between Serbs, Croatians, Bosnian Muslims, and Kosovars; separatist mobilization among French-speaking Québécois; racially based riots in Los Angeles; Basque terrorism in Spain; and Protestant-Catholic strife in Northern

Ireland all have demonstrated clearly that interethnic tensions and violence do erupt in Western industrial democracies and in former communist countries. But ethnically based confrontations have been particularly prevalent and cruel in Africa, Asia, and other parts of the developing world. Brutal struggles pitting Hindus against Sikhs or Muslims in India, Islamic Arabs against Christian or Animist Blacks in Sudan, Kurds against Arabs in Iraq, and Hutu against Tutsi in Rwanda and Burundi are but a few recent examples.

DEFINING ETHNICITY

While it is difficult to define ethnicity precisely, certain common qualities set individual ethnicities apart. They generally have (or believe themselves to have) a common history, traditions, beliefs, and values that unite their members and distinguish them from other cultures.[5] J.E. Brown's cynical definition of a nation can be applied to a variety of ethnic identities: "A group of people united by a common error about their ancestry and a common dislike of their neighbors."[6] In other words, ethnicity requires a subjective group consciousness that enables its members to establish mental boundaries between themselves and "others." Pakistanis in Uganda, Chinese in Malaysia, Kurds in Iraq, Hmong in Laos, or highland Indians in Ecuador each join together in political organizations, business groups, social clubs, or mutual-benefit societies. This does not mean that these ethnic groups are necessarily fully homogeneous or politically united; often they are divided by class, ideology, religion, or other differences. Palestinians, for example, are split between Islamic fundamentalists and more secular Arabs, between hard-line opponents of Israel and accomodationists. Sri Lanka's Tamil population is divided between those who have lived in the country for centuries and those brought from India in the nineteenth century to work the tea plantations. Indian Muslims and American Blacks are each separated by class and other cleavages. Still, the factors that bind together an ethnic group are more powerful than those that divide it. Thus, important as class distinctions may be, Sikh peasants in India identify more closely with Sikh businessmen than with Hindu peasants. As Cynthia Enloe has noted, "Of all the groups that men [or women] attach themselves to, ethnic groups seem the most encompassing and enduring."[7]

In some cases, ethnic classifications were originally artificially imposed by outsiders. In the Belgian Congo, for example, White explorers, colonial administrators, missionaries, and anthropologists erroneously lumped together people of the upper Congo into an imagined tribe (or ethnicity) called the Bangala. After a number of decades, the "myth of the Bangala" took on a life of its own as migrants from the upper Congo settling in the city of Kenshasa joined together politically under the ethnic banner that had been externally imposed on them.[8] Similarly, the classification of "Colored" used to denote racially mixed South Africans was an artificial construct established by the old White regime. Once individuals begin to accept in some manner the group label imposed on them, however, even such created ethnic classifications become politically relevant.[9]

Sometimes an ethnic group's history may be submerged or may remain relatively unrecognized for a prolonged period only to be revitalized at a later date. In the United States, since the 1960s there has been a flowering of Black history, Afrocentric consciousness, and African-American ethnic pride. That, in turn, contributed to the emergence of greater Black consciousness and Black Power movements in nations such as Jamaica and Brazil.

Ethnic groups may have their own social clubs, soccer teams, schools, or cemeteries. For the insecure Peruvian Indian recently arrived in Lima from her rural village, or the Yoruba seeking a job in Lagos, ethnically based social clubs may be the key to finding employment and housing in an otherwise cold and inhospitable city. In the threatening environment often associated with modernization and social change, "fear, anxiety and insecurity at the individual level can be reduced within the womb of the ethnic collectivity."[10] At the same time, however, ethnic consciousness often creates barriers between groups. Interreligious or interracial marriages, for example, may be frowned upon by both sides. In such countries as Canada, Malaysia, and Trinidad, ethnic divisions are managed relatively amicably and peacefully. More frequently, however, they are not. In multi-ethnic countries such as the United States, India, Liberia, and the Congo, common consciousness and culture bind together certain religious, caste, tribal, and racial groups while creating a barrier with other ethnicities.

ETHNIC AND STATE BOUNDARIES

Were the world composed of relatively homogenous nations such as Uruguay, South Korea, or Sweden, ethnically based wars would undoubtedly continue between states, but there would be no internal strife based on communal antagonisms.[11] In other words, an underlying cause of internal ethnic conflict is that boundaries for states (self-governing countries) and nations (distinct cultural-linguistic groups such as Serbs, Russians, or Kurds) or other ethnicities so frequently fail to coincide.[12] Had large numbers of Serbs and Croations not lived in Bosnia, there probably would not have been such extensive carnage in that nation. The absence of an independent state to house the Kurdish nation has precipitated ongoing confrontations in Iraq, Turkey, and Iran. Sikh militants in the Indian state of Punjab demand the creation of an independent Sikh state. In all of these cases, ethnonational boundaries and political boundaries do not correspond. When a minority (or, on occasion, majority) group feels it has been denied its fair share of political and economic power, it will resort to some form of protest or confrontation.

A look at the world's population map, particularly for the Third World, reveals how many independent nation-states are composed of multiple ethnic groups, many of whom are uncomfortable with or hostile toward each other. One study of 132 countries throughout the world revealed that only 12 of them (9 percent) are ethnically homogeneous, with another 25 (19 percent) overwhelmingly populated by a single ethnic group. The remaining 72 percent of the world's nations, then, have substantial minority group populations. Indeed, in 39 countries (30 percent of the total) no single ethnic group accounts for half of the state's population.[13] This pattern is most striking in sub-Saharan Africa, where virtually every country is composed of several tribal or ethnic groups.[14] For example, it is estimated that Nigeria, the most populous Black African state, has more than 200 ethnic or linguistic groups.[15]

Africans often attribute their continent's legacy of ethnic conflict to the European colonizers who divided the region into administrative units little connected with ethnic identities. In some areas, antagonistic ethnic groups were thrown together in a single colonial unit, while elsewhere individual tribes were split between two future countries. In both Africa and Asia, colonial powers often exacerbated ethnic tensions by favoring some groups over others. Yet colonialism must be seen as but one of many factors contributing to ethnic strife. Given the enormous number of tribal or ethnic groups in Africa, even if the European powers had exhibited greater ethnic sensibility, some form of multi-ethnic nations would inevitably have developed. The alternative would have been the creation of hundreds of small states that were not economically viable.

Ironically, the breakdown of European colonialism has also led to some singularly unhappy ethnic marriages. When the Portuguese withdrew from East Timor in 1975, the world community allowed neighboring Indonesia to annex it against the will of the local population. Faced with opposition to its rule, Indonesia introduced repressive measures that resulted in the death of perhaps 150,000 East Timorese (some 25 percent of their population) due to starvation, disease, or execution. Similarly, following Italian colonization and a brief British occupation in the 1940s, Eritrea was forcibly merged with Ethiopia. The Eritrean people were barely consulted and they subsequently began a long, ultimately successful struggle for independence.[16] The result was a three-decade-long civil war leading to the starvation of hundreds of thousands of people. Ultimately, the Ethiopian army fell to rebel forces from the provinces of Eritrea and Tigray.[17] The associated collapse of the Ethiopian revolutionary government led to independence for those two regions.

TYPES OF ETHNIC-CULTURAL DIVISIONS

In order to better comprehend the variety of ethnic tensions that pervade much of the developing world today, we will first classify ethnicities according to a set of overlapping categories: nationality, tribe, race, religion, and caste.[18]

Nationality

In ethnic analysis the term nation takes on a special meaning somewhat distinct from its more common usage depicting a sovereign state. It refers instead to a population with its own language, cultural traditions, and historical aspirations. It is frequently associated with the belief that "the interests and values of this nation take priority over all other interests and values."[19] As opposed to other types of ethnicity, nationalities often claim sovereignty over a specific geographic area. As we have seen, national boundaries, as here defined, often do not coincide with those of sovereign states. Thus, for example, Russia, India, Cyprus, and Sri Lanka are all sovereign states (i.e., independent countries) that encompass several distinct nationalities (cultural identities). Conversely the Chinese are a nationality that, through migration, has spilled over to several East Asian states and to other parts of the world. The Kurds also reside in several countries, including Iraq, Turkey, and Iran. Unlike the Chinese, however, they are a nation without a state of their own.

As with many types of ethnicity, the political significance of national identity is grounded in highly subjective factors. That is to say, nationality becomes politically important when members believe themselves to have a common history and destiny that both unites them and distinguishes them from other ethnicities in their country. Perhaps the most fundamental element here is the extent to which groups maintain a distinct spoken language. Because French Canadians, Kurds, and Chinese in Southeast Asia have maintained their "mother tongues," their national identities remain politically salient. Chicano nationalists in Texas, California, and New Mexico have sought to protect Mexican-American rights and cultural integrity, as some have run for local office under the banner of la raza unida ("the united race"). In Canada, the current Parti Québécois provincial government favors an independent Quebec ruled by French speakers. Chinese in Southeast Asia have maintained their own cultural and political organizations while suffering serious repression in countries such as Vietnam and Indonesia. On the other hand, whenever migrants to countries such as the United States or Australia fully assimilate into a new language and culture (gradually dropping their original language), their prior national identity becomes far less politically significant.

In its most limited form, nationalist leaders may simply seek to preserve their people's cultural identity and to promote their collective economic and political interests. The Lebanese in Brazil, the Irish in Liverpool, or the East Indians in Guyana and Trinidad have entertained no vision of self-governance. Nationalist aspirations become far more volatile, however, when they seek to create an independent ethnic state. Separatist movements are most likely to arise when an ethnic minority is concentrated in a particular part of the country and represents a majority of the population in that region.

Those conditions exist in Sri Lanka, where the long-standing Tamil minority is concentrated in the country's northern and eastern provinces, particularly the Jaffna region. As in most domestic controversies between nationalities, language issues precipitated the conflict. In 1956, not long after Sri Lankan independence, Sinhalese replaced English as the country's official language. While Tamil never ceased being used by government bureaucrats in the northeast provinces and while the language was given legal status in 1978, many Tamils, particularly those aspiring to government jobs, felt victimized. Religious differences between the largely Hindu Tamils and the Buddhist Sinhalese majority augment their language and cultural divisions. As early as 1949, leaders of the Tamil minority (some 18 percent of the nation's population) called for a federal system that would grant Tamil areas substantial autonomy.[20] Sinhalese nationalists, in turn, tried to impose their language on the entire nation. From the 1950s through the late 1980s Tamil nationalism took on increasingly strident and violent tones. Early calls for separatism (a degree of self-rule within the Sri Lankan state) were superseded in time by demands for secession and the creation of a sovereign Tamil state called Eelam. By the late 1980s, the most powerful force in predominantly Tamil areas was the Liberation Tigers of Tamil Eelam (better known as the LTTE or Tamil Tigers), a secessionist force engaged in terrorism and guerrilla warfare.

In 1987, following a major government offensive against the LTTE, India (which has its own Tamil minority population) intervened militarily. The resulting Indo-Lanka Peace Accord called for a multi-ethnic, multilingual Sri Lankan state with greater regional autonomy benefiting Tamil areas. Though signed by the Indian and Sri Lankan governments and supported by most Tamils, the accord was rejected by many Sinhalese, particularly the nationalist group JVP (National Liberation Front). From 1987 to 1989 the JVP launched their own campaign of strikes, school boycotts, and terrorism, resulting in thousands of deaths.

A brutal government campaign crushed the JVP but the struggle against the Tamil Tigers has continued. While many Tamils welcomed the Indo-Lanka accord, the Tigers viewed it as inadequate and began a bloody guerrilla war, first against the 60,000-man Indian army of occupation, and then, after the withdrawal of Indian troops in 1990, against moderate Tamil groups. The Tigers are believed to be behind the 1993 assassination of Sri Lankan president Ranasinghe Premadasa in a suicide bombing, and they remain an active force. While the level of conflict has declined since the mid-1990s, fighting and periodic acts of terrorism continue.

Tribe

The very use of the term tribe is fairly controversial. Many anthropologists and political scientists find it arbitrary and unhelpful. They note that earlier cultural anthropologists working in Africa, parts of South Asia, and Australia-New Zealand frequently assumed that the social characteristics of a small group of people they were studying could simply be extended to a larger unit of people they called a "tribe."[21] We spoke previously in this regard about the myth of the Bangala in the upper Congo. An additional criticism of the term is that it has been used to describe groups as large as the 15 million Yorubas who would be called a nation in other parts of the world. Hence, many scholars prefer the term ethnicity.

However, the term tribe continues to be used, not only by scholars of ethnic politics, but by political leaders in Africa and Asia as well. For example, in describing the problems of his country, former Ugandan president Milton Obote lamented "the pull of the tribal force."[22] We will use the term tribe to describe subnational groups that share a collective identity and language and believe themselves to hold a common lineage. In India, Vietnam, Burma, and other parts of Asia, tribe refers to nonliterate hill peoples, such as the Laotian Hmong, living very traditional lifestyles in relative isolation from modern society. The term has also been used, of course, regarding North American Indians as well as the lowland (Amazonian) Indians of South America. In none of these regions do we use the term in a pejorative sense.

Intertribal conflict has on a number of occasions sparked great violence in Africa, affecting more than half the countries in that continent at some time. Countries such as Nigeria, Ethiopia, Rwanda, Burundi, Uganda, Sudan, and Congo (Zaire) have been torn apart by civil wars that have been largely or partially ethnically based. In Liberia, Angola, and Mozambique, civil conflicts initially fought over other issues were aggravated by overlapping ethnic tensions. From the time of independence, Nigeria experienced antagonism between the northern Muslims and ethnic groups from other regions of the country. With 50 percent of the country's population, the Hausa-Fulani and other northern tribes were a powerful force in the political system, resented by southerners such as the Ibo, who considered them backward.[23] Northerners, in turn, feared the influence of the more modern and commercially successful Ibo, who dominated the East. Each of the three major ethnic groups (Hausa-Fulani, Ibo, and Yoruba) dominated one region of the country, casting a shadow over smaller tribes in their area. Each, in turn, feared domination by the other.[24]

Two military coups in 1966 intensified friction between officers of differing ethnic backgrounds and sparked violence against the many Ibos living in the north. In fear of their lives, hundreds of thousands of Ibo (perhaps as many as 2 million) fled to their homeland. In May 1967 Colonel Chukwuemeka Ojukwa, an Ibo military leader, declared that Eastern Nigeria was withdrawing from the country to become the independent nation of Biafra. Backed by the Organization of African Unity (OAU), the central Nigerian government was determined not to let Biafra secede.[25] Despite its initial military success, the Biafran army ultimately suffered from the antipathy that smaller eastern tribes tended to feel toward the Ibo. A number of them supported the federal army. Ultimately, the federal armed forces surrounded Biafra and gradually reduced its territory. Tens of thousands of Ibos starved to death in a pattern of war and famine that subsequently became tragically familiar in other parts of Africa. When Biafra finally did surrender in early 1970, however, the Nigerian military government was impressively disciplined and free of vengeance. Since that time, the Ibos have been successfully reintegrated into Nigerian society, though tensions and occasional violence persist.

Unfortunately, the Nigerian conflict was but one of the earliest cases of civil war that have developed between tribal and cultural groups in Africa during the past decades. Another was the long and bitter fight by the Eritreans and Tigrayans to secede from Ethiopia. Burundi's ruling Tutsi minority has crushed a series of uprisings by the majority Hutu (85 percent of the population) over the last three decades, massacring perhaps 100,000 people in 1972 alone.[26] In 1993, when a Tutsi soldier assassinated Melchior Ndadaye, a Hutu who was the country's first elected president, new intertribal bloodshed erupted. One year later, the death of neighboring Rwanda's president in a plane crash set off an orgy of violence in that country as well. A government-directed massacre aimed primarily at the minority Tutsis resulted in the death of perhaps 500,000 people, most of whom were beaten or hacked to death by local militia and villagers.[27] Eventually, the Tutsis'revolutionary army gained control of the country and jailed thousands of Hutus. Hundreds of thousands more fled to neighboring Congo where many of them were massacred by the anti-Hutu regime of Laurent Kabila.

In cases such as the Angolan and Mozambiquan civil wars, external intervention intensified internal splits and added to the carnage. Cold War superpowers often armed the opposing sides or interceded through surrogates. For example, acting in consort with the Soviet Union, the Cubans provided military assistance to the central governments of Ethiopia, Angola, and Mozambique. The United States armed UNITA, the Angolan rebel force, while the South African military supported Mozambique's bloody RENAMO guerrillas, and Belgium and France helped arm the Rwandan regime. In each of those countries, hundreds of thousands perished from warfare or starvation. While the end of the Cold War may ultimately reduce external intervention in Africa's tribal conflicts, the bitter war in Liberia demonstrates that the "New World (Dis)Order" will still include African interethnic violence for the foreseeable future. And during the late 1990s, Rwanda, Uganda, Zimbabwe, and Angola intervened militarily in the ethnically related civil wars in the Congo.

Corrupt dictators have also launched campaigns against tribal minorities in order to curry favor among more powerful ethnic groups and, thereby, deflect protest against their own government. Thus, in recent years Kenyan President Daniel arap Moi has brutalized the Kikuyu and Congolese President Laurent Kabila has massacred the Hutu minority in his country for precisely that purpose.

Race

Race is usually the most visible type of ethnic division within society. Thus, the visitor to South Africa can immediately know whether he or she is in a Black township or a White neighborhood, just as the traveler in Guyana can easily distinguish between a Black or East Indian community. In other instances, however, racial distinctions are subtler and more elusive. The Aymara-speaking woman in La Paz, Bolivia, who wears a bowler hat and a distinctive Indian skirt, would surely be classified as an Indian. Yet her Spanish-speaking son, teaching at a nearby high school or university and wearing a suit, is considered a Mestizo. Many African Americans or South African Coloreds of mixed racial origin are physically indistinguishable from Whites. Unlike other ethnic divisions, racial divisions are not necessarily linked to language or cultural differences.

We have noted that cultural identity involves a common set of values and customs, and a shared sense of history and destiny. Of course, not all people of the same race living in a particular country enjoy that sense of community. Serbs, Croats, Bosnian Muslims, and Kosovars in the former Yugoslavia are all White; Lebanese Shi'ites and Christians are Arabs; and Ethiopia's Amharic majority and the Eritreans who seceded are both Black. Yet in none of these cases do those with common racial backgrounds share a common cultural bond. Only when people live in multiracial settings do individual racial groups develop a sense of ethnicity. "There was no common sense of being 'African,' 'European,'or [American] 'Indian,'" notes Crawford Young, "prior to the creation of multiracial communities by the population movements of the imperial age."[28] Slavery and other manifestations of Western imperialism in the Third World were associated with a wide range of negative racial stereotypes of Asians, Africans, and Amerindians. The subsequent migration of Asians to East Africa and the Caribbean created further racial cleavages.

South Africa presented the most notorious and most intractable example of racially based political conflict. From its colonization by the British until the 1994 transition to majority rule, the country was dominated by a White minority constituting, as of the 1990s, some 15 percent of the population. In the years after World War II, political power shifted from English-speaking Whites to the more conservative Afrikaners, who had descended primarily from Dutch settlers (and who represented about 60 percent of the White population).[29] Blacks, while constituting about 70 percent of the nation's population, were denied fundamental legal and economic rights, including the ability to vote or to hold national political office.

Until renounced by President F. W. de Klerk's administration (the last White minority government), the legal centerpiece of South African racial policy was apartheid ("separateness"). It rigidly segregated employment, public facilities, and housing, while calling for the creation of eight allegedly self-ruling "homelands" where the nation's Blacks would be settled. In fact, these homelands, consisting of desolate rural regions, could not possibly support the country's Black population. Moreover, since important sectors of the South African economy, most notably the mines, are dependent on Black labor, the geographical segregation envisioned by apartheid was implausible even from the perspective of the White business community. The millions of Blacks who continued to live outside the homelands were denied the right to own land or to enjoy fundamental civil liberties.

The South African social and political hierarchy was based on a fourfold racial classification that defied international ethical standards and often fell victim to its own logical contradictions. Blacks, of course, were subjected to the greatest level of legal discrimination. "Coloreds," constituting less than 10 percent of the population, and Asians (about 3 percent) had greater legal rights than Blacks, but still ranked well below Whites. The Constitutional Act of 1983 established a three-house Parliament for Whites, Coloreds, and Asians. The powers of the non-White houses, however, were quite limited.

Beginning in the 1980s, cracks developed in South Africa's separation policies as many middle-class Coloreds and Asians moved into "Whites only" neighborhoods by subletting from Whites. Hoping to isolate Colored professionals and business people from the Black population, the Government often turned a blind eye to such violations while simultaneously brutally repressing Black civil rights demonstrations in the townships.

By the late 1980s, apartheid and White dominance were under intense domestic and international pressures. South Africa was an international pariah, subject to diplomatic and cultural isolation, including a United Nations boycott on trade, travel, and investment. The country's athletes of any race could not compete in the Olympics or other international sporting events. Though slow to take effect, economic sanctions, particularly restrictions on investment, eventually began to limit economic growth. Constant unrest in the Black townships, coupled with international isolation and a worldwide trend toward democracy, all compounded the pressures for change.[30] A growing number of powerful voices among the White economic, legal, and intellectual elite (including Afrikaners) pressed the government for racial reform.

Thus, in the early 1990s, the de Klerk administration came to recognize that apartheid was no longer viable, gradually rescinding a variety of segregation laws. At the same time, it legalized the primary Black opposition group, the African National Congress (ANC) and two other radical organizations after decades of banishment. The Congress's legendary leader, Nelson Mandela, perhaps the world's most renowned political prisoner, was released along with hundreds of other political prisoners. These changes, coupled with the ANC's suspension of armed struggle, opened the door to a new Constitution enfranchising the Black majority and ending White minority rule.

In December 1991 the Convention for a Democratic South Africa (CODESA) brought together the government, the ANC, the Zulu-based Inkatha Freedom party (headed by Chief Mangosuthu Gatsha Buthelezi), and 16 smaller groups for discussion of the new political order. Public opinion among Whites was somewhat mixed, but generally supportive. Nelson Mandela expressed amazement at the hundreds of Whites who lined the road to cheer him when he was released from prison. In a 1992 national referendum called by de Klerk, nearly 70 percent of all White voters endorsed negotiations with the ANC and other Black groups. And in early 1993, the government and the ANC announced agreement on the election of a constitutional assembly to create a Black-led political system. Universal suffrage has ensured a Black majority in the assembly, but Whites were guaranteed special minority protection until 1999. In May 1994 Nelson Mandela was elected president of South Africa by the ANC parliamentary majority.

The road toward multiracial democracy remains difficult. Blacks have discovered that majority rule does not guarantee them improved living standards, and they could turn against the more affluent White and Asian minorities some day. President Mandela's government has implemented moderate economic policies in an attempt to reassure the White business community. Over time, however, if Black living conditions do not improve and if there is no substantial redistribution of economic resources, the ANC's Black constituency may demand more radical policies. And tribally based violence among Blacks could also resurface. Prior to the 1994 transition, violence within the Black community took a terrible toll, often pitting the more radical ANC (primarily backed by individuals of Xhosa ethnicity) against the conservative, Zulu-dominated Inkatha party. Some of that violence, it was subsequently revealed, was fomented by the outgoing White government's security forces. By including Inkatha in his government, Mandela quieted the situation. Indeed, South Africa has impressively contained and soothed earlier ethnic hostilities to this point. But, remaining tensions lie just beneath the surface.

Religion

Because of the deeply felt beliefs it represents, religion has frequently been the source of bitter communal strife. The likelihood of conflict between religious groups is influenced by at least two important factors: the extent to which one religious community feels dominated by another, and the degree to which either religion believes that it represents the only true faith, making alternate theologies unacceptable. Thus, for example, Catholics and Protestants coexist rather harmoniously in the United States and Germany because neither of these conditions applies. On the other hand, in Northern Ireland, where Catholics have resented the Protestants'political and economic power, years of bloody strife preceded the recent peace treaty.

In 1992, Hindu fundamentalists destroyed a sixteenth-century Muslim mosque in the northern Indian town of Ayodhya. As in many such clashes, the incident originated in centuries-old beliefs and hostilities.[31] The Ayodhya mosque had been built by the Mogul emperor Babur on the spot where many Hindus believe their god Ram had been born some 5,000 years earlier. To the Hindu political party, the Bharatiya Janata, and the militant World Hindu Council the building was a symbol of foreign Islamic domination during hundreds of years of Mogul rule prior to British colonialism. Indeed, two years prior to the attack on the mosque, Prime Minister Vishwanath Pratap Singh's National Front coalition government had been forced to resign over its refusal to have it razed and replaced with a Hindu temple. Within days of the assault, rioting in much of north and central India left perhaps 2,000 dead.

Ironically, some of the worst Hindu-Muslim bloodshed took place in Bombay, India's financial and cultural center and one of the most modern and least sectarian cities in the country. An extremist Hindu group, Shiv Sena, with some 30,000 armed members in Bombay was believed responsible for much of the city's violence. Not only have city authorities failed to prosecute Shiv Sena's leader subsequently, but he is protected by the Bombay police. In Islamic Pakistan crowds attacked dozens of Hindu temples, while in Bangladesh Muslims attacked shops owned by Hindus and burned the Air India offices.

To be sure, India and Pakistan were born of religious violence and neither has been free of it since. Although both had been part of a single British colony, the Muslim League made it clear during negotiations for independence in the 1940s that it wanted its own country. Using language that classically defines an ethnic group, League leader Mohammed Ali Jinnah declared: "We are a nation with our own distinctive culture and civilization, language and literature . . . customs . . . history and tradition."[32] In 1946, as independence approached, political conflict between the Muslim League and the Congress Party (a secular party led primarily by Hindus) touched off Hindu-Muslim communal violence that left thousands dead. Finally, the British reluctantly divided their crown jewel into two countries: India, with roughly 300 million Hindus and 40 million Muslims, and Pakistan, with approximately 60 million Muslims and 20 million Hindus. No sooner had independence been declared, on August 15, 1947, when horrendous interreligious massacres began in both countries. In Punjab, the center of the violence, both Hindus and Sikhs battled Muslims.[33] Whole villages were destroyed. As many as 1 million people may have been killed in one of the twentieth century's worst ethnic eruptions. In addition, perhaps 12 million refugees from both countries fled across the border to join their coreligionists.[34] The creation of Pakistan as a Muslim state, however, ultimately failed to create a sense of nationhood for all its citizens. Two decades later the eastern region of the country broke away to form Bangladesh. Meanwhile, Muslim separatists in the Indian state of Kashmir are currently waging guerrilla warfare designed to achieve either Kashmiri independence or unity with Pakistan.

Interreligious hostilities have continued in India since independence, taking a heavy toll on its political system. Since the late 1970s, for example, Sikh militants have demanded the creation of an independent Sikh nation, called Khalistan, in the state of Punjab (where Sikhs constitute 55 to 60 percent of the population). Ironically, many analysts charge that the ruling Congress Party and its leader, Indira Gandhi, secretly encouraged the most extremist Sikh organization, the outlawed Dal Khalsa, in order to discredit the cause of Sikh autonomy and the more moderate Akali Dal Party.[35] If so, that proved to be a grave miscalculation. Sikh terrorism (including random murder of Hindu civilians) countered by police repression created a spiraling cycle of violence. In 1984, government troops attacked the holy Golden Temple of Amristar where militant Sikh leader Sant Jarnail Singh Bhindranwale and his followers were holed up. In a three-day battle, over 1,000 people, including Bhindranwale, were killed. Thousands of Sikh troops in the Indian armed forces mutinied, some of them battling loyal amy units. Finally, on October 31, months after the attack on the Golden Temple, two Sikh members of Prime Minister Indira Gandhi's personal bodyguard assassinated her. In the ensuing rioting, Hindu mobs killed thousands of Sikhs. Despite the attempts at reconciliation by Indira's son Rajiv Gandhi, who succeeded her as prime minister, government repression and Sikh terrorism continued unabated. By the 1990s, after some 20,000 deaths on both sides, the Indian military seemed to have contained the separatist movement.

During the 1970s and 1980s, Lebanon was a battlefield for warring religious factions. Among the 17 religious communities that officially shared political power after independence, the most important were the Maronites (a Catholic sect), Armenians (Christians, primarily non-Catholics), Shi'ite Muslims, Sunni Muslims, and Druze (a Muslim sect). Ironically, for decades the country was considered "the Switzerland of the Middle East," a bastion of peace and economic prosperity in the midst of an otherwise troubled region. The dominant Maronite and Sunni populations had politically coexisted under the terms of a power-sharing arrangement first adopted in the 1920s and reinforced at the time of Lebanese independence by the national pact of 1943.

That arrangement broke down in the 1970s due to Muslim discontent, particularly among the Shi'ites. The long-standing power-sharing arrangement between Christians and Muslims no longer reflected their relative population strength. Muslims, with between 55 and 70 percent of the population (depending on which estimate one believed), had been allocated only 50 percent of the nation's bureaucratic and political posts. Religious, economic, and political differences also separated the Shi'ites from the more powerful Sunni Muslims. Living primarily in the rural south, the Shi'ites suffered from a far lower standard of living and an illiteracy rate perhaps triple that of the Christians. Though the Shi'ites were the single largest religious group in the country, they held less than 20 percent of the seats in Parliament. The nation's two most important political posts—president and prime minister—were reserved for a Maronite Christian and Sunni, respectively.[36]

Tensions were further exacerbated by external forces. The arrival of large numbers of Palestinian refugees, including armed PLO militia, radicalized the country's political debate. Many economically deprived Shi'ites were attracted to the revolutionary rhetoric espoused by Palestinian groups. On the other hand, Christians, though they had sympathized earlier with the Palestinians, observed that PLO attacks on Israel provoked retaliatory Israeli raids on Lebanon. As Israel began to mount military assaults against Palestinian forces in southern Lebanon, Shi'ite leader Musa Sadr created Amal (the Battalions of the Lebanese Resistance) to defend the region. Israel, in turn, allied itself with Christian militias who feared both Shi'ite radicalism and the Palestinian guerrilla fighters. Initially, Syria backed the Palestinian armed forces.[37]

By 1975, clashes between Palestinian guerrillas and Christian militias engulfed Lebanon in a civil war that lasted until 1990 and could conceivably resurface at some future time. The country's religious conflict had elements of class struggle as well, with Christians being the most affluent community and the Shi'ites seeing themselves as the oppressed poor. Palestinian national aspirations, temporary Israeli occupation of southern Lebanon, and Syrian military domain over much of the country all added to the bloodshed. Over time alliances sometimes shifted, with Shi'ites and Syrians, for example, supporting the Palestinians at some points and fighting them at others.

Caste

Unlike racial, religious, or national divisions, stratification based on caste is found in only a small number of societies. Caste differentiations are most prevalent in India (among Hindus) but can be found in some of the neighboring countries of South Asia and, in a different form, in West Africa as well. Caste systems have three fundamental properties. First, they involve a rigid social hierarchy—people are born into a particular caste rank and remain there permanently. Second, they are endogamous—members marry within their own caste. And finally, they are ascriptive—an individual's social status as defined by caste is largely unrelated to his or her educational or occupational achievement.[38]

In its worse manifestations, the caste system has generated tremendous injustices. For example, periodically the Indian press reports instances of powerful rural Brahmans (the highest caste) killing untouchables (those below the caste system) without any legal punishment. Over time, however, the effects of modernization and the Indian government's legislation against caste discrimination have modified its effects somewhat. In urban areas social status is not as closely linked to caste origin as it once was. In the political sphere, for example, elected officials or bureaucrats of lower-caste or even untouchable origin now serve in important government positions. Indeed, India's competitive electoral system has given birth to political machines based on caste affiliation.[39] Since about 60 percent of the country's Hindus are in the lower, Sudra, caste and another 20 percent are untouchables, machines tied to these groups have obvious political strength. Caste associations also function as interest groups defending the needs of their members.

INDEPENDENCE, MODERNIZATION, AND ETHNIC TENSION

In the United States, with its history as a "melting pot" for a wide variety of immigrant groups, we often assume that the process of social modernization—entailing higher literacy, urbanization, and the spread of mass communication—brings with it greater ethnic integration and harmony.[40] Yet in Africa and Asia, the achievement of national independence and the subsequent modernization of society have frequently intensified and politicized ethnic hostilities. Indeed, Crawford Young notes that "cultural pluralism as a political phenomenon" was not significant in traditional Third World societies but, rather, emerged "from such social processes as urbanization, the revolution in communications and spread of modern education."[41]

During the era of European colonialism, ethnic divisions in Africa and Asia were kept somewhat in check by the independence movement's desire to create a common front against the Europeans. "The transcendent obligation of resistance to the colonizer . . . largely obscure[d] the vitality of ethnicity as a basis of social solidarity."[42] After independence, however, previously submerged ethnic rivalries sprang to the surface.[43] In the new political order different religious, racial, tribal, or national groups have competed with each other for such state resources as roads, schools, medical clinics, irrigation projects, and civil service employment.

More recently, the migration of rural villagers to urban centers has brought many ethnic groups into close proximity for the first time. Furthermore, urbanization, rising educational levels, together with the spread of mass communications have politicized previously unmobilized sectors of the population. Because many of them identify with competing caste, religious, national, or tribal groups, their newly acquired political awareness often brings them into conflict with each other. Furthermore, the spread of higher education, rather than creating greater harmony, often creates a class of ethnically chauvinistic intellectuals who become the driving force for intergroup struggle. Hence, for all of these reasons, ethnic tensions have remained a potent and often growing phenomenon in the developing world.

LEVELS OF INTERETHNIC CONFLICT

While most countries are ethnically heterogenous, there are wide variations in the ways ethnicities relate to each other. In some cases, people of different races or religions interact fairly amicably. In others, deep resentments have inspired the most horrific barbarities. Having examined various types of ethnic cleavages in society, we will now examine the nature and intensity of interethnic conflict. As a measure of these relations, we will consider such indicators as the frequency of interethnic friendships or marriages, the prevalence of political parties or trade unions segregated by (or even based upon) ethnic groupings, and the correlation between ethnicity and social class.

Relative Harmony

Industrial democracies are more likely to have records of amicable ethnic relations than are LDCs. In Switzerland, for example, German-, French-, and Italian-speaking citizens have lived together peacefully for centuries. Since linguistic divisions within states are the most likely to polarize, the Swiss experience is particularly impressive.[44] Relative harmony also prevails in the United States and Canada, which have fairly successfully assimilated a variety of ethnic immigrants. In North Dakota or Saskatchewan, for example, little notice is taken when a person of Ukrainian or German Catholic origin marries a Lutheran of Norwegian ancestry. Of course, racial divisions in the United States have been more conflictual.

Instances of relative ethnic harmony in developing countries are less common. However, in Brazil and in Cuba and other Caribbean nations, relations between Blacks and Whites are generally more harmonious than in the United States. Interracial dating and marriages, for example, are quite common, particularly among lower-income groups. Still, even in these nations historical legacies of discrimination maintain a clear social hierarchy between races. While many Black Dominicans, Brazilians, and Panamanians can be found in the middle class, most remain mired in the lower class and virtually none make it to the upper echelons of the political and economic order.

In short, even the countries classified as harmonious are only so categorized relative to other, more conflict-ridden societies. Glaring examples of interethnic discrimination and tension persist. In Cuba, for example, despite a long history of interracial marriage and government efforts against racial discrimination since the Revolution, Blacks have yet to attain many political leadership positions. There and elsewhere in the Caribbean racial slurs remain fairly common.[45] In the United States, the comparatively amicable interaction between most White ethnic groups stands in stark contrast to the country's ongoing racial divide. And Canada, perhaps more of a melting pot than the United States, has not really resolved the vexing problems of French separatism in Quebec.

Uneasy Balance

In developing nations such as Trinidad or Malaysia, divisions between the principle ethnic groups are somewhat sharper than in our previous category. While still generally peaceful, interethnic relations are at times quite strained. In Malaysia, the Muslim Malay majority has dominated the political system and the bureaucracy while the Chinese minority has prevailed in the private sector. Racial riots in 1969 led to the New Economic Policy, designed in part to redistribute more of the country's wealth to the Malays. Fearful of Chinese domination, the Malays have also benefited from a system of ethnic preferences in education and the civil service.[46] Today the two communities continue to maintain a social distance and some analysts see signs of slowly growing communal antagonisms. Thus, it remains to be seen if the country's current economic crisis will reignite ethnic tensions.

The Caribbean nation of Trinidad and Tobago offers another interesting example of uneasy balance. During the second half of the nineteenth century, British colonial authorities encouraged the migration of indentured plantation workers from India who joined the Black majority and the small White elite. Contrary to the usual Caribbean practice of extensive racial mixing, there was little intermarriage or childbearing between Blacks and East Indians.[47] Although there was little overt hostility, each group did develop negative stereotypes of the other.[48] Following Trinidadian independence in 1962, ethnic tensions increased as Blacks and Indians began to compete for state resources. Most of the important political, civil service, military, and police positions since that time have been held by Blacks, who predominate in the country's urban middle class and working class. The upper ranks of the business community continue to be dominated by the small White minority. Until recent decades much of the East Indian population belonged to one of two groups: middle- and upper-middle-class urban merchants and businessmen, some of whom exercise considerable economic power; and a large, impoverished rural population of farm workers and small farmers.

Trinidadian politics do not manifest the same overt ethnic appeals that characterize many LDCs, but most political parties and unions represent primarily one race. For more than two decades (1962 to 1986) the national government was headed by the predominantly Black People's National Movement (PNM). During that time the opposition was led by various Indian-dominated parties, including the Democratic Labour Party (DLP) and the United Labour Front (ULF). Major labor unions tended to be either primarily Black or East Indian.[49] Only in 1986 did the newly formed National Alliance for Reconstruction (NAR) finally dislodge the PNM from power by forging an electoral alliance between Indian voters and the Black middle and upper-middle classes.[50]While Black and Indian political and labor leaders have cooperated periodically over the years in efforts such as this, the two communities continue to maintain their social, political, and economic distance.

Enforced Hierarchy (Ethnic Repression)

Uneasy ethnic balances are maintained in countries such as Malaysia and Trinidad in part because political and economic power each tend to be controlled by different ethnicities. Enforced hierarchies, however, involve the concentration of both forms of power in the hands of the ruling ethnic group. Undoubtedly, South African apartheid represented the most blatant example of such a relationship. Through the 1980s Whites dominated both the private sector and the state, including the courts, police, and armed forces. Blacks were denied the most basic rights of citizenship. Until the dismemberment of apartheid legislation, the legal system prohibited or restricted interracial marriage, sexual relations, and housing.

In Latin American nations with large Indian populations, such as Guatemala, Ecuador, and Peru, there exists a less overt but still significant form of hierarchy. Until recently, when opportunities for indigenous peoples have improved, being Indian usually meant being a peasant at the bottom of the socioeconomic hierarchy. Even today, virtually all positions of political and economic influence are held by Whites or Mestizos (persons of mixed cultural backgrounds). Yet racial tensions are mitigated by the practice of defining Indians and Mestizos primarily in cultural rather than genetic terms, thereby allowing for some upward mobility. That is to say, an Indian who moves to the city, adopts Western dress, and speaks and reads Spanish is accepted as a Mestizo. And in the rural highlands of Ecuador or Peru, many peasant communities that spoke Quechua a generation ago have switched to Spanish in a process of mestizaje (becoming Mestizo). Over time, then, Mestizos have progressively increased as a proportion of the population while the percentage speaking Indian languages has diminished. Of course, until quite recently this meant that Indians normally could only enjoy upward mobility by abandoning their own culture.[51]

In these circumstances, racial and class distinctions are closely intertwined. Those higher on the social ladder tend to be lighter skinned, those at the lower ranks of society are generally darker. A study of more than 80 members of the Ecuadorian industrial and commercial elite revealed only one business leader who admitted to having any Indian ancestry at all, though a few others likely had some small proportion.[52] Similarly, in Brazil being Black is largely synonymous with being poor. Indeed, Blacks who rise to the middle or upper-middle class often are no longer considered Black by their peers. While upward mobility through the class-race hierarchy is possible, it remains difficult. Racial prejudice shapes social relationships and creates subtle—or not so subtle—barriers to equality.

Unlike South Africa's old social order, the racial hierarchy in Latin America is not legally enforced, nor has it normally required a comparably repressive police and military apparatus. In Guatemala, however, decades of revolutionary insurrection and government repression have taken a tremendous toll on the nation's Indian communities. Viewing peasant communities as breeding grounds for leftist guerrillas, successive military regimes massacred tens of thousands of peasants in a policy bordering on genocide. Fortunately, since the 1990s a peace treaty with the guerrillas has curtailed such violence.[53] Indian villages also suffered from the Peruvian military's recent war against the Maoist Shining Path guerrillas. Guerrilla organizers benefited from the Indian peasantry's resentment against the White-Mestizo power structure but, following their hard-line Marxist ideology, they insisted that they were engaged in class struggle rather than racial conflict.[54]

Systematic Violence

In much of Africa, Asia, and elsewhere ethnic hostilities have boiled over into violence and even civil war. Often, these clashes occur when ethnic tensions are reinforced by class antagonisms. In Northern Ireland, for example, many Catholics have resented Ulster Protestant dominance of the region's economic and political structures (the peace treaty will change the political situation but not the economic). Antipathy between Lebanon's Christian and Muslim communities was fueled by the Christians' economic superiority. In Nigeria, many Islamic northerners have taken exception to the economic success of the Christian Ibos.

Interethnic violence may also emerge when one group dominates the political system. For example, at various times Sunnis in Iraq, Arabs in Sudan and Mauritania, Amharics in Ethiopia, and descendants of U.S. slaves in Liberia have benefited disproportionately from state expenditures and employment. A shift in political power from one ethnicity to another may bring retribution against the former ruling group. Thus, when General Idi Amin seized power in Uganda, he ordered the slaughter of Langi and Acholi soldiers who were identified with the regime of ousted president Milton Obote. Following the overthrow of the

Communist government in Afghanistan, the country began to disintegrate as Tajiks, Hazars, and Uzbeks challenged the long-standing political dominance of the Pathan population.

ETHNIC PLURALISM AND DEMOCRACY

One of the most important and hopeful developments in Third World politics during the closing decades of the twentieth century was the rise of democracy or partial democracy in nations previously governed by authoritarian regimes (see Chapter 10). But democracy is far harder, though not impossible to maintain in multi-ethnic countries. As we have seen, in Lebanon, civil war between Christians and Muslims destroyed one of the most enduring democracies in the Middle East. And democracy could only be established in South Africa after White oppression of the Black majority had ended. Explaining the failures of democracy in Africa and Asia during the 1960s and 1970s, Alvin Rabushka and Kenneth Shepsle concluded that democracy "is simply not viable in an environment of intense ethnic preference."[55] By this they refer to societies in which certain ethnic groups receive special privileges while others suffer discrimination.

Worldwide, democracy has fared best either in countries which are relatively ethnically homogeneous (such as Finland, Denmark, and Japan which until recent decades have had few ethnic minorities) or in countries of "new settlement" (such as the United States, Canada, and Australia), populated by immigrants who have created a new, common culture.[56] In Africa and Asia where many countries labor under strong ethnic divisions, democracy and increased mass political participation may unleash ethnic hostilities as cynical politicians use ethnic appeals and stir up ethnic hatreds to secure votes.

Ethnic pluralism is more likely to hinder democracy in poorer countries where different groups contend for limited government resources in "the politics of scarcity." But this simply means that democracy is more difficult to achieve in such situations. It is not impossible. Despite its history of religiously based violence, India, one of the world's most ethnically diverse countries, has maintained democratic government for most of its half-century of independence. Trinidad-Tobago, a country divided by religion and race, has been among the Third World's most democratic countries. What is needed to accommodate ethnic pluralism and resolve tensions is mature and enlightened political leadership, a spirit of compromise, and the implementation of politically negotiated solutions such as federalism and consociational democracy, discussed below.

OUTCOMES AND RESOLUTIONS

When ethnic antagonisms arise from competition for state resources or from a group's demand for greater autonomy, a number of outcomes are possible. While some are entirely peaceful, many others are born of intense violence. And while some resolutions are successful, others do not endure. Potential solutions are always circumscribed and constrained by the political culture and the intensity of ethnic cleavages. Both historical enmities and patterns of cooperation weigh heavily on contemporary political leaders. Within these constraints, however, political creativity and statecraft are critical ingredients for a successful solution. Political elites may choose to play on ethnic hatreds and rivalries for their own advantage, or they may seek negotiated solutions. For example, the unexpectedly smooth and peaceful dismantling of White minority rule in South Africa was greatly facilitated by the skilled leadership of Nelson Mandela and F. W. de Klerk. All too often, however, self-serving and chauvinistic leadership makes a bad situation worse. In Bosnia, for example, where Serbs and Muslims had enjoyed a relatively amicable relationship in the not-too-distant past, extremist leaders, such as Serb President Slobodan Milosevic, have aroused ethnic hostilities in order to build their own political power base while bringing the country to ruin. Similarly, the brutal 1994 massacres in Rwanda were overwhelmingly directed from above. The government induced Hutu villagers to attack their Tutsi neighbors with whom they had lived peacefully, and had often intermarried, for many years.

Examination of intense ethnic conflict in the developing world reveals several types of resolutions. While the options presented here are not exhaustive, they cover a wide range of Third World experiences.

Power Sharing: Federalism and Consociationalism

Power-sharing arrangements seek to create ethnic tranquility and stability by constitutionally dividing political power among major ethnic groups. Often such settlements result from protracted negotiation and constitutional debate. When introduced into the constitution at the time of independence, power sharing offers the hope of heading off interethnic violence before it gets started. Unfortunately, however, such arrangements often break down and fail to prevent conflict.

Federalism, the primary form of power sharing, is "a system of government [that] emanates from the desire of people to form a union without necessarily losing their various identities."[57] It may involve the creation of autonomous or semiautonomous regions, each of which is governed by a particular ethnicity.[58] For example, prior to its collapse, Yugoslavia consisted of six autonomous republics governed by individual nationalities, such as Serbs, Croats, Montenegrans, and Slovenes. At the national level, the Constitution mandated power sharing between the various republics. That compromise began to unravel in the 1970s, however, following the death of Marshal Joseph Broz Tito, the country's long-term strong man. It collapsed completely in the early 1990s when the Communist party lost its grip on several republics. The Soviet Union represented another federalist effort that lasted for nearly 70 years but also disintegrated with the demise of Communist party rule. It should be noted, however, that Soviet federalism was fraudulent, since Moscow exercised firm control over the ethnically based republics while Russians (constituting slightly over half the Soviet population) dominated the union.

Industrial democracies have had greater success with ethnically based federalism. Switzerland's 22 cantons are each dominated by one of the country's three language groups. German, French, and Italian cantons coexist rather harmoniously. Canada's federalism, though not based on ethnic divisions, has allowed French-speaking Quebec a substantial amount of autonomy on language and other cultural matters. Although the country's constitutional arrangement has not satisfied Québécois nationalists, it has accommodated many of their demands and, at least until now, has induced the province's voters to reject independence. Whether such harmony can be maintained in the future remains to be seen, particularly as the French-nationalist party has governed Quebec since 1994 and continues to advocate independence. On two occasions Quebec's voters have rejected that option. But the margin of defeat has narrowed and a third plebiscite sometime in the future could yield a different result.

In the developing world, power sharing has had a spotty record, at best. After independence, Nigeria sought to accommodate its ethnic divisions through federalism. As previously noted, the country's northern region was dominated by the Hausa-Fulani, the east by the Ibos, and the west, to a lesser extent, by the Yoruba. While the Biafran war took a terrible toll, a new federal solution has subsequently taken hold. On the other hand, Pakistani federalism failed to overcome the tensions between the country's more powerful western region (populated largely by Punjabi speakers) and the Bengali-speaking east. In 1971, relations between the two regions broke down completely, resulting in the massacre of some 500,000 Bengalis by western Pakistani troops.[59] When India went to war with Pakistan, the eastern region was able to secede and form the new nation of Bangladesh. Federalist arrangements also failed to prevent the breakup of Ethiopia because they were not adequately supported by the central government.[60]

Consociationalism offers another potential solution to ethnic tensions. Like other forms of federalism, however, it has had limited success. Consociational democracy in plural (multi-ethnic) societies entails a careful division of political power designed to protect the rights of all participants.[61] It involves the following components:

1. The leaders of all important ethnic groups form a ruling coalition at the national level.
2. Each group's leaders have veto power over government policy, or at least over policies that affect their constituents.
3. Government funds and positions, such as the civil service, are divided between ethnicities on a proportional basis.
4. Each ethnic group is afforded a high degree of autonomy over its own affairs and over the region it populates.[62]

Thus, consociational democracy consciously rejects pure majority rule. Instead, it seeks to create a framework for stability and peace by guaranteeing minorities a share of political power and, if need be, a veto to protect them against the majority. Not surprisingly, negotiators for South Africa's outgoing White government insisted on consociational features in the country's new constitution that would provide protective guarantees for the White minority in the new Black-led regime. The irony of those demands can hardly be lost on South African Blacks, who enjoyed no such protection under White rule.

Arend Lijphart notes that the very success of consociational systems in reducing ethnic antagonisms often causes them to wither away. For example, after World War II, the Netherlands, Austria, Belgium, and Switzerland all crafted consociational democracies to manage internal ethnic divisions. Since the late 1950s, however, all have moved away from these arrangements as ethnic divisions (with the exception of Belgium) have diminished, largely as the result of consociationalism. Such success requires a high level of elite consensus across ethnic lines. Indeed, a degree of mutual trust and cooperation between the leaders of contending ethnic groups is the key to consociational democracy. Trust is not easy to establish, however, and becomes ever more difficult to attain after interethnic tensions erupt in bloodshed.

Consociational democracy has been tried for periods of time in several developing nations, including Cyprus and Malaysia. Perhaps the most widely known effort has been in Lebanon. From independence in 1943 until civil war erupted in 1975, government positions and political authority were divided proportionally between the nation's Muslim and Christian communities. Ultimately the system broke down, in part because formulas for the proportional division of government posts were not adjusted to reflect the rapid population growth of Shi'ites and other Muslims over the years. After 15 years of fighting that left that once-admired Middle Eastern democracy shattered, Lebanon's civil war came to an end in 1990. The settlement, largely brokered by Syria, restored consociational rule, with a division of government positions that more accurately reflect the increased size of the country's Islamic population.

Secession

When power sharing or other compromises fail, disgruntled ethnic minorities may seek to withdraw from the country in order to form their own state or to join their ethnic brothers and sisters in a neighboring country. As one author has put it, "Secession, like divorce, is an ultimate act of alienation."[63] It offers a potential way out of the failed "marriage" of ethnic groups within a nation-state. Unfortunately, however, like many divorces, secessionist movements provoke bitterness and hostility.

Ralph Premdas indicates that such movements have several characteristics:

1. An ethnic group, defined by factors such as language, religion, culture, or race, claims the right of self-determination. In other words, secession is not just a demand for greater autonomy from the central government, but rather an insistence on full independence. It should be noted, however, that ethnic groups often begin by seeking only autonomy and then expand their goal to full independence when their more modest objectives are denied.

2. The ethnicity has a defined territorial base that it claims as its homeland.
3. There must be some organized struggle.[64]

Given the many ethnically conflicted states in the developing world, we should not be surprised to find a large number of secessionist movements in the LDCs. Central governments faced with such breakaway efforts virtually always seeks to repress them since they are unwilling to part with some of their country's territory or resources just as the Abraham Lincoln was unwilling to part with the confederacy. This chapter previously examined secessionist struggles by Tamils in Sri Lanka, Ibos in Nigeria, Eritreans in Ethiopia, and Sikhs in northern India. To that list could be added Palestinians seeking their own state in the West Bank and Gaza,[65] Blacks in southern Sudan, Karens in Myanmar (Burma), Moros in the Philippines, and a host of others.

Following the Gulf War, the world's attention focused on the plight of Iraq's Kurdish population and their persecution by the government of Saddam Hussein. The Kurdish secessionist movement, however, transcends the borders of Iraq and precedes Saddam. Residing in a largely mountainous region which they call Kurdistan, more than 20 million Kurds live in Turkey, Iraq, and Iran, with smaller communities in Syria and parts of the former Soviet Union.[66] Separatist efforts date to the collapse of the Ottoman Empire at the close of World War I. Over the years, the Kurds have been subjected to severe repression in those Middle East nations and today still have little prospect of attaining the independent Kurdistan that so many of them desire.

While secession is a potential solution for ethnic minorities that are repressed or that feel aggrieved, hardly ever have Third World secessionist movements succeeded (though they have in the Soviet Union, Yugoslavia, and Czechoslovakia). The breakaway of Bengali-dominated East Pakistan to form Bangladesh is a rare successful case. As we have noted, however, this required outside military intervention. Eritrea also achieved independence from Ethiopia in 1993 after decades of struggle. And, as Israel transfers Gaza and parts of the West Bank to the PLO, a Palestinian-ruled entity of some kind may be emerging. More often than not, however, the most that secessionist movements can hope to achieve is greater autonomy or government recognition of their people's rights.

Outside Intervention

"If the Bosnian Muslims had been needle-nosed dolphins," Edward Luttwak asked, "would the world have allowed the Croats and Serbs to slaughter them by the tens of thousands."[67] His soul-searching question raises important ethical and pragmatic issues. A number of historians have noted, in retrospect, how often the United States and Western European nations failed to avail themselves of opportunities to save Jews from the Nazi Holocaust. More recently, many have wondered how the world could have stood by and allowed (or even indirectly abetted) acts of ethnic genocide in Bosnia, Kosovo, Indonesia, Rwanda, the

Congo, and Sudan while the mass media documented the carnage so graphically (either during or shortly after the fact).

Unless a sovereign government (often the perpetrator of the ethnic violence) invites outsiders in, external intervention raises a number of difficult questions: At what point, if any, do other nations or international organizations such as the U.N., NATO, and the Organization of African Unity have the right to violate a nation's sovereignty in order to save innocent lives? (For example, did the United Nations have the right to send troops to Alabama or Mississippi during the height of the civil rights' movement and the associated antiblack violence of the 1960s?). Under what circumstances can outside intervention (including military intervention) save lives and impose a durable solution and when will its efforts be futile or its success short-lived? How long a commitment of peace-keeping troops and economic aid are intervening countries prepared to assume? What kind of military losses are they prepared to take?[68]

To be sure, some otherwise intractable ethnic conflicts have had resolutions imposed on them through external intervention. The intervening power is often a neighboring state that either has ties to one of the warring ethnic groups or has a strategic interest in the country it invades. For example, India interceded on behalf of the Bengalis in Pakistan's east. Without that intervention, the nation of Bangladesh could not have been born. The Turkish invasion of Cyprus imposed an ethnic settlement by partitioning the island between its Greek and Turkish communities. And, while long-term Syrian intervention in Lebanon initially aggravated that nation's 15-year civil war, ultimately it was the might of the Syrian military that brought the conflict to an end. And, after an agonizing delay, U.S. and NATO forces have halted to the ethnic violence in Bosnia (at least for now).

But in many cases, externally imposed solutions are not necessarily desirable, nor do they always last. In the wake of the Gulf War, U.S. air power has created a "no fly zone" in northern Iraq, affording the Kurds a certain degree of autonomy. It is not clear, however, whether this solution is viable over the long run. Indeed, the Kurds have bitter memories of past aid extended to them by the United States. During the early 1970s, the United States secretly channeled aid to the Iraqi Kurds in order to support a rebellion that would destabilize or topple that country's government. Kurdish needs, however, were clearly secondary to U.S. policy objectives. One of those primary goals was to aid Reza Shah, the American ally then ruling Iran. However, in 1975, when Iran temporarily resolved its differences with Iraq, the United States withdrew aid for the Kurdish rebellion in response to the Shah's request. As a consequence, thousands of Iraqi Kurdish families were driven from their homes or killed.[69] Other external interventions have also had unhappy results. In recent years, central African nations such as Uganda and Rwanda have supported rival tribal armies in neighboring countries so as to advance their own geopolitical interests.

As we have seen, India's attempt to settle the Tamil-Sinhalese conflict in Sri Lanka only triggered increased bloodshed on both sides. After the invasion much of the violence by Tamil separatists was directed at the Indian army, and Tamil bitterness subsequently resulted in the assassination of Indian prime minister Rajiv Gandhi. Despite a truce in Bosnia, Serbian war criminals (including former political leaders) remain at large, in the face of indictments by international human rights courts, and extremist politicians remain dominant in the Serbian and Croatian communities. Thus, it is far from certain that peace will last once external peace keepers are removed, as they inevitably will be.

More generally, Glynne Evans notes that

> A half-hearted [outside] military response [to ethnic conflict] without any under-lying political action is a poor option.... Conflicts with a high degree of ethnic mobi-lization last for generations rather than years, and are intense in their impact... as neighbors turn on neighbors. An intervention for humanitarian purpose in such cases becomes a major military commitment, and one of long duration.[70]

Recent experience in Bosnia, Kosovo, Rwanda, the Congo and elsewhere suggests that this is a commitment which neither the U.S. nor European publics are probably prepared to make.

Settlement through Exhaustion

Ultimately, many ethnic conflicts are resolved less through statecraft, constitutional arrangements, or external intervention than through the exhaustion of the warring parties. Although the weight of Syrian military power was critical in terminating Lebanon's prolonged civil war, the weariness of Beirut's population after 15 years of devastating destruction also played an important role. The same exhaustion may now be producing peace in Sri Lanka. While the Ugandan government continues to clash periodically with the Acholi and Langi tribes, there seems little inclination to return to the ethnically based bloodshed of the Amin and Obote regimes. And exhaustion was an important force driving both sides in Mozambique and Angola toward a U.N.-brokered peace treaty that halted (at least into 1999) their long and bitter civil wars.

Toward a Peaceful Resolution of Conflict

If developing nations are to avoid the horrors of civil war, dissolution into break-away states, or foreign intervention, they must arrive at legal, political, and social solutions that can constrain ethnic tensions. A 1991 conference of U.S. foreign assistance officials and scholars proposed the following measures

- Writing a new constitution [that] offers the possibility of creating new institutional arrangements, such as federalism, for power-sharing between . . . ethnic groups.
- Establishing protection for ethnic minority rights, not only through constitutional and legal guarantees but also through civic education. . . .
- Creating electoral systems with incentives for cooperation and accommodation among groups. . . .[71]

While these recommendations outline goals that are obviously desirable, the devil is in the implementation.

CONCLUSION

It has become somewhat cliché for scholars, journalists, and statesmen to declare that with the end of the Cold War, domestic ethnic conflict has become the greatest threat to world peace. The media are replete with stories of how the collapse of Communism has unleashed the forces of ethnic struggle. The full fury of ethnic tensions has reemerged in the former states of Yugoslavia and the USSR as well as other parts of Eastern Europe. But in the Third World, ethnic hostilities are not a new phenomenon; they have been the greatest source of conflict since independence. As we have seen, modernization offers no easy solution for solving these confrontations. Quite the contrary, urbanization, the spread of literacy, and increased media exposure often seem to fan the fires of ethnic division. Crafting peaceful solutions for multicultural societies will remain one of the greatest challenges facing Third World leaders in this coming century.

DISCUSSION QUESTIONS

1. What do we mean by ethnicity and what are some of the most important types of ethnic identification?
2. Discuss the effect that modernization has had on ethnic identification and ethnic conflict.
3. What are some factors that may cause interethnic relations to become violent?
4. How might outside intervention reduce or increase ethnic tension? Cite some specific successful examples of such intervention and some failures.

NOTES

1. Crawford Young, *The Politics of Cultural Pluralism* (Madison: University of Wisconsin Press, 1976), pp. 23–26. The quote appears on p. 23.
2. Analysis of the years 1958 to 1966, for example, shows that of 164 conflicts with significant violence only 15 involved clashes between two or more states. Most involved ethnic conflict within countries. See Abdul A. Said and Luiz R. Simmons, "The Ethnic Factor in World Politics," in *Ethnicity in an International Context*, ed. Said and Simmons (New Brunswick, NJ: Transaction Books, 1976), p. 16.
3. During this period, only two or three international conflicts—the Iran-Iraq War and the Soviet war in Afghanistan, and perhaps the Gulf War—had comparable death tolls. Ironically the last two were followed by internal ethnic violence. Of course, some brutal civil wars, such as those in El Salvador and Nicaragua, have not been ethnically related.
4. One study estimated some 10 million deaths as of the early 1970s. Harold Isaacs, *Idols of the Tribe: Group Identity and Political Change* (New York: Harper & Row, 1975), p. 3.
5. Donald Rothchild and Victor A. Olorunsola, "Managing Competing State and Ethnic Claims," in *State versus Ethnic Claims: African Policy Dilemmas*, ed. Rothchild and Olorunsola (Boulder, CO: Westview Press, 1983), p. 20.

6. Quoted in Francine Friedman, *The Bosnian Muslims: Denial of a Nation* (Boulder, CO: Westview Press, 1996), p. 1.

7. Cynthia Enloe, *Ethnic Conflict and Political Development* (Boston: Little, Brown, 1973), p. 15.

8. Charles W. Anderson, Fred R. von der Mehden, and Crawford Young, *Issues of Political Development*, 2d ed. (Upper Saddle River, NJ: Prentice Hall, 1974), pp. 31–33; Crawford Young, *Politics in the Congo* (Princeton, NJ: Princeton University Press, 1965), Chapter 11.

9. Donald Horowitz, *A Democratic South Africa?: Constitutional Engineering in a Divided Society* (Berkeley: University of California Press, 1991), pp. 44–48.

10. Young, *Cultural Pluralism*, p. 20.

11. With the spread of migration across state borders, even countries like Sweden (with an upsurge of Third World and Eastern European migrants) are no longer fully homogeneous.

12. Uri Ra'anan, "Nation and State: Order Out of Chaos," in *State and Nation in Multiethnic Societies*, ed. Uri Ra'anan et al. (Manchester and New York: Manchester University Press, 1991), pp. 4–7.

13. Said and Simmons, *Ethnicity in an International Context*, p. 10.

14. Scholars specializing in African culture and politics tend to reject the use of the term tribe to describe the region's various cultural-linguistic groups; they prefer the term ethnicity. Tribe is used here because it is a term more familiar to readers and one still used in much of the ethnic literature. It also avoids confusion with the more broadly used sense of the word ethnicity. More will be said of this later in the chapter.

15. Omo Omoruyi, "State Creation and Ethnicity in a Federal (Plural) System: Nigeria's Search for Parity," in *Ethnicity, Politics, and Development*, ed. Dennis L. Thompson and Dov Ronen (Boulder, CO: Lynne Rienner Publishers, 1986), p. 120. Since social scientists do not agree on what constitutes a distinct ethnic group, other calculations would be far different.

16. Crawford Young, "Comparative Claims to Political Sovereignty: Biafra, Katanga, Eritrea," in *State versus Ethnic Claims*, pp. 211–219.

17. On Ethiopia and the secessionist wars, see Christopher Clapham, *Transformation and Continuity in Revolutionary Ethiopia* (Cambridge, England: Cambridge University Press, 1988), and J. Markakis, *National and Class Conflict in the Horn of Africa* (Cambridge, England: Cambridge University Press, 1987). Subsequent events have superseded the material in both books.

18. Scholars such as Crawford Young maintain that "caste, race and religion belong to a larger genus . . . called cultural pluralism."

19. John Breuilly, *Nationalism and the State* (Manchester, England: Manchester University Press, 1982), p. 3.

20. S. W. R. de A. Samarasinghe, "The Dynamics of Separatism: The Case of Sri Lanka," and K. M. de Silva, "Separatism in Sri Lanka: The 'Traditional Homelands' of the Tamils," in *Secessionist Movements in Comparative Perspective,* ed. Ralph R. Premdas, S. W. R. de A. Samarasinghe, and Alan B. Anderson (London: Pinter Publishers, 1990), pp. 32–67; also, K. M. de Silva, *Managing Ethnic Tensions in Multi-Ethnic Societies: Sri Lanka 1880–1985* (Lanham, MD: University Press of America, 1986).

21. Aidan Southall, "The Illusion of Tribe," in *The Passing of Tribal Man in Africa, Journal of African and Asian Studies* 5 (special issue), nos. 1–2 (January–April 1970): 28–50. Cited by Young, *Politics of Cultural Pluralism*, p. 19.

22. Milton Obote, *Proposals for New Methods of Election of Representatives of the People to Parliament* (Kampala, Uganda: Milton Obote Foundation, 1970), p. 6. Quoted in Donald Rothchild, "Hegemonial Exchange: An Alternative Model for Managing Conflict in Mid-

dle Africa," in *Ethnicity, Politics and Development*, p. 77. The term tribe is used by various scholars in this volume as well as in Enloe, *Ethnic Conflict*.

23. Dov Ronen, *The Quest for Self Determination* (New Haven, CT: Yale University Press, 1976), pp. 79–86.

24. Young, "Comparative Claims to Political Sovereignty," pp. 204–211; Enloe, *Ethnic Conflict*, pp. 89–92.

25. Frederick Forsyth, *The Biafran Story* (Baltimore, MD: Penguin Books, 1969).

26. Basil Davidson, *The Black Man's Burden* (New York: Times Books, 1992), p. 250.

27. Gérard Prunier, *The Rwanda Crisis: 1959–1994* (London: Hurst & Company, 1995).

28. Anderson, von der Mehden, and Young, *Issues of Political Development*, p. 21.

29. Horowitz, *A Democratic South Africa*, p. 47.

30. Khehla Shubane, "South Africa: A New Government in the Making?" *Current History* 91 (May 1992): 202–207; Pauline H. Baker, "South Africa on the Move," *Current History* 89 (May 1990): 197–200, 232–233.

31. *New York Times*, December 8, 1992, p. 1.

32. Cited in T. Walker Wallbank, *A Short History of India and Pakistan* (New York: Mentor, 1958), p. 196.

33. Originating in the fifteenth century, the Sikh religion is related to both Hindu and Islam.

34. Bernard E. Brown, "The Government of India," in *Introduction to Comparative Government*, 2d ed., ed. Michael Curtis et al. (New York: Harper Collins, 1990), pp. 479–480; Robert L. Hardgrave Jr., *India: Government and Politics in a Developing Nation*, 3d. ed. (New York: Harcourt Brace Jovanovitch, 1980), pp. 40–42. Hardgrave offers an estimate of half a million dead.

35. Mohammed Ayoob, "Dateline India: The Deepening Crisis," *Foreign Policy* 85 (Winter 1991–1992): 173; Surendra Chopra, "Ethnic Identity in a Plural Society: A Case Study of System Breakdown in the Punjab," in *Ethnicity, Politics, and Development*, pp. 196–197.

36. Elizabeth Picard, "Political Identities and Communal Identities: Shifting Mobilization Among the Lebanese Shi'a Through Ten Years of War, 1975–1985," in *Ethnicity, Politics, and Development*, pp. 159–175. In the absence of dependable census information, estimates of Lebanon's religious composition varied widely.

37. Ronald D. McLaurin, "Lebanon: Into or Out of Oblivion?" *Current History* 91 (January 1992): 29–30.

38. Young, *Cultural Pluralism*, pp. 20–21, 60–64.

39. Lloyd and Susanne Rudolph, *The Modernity of Tradition* (Chicago: University of Chicago Press, 1967).

40. Of course, the American image as a successful melting pot has often been exaggerated. Serious racial tensions continue to divide society. In recent decades, substantial numbers of Hispanic immigrants have found it difficult to integrate into the mainstream of American life. And various forms of prejudice abound against Asian Americans and other non-Whites.

41. Young, *Cultural Pluralism*, p. 65.

42. Anderson, von der Mehden, and Young, *Issues*, p. 29.

43. A similar process is currently taking place in Eastern Europe, where the collapse of the Soviet multinational empire and the removal of repressive political systems have unleashed ethnic conflict in Bosnia, the former Soviet Union, and elsewhere.

44. Karl W. Deutsch, *Nationalism and Social Communication* (Boston: MIT Press and John Wiley and Sons, 1953).

45. The Cuban government has been much more explicit in its campaigns against sexism than against racism. It tends to insist that pre-Revolutionary racial divisions were merely surrogates for class divisions. Consequently, it erroneously maintains that the social and economic gains the Revolution has brought the lower classes have, by themselves, ended racism.

46. Gordon Means, "Ethnic Preference Policies in Malaysia," in *Ethnic Preference and Public Policy in Developing States*, ed. Neil Nevitte and Charles H. Kennedy (Boulder, CO: Lynne Rienner Publishers, 1986), pp. 95–115; Young, *Cultural Pluralism*, pp. 121–124.

47. The designation "East Indian" is used in Trinidad, Guyana, and other Caribbean nations to distinguish them from indigenous American Indians in the hemisphere.

48. Bridget Brereton, "The Foundations of Prejudice: Indians and Africans in 19th Century Trinidad," *Caribbean Issues* 1, no. 1 (1974): 15–28; John Gaffar LaGuerre, "Race Relations in Trinidad and Tobago," in *Trinidad and Tobago: The Independence Experience 1962-1987*, ed. Selwyn Ryan (St. Augustine, Trinidad: University of the West Indies, 1988), p. 195.

49. Selwyn D. Ryan, *Race and Nationalism in Trinidad and Tobago* (Toronto: University of Toronto Press, 1972).

50. Kevin Yelvington, "Trinidad and Tobago, 1988–89," in *Latin American and Caribbean Contemporary Record*, ed. James Malloy and Eduardo Gamarra (New York: Holmes and Meier, 1991).

51. For the first time in Ecuador, Bolivia, and Peru, bureaucrats in some government agencies are wearing Indian dress and speaking Aymara or Quechua (though much of their work is still conducted in Spanish).

52. Howard Handelman, "The Origins of the Ecuadorian Bourgeoisie: A Generational Transformation," paper presented at the XVII International Congress of the Latin American Studies Association, Los Angeles, 1992.

53. Susanne Jonas, *The Battle for Guatemala* (Boulder, CO: Westview Press, 1991).

54. D. Scott Palmer, The Shining Path of Peru (New York: St. Martin's Press, 1992).

55. From *Politics in Plural Societies*. Quoted in Larry Diamond and Marc F. Plattner (ed.), *Nationalism, Ethnic Conflict, and Democracy* (Baltimore, MD: Johns Hopkins University Press, 1994), p. xix.

56. Francis Fukuyama, "Comments on Nationalism and Democracy," in *Nationalism, Ethnic Conflict and Democracy*, ed.Diamond and Plattner, pp. 23–28.

57. J. Isawa Elaigwu and Victor A. Olorunsola, "Federalism and the Politics of Compromise," in *State versus Ethnic Claims*, p. 282.

58. Enloe, *Ethnic Conflict*, pp. 89–134.

59. Ibid., p. 111.

60. Young, "Comparative Claims to Political Sovereignty."

61. Consociationalism can exist between conflicting groups other than ethnicities, but we will confine our discussion of it to that area.

62. Arend Lijphart, *Democracy in Plural Societies* (New Haven, CT: Yale University Press, 1977), pp. 25–40.

63. Ralph R. Premdas, "Secessionist Movements in Comparative Perspective," in *Secessionist Movements*, p. 12.

64. Ibid., pp. 14–16.

65. This is a somewhat distinct case since these areas are not part of Israel but are, rather, under Israeli military occupation. Similarly, West Bank and Gaza Palestinians are not citizens of Israel in the way that Sikhs or Ibos are citizens of India or Nigeria.

66. Kurdish leaders have claimed that their people number 35 million, but this is considered an exaggeration. National governments cite figures that are too low. Laura Donnandieu Aguado, "The National Liberation Movement of the Kurds in the Middle East," in *Secessionist Movements; Nader Entessar, Kurdish Ethnonationalism* (Boulder, CO: Lynne Rienner Publishers, 1992), pp. 1–10.

67. Edward Luttwak, "If Bosnians Were Dolphins...," *Commentary* 96 (October 1993), p. 27.

68. When television news recorded a crowd of Somali civilians and militia dragging the bodies of several recently killed American marines, the United States quickly withdrew its peacekeeping force from that nation. Fears of similar scenes in Bosnia or Serbia helped explain why the United States hesitated to intervene in that area for so long despite the horrendous massacres of civilians, particularly Muslims

69. Entessar, *Kurdish Ethnonationalism*, pp. 119–127. The Pike Commission of the U.S. House of Representatives revealed details of U.S. involvement with the abortive Kurdish revolt.

70. Glynne Evans, *Responding to Crises in the African Great Lakes* (New York: Oxford University Press, Adelphia Paper 33, 1997), p. 75.

71. Project on Democratization, "Democratization and Ethnic Conflict" (Washington, DC: National Academy Press, 1992), p. 16.

4

⸜⸝

WOMEN
AND
DEVELOPMENT

Following the victory of the Chinese Communists in 1949, revolutionary leaders seeking to enroll women in the new order observed, "Women Hold Up Half the Sky." Yet for many years, scholars, Third World governments, and Western development agencies appeared strangely oblivious to women's role in the development process. Studies of political and economic change in the LDCs usually said little or nothing about women's issues. In the past two to three decades, however, two factors have contributed to a new understanding of women in developing nations: the emergence of feminist or gender-related social science research, and the growing recognition by policy planners that women play a distinct and important role in the modernization process.

Gender-related economic and political analysis is instructive in the same way that class analysis or examination of ethnic divisions can be. To begin with, Third World women are largely relegated to particular occupations. The vast majority work in agriculture or the "informal sector."[1] Those who work in industry are disproportionately found in labor-intensive (and low-wage) industries such as apparel and electronics in the Far East and Southeast Asia, and in assembly plants in Mexico and the Caribbean. Like their counterparts in industrialized nations, Third World professional women are overrepresented in nurturing professions such as nursing and teaching. Such divisions between "women's work" and "men's work" have obvious economic and political implications. Women are also highly underrepresented in the political arena. Not only do they hold far less than their share of government posts, but also their percentage diminishes as one moves up the ladder of political power.

While evidence of gender inequality and exploitation of women exists in most societies, some of its worst manifestations can be found in parts of the developing world. In their most horrifying form, the litany of injustices includes forced (and painful) female circumcision in Islamic areas of Africa; the virtual enslavement (and frequent rape) of women working in Pakistan's brick-making industry; the sale of child brides for dowries in India; wife beatings in Zambia and the Andes; the murder of some 5,000 women annually in India by husbands dissatisfied with the size of their dowries;[2] a judicial system in Brazil that virtually never convicts men who kill their wives; and economic conditions that force large numbers of Third World women into prostitution. Less chilling, but no less significant, examples of gender inequality include divorce laws that greatly favor husbands; barriers to women seeking commercial credit for small businesses; the double day that working women typically face (coming home after a day's work and having to do all the housework and child care); and the restricted opportunities for women in government, universities, the professions, and higher-paid blue-collar jobs.

The study of women in the developing world, however, is by no means confined to questions of inequality and victimization. After years of neglect, many international agencies and government planners have begun to recognize women's special status and needs in development projects. Nor have women been passive subjects who are "acted upon." Their political mobilization has ranged from the quiet subversion common to oppressed groups to more open assertion of political, economic, and social rights. A growing body of scholarly literature now focuses on women's empowerment. Throughout Latin America, for example, women have played a decisive role in the independent grassroots political organizations, known as "new social movements," that have burst upon the scene since the 1970s. Focusing on gender issues, human rights, poverty, and a range of other concerns, NSMs have provided an important alternative to traditional organizations such as political parties and unions.[3] Elsewhere, revolutionary movements in countries such as El Salvador, Nicaragua, and China have opened up opportunities for female activism and leadership that had not previously existed in traditional society. And in nations as diverse as India, the Philippines, Haiti, and Bolivia, women have headed the national governments. All of these aspects of women's economic and political activity deserve our attention.

THE POLITICAL AND SOCIO-ECONOMIC STATUS OF THIRD WORLD WOMEN

Table 4.1 offers several indicators of women's political and socioeconomic status in a number of representative LDCs. First, in each country the Human Development Indices (HDIs) of the female and male populations were compared. (The HDI is a composite index of per capita income, income distribution, education, and life expectancy.) As expected, those figures (not shown in the table) reveal that women regularly score lower. Next, all of the world's nations (with avail-

Table 4.1　Women's Political and SocioEconomic Standing in the Third World

Country	Gender Development Index (GDI) Rank	Women's Income as a Percent of Men's	Gender Empowerment (GEM) Rank	Percent Women in Parliament
Chile	46	22%	61	7.2%
Cuba	69	31	25	22.8
Mexico	66	26	37	14.2
S. Korea	37	29	83	3.0
Thailand	40	37	60	6.6
China	93	38	33	21.0
India	128	25	100	2.6
Egypt	111	25	88	12.5
Zimbabwe	118	38	56	14.7

Source: UNDP, *Human Development Report 1998* (New York: Oxford University Press), pp. 133–135.

able data), underdeveloped and developed alike, were ranked from first through roughly one-hundred fortieth according to how narrow or wide the gap was between women and men. The country with the world's narrowest gap (Norway) was ranked first and those with the highest gaps (such as India and Zimbabwe) received the highest score. Column 1 (GDI) of our table offers that ranking. Countries in East Asia had some of the best scores (South Korea, with 37, led the LDCs, with Thailand close behind). The Latin American nations shown here (Cuba, Mexico and, especially, Chile) were also above average. And countries in Africa and South Asia (India, Egypt and Zimbabwe) had the highest gender gap.

Column 2 compares average women's incomes with those of men. In none of the countries shown here did women earn as much as 40 percent of men's earnings. Interestingly, women performed most strongly (or, better put, least weakly) in China and Zimbabwe (38 percent), countries toward the bottom of the list on the GDI rankings (column 1). This may reflect inaccuracies in column 2 due to problems in recording women's incomes (discussed below).

The last two columns measure women's political power and influence. Column 4 indicates what percentage of the seats in the nation's parliament (or congress) were held by women at the time the data were collected. While no LDC's parliament has female representation comparable to Norway and Sweden (where close to 40 percent of the seats are held by women), countries such as Cuba (22.8 percent), China (21 percent), Zimbabwe and Mexico (both with 14 percent) outperform the United States by a considerable margin. India, once again, trails the pack (2.6 percent). South Korea, which fared so well on GDI, does very poorly here.

And column 3 (GEM) is based on a composite measure of women's political and economic empowerment. After comparing various measures of economic and political power by gender, a combined score was developed and all the countries of the world with data were ranked. As with parliamentary representation, the communist nations of Cuba and China ranked highest in this dimension (indeed, Cuba's twenty-fifth ranking placed it ahead of a number of developed countries). Latin American countries (Cuba, Mexico, and Chile) tended to rank well, while India and Egypt ranked lowest.

Finally, it should be noted that any analysis of the condition of women in developing nations must begin by recognizing that most official statistics "reflect a gross underestimation of [their] participation in economic activity."[4] For one thing, the long and difficult hours women spend working at home to maintain their families are not reflected in government economic data. Moreover, women who engage in income-earning activity often work in areas that are not officially counted either. For example, in villages throughout the developing world, peasant women play a key role in agricultural production either as part of a broader family effort or as the primary food producer. Much of this, particularly production consumed by the household rather than sold on the market, is officially overlooked. Many women in urban areas work in small-scale trade or other parts of the informal sector that escape government scrutiny and only show up in estimates of the work force.

Colonialism, Modernization, and the Economic Status of Women

Often Westerners associate traditional religious and cultural values with rigid social and economic systems that relegate women to an inferior rank. This frequently leads them to assume that the imposition of European colonialism in Africa and Asia and the subsequent spread of modernization and Western ideas offered women greater opportunities and improved social standing. But, while modernization theorists would have us believe that urbanization, industrialization, and the diffusion of Western values and lifestyles have an emancipating effect, many "feminist scholars [often oriented toward dependency theory] have produced a wealth of literature that suggests that political and economic modernization have overwhelmingly negative effects for women."[5]

While the status of women in precolonial Africa varied greatly, the consequence of European colonialism was frequently to reverse or further diminish their position in society. It must be remembered that colonial rule was introduced at a time (the nineteenth century) when Victorian England and other European societies had rather restricted views of women's roles.[6] Consequently, colonial administrators in Africa and Asia were often less equitable in their treatment of women than were traditional societies. In some West African cultures, for example, women could serve as chiefs or hold other important political positions. However, as the influence of such traditional leaders declined under colonialism (and continued to decrease after independence), these women lost their influence to male-dominated colonial or national governments. Among the Nigerian Ibo, women had exercised significant political power prior to British colonialism. Colonial administrators, however, viewed politics as "a man's concern" and, consequently, female political influence declined. [7]

At the same time, the introduction of commercialized agriculture contributed to the loss of women's economic power. In Asia as well as Africa, that commercialization often led to the granting of government titles to the land. Frequently the effect was to transfer farm land that had been controlled by women to male ownership.[8] In addition, as families moved from subsistence (family consumption) agriculture to commercial agriculture and as commercial plantations were developed by foreigners, men were more likely to do the farming than before. Commercialization also made farmers more dependent on the state for credit and for technical training. In the colonial period and in the early decades of independence, women found themselves frozen out of such aid. In Uganda, for example, it was women farmers who first began cotton cultivation. Yet in 1923 the British administrator in charge of agriculture declared that "cotton growing [can] not be left to the women and old people."[9] Consequently, as new technologies were introduced for cotton growing, they were taught only to men, ultimately driving women out of that occupation. After independence, a similar pattern continued in most of Africa and Asia. Government extension agents offered modern technologies, credits, and other assistance fairly exclusively to men. Foreign aid programs were often no less sexist. Thus, when a Taiwanese foreign aid team went to Senegal to improve rice cultivation, they trained only men even though women did most of the rice cultivation. As a result, the men ignored the instructors, the women were not taught, and the new techniques never took hold.[10]

Women in the Countryside

Agriculture represents a major area of female economic activity in the developing world. United Nations data on sub-Saharan Africa, for example, suggested that not long ago 60 to 70 percent of all food production and 50 percent of all animal husbandry were carried out by women.[11] Other country-specific studies in Africa have shown a smaller but still very significant female contribution to family farming. Ester Boserup's early landmark study indicated that in Ghana, Sierra Leone, and Liberia, for example, women contributed approximately 40 percent of family labor in agriculture. In the Muslim north African countries of Algeria and Tunisia, women put in close to 40 percent of family farm labor, with another 20 percent done jointly by men and women. In Asian nations such as Thailand and South Korea, women contributed close to half of all family farm labor, though the proportion was much lower in Taiwan, India, and the Philippines. In Latin America, by contrast, the percentage of purely female farm labor was generally well below 10 percent. But in countries such as Chile, Cuba, Costa Rica, El Salvador, and Mexico, 54 to 69 percent was done jointly by men and women.[12] A more recent study suggested that women contributed over 60 percent of agricultural labor in Africa and Asia and 40 percent in Latin America.[13]

Despite the importance of women in farming, "too little attention has been given by researchers and administrators or planners to women and the roles they play in rural society."[14] While male "heads of household" in regions such as Latin

America and South Asia are often employed off the family farm, thereby leaving its cultivation to their wives, government planners have often clung to "the myth of the ever-present male head."[15] Consequently, agricultural extension workers have often neglected female farmers. Yet in Kenya alone, a study conducted by the United Nations' International Labor Office in the 1970s estimated that 525,000 rural households were headed by women whose husbands had migrated to urban areas.[16]

In the years since the United Nations' "Decade for Women" (1975 to 1985), international agencies and Third World government planners have developed greater consciousness of the role of women in rural development. Thus, the 1985 conference in Nairobi, Kenya, concluding the Decade for Women, was the second largest U.N. conference ever held. At the United Nations, the World Bank, the United States' Agency for International Development (AID), and many Nongovernment Organizations (NGOs), rural development programs that previously focused narrowly on agricultural production have often given way to Integrated Rural Development Programs (IRDPs) designed to promote agricultural production, education, sanitation, and health care simultaneously. Increasingly these programs have recognized the necessity of addressing the role of rural women. AID established an office for Women in Development to better address women's needs in U.S. foreign aid projects. The results of these efforts have been mixed. Some projects have been very successful while others suffered from poor planning or understanding of the cultural milieu. Thus, for example, one study of an IRDP project in India found that its effectiveness was diminished by the absence of female administrators and by inadequate early educational opportunities for women participants.[17] Cornelia Butler Flora's survey of projects designed to generate income for rural women in Latin America found that the programs often produced low-paying jobs with limited economic benefit for the women employed. Still, despite the weak economic record of these projects, Flora argues that the women's organizations that they establish can serve as the basis for their members' political and social mobilization.[18]

Ultimately, it appears that only the increased political mobilization of urban and rural Third World women is likely to make their governments more responsive to their demands. In a number of LDCs, there are signs of progress. For example, many planners concerned with population control now recognize that it is insufficient merely to make family planning services available. Indeed, reduced fertility rates are closely tied to increased educational levels and greater occupational opportunities for women. At the 1994 United Nations Conference on Population and Development that linkage was established as a central theme of world population control efforts.

Urbanization and the Status of Women

The negative effects of modernization on women have certainly not been limited to agriculture. In her study of Ghana's Ga tribe, Claire Robertson found that women's status declined when families moved to the capital city of Accra and

entered a more modern, urbanized environment. Whereas economic cooperation between spouses had previously been common in rural villages (largely in
fishing and farming), it was less frequent among urban migrants. In the cities,
men had greater access to education and to higher-paying jobs, thereby giving
them a level of economic security that they had not heretofore enjoyed. Women
tended to be more dependent on their husbands and to own less of the family's
property than they had before migrating to the city.[19]

In many Latin American nations women constitute the majority of
migrants from the countryside to urban centers, where they are often able to
secure employment only at the low end of the wage scale. In much of the region
the female migrants' most common form of employment is domestic service,
for which they rarely receive even the legal minimum wage. Thus, Mexican
census figures in the 1970s indicated that 25 percent of all women in the work
force were either maids in private homes or cleaning women in commercial
establishments and hotels (that percentage has likely declined since).[20] A second important area of employment is in the informal sector, including activities such as street vending and recycling newspapers, bottles, and cans. While
some informal sector workers earn higher incomes than blue-collar laborers,
many fall below the poverty line. Finally, in newly industrializing countries,
women are frequently employed in low-wage, labor-intensive manufacturing
such as textiles. However, as factories in the developing world become more
technologically sophisticated and as wages rise, women tend to be employed
less frequently than men.[21]

In East Asia, the industrial boom from the 1980s to late 1990s opened up
additional employment opportunities for women, particularly in such labor-
intensive industries as apparel and electronics. For several reasons firms in those
industries often prefer to hire young, unmarried women: Many of the jobs require
manual dexterity, which employers associate with women; lacking a family to
support, women are often willing to work for lower wages; and, finally, women
are less likely to unionize. The current economic crisis in that region has caused
numerous plant closings and the dismissal of female (and male) labor.

Throughout the developing world, women have fewer educational opportunities than men, a deficit that, in turn, limits their occupational possibilities.
All too often, poverty and the lack of vocational skills force desperate women
into prostitution in order support themselves or their children. A study of
Manilla, the Philippines, and Bangkok, Thailand indicated that 7 to 9 percent of
female employment was "prostitution related."[22] Despite Thailand's economic
boom, rural poverty drove many young female migrants to work in Bangkok's
thriving "sex tourism" industry. That country's severe economic crisis since 1997
has pushed many more women into that realm. In the squatter settlements of
Nairobi, impoverished Kenyan women are rarely equipped to attain employment in the modern sector of the economy. Consequently, illegal brewing of beer
and prostitution are the two major sources of female employment.[23]

On a more hopeful note, research on the South Asian labor market indicates that increased education has offered many poorer urban women a vehicle for improving their occupational status.[24] Spurred on by the United Nations' Decade for Women, India's Ministry of Labor, with assistance from the International Labor Organization and the Swedish government, has begun an extensive vocational training program for urban women.[25]

Among middle- and upper-class women, educational and occupational opportunities are more comparable to those of men with the same social status. There are, however, interesting differences between countries and regions. A number of years ago, Ester Boserup presented data on the proportion of people between the ages of 15 and 24 who were still in school (essentially high school and university). Not surprisingly, the overall rate of school attendance in individual countries was linked to the nation's level of economic development. In other words, more economically developed countries like Costa Rica, Singapore, and South Korea had higher overall rates of high school and university attendance than did poorer nations. However, cultural rather than economic factors seemed to determine what proportion of these students were women. In Latin American nations, about half of the student population was female regardless of whether the country was more developed (Venezuela, Panama) or comparatively poor (Honduras, El Salvador). In Asia, women made up nearly half of the 15- to 24-year-old students in the Philippines and Hong Kong, but under one-third in India, Malaysia, and Indonesia. The proportion of women attending high school or college in Africa and the Middle East was generally quite low, frequently under 25 percent. As a consequence of these educational patterns, women constitute a far higher percentage of professionals in Latin America than in other parts of the Third World.[26] To a large extent women professionals remain concentrated in such traditional nurturing professions as teaching and nursing. However, in more modernized countries such as Chile, Argentina, and Uruguay, they are significantly represented in other fields such as university teaching, medicine, and law. Over half of all Argentine doctors, for example, are female.[27]

Women and Economic Crisis

During the 1980s Africa, Latin America, and parts of Asia suffered harsh economic dislocations from which many nations have not yet recovered. A severe debt crisis in Latin America forced most of the region's governments to impose painful economic stabilization and adjustment programs that sharply reduced living standards (see Chapter 9). Civil war, drought, and debt devastated much of Africa. And, the end of the 1990s witnessed a severe economic decline in Thailand, Indonesia, South Korea, Malaysia, and other parts of East and Southeast Asia. In a number of ways women suffered disproportionately from the economic crises in these countries.

As large numbers of male wage earners either lost their jobs or experienced declining real wages,[28] women already engaged in housework and child care needed outside jobs to supplement family income. In Tanzania, for example, real wages declined 65 percent between 1974 and 1988. By the end of that period a worker's average monthly salary could feed a family of six for only three days. For many, the only way of avoiding starvation was for women who had not previously worked outside the home to seek additional income. Consequently, there was a dramatic surge in the number of urban women forming small businesses or otherwise entering the informal sector. One survey indicated that for a typical low-income family in the capital city of Dar es Salaam only 10 percent of family earnings came from wages while the remaining 90 percent came from the informal sector, much of it earned by women.[29]

Nicaragua, which experienced a devastating civil war and Latin America's most severe economic crisis in the 1980s, had a similar experience. In the capital city of Managua, the number of women working increased significantly. They were employed disproportionately in the informal sector (including black market sales of rationed goods) for two reasons: first the collapse of real wages in the formal sector (where, like Tanzania, a monthly wage was totally inadequate to support a family); second, the greater ease of combining informal activities such as street vending with housework and child care (it is common, for example, to see female vendors in Latin America caring for their children while working at their stalls). Although it has long been assumed that most women in the informal sector are supplementing their husbands' incomes, in Nicaragua this was not the case. Even in normal times many Nicaraguan mothers are single (divorced, separated, or never wed) and many more were widowed by the Contra war. Consequently a large portion of the women in Managua's informal sector are their family's primary breadwinners.[30]

The Tanzanian and Nicaraguan experiences have been repeated recently in Indonesia and Thailand as well as other parts of the developing world. While at one level increased female participation in the paid work force associated with economic crises can be viewed as a liberating factor, it often brings women problems not shared by men. The most obvious and widespread difficulty is what has been referred to as the double day. Poor women with families generally find that when they begin gainful employment (often out of necessity) they still must put in long hours at home cleaning, cooking, shopping, and caring for their children. Cuba is the only nation in the world whose laws require both spouses to share housework equally. And even there compliance is quite uneven.

There is, however, one segment of women in the Third World who have some advantages over their First World peers in pursuing their careers. Middle- and upper-class women often benefit from the ready availability of very poorly paid domestic servants who care for their children and home while they themselves work in the professions or in business. In that rather limited case, one women's poverty becomes another's advantage.

WOMEN AND POLITICS

Many of the same prejudices and traditions that have negatively affected women's socioeconomic position have also disadvantaged them politically. In Latin America, for example, women received the right to vote substantially later than in industrial democracies. Whereas the United States and most European democracies enacted female suffrage in the years following World War I,[31] only 7 of 20 Latin American countries allowed women the vote before the close of World War II. Ecuador was the first nation in that region to extend the franchise (1929) and Paraguay the last (1961).[32] In Africa and Asia the situation was somewhat different. Since most of the countries in those regions received independence in the decades after World War II, when female suffrage was a universally accepted principle, women were usually granted the vote from the onset. Saudi Arabia remains a notable exception, with women still lacking the vote. Given the low number of democratically elected governments in Asia and Africa until recently, however, the value of the franchise to women—or even to men—had been somewhat limited.

In many parts of Africa, Asia, and the Middle East, traditional cultural values have limited women's participation in the political system. One study of transitional Hindu families (partially traditional and partly modernized) revealed an important generational difference between women who had completed a university education at the time of Indian independence and their more traditional mothers. The women analyzed in this study were the daughters of relatively Westernized fathers who worked for the Indian civil service and who were quite politically involved. Their mothers, on the other hand, generally spoke no English, believed in female submissiveness, and were quite apolitical.[33] In contrast, the university-educated daughters were far more politically involved than their mothers. In the absence of such educational opportunities, political participation levels remain low for the majority of poor women in South Asia, the Middle East, and much of Africa, all of whom lack the resources available to women from more affluent families.

Indeed, social class influences are as important as gender considerations in predicting a particular woman's political involvement. Among highly educated, Westernized women born to elite Third World families, political involvement may be as great or greater than for their cohorts in the Western world. It is worth noting, for example, that all of the countries of the Indian subcontinent—India, Pakistan, and Bangladesh—as well as neighboring Sri Lanka have had female prime ministers, a record not nearly equaled by North America or Western Europe. Until recently, the proportion of women in the Indian parliament was substantially higher than in the U.S. Congress. In Africa elite women were slow to attain cabinet-level positions but were very visible in United Nations delegations. Thus, for example, the first women to serve as president of the General Assembly and the first to preside over the Security Council were both from

Africa.[34] And, in the 1993 Mexican gubernatorial race in the Yucatan, the two leading political parties fielded female candidates.

Middle-class women have also benefited in many ways from elements of Western lifestyles. For example, the greater availability of birth control devices "has ruptured [women's] previously existing physiological fatalism," enabling them to work outside the home and involve themselves in political movements.[35]

But modernization has not always been politically beneficial to the mass of underprivileged Third World women. Indeed, in Africa, where traditional cultures often featured women's organizations and production techniques that bound women together, urbanization and the absence of extended families has often deprived women of the organizational foundations they had previously enjoyed. In Nigeria, Africa's most populous sub-Saharan nation, women in the urban informal sector have been less prone to demonstrate politically since independence than they were under colonial rule.[36] Throughout the developing world, the mechanization and commercialization of agriculture and the accompanying decline of traditional labor relations has frequently deprived rural women of their specialized labor functions. In doing so, these changes may, at least temporarily, reduce women's political influence.

In short, because the developing world encompasses so wide a variety of cultural traditions, and because social change has impinged so differently on the various social classes and sectors within individual nations, there can be no simple generalizations about the way in which modernization has influenced the political status of Third World women. Thus, for example, modernization theory would lead us to expect that more socioeconomically developed countries would be more likely to grant political rights to women than would their poorer counterparts. If we look at Latin America, however, we find that there is only a mild correlation between a country's literacy rate or its GNP per capita and the year in which it extended the vote to women.[37] Thus, the spread of education alone does not seem to guarantee women greater political equality. It does appear, however, that in countries such as China, Costa Rica, and Cuba, extensive mass educational programs coupled with conscious efforts to change traditional values have contributed to greater political opportunities and equity for women.[38]

Women at the Grass-roots Level

Perhaps women have most powerfully influenced Third World politics when acting through grass-roots organizations in their own neighborhoods and communities. Community-based groups may afford them opportunities for participation and leadership that are usually lacking at the national or regional level. Moreover, for poor women who may not have day care and who often cannot travel far, neighborhood or village organizations have the obvious advantage of physical proximity to their homes. Most important, many of the issues these associations focus upon—such as housing, health care, clean drinking water, and educating children—are of particular interest to women. Hence, many traditional women who are not particularly politically oriented or who would never consider political-party activity are attracted to these groups because of their obvious relevance to their lives.

Since the 1970s grass-roots organizations representing poor and middle class women have emerged in various parts of the Third World. Some represent women exclusively, while others have members of both sexes but are often led by women or contain women's wings.[39] Jana Everett studied a number of Indian community groups in urban and rural settings, finding both similarities and differences. In both areas, the organizations were initially led by politically experienced, middle-class women committed to organizing the poor. But subsequent surveys of the low-income women who joined these groups showed that their activity had increased their political awareness, confidence, and assertiveness. Thus, as in grass-roots movements generally, activism frequently induces broader participation in the political system.

Beyond these similarities, however, the tactics and goals of urban and rural groups often differed. The Self-Employed Women's Association (SEWA) of Madras and the Annapurna Mahila Mandal of Bombay (named after the Goddess of Food) represented urban women involved in home-based production, street vending of food, and other informal sector activities. Serving extremely poor women who were unable to secure government services, their tactics were quite moderate and peaceful. To begin with, they operated through normal patron-client relations, working within the system to seek government help. Their objectives were also fairly conventional, including enforcement of minimum-wage laws and securing loans for women with very small businesses who had previously been unable to attain credit from private banks or government agencies.

In contrast, Everett's examination of six organizations representing the rural poor (including underprivileged tribal people) uncovered more militant activity. For example, at an early training session for women in a Bhil tribal organization, members complained about alcoholism among the men in their villages and the associated wife beating. Emboldened by their own discussion, the women spontaneously marched to an illegal liquor still and smashed it. They then encircled the local police inspector to protest his failure to take action against illegal liquor production.[40]

In general, rural grass-roots groups are more likely than urban organizations to stage protest demonstrations or other direct action and more prone to demand some form of economic redistribution such as land reform. Armita Basu's study of women's rural protest in the Indian state of Maharashtra found evidence of equal militancy. After a woman was unable to get help from the police against a local landlord who had beaten her severely for reprimanding him for abusive behavior, a crowd of 300 women and 150 men "smeared his face with cow dung . . . and paraded him through the surrounding villages."[41] The rural women's greater militancy likely resulted from the more repressive political atmosphere in which they operated. Village political and economic elites are usually less willing than their urban counterparts to allow the poor to act through normal political channels.

Social movements often develop as a response to a particular crisis or danger. For example, the 1985 earthquake that destroyed large sections of Mexico City had a particularly devastating effect on seamstresses in the city's apparel industry. The quake hit early in the morning when most people had not yet left for work, but seamstresses work longer hours so many of them were trapped under rubble at their places of employment. To their horror, some found that their employers were more interested in saving their sewing machines than in bringing out endangered employees. The clothing workers subsequently formed their own labor union led by women from their ranks, independent of the government-affiliated federation to which most Mexican unions belong. With more honest leadership than typically exists in the Mexican labor movement, the union not only bargains with employers and the government for better working conditions but also provides day care and related services for its members.

In Latin America, one of the major catalysts for the grass-roots political activity that sprung up during the 1970s and 1980s was opposition to the authoritarian military governments that swept the region at that time. In Argentina, Brazil, Chile, and Uruguay, bureaucratic-authoritarian (BA) regimes halted the electoral process, banned political party and union activity, (particularly by the Left), and arrested, tortured, and killed large numbers of suspected "subversives." At the same time, a major debt crisis in the 1980s coupled with harsh state economic measures designed to control inflation produced the worst recession since the 1930s and resulted in a precipitous decline in popular living standards. In all of these countries women played an important role in antiauthoritarian social movements that helped pave the way for the restoration of democracy.

The women's movement in these countries incorporated three types of political organizations, all largely urban based. First, it included feminists coming primarily from middle- or upper-middle-class families with a heavy representation of professional women. Many of them had been active in Leftist political parties but had become disillusioned by the Left's lack of concern for women's issues. Second, neighborhood organizations represented women from the country's urban slums. In the face of the severe economic crisis, self-help groups were formed for activities such as opening communal kitchens and infant nutrition centers. Though not previously highly politicized, over time members of these grass-roots groups often expanded their initial goals to demand more equitable distribution of state resources and the return of democratic government. Finally, a third movement sought to stop or uncover government violations of human rights. Organizations such as Argentina's famed Mothers of the Plaza de Mayo regularly marched in defiance of government rules to demand an accounting of their missing children and grandchildren. Responding to wide-scale imprisonments, torture, disappearances, and death-squad assassinations, women formed a major component of the human rights movement. Of the three strands of the women's movement, this was the most socially integrated, joining activists from both the middle class and working class. Often human rights groups were linked to the Catholic Church or to Christian organizations such as Base Communities.[42]

One of the most important women's political movements emerged in Brazil. Several factors contributed to this phenomenon. First was the rapid expansion of women's educational opportunities, beginning in the early 1960s prior to the military takeover, and continuing through the 1980s. Between 1969 and 1975 the number of men attending Brazilian universities doubled, while the number of women increased fivefold. By 1980, nearly half of all university students in the country were female. Women also constituted a growing proportion of the nation's professionals, with their numbers swelling from 19,000 in 1970 to over 95,000 in 1980.[43] Paid significantly less than their male counterparts, they were the nucleus of the new feminist movement. Their leaders were highly politicized and had usually worked with Leftist political parties. During the intense military repression of the late 1960s a number of them were forced into exile, often leaving for Western Europe or Chile, where they were exposed to more sophisticated feminist organizations. When Brazil's political system began to open up in the mid 1970s, they returned home to start a movement there.

In the absence of democratic elections, grass-roots movements such as tenants' associations offered one of the only means by which the urban poor might pressure the government. In slums and shantytowns throughout the country, radical priests, nuns, and parishioners (often committed to liberation theology) organized Christian Base Communities that combined Catholic beliefs and social activism. Leftist activists also helped organize the poor. A study of these grass-roots movements in São Paulo, Brazil's largest city, revealed that most of the members and leaders were women.[44] Typically, such organizations focused on their members' economic needs—jobs, health care, and food—and had little initial concern with feminist issues. Indeed, Church leaders were usually hostile to feminism and most leftist groups were rather indifferent, viewing gender divisions as secondary to class conflict. In time, however, many poor women came to share their middle-class counterparts' concern about questions of sexuality, household equality, and protection against abuse by husbands and companions.

In the late 1970s, the women's movement's third strand emerged, concerned with government violations of human rights. Freed political prisoners, political party activists (frequently from the Left), and progressive elements of the Catholic Church all played leadership roles. Interestingly, this was one of the only areas in which women's groups had an advantage over comparable groups led by men. Because the government viewed women as inherently less political then men, they allowed their human rights groups greater freedom than other protest movements had.

When the Brazilian military government engineered a transition to democracy in the 1980s, women politicians played an important role in the major opposition party, the PMDB. Female voters also were an important base of party support. Yet the restoration of Brazilian democracy removed some of the motivation for unity among disparate wings of the women's movement and presented them with new challenges. As middle-class women activists became more involved with political parties in the new democratic order, they tended to loose their contacts with community groups representing the urban poor. Indeed, in many Latin American nations the restoration of democracy had the ironic effect of demobilizing women.

Women as Political Leaders

In political systems throughout the world (except, perhaps, for Scandinavia) women are severely underrepresented in political leadership positions. The Third World is surely no exception. During the mid-1980s, for instance, women constituted only 6 percent of the national legislators in Africa and only 2 percent of all cabinet members. Throughout the developing (and developed) world, "United Nations surveys repeatedly show that even in countries where women are active professionally, their level of responsibility as policymakers and planners is low."[45]

Furthermore, an examination of the small number of women who have reached high leadership positions reveals that they tend to be confined to posts popularly associated with female qualities. For example, most of the African women who held cabinet posts in the 1980s were in charge of education, women's affairs, health, or social welfare, areas traditionally viewed as compatible with women's "nurturing role."[46] In her study of Chilean and Peruvian female political leaders, Elsa Chaney discovered a pattern common to much of Latin America. Women political leaders were forced to legitimize their activism outside the home by presenting themselves as *supermadres* ("supermothers") who were using their political position to nurture their constituents (their extended family). That image had been painted eloquently years earlier by Argentina's legendary political leader Eva Perón (Evita):

> In this great house of the Motherland [Argentina], I am just like any other woman in any other of the innumerable houses of my people. Just like all of them I rise early thinking about my husband and about my children. . . . I so truly feel myself the mother of my people.[47]

Chaney's survey of 167 Chilean and Peruvian female political officials showed that half of them felt that certain government posts (such as education and health) were more appropriate for women, while others should be held by men (finance and defense, for example). Only 13 percent of the women she interviewed believed that gender roles were irrelevant to the type of political post one holds, while another 37 percent were ambivalent.[48] Of course, it is not only in developing nations that women tend to be restricted to political positions associated with their gender stereotypes. Until fairly recently, women cabinet members in the United States normally held such posts as Labor, Education, and Health and Human Services. Recent appointments of women to the powerful positions of U.S. Attorney General, U.S. Secretary of State, and Canadian Defense Minister constitute important breakthroughs in this regard.

Another factor limiting female political leaders is a somewhat permeable "glass ceiling" that tends to concentrate them at lower levels. Thus, for the most part women are more likely to get elected to local or state legislatures than to the national parliament. There are, of course, some notable exceptions to this rule. Despite the generally inferior status of women in India, many of them in the country's Westernized, upper-caste elite have achieved considerable political success. During the 1960s and 1970s the percentage of women in the Indian parliament was between 2.5 to 4 times as high as the proportion of women in the U.S. House of Representatives.[49] Indeed, the ability of women to rise to the top of the political system in South Asia is striking, particularly when one considers their generally lamentable position in society as a whole.

All three nations on the Indian subcontinent along with closely neighboring Sri Lanka have had women prime ministers. The most prominent member of this group was Indira Gandhi, who dominated Indian politics from 1966 until her assassination in 1984 (when she was succeeded by her son Rajiv). In recent decades women have been prime ministers in Pakistan (Benazir Bhutto), Sri Lanka (Sirimavo Bandaranaike), and Bangladesh (Khaleda Zia). Other prominent female Asian leaders include former Filipino president Corazón Aquino and Burmese opposition leader Daw Aung San Suu Kyi, winner of the 1991 Nobel Peace Prize. No other Third World region matches Asia's array of women leaders, but Latin America has produced Eva Perón, as well as former presidents Isabel Perón (Argentina), Violeta Chamorro (Nicaragua), and Ertha Pascal-Trouillot, who served briefly as Haiti's provisional president.

Two cautions must be considered about the political success of these leaders. First, most represent a tiny elite of highly educated, upper-class women. Thus, for example, Pakistan's Benazir Bhutto and Burma's Aung San Suu Kyi were educated, respectively, at Harvard and Oxford universities. Secondly, in almost all cases they were the wives, widows, or daughters of charismatic national leaders. Indira Gandhi was the daughter of India's first prime minister, Jawaharal Nehru, a legendary figure who led his nation for 15 years. Sri Lankan prime minister Sirimavo Bandaranaike was the widow of a slain prime minister, while Benazir Bhutto is the daughter of another former Pakistani prime minister (executed by the military) and Corazón Aquino is the widow of an assassinated opposition leader. Bangladesh's prime minister and opposition leader are, respectively, the widow and daughter of assassinated heads of government. Aung San Suu Kyi is the daughter of Burma's most revered independence leader and both Eva and Isabel Perón were married at some time to Argentina's charismatic hero Juan Perón. Former Nicaraguan president Violeta Chamorro is the widow of a famed newspaper editor whose assassination helped spark the Nicaraguan Revolution.[50]

This does not imply that all of these women lacked political ability or leadership qualities. Indira Gandhi was widely recognized as one of the world's most accomplished political leaders and Violeta Chamorro helped heal the wounds of her country's civil war.[51] What the evidence demonstrates, however, is that no matter how highly skilled Third World women may be, they have only been able to reach the top of their political systems as successors to their fathers or husbands.[52] For now, then, the glass ceiling remains in place for most Third World women in politics, with the notable exception of this elite minority.

Women and Revolutionary Change

The political, economic, and social changes brought about by revolutions in the LDCs often present women with rather unique opportunities that merit special attention. For one thing, revolutions tend to alter or tear down many of the traditional social structures and values that had previously oppressed women. When the Communists came to power in China, for example, they eliminated the last vestiges of foot binding for young women and prohibited the sale of women and girls as wives, concubines, or prostitutes.[53] In addition, most revolutionary armies and parties create social structures that are open to women and present greater opportunities for upward mobility. For example, women held important military command positions in both the Nicaraguan Sandinistas and the Salvadorian FMLN during their guerrilla struggles.

Indeed, because of their need for soldiers and their willingness to violate traditional gender roles, many guerrilla armies include significant numbers of women. For example, in the Eritrean People's Liberation Front (EPLF), which carried out a 30-year struggle for independence from Ethiopia, women constituted some 30 percent of the army and 11 percent of the delegates to the First EPLF Congress.[54] Similarly, it is estimated that women constituted 20 to 30 percent of the Sandinista forces in Nicaragua, perhaps 25 percent of Uruguay's Tupamaros, and a significant proportion of the FMLN guerrillas in El Salvador.[55] Because guerrilla armies such as the Sandinistas continued to play a central political role in society after the revolutionary party took power, their high level of gender integration has had long-term consequences that have transcended the military struggle.

After the Communist victory in China, Party Chairman Mao Zedong and the All-China Women's Federation assigned women an important role in rebuilding the nation's economy.[56] Consequently, many women who had long been confined to their homes entered the industrial work force, not because of a feminist agenda but because the government needed to reconstruct an economy devastated by three decades of war. But while the opportunity to work outside the home was obviously beneficial, women failed to attain the occupational equality called for by the government. In both collective farms and industry they continued to hold less-skilled, lower-paying jobs than men.

Radical regimes such as those in China, Vietnam, and Cuba emphasize the transformation of traditional cultural values through education and propaganda. Combating long-standing prejudices against women is a part of that process. But even these societies find it difficult to eradicate long-standing sexist attitudes. China's 1950 Marriage Law decreed that women could only wed under their own free will and granted women equal rights within the family, but enforcement of the Marriage Law has been considerably less than perfect, especially in rural areas. Furthermore, during the Maoist era (1949–1976) the government's commitment to new values varied considerably as the country swung between periods of ideological fervor and eras of pragmatism. During radical phases, such as the Great Leap Forward and the Cultural Revolution, state policy supported female liberation and lambasted traditional Chinese prejudices toward women. Following these periods of mass mobilization and turmoil, however, when party leadership wished to restore stability, the government reverted to more traditional values, extolling the importance of motherhood and the family.

Since the late 1970s, Deng Xiaoping's pragmatic state policies have stressed economic growth more than gender equality. As many Chinese factories have begun to abandon a policy of guaranteed lifetime employment (the "iron rice bowl") in their quest for higher efficiency, the first workers to be fired have more likely been women than men (though it is also true that women are disproportionately employed in the thriving industrial export sector).[57] Nothing more clearly shows the enduring influence of sexism in Chinese culture, however, than the question of population control. Troubled by the country's enormous population (over 1.2 billion people at the start of the twenty-first century), the government has been pressuring the Chinese people to have only one child per family. In rural China, where girls are considered less desirable than boys, this has apparently led to significant infanticide against female babies by parents who want their single child to be a boy.[58] In addition, some observers have noted that a disproportionate share of the abandoned children in rural orphanages are female.

The Cuban Revolutionary government has very actively sought to improve the status of women and to combat traditional male values of machismo. In 1960 the Federation of Cuban Women (FMC) was founded to mobilize women behind the Revolution and give them a voice in the political process. Since the Federation's long-time leader, Vilma Espín, is Fidel Castro's sister-in-law as well as the wife of Cuba's second most powerful leader, Raúl Castro, the FMC had a direct line to the center of power. Espín, a graduate of MIT, also had a distinguished career as a guerrilla officer in Cuba's revolutionary struggle. Officially representing 70 percent of Cuban women, the FMC has successfully encouraged many of them to seek employment and to participate politically. Thus, from 1970 to 1979 the proportion of women in the work force rose from 17.8 percent to 30.9 percent with impressive gains in the professions.[59] In the political sphere, women have been particularly active in the neighborhood-based Committees for Defense of the Revolutions (CDRs). The CDRs (to which some 80 percent of Cuba's adult population belong) promote revolutionary values including gender equality. Some men who refuse to let their wives work or who don't put in their share of the housework find themselves denounced for machismo at CDR meetings (perhaps by their wives or even their mothers) and castigated by their peers for their nonrevolutionary values. By the early 1980s, women represented half the local CDR leaders, 46 percent of the leaders of labor union locals, and 22 percent of the delegates to the National Assembly (the national congress).[60]

But revolutions are no panacea for women's problems. Often radical rhetoric exceeds actual accomplishments. Cuba, like China, demonstrates that even egalitarian revolutions fail to achieve full gender equality. Thus, despite their prominence in local CDR and labor union structures, Cuban women have rarely penetrated the top ranks of national political leadership, such as the State Council (in effect, the president's cabinet) or the Central Committee and the powerful Politburo of the Communist Party. An analysis in the early 1980s showed that only 8.9 percent of Central Committee members were female.[61] Similarly, while Cubans pay lip service to the Family Code, few men live up to its requirement that spouses share equally in domestic tasks. Change has been limited by ingrained male attitudes and most women's obvious reluctance to complain to the local CDR (composed of their neighbors) about their husband's noncompliance with the law. As one sympathetic observer has noted, "It must take an extremely confident women to bring her husband to public censure for failure to honor the code."[62] Chauvinist attitudes linger there as they do in other revolutionary societies.

CONCLUSION

Our analysis to this point reveals that the political and economic status of Third World women is anything but uniform. Their position varies considerably from region to region and country to country. Within individual countries a woman's condition differs according to her social class or ethnicity. Three factors seem particularly relevant in this regard: the prevailing cultural values, the level of socioeconomic modernization, and the type of political regime in place.

Religious and other cultural factors ultimately set limits on Third World women and influence the opportunities available to them. This is most manifestly true in fundamentalist Islamic states such as Iran, Sudan, and Afghanistan as well as conservative Islamic nations such as Saudi Arabia. In the most extreme example, Afghanistan's government has prohibited female employment outside the home and virtually confined women to their households. In doing so, they have denied one of the world's poorest nations a substantial portion of its small core of teachers and health care workers. While educational and professional opportunities exist for a small female elite in Iran and Saudi Arabia, most women are marginalized from the mainstream of economic life. Political leadership in all these countries is an exclusively male preserve. Cultural restraints are more subtle in East Asia, where Ester Boserup found that even in modern societies such as Singapore and Hong Kong, women had lower than expected rates of university attendance.

Contrary to expectations, economic modernization has often had an adverse effect on women in the LDCs. In Africa, for example, the commercialization and mechanization of agriculture has generally benefited male cultivators dispro-portionately, frequently at the expense of women farmers. In East and Southeast Asia, rapid industrialization based on cheap labor has led to higher wages for some female laborers and exploitation of others.[63] Yet while the initial impact of modernization may be negative for many poor women, its longer-term impact—including a growing middle class, wider educational opportunities, and, hope-fully, more egalitarian values—may benefit many women in the long run. It should be noted that the more modernized nations of Latin America—including Argentina, Chile, Mexico, and Uruguay—have the largest number of female polit-ical leaders and professionals.

Finally, the status of women is strongly influenced by the type of political regime and economic system that prevails in their country. Women seem to fare poorly under right-wing, authoritarian military regimes such as those that dom-inated much of South America in the 1970s and early 1980s and to benefit from leftist regimes. Ironically, however, while women suffered under the former mil-itary dictatorships in Chile, Argentina, and Brazil, they played important roles in the social movements seeking to protect human rights and to provide services for the poor. Revolutionary regimes, with their ideological commitment to equality, have often championed women's rights. However, while the revolutionary process has undoubtedly benefited many women in countries such as China, Vietnam, Cuba, and Nicaragua, obvious gender inequalities remain in those societies. To some extent this reflects the heritage of deeply entrenched cultural values as well as continued male dominance of the political system. At the same time, it also stems from the Marxist belief that all societal inequalities—whether based on gen-der, race, religion, or the like—are all derived from class divisions. Hence, there is a tendency to underestimate gender-based injustices and to assume that, in time, the eradication of capitalism will inevitably end serious sexism.

Since full gender equality does not exist yet in advanced industrial democracies (with only small democracies such as Iceland, the Netherlands, Fin-land, Denmark, Norway, and Sweden coming close), it seems unlikely that the process of socioeconomic modernization or the spread of democratic norms will automatically bring gender equality to the developing world. Both negative and positive consequences can be expected. In the short run, economic moderniza-tion, particularly in the area of agriculture, will likely be detrimental to many low-income women. In countries suffering economic difficulties such as debt crises or internal strife, women will doubtless continue to bear an unequal bur-den. And the spread of Islamic fundamentalism in many parts of the Middle East and Africa does not bode well for women's rights in those regions.

At the same time, however, as modernization and the spread of education produce a larger middle class and increasing numbers of literate women among the poor, women will become increasingly conscious of their rights and oppor-tunities and will be more capable of defending them. In many Third World nations women's rights movements have grown where none existed or were even conceivable a decade or two earlier. Like many other worldwide political movements carried from nation to nation by the mass media and scholarly publications, the feminist movement has extended itself through the demonstration effect. Women in more traditional societies like Bolivia or Jordan are also influenced by the women's movements that first arose in more progressive societies such as Chile or Lebanon. In each case, however, the movement has taken on a distinct character, particularly distinguishing itself from Western feminism. The women's movement was born in the Western world a mere three to four decades ago, and one can only speculate as to its influence in the Third World three decades into the future.

DISCUSSION QUESTIONS

1. Explain how the focus of research on gender in the developing world has moved from the study of oppression to the study of empowerment. What does this change reflect?

2. What occupations attract the highest proportions of Third World women? Why do many women gravitate toward those occupations?

3. Discuss the ways in which modernization has affected women of differing social status in distinct ways.

4. What is the most common characteristic of female heads of government in the Third World? To what extent has their assumption of power substantially improved the status of other women in their nations?

5. Discuss the reasons why Latin American women organized grass-roots political and social movements in the 1980s. What social classes were most mobilized in this period and what issues motivated mobilization of different classes?

NOTES

1. The informal sector, including a vast number of street vendors and small businesses, is the part of the economy that is "unregulated by the institutions of society [most notably the state], in a legal and social environment in which similar activities are regulated" and taxed. See Manuel Castells and Alejandro Portes, "World Underneath: The Origins, Dynamics and Effects of the Informal Economy," in *The Informal Economy: Studies in Advanced and Developing Economies*, ed. Alejandro Portes, Manuel Castells, and Lauren A. Benton (Baltimore, MD: Johns Hopkins University Press, 1989), p. 12. Of course, men constitute much of the informal sector, but women are disproportionately represented.

2. *New York Times*, December 30, 1993, p. 5.

3. Arturo Escobar and Sonia E. Alvarez, eds., *The Making of Social Movements in Latin America: Identity, Strategy and Democracy* (Boulder, CO: Westview Press, 1992); June Nash, "Women's Social Movements in Latin America," *Gender and Society* 4, no. 3 (September 1990): 338–353.

4. Lourdes Benería, "Accounting for Women's Work," in *Women and Development: The Sexual Division of Labor in Rural Societies*, ed. Lourdes Benería (New York: Praeger, 1982), p. 120.

5. Sonia E. Alvarez, *Engendering Democracy in Brazil: Women's Movements in Transition Politics* (Princeton, NJ: Princeton University Press, 1990), p. 4, fn. 2.

6. Paul Cammack, David Pool, and William Tordoff, *Third World Politics: A Comparative Introduction* (Baltimore, MD: Johns Hopkins University Press, 1988), pp. 184–193.

7. Leith Mullings, "Women and Economic Change in Africa," in *Women in Africa: Studies in Social and Economic Change*, ed. Nancy J. Hafkin and Edna G. Bray (Stanford, CA: Stanford University Press, 1976), pp. 239–264.

8. Margo Lovett, "Gender Relations, Class Formation, and the Colonial State in Africa," in *Women and the State in Africa*, ed. Jane L. Parpart and Kathleen A. Staudt (Boulder, CO: Lynne Rienner Publishers, 1989), pp. 37–39.

9. Ester Boserup, *Women's Role in Economic Development* (London: George Allen and Unwin, 1970), p. 54.

10. Ibid., p. 55.

11. Cited in Esther Trenchard, "Rural Women's Work in Sub-Saharan Africa and the Implications for Nutrition," in *Geography of Gender in the Third World*, ed. Janet Henshall Momsen and Janet G. Townsend (London: SUNY Press, 1987), p. 155: and Marie-Angélique Savané, "Women and Rural Development in Africa," in *Women in Rural Development: Critical Issues* (Geneva: International Labour Office, 1980), p. 27. The findings of any given study are undoubtedly less precise than its tables may suggest since female labor participation in developing nations is hard to measure and varies considerably from place to place. Yet the research generally shows similar patterns.

12. Boserup, *Women's Role*, pp. 27–28. For other estimates see Joan Mencher, "Women in Agriculture," in *Food Policy: Framework for Analysis*, ed. Charles K. Mann and Barbara Huddleston (Bloomington, IN: Indiana University Press, 1986), p. 39.

13. A. Bandarage, "Women in Development: Liberalism, Marxism and Marxism-Feminism," *Development and Change* 15, no. 3 (1984).

14. Nici Nelson, *Why Has Development Neglected Rural Women?* (Oxford, England: Pergamon Press, 1979), p. 4.

15. Ibid., pp. 45–47.

16. Savané, *Women in Rural Development*, p. 27.

17. Leena Mehendale, "The Integrated Rural Development Programme for Women in Developing Countries: A Case Study" in *Women, Development and Survival in the Third World*, ed. Haleh Afshar (New York: Longman, 1991), pp. 223–238.

18. Cornelia Butler Flora, "Income Generation Projects for Rural Women," in *Rural Women and State Policy: Feminist Perspectives on Latin American Agricultural Development*, ed. Carmen Diana Deere and Magdalena León de Leal (Boulder, CO: Westview Press, 1987), pp. 212–238.

19. Claire Robertson, "Ga Women and Socioeconomic Change in Accra, Ghana," in *Women in Africa*, pp. 111–133.

20. Gloria González Salazar, "Participation of Women in the Mexican Labor Force," in *Sex and Class in Latin America*, ed. June Nash and Helen I. Safa (New York: J. F. Bergin Publishers, 1980), p. 187. The proportions may well have changed somewhat since then.

21. Heleieth I. B. Saffioti, "Technological Change in Brazil: Its Effect on Men and Women in Two Firms," in *Women and Change in Latin America*, ed. June Nash and Helen I. Safa (South Hadley, MA: Bergin & Garvey Publishers, 1985), pp. 110–111; Commack, Pool, and Tordoff, *Third World Politics*, pp. 195–196.

22. Cited in Alan Gilbert and Josef Gugler, *Cities, Poverty and Development: Urbanization in the Third World*, 2d ed. (New York: Oxford University Press, 1992), p. 104, fn. 29.

23. Nici Nelson, "How Women and Men Get By: The Sexual Division of Labour in the Informal Sector of a Nairobi Squatter Settlement," in *The Urbanization of the Third World*, ed. Josef Gugler (New York: Oxford University Press, 1988), pp. 183–203.

24. Shahnaz Kazi, "Some Measures of the Status of Women in the Course of Development in South Asia," in *Women in Development in South Asia*, ed. V. Kanesalingam (New Delhi, India: Macmillan India Limited, 1989), pp. 19–52.

25. Mary C. Muller, "Vocational Training for Women of India," in *Third World at the Crossroads*, ed. Sheikh R. Ali (New York: Praeger, 1989), pp. 87–94.

26. Boserup, *Women's Role*, pp. 119–128.

27. It should be noted, however, that in countries such as Argentina and Russia, where women constitute a high proportion of the medical profession, medicine is not nearly as lucrative an occupation as in the United States. The most financially rewarding jobs in Argentina, such as business executives, are still largely male.

28. The real wage is a measure of the purchasing power of individual or family earnings. It factors in earnings and changes in the cost of living.

29. Aili Mari Tripp, "The Impact of Crisis and Economic Reform on Women in Urban Tanzania," in *Unequal Burden: Economic Crisis, Persistent Poverty, and Women's Work*, ed. Lourdes Benería and Shelley Feldman (Boulder, CO: Westview Press, 1992), pp. 163–166.

30. Paola Pérez-Alemán, "Economic Crisis and Women in Nicaragua," in *Unequal Burden*, pp. 239–247.

31. Only Finland and Norway granted women the vote prior to World War I. Female suffrage was enacted in the United States in 1920 at about the same time as most West European democracies. On the other hand, women were not able to vote in Swiss national elections until 1972, nor in the small European state of Liechtenstein until 1986.

32. On women's suffrage in Europe and the United States, see Vicky Randall, *Women and Politics: An International Perspective*, 2d ed. (Chicago: University of Chicago Press, 1987), pp. 5, 51, 209–211; on Latin America, see Jane Jaquette, "Female Political Participation in Latin America," in *Sex and Class in Latin America*, p. 223; also, Francesca Miller, *Latin American Women and the Search for Social Justice* (Hanover, NH: University Press of New England, 1991), pp. 96–101.

33. Rama Mehta, *The Western Educated Hindu Woman* (New York: Asia Publishing House, 1970), pp. 16–32.

34. Judith Van Allen, "Memsahib, Militante, Femme Libre: Political and Apolitical Styles of Modern African Women," in *Women in Politics*, ed. Jane S. Jaquette (New York: John Wiley and Sons, 1974), p. 310.

35. Lourdes Arizpe, "Foreword: Democracy for a Small Two-Gender Planet," in *Women and Social Change in Latin America*, ed. Elizabeth Jelin (London and Atlantic Highlands, NJ: Zed Books, 1990), p. xv.

36. Nina Mba, "Kaba and Khaki: Women and the Militarized State in Nigeria," in *Women and the State in Africa*, p, 86.

37. Jaquette, "Female Political Participation," p. 223.

38. See, for example, JoAnn Aviel, "Changing the Political Role of Women: A Costa Rican Case Study," in *Women in Politics*, pp. 281–303.

39. See, for example, Amy Conger Lind, "Power, Gender and Development: Popular Women's Organizations and the Politics of Needs in Ecuador," in *The Making of Social Movements*, pp. 134–149.

40. Jana Everett, "Incorporation Versus Conflict: Lower Class Women, Collective Action, and the State in India," in *Women, the State and Development*, ed. Sue Ellen M. Charlton, Jana Everett, and Kathleen Staudt (Albany: State University of New York Press, 1989), p. 163.

41. Armita Basu, *Two Faces of Protest: Contrasting Modes of Women's Activism* (Berkeley: University of California Press, 1992), p. 3.

42. Jane S. Jaquette, introduction to *The Women's Movement in Latin America: Feminism and the Transition to Democracy*, ed. Jane S. Jaquette (Boston: Unwin Hyman, 1989), p. 6. This section draws heavily on Jaquette's book and on Alvarez, *Engendering Democracy in Brazil*.

43. Sonia E. Alvarez, "Women's Movements and Gender Politics in the Brazilian Transition," in *The Women's Movement in Latin America*, pp. 19–20; see also Alvarez, *Engendering Democracy in Brazil*.

44. Teresa Pires de Rio Caldeira, "Women, Daily Life and Politics," in *Women and Social Change in Latin America*, ed. Elizabeth Jelin (London and Atlantic Highlands, NJ: Zed Books Ltd., 1990), pp. 47–79.

45. Elsa M. Chaney, *Supermadre: Women in Politics in Latin America* (Austin: University of Texas Press, 1979), p. 4.

46. Jane L. Parpart and Kathleen A. Staudt, "Women and the State in Africa," in *Women and the State in Africa*, p. 8.

47. Quoted in Chaney, *Supermadre*, p. 21.

48. Ibid., p. 141.

49. Manjulika Koshal, "Indira Gandhi as Head of Government," in *Asian Women in Transition*, ed. Sylvia A. Chipp and Justin J. Green (University Park, PA: Pennsylvania State University Press, 1980), p. 253. It should be noted that women were highly underrepresented in both bodies, just less so in India for that period. As Table 4.1 indicates, India's comparative ranking on female representation is considerably lower.

50. It is worth noting a similar pattern in the United States until recently. Vicky Randall notes that between 1917 and 1976, 73 percent of female senators and 50 percent of women congressional representatives were the widows of men who held seats. See *Women and Politics*, p. 132.

51. To be sure, some of the aforementioned group, most notably Isabel Perón, were far less capable.

52. Of course, it is also true that until the 1970s almost all women governors and senators in the United States were the widows of men who had formerly held those posts. Only relatively recently have American women attained those positions totally on their own.

53. Delia Davin, "Chinese Models of Development and Their Implications for Women," in *Women, Development and Survival*, p. 32.

54. National Union of Eritrean Women, "Women and Revolution in Eritrea," in *Third World: Second Sex*, ed. Miranda Davis (London: Zed Press, 1983), p. 114.

55. *Envio* (Managua) 6, p. 78, quoted in Mary Stead, "Women, War and Underdevelopment in Nicaragua," *Women, Development and Survival*, p. 53; Randall, *Woman and Politics*, p. 61.

56. Bee-Lan Chan Wang, "Chinese Women: The Relative Influences of Ideological Revolution, Economic Growth and Cultural Change," in *Comparative Perspectives of Third World Women: The Impact of Race, Sex and Class*, ed. Beverly Lindsay (New York: Praeger Publishers, 1980), pp. 99–104; see also Delia Davin, "Chinese Models of Development," in *Women, Development and Survival*.

57. *New York Times*, May 11, 1993.

58. *New York Times*, April 25, 1993 and July 21, 1993. Thus, demographers have found a higher than normal ratio of male births to female births reported to the government. Some of the discrepancy may be caused by girls who are born and not reported, but part is probably due to female infanticide.

59. Isabel Larguia and John Domoulin, "Women's Equality in the Cuban Revolution," in *Women and Change in Latin America*, pp. 344, 363.

60. Ibid., p. 360. There is an extensive literature on women in Revolutionary Cuba, most of it written from a strongly pro-Revolutionary perspective. See Margaret E. Leahy, *Development Strategies and the Status of Women* (Boulder, CO: Lynne Rienner Publishers, 1986), pp. 91–116; Lois M. Smith and Alfred Padula, "The Cuban Family in the 1980s," in *Transformation and Struggle: Cuba Faces the 1990s,* ed. Sandor Halebsky and John M. Kirk (New York: Praeger, 1990), pp. 176–188; and Max Azicri, "Women's Development through Revolutionary Mobilization," in *The Cuba Reader: The Making of a Revolutionary Society*, ed, Philip Brenner et al. (New York: Grove Press, 1989), pp. 457–470. For a different viewpoint, see Julie Marie Bunck, "The Cuban Revolution and Women's Rights," in *Cuban Communism*, 7th ed., ed. Irving Louis Horowitz (New Brunswick, NJ: Transaction Publishers, 1989), pp. 443–465.

61. Randall, *Women and Politics*, p. 103.

62. Johnetta Cole, "Women in Cuba," in *Comparative Perspectives of Third World Women*, p. 176.

63. Linda Y. C. Lim, "Capitalism, Imperialism and Patriarchy: The Dilemma of Third World Women in Multinational Factories," in *Women, Men and the International Division of Labor*, ed. June Nash and María Patricia Fernández-Kelly (Albany: SUNY Press, 1983).

5

❧

AGRARIAN REFORM
AND THE POLITICS
OF RURAL CHANGE

When we speak of "the people" of Africa and Asia, in large part we are talking about the peasantry. Despite substantial urbanization in recent decades (see Chapter 6), much of the developing world remains primarily rural. According to one relatively recent estimate, close to 60 percent of Third World families earn their livelihood from agriculture.[1] And it is in the countryside where some of the worst aspects of political and economic underdevelopment prevail. In nations as distinct as China and Mexico, rural annual incomes are 20 to 25 percent that of urban earnings. Sharp urban-rural gaps also exist in literacy, life expectancy, and the availability of health care. Rural villagers are less likely than their urban cousins to have safe drinking water, electricity, or schools for their children.

The proportion of the population living in rural areas within particular developing countries is generally substantially higher than it is in the First World, but varies greatly. The proportion ranges from under one-third in Venezuela, Argentina, Brazil, and Zambia; to almost two-thirds in Malaysia, Yemen, Nigeria, Ghana, and Bolivia; and to 70 percent or more in much of Africa and in the world's population giants, China and India.

More than 1 billion rural inhabitants live in "absolute poverty," defined as suffering from malnutrition, high infant mortality rates, inadequate housing, and pervasive illiteracy.[2] In the countryside of Malawi, Rwanda, the Congo, Bangladesh, and Haiti, more than 80 percent of the rural population fall in this category.[3]

Because of the rural sector's great size, we should not be surprised to find that it contributes a larger share of GNP (or GDP) in the LDCs than it does in industrialized nations. Agricultural output constitutes 35 percent of GDP in the poorest Third World nations, 22 percent in middle-level countries, and 10 percent in the more advanced developing countries, compared to only 3 percent in industrialized democracies.[4] At the same time, however, the farm population's per capita output is far lower than the urban sector's.

In most of the developing world, political power, like economic dominance, is concentrated in the cities. Consequently, government policy—on issues ranging from social expenditures to agricultural pricing—has a predictable urban bias. As noted in Chapter 1, dependency theorists maintain that the exploitative relationship between the core (developed, capitalist nations) and the periphery (developing world) is replicated in the links between city and countryside in the Third World.[5] Resolving political and economic tensions between urban and rural areas as well as class tensions within the countryside remains one of the primary challenges facing most LDCs.

RURAL CLASS STRUCTURES

Within the rural sector there is usually a substantial disparity in ownership of or access to farm land. Particularly in Latin America and parts of South Asia, agricultural property tends to be concentrated in a relatively small number of hands. These inequalities have contributed to substantial rural poverty and created rigid class systems in countries such as El Salvador, Colombia, and the Philippines, as well as parts of India. African nations—with the exception of a few, like South Africa, Morocco, Kenya, and prerevolutionary Ethiopia—have a more equitable pattern of land distribution, though they still suffer from sharp urban-rural gaps and intense rural poverty.

At the apex of the rural class system stand the large and powerful land owners, sometimes known as the oligarchy. Large Filipino sugar growers and Argentine cattle magnates, for example, have exercised considerable political power in national politics for many decades. In El Salvador, the most influential coffee producers have long dominated the country's political system together with the military. Land concentration has been most intense in Latin America, with its tradition of large estates (latifundia) dating back to the Spanish colonial era and the early decades of independence. In the Philippines, Sri Lanka, Pakistan, Bangladesh, and parts of India, Indonesia and Thailand, reactionary landed elites have also contributed to rural backwardness and poverty.

In recent decades, the national economic and political power of large, rural landlords has often declined considerably. Thus, in industrializing nations such as Mexico, Brazil, and Thailand, the economic importance of agribusiness has diminished relative to the industrial and commercial sectors'. Consequently, many wealthy land-owning families have diversified into those other sectors of the economy or left agriculture entirely. In other countries, agrarian reform has weakened or even destroyed the power of the rural oligarchy.[6]

These changes have been most sweeping (and often brutal) in countries that have experienced peasant-based revolutions. Following China's Revolution, for example, the nation's landlords were stripped of their wealth, while untold thousands were executed. After the Communist victory in Vietnam, landlords were sent to prison camps for "political reeducation." Elsewhere, in nonrevolutionary societies such as Peru's and South Korea's, comprehensive but peaceful agrarian reforms have also undermined the landed aristocracy.

At the local and regional levels, however, many landlords in Asia and Latin America continue to exercise considerable influence. For example, upper-caste land owners in the Indian state of Bihar and cattle barons in the Brazilian interior retain virtually unchallenged power in their domain. At times they intimidate or murder peasant organizers and union leaders without fear of legal sanctions. Such was the fate of Chico Mendes, the renowned Brazilian union leader who had organized Amazonian rubber-tree tappers against powerful cattle ranchers who were clearing the forest and destroying the local habitat. Despite his impressive international stature (he was honored, for example, by Turner Broadcasting and various U.S. Senators) and his links to U.S. environmental groups, Mendes was murdered by hired gunmen. Only after a sustained international outcry were his murderers brought to trial.

On the rung beneath the landed elite in the rural hierarchy we find middle-sized landlords and "rich" peasants. The second group (sometimes called Kulaks) is composed of peasants who, unlike the landlords, work the land themselves. Unlike poorer peasants, however, they are sufficiently affluent to hire labor as well. While neither middle-sized landlords nor rich peasants are part of the national power elite, in countries such as India they exercise considerable influence as activists in political parties and interest groups.[7] Indeed, in much of Asia, where the biggest agricultural holdings are not nearly as large as those in Latin America, middle-sized landlords are a potent political force. Together with rich peasants they are often village political leaders. Moreover, their influence is magnified further by extended family and clan networks.

At the bottom of the socioeconomic ladder, the rural poor—including peasants who own small plots of land, tenant farmers, and farm workers—are generally the Third World's most impoverished and least powerful group. Peasants are defined as family farmers (mostly poor) who maintain a traditional lifestyle distinct from that of city dwellers. Their links to the outside world—including the government, military, church, and market economy—are largely controlled by influential individuals and institutions outside the peasant community.[8] Because many peasants are illiterate or semiliterate, need others to transport their crops, and lack easy access to credit, they are dependent on government bureaucrats, merchants, and money lenders who frequently exploit them. Thus, as Eric Wolf has noted, "Peasant denotes an asymmetrical structural relationship between the producers of surplus [peasants] and controllers [landlords, merchants, tax collectors]."[9]

Poor peasants may further be subdivided into those who own small plots of land for family cultivation (smallholders) and the landless. The ranks of the landless, in turn, include tenant farmers (who enter into various types of rental arrangements with landlords) and hired farm laborers. It should be noted that these activities are not mutually exclusive. Smallholders, for example, may supplement their incomes by working as farm laborers or renting land as tenants. On the whole it is the landless who constitute the poorest of the rural poor. They constitute as little as 10 percent of agricultural families in Kenya and Sierra Leone, but rise to 25 to 35 percent in Mexico, Peru, Turkey, and Cameroon, and to 50 to 70 percent in India, Bangladesh, Pakistan, the Philippines, Iraq, the Dominican Republic, and Brazil.[10] Not surprisingly, then, in much of Asia and Latin America, where concentration of land ownership and associated peasant landlessness are particularly high, the issue of land reform has often been at the center of rural politics.

PEASANT POLITICS

Despite their vast numbers, peasants usually play a rather muted role in Third World politics. Because most LDCs don't have competitive national elections, those numbers do not convert readily into political influence. The peasantry's political leverage is also limited by their poverty, lack of education, dependency on outsiders, and physical isolation from each other and from the centers of national power. Cultural values stressing caution and conservatism may further constrain peasant political behavior.

Karl Marx's analysis of nineteenth-century European rural society questioned the peasants' capacity for political change and dismissed their revolutionary potential. In his *Eighteenth Brumaire* he cited their lack of class consciousness and solidarity, disparagingly referring to smallholders as a "sack of potatoes." Dismayed by their alleged conservatism, he dismissed them as "the class that represents the barbarism in civilization."[11] More recently, Robert Redfield's classic study of peasants in the developing world portrayed them in similar terms. "In every part of the world," he argued, "generally speaking, peasants have been a conservative factor in social change, a brake on revolution."[12]

Indeed, over the years a number of prominent anthropological studies have depicted peasant political culture as fatalistic and atomized. Individual peasants and their families, it is said, question the capacity of collective political action to better their fate.[13] Describing the reaction of Indian villagers to local government authorities, Phyllis Arora noted a sense of powerlessness resulting in political apathy. "Helplessness is . . . evoked by the presence of the district officer. The peasant tends to feel that all he [or she] can do before such authority . . . is petition for redress of grievances. . . . In the ultimate analysis, however, . . . the peasant feels at the mercy of the whims of the [political] authorities."[14] More recently, Western journalists visiting peasant communities in China have been struck by the villagers' lack of political involvement and their insularity from national political debate.[15]

To be sure, there is often an underlying conservatism in Third World rural society. To some extent this may reflect a suspicion of external values, a distrust grounded in religious beliefs and other long-standing traditions. The maintenance of a distinct peasant culture depends, to some extent, on rejection of outside influences. But it is important to recognize that oftentimes peasant suspicion of social change is both understandable and rational. Struggling on the margins of economic survival, the rural poor have often found that commercialization and mechanization of agriculture, as well as other aspects of rural modernization, have affected them adversely. In rural Pakistan, for example, the introduction of tractors improved the output and income of those farmers who could afford them. As a consequence, however, many tenant farmers were forced off the land and the net result was to increase the concentration of farm property in fewer hands.[16] Parallel examples from elsewhere in the developing world are legion. Small wonder, then, that peasants are often suspicious of change.

This does not mean, however, that they are incapable of standing up to landlords and government authorities who repress them—far from it. Examples of peasant resistance are commonplace, ranging from the most restrained to the most radical. James C. Scott has demonstrated that many peasants in Southeast Asia who appear to accept the established order actually engage in unobtrusive "everyday forms of resistance," such as theft and vandalism against their landlords, foot dragging, and false deference.[17] Elsewhere peasants have presented their political demands more openly and aggressively. Since the mid-1990s, in the Mexican state of Chiapas, Zapatista peasant rebels, drawn from the area's Indian communities, have accelerated the nation's pro-democracy movement and forced the government to the negotiating table. Similarly, peasant demonstrators and voters have been a force for change in parts of India. And, contrary to Marx's expectations, the allegedly conservative peasantry were critical actors in most twentieth-century revolutions. In the Marxist revolutions that swept Russia, China, Vietnam, and Cuba, as well as in Bolivia's and Mexico's more centrist insurgencies, peasants played a decisive role.[18] More recently, they have been the backbone of guerrilla movements in the Philippines, Afghanistan, Cambodia, El Salvador, and Peru.

The role of the peasantry in revolutionary movements will be examined at greater length in Chapter 7. For now, however, suffice it to say that peasants are neither inherently conservative nor intrinsically radical. Rather, they vary considerably in their capacity for collective political action and in their ideological propensities.

To understand why so many peasants accept the political status quo while others choose to resist or even rebel, we must first examine the relationship between the powerful and the weak in the countryside. Although landlords in traditional settings frequently exploit their tenants or neighboring small holders, mutually understood boundaries normally limit the extent of that exploitation. Links between landlords and peasants are usually grounded in long-standing patron-client relationships involving reciprocal obligations.

Despite the landlords' superior power, these relationships are not exclusively exploitative. For example, landowners frequently provide their tenants with land and financial credit in return for labor on the estate. They may fund religious festivals or serve as godparents for their tenants' children.

As long as landlords and other members of the rural power elite fulfill their obligations, peasants generally accept the traditional order despite its many injustices. However, should rural modernization and the commercialization of agriculture induce rural patrons to cease discharging their traditional responsibilities, the peasantry may conclude that the previously existing "moral economy" has failed them.[19] Eric Wolf has noted that the transition from feudal or semifeudal rural social relations to capitalist economic arrangements frequently strips the peasantry of the certainty and protection afforded them by the old order. The result is often rural upheaval. Thus, he argues, the origins of Communist revolutions in China, Vietnam, Cuba, and other Third World nations lay in the threat that the spread of rural capitalism posed to the peasants' traditional way of life.[20]

This does not suggest that rural modernization and the transition to capitalism always radicalize the peasantry or drive them to revolutionary activity. But when peasants feel that their traditional way of life is threatened they will resist change or at least try to channel it in ways more beneficial to their interests. How effectively they engage in collective political action and how radical or moderate their demands are depends on a variety of factors: the extent to which they perceive themselves to be exploited; how desperate their economic condition is; the degree of internal cohesion and cooperation within their communities; their ability to form political linkages with peasants in neighboring villages or in other parts of the country; the extent to which they forge political ties with nonpeasant groups and leaders; the type of outside groups they ally with (be it the Catholic Church in the Philippines or Maoist revolutionaries in Peru); the responsiveness of the political system to their demands; and the variety of political options that the political order affords them.

The last two factors suggest that the probability of radical peasant insurrection depends as much on the quality of a country's political system as it does on the nature of the peasantry. Given a meaningful opportunity to implement change peacefully, peasants rarely opt for revolution. Rebellion—which brings obvious danger to their own lives and the lives of their families—is an act of desperation entered into only when other options are unavailable. It is largely for that reason that no democratic political system has ever been toppled by a revolutionary insurgency.

In recent decades, the spread of the mass media in the countryside, increased rural educational levels, and the broadening of the franchise in many LDCs (such as extension of the vote to illiterates) have greatly increased peasant voting power in democratic and semidemocratic countries. In countries such as India, South Korea, Nicaragua, and Ecuador, politicians must now take the peasant vote more seriously. With rising educational levels and more information at their disposal, peasants can more effectively press their demands. Still, such voting power is of little use in the single-party or no-party governments that still predominate in Africa, the Middle East, and much of Asia. And even in competitive party systems, the peasantry's political power is not proportional to the size of its population.

Ultimately, the range of peasant activity runs the gamut from far left to far right, from peaceful to violent. As Samuel Huntington has noted, "The peasantry . . . may be the bulwark of the status quo or the shock troops of revolution. Which role the peasant plays is determined by the extent to which the existing system meets his immediate economic and material needs as he sees them."[21] In India, many peasants vote for conservative political parties, including a neofascist Hindu movement. In Latin America, on the other hand, peasants often vote for moderately left-of-center candidates such as Social Democrats, Christian Democrats, and populists. And in countries such as China, Vietnam, Nicaragua, and Peru many peasants have supported revolutionary insurrections. Whatever their political bent, the peasants' economic and political concerns usually revolve around four broad issues: crop prices (i.e., what they are paid for their production), consumer prices, taxes, and the availability of land.[22] The issue of land has been the most volatile and the most critical to the political stability of many Third World nations, and it is to this issue that we will now turn our attention.

THE POLITICS OF AGRARIAN REFORM

In areas of the Third World where land ownership is more highly concentrated, the issue of agrarian reform has frequently been at the top of the rural political agenda. To be sure, the pressure for such reform has waxed and waned, and other models of rural development have been more popular in recent decades. Still, the issue of agrarian reform lingers. Normally, it involves redistribution of farmland from landlords to landless peasants or to smallholders who need larger plots to support their families. In other instances, it entails distribution of public property, including previously uncultivated lands. To stand a meaningful chance of increasing agricultural production, improving rural living standards, and establishing political stability, government land redistribution must be accompanied by supplementary aid to program beneficiaries. This includes technical assistance, commercial credit, transportation, and enhanced access to markets. Unfortunately, agrarian reform programs often fail to provide these additional supports in sufficient quantities. Furthermore, the amount of land distributed is frequently inadequate to meet the peasants' needs. Thus, with such notable exceptions as Japan, Taiwan, and South Korea, land reforms have often fallen short of their goals.

Patterns of Land Concentration

In the early 1990s, an estimated 100 million Third World, rural families (some 500 million people) earned most of their income on farmland that they did not own.[23] In addition, millions of smallholders lack sufficient land to support their families adequately. In countries such as Bangladesh, Rwanda, El Salvador, and Peru, the ratio of rural families to arable land is so high that even an equitable distribution of farmland would fail to meet all of the peasantry's needs. But in many LDCs landlessness and land shortages are primarily attributable to the concentration of agricultural land in a limited number of hands.

Maldistribution of land is most pronounced in Latin America, where large estates, sometimes measuring thousands of acres, contain a substantial proportion of the region's farmland. In Brazil, for example, a mere 2 percent of the nation's farms, each exceeding 1,000 hectares, (2,500 acres)[24] contain 57 percent of all farmland.[25] Vast cattle and citrus estates have been cut out of the Amazonian interior, some covering several hundred thousand acres. In the Dominican Republic, where holdings are not nearly as vast, farms over 50 hectares in size constitute less than 2 percent of the nation's agricultural units; nevertheless, they control over 55 percent of the country's farmland. The largest of these estates—each with holdings exceeding 500 hectares—represent a mere 0.1 percent of all Dominican farms, but possess 27 percent of the nation's agricultural land. At the other end of the spectrum, peasant smallholders (owning units of 5 hectares or less) possess nearly 82 percent of the country's farms but merely 12.2 percent of its farmland.[26] Similar patterns prevail in much of Latin America. Prior to the 1979 Sandinista Revolution, 43 percent of Nicaragua's rural families were landless. At the same time, a mere 2 percent of the rural population owned 36 percent of the land. About one-fifth of Nicaragua's agricultural area belonged to the ruling Somoza family.[27]

With different historical traditions and far higher population density, Asia does not have agricultural estates of the same magnitude. In nations such as Indonesia, India, and Pakistan, farm holdings rarely exceed 50 hectares.[28] Still, a high proportion of agricultural land is often concentrated in relatively few hands. For example, in Bangladesh, one of the world's most densely populated countries, the largest farms are relatively small, rarely exceeding 5 to 10 hectares. Yet, less than 3 percent of the nation's rural households control over 25 percent of the nation's farmland. In the Philippines, virtually identical data show 3.4 percent of the country's farms accounting for 26 percent of the land.[29]

The Case for Agrarian Reform

Given the powerful vested interests opposing land redistribution, advocates of agrarian reform have needed to justify their objectives on a variety of grounds, including social justice and equity, greater political stability, improved agricultural productivity, economic growth, and preservation of the environment. An examination of each of these arguments reveals the complexity of the debate.

Social Justice Because of the maldistribution of agricultural holdings in Latin America and parts of Africa and Asia, a prima facie case can be made for some type of land redistribution in terms of social justice and human rights.[30] As noted, the millions of rural families with little or no land are generally among the poorest of the Third World's poor. They are frequently trapped in a web of poverty, malnutrition, and illiteracy from which there is little escape. They are usually politically powerless as well, controlled by landlords, local political bosses, the police, or the military. For them agrarian reform is a fundamental step toward achieving greater political and socioeconomic equity.[31]

Political Stability From the perspective of Third World policy makers and their foreign advisors, a more compelling goal of agrarian reform has been curtailing peasant unrest. Samuel Huntington most starkly linked reform to political stability:

> Where the conditions of land tenure are equitable and provide a viable living for the peasant, revolution is unlikely. Where they are inequitable and where the peasant lives in poverty and suffering, revolution is likely, if not inevitable, unless the government takes prompt measures to remedy those conditions.[32]

Indeed, statistical analyses indicate that the likelihood of revolutionary activity in various developing countries increases where there is high inequality of land ownership and where there is a significant proportion of landless peasants.[33]

In the absence of peasant unrest, however, policy makers have tended to be relatively indifferent to the injustices of land tenure patterns. Throughout the Cold War, for example, the United States tended to press its allies in Asia and Latin America for agrarian reform only when it was apprehensive about instability and the prospects of leftist revolution. Following World War II, the U.S. occupation command in Japan oversaw a major land reform designed to establish the basis for stable democracy. Shortly thereafter, American support contributed to Taiwan's and South Korea's highly successful agrarian reforms. During the 1960s, in the wake of the Cuban Revolution, the Kennedy administration formulated the Alliance for Progress for Latin America, which repeatedly articulated the desirability of land reform in the region, though it achieved only limited success in that regard. During the 1980s, the United States encouraged agrarian reform in El Salvador, again with mixed results.

What almost all of these cases had in common was America's desire to forestall communist insurgency or other forms of peasant insurrection. However, where the peasantry was not mobilized or where pro-U.S. dictators dominated the political system (such as Alfredo Stroessner in Paraguay and Ferdinand Marcos in the Philippines), the United States was usually rather indifferent to inequitable land distribution patterns.

Productivity One of the most hotly debated aspects of land reform has been its effect on agricultural productivity. Opponents of change maintain that land redistribution lowers agricultural output, thereby diminishing food supplies for the cities and curtailing export earnings. Citing "economies of scale," they argue that large agricultural units are generally more productive because they can be more easily mechanized and can use rural infrastructure (such as irrigation or roads) more efficiently. Second, they insist that peasant cultivators lack the education and know-how of large landowners. Thus, one of Ecuador's most powerful and most progressive landowners (and a former national president) told this author that he had voluntarily given some of his land to the peasants on his estate but, unfortunately, had found them incapable of using it properly. Finally, some opponents of reform contend that if large agroexport estates were divided into smallholder plots, peasants would switch to cultivation of subsistence food crops, thereby denying the country much-needed foreign exchange.

Proponents of agrarian reform counter that it is smallholders who are actually the more efficient producers. Although a growing number of landowners now study agricultural sciences and employ modern productive techniques, many of the landed elite still farm their land very inefficiently. Because land is an important source of prestige and political power in rural societies, landlords often own more than they can effectively cultivate. Peasant cultivators, on the other hand, tend to farm their plots very intensively because their families' living standards depend on raising productivity.

This does not imply, however, that small peasant-run units are always more efficient. The comparative productivity of large and small farms varies according to their owner's farming skills and the crop or animal being raised. Land reform in Taiwan, South Korea, and Japan did not adversely affect production because tenant farmers on the large estates already had substantial decision-making responsibility over agricultural production prior to the reforms. Consequently, they were well qualified to use the land efficiently as soon as it was distributed to them. Conversely, Latin American peasants living on latifundia are more tightly controlled and permitted less managerial authority. Consequently, land transfers there sometimes generate short-term declines in efficiency.[34] Peasant beneficiaries in such regions may require more government technical assistance in their transformation to landowners.

The comparative efficiency of landlords and peasant smallholders also varies according to crop or animal product. For example, production of meat, wheat, or sugar is more likely to benefit from economies of scale (i.e., output is more responsive to heavy capital inputs). On the other hand, most of the grains, tubers, fruits, and vegetables that constitute the core of Third World food supplies, along with some exports such as coffee, do best with labor-intensive cultivation on small farm units.

These variations notwithstanding, data collected in Asia and Latin America since the 1950s reveal that labor-intensive smallholders generally have higher yields per acre than do large-scale, capital-intensive (mechanized) producers.[35] For example, a recent study of Brazilian agriculture found that the larger the farm, the lower its output per hectare of land and per input of capital (such as machinery).[36] Similar relationships have been discovered in countries as diverse as Colombia, Malaysia, the Philippines, Pakistan, and India.[37]

The economic efficiency of small farms may surprise many Americans accustomed to believing that larger units are inherently more productive. But in underdeveloped rural areas with a surplus of labor (i.e., many people who are underemployed and who will work for low wages), it is cost effective to use family or hired labor intensively. Out of economic necessity, peasant cultivators work hard, exploiting their own family labor. On the other hand, large estates are generally farmed by tenants or hired laborers who gain little from raising productivity. That difference in motivation may explain why the agricultural yields of peasant land owners in Japan, South Korea, and Taiwan and of near-owners in China are generally over twice as high as those of Filipino tenant farmers with comparable plots of land.[38]

During the past two decades the disparity in agricultural productivity between large and small units has diminished somewhat. By using more advanced technology, such as green revolution seeds and complementary irrigation, some large farmers have narrowed the efficiency gap.[39] But, even were the disparity to be eliminated entirely, smallholding operations would still be more efficient for the country in another sense. Owners of larger farms often need to import machinery, fuel, and chemicals, thereby drawing upon scarce foreign exchange. Even when they purchase these items domestically, they spend funds that could better be invested elsewhere. On the other hand, peasant farms utilize family labor intensively, a cheap input found in abundance. It is for this reason that the former president of the Overseas Development Council argued, "a land and capital scarce (but population plentiful) country should favor 40 two and a half acre farms over a single-owner 100-acre farm in order to make optimum use of available land, labor and capital."[40]

Economic Growth Beyond its positive effect on agricultural productivity, land redistribution often has broader beneficial consequences for the economies of developing nations. A number of countries that have undertaken extensive agrarian reforms, such as Bolivia and Cuba, have slowed the tide of peasant migration to the cities. Giving peasants an economic stake in the countryside has reduced rural-to-urban migration, thereby alleviating the tremendous strain on infrastructure and social fabric currently being experienced by many Third World cities (see Chapter 6).

When successfully implemented, land reform improves the living standards of many rural poor. As their purchasing power increases, they consume more of their country's manufactured goods, thereby stimulating industrial growth.[41] It is no coincidence, then, that postwar economic development in Japan, Taiwan, and South Korea initially followed on the heels of agrarian reform.[42] In Korea, for example, the expansion of rural purchasing power helped stimulate the nation's electronics industry, setting the stage for subsequent export. Today, over 90 percent of South Korea's rural families (almost all of them peasant smallholders) own television sets and many are now switching to color televisions. Such affluence stands in stark contrast to the rural poverty found in much of the Third World.

Agrarian reform has also contributed to comparatively high income equality in those same East Asian nations (though other factors contributed as well). That equality and pervasive purchasing power, in turn, has been a significant ingredient in the region's dramatic economic development. In contrast, Latin America's concentrated pattern of farmland ownership is partially responsible for its highly inequitable distribution of income, ultimately adversely affecting economic growth.

Environmental Preservation An increasingly urgent argument for agrarian reform relates to the preservation of the environment. Each year in Brazil, an area of the Amazonian tropical forest approximately the size of New York State is being destroyed. The burning of those trees to clear the land for ranching or agriculture is believed to contribute substantially to the greenhouse effect on world climate (see chapter 9). Other environmental consequences are related to the Amazonian forest's contribution to the world's oxygen supply. Although a substantial portion of this devastation is caused by large-scale farmers and ranchers, peasant settlers also contribute to the process. Driven by poverty from the nation's poorest regions, land-hungry peasants colonize the jungle in search of a better life. Once there, many of them find that the jungle soil quickly looses its nutrients. Consequently, they move on, clearing new forest land. Agrarian reform in Brazil's nonforest regions would reduce landlessness, give tenant farmers a stake in the land they already farm, and thereby reduce migration to the Amazonian basin.

Similar arguments have been advanced for land reform in other parts of the world. While Bangladeshi farmers enjoy extremely fertile soil, concentration of ownership has forced landless peasants to push the frontiers of farming beyond their desirable limits. In their search for farmland, many move to unsafe coastal regions not suitable for habitation. There they fall victim to the typhoons that periodically sweep across the region, killing thousands of people.

Only recently have government policy makers and international aid agencies begun to relate agrarian reform to ecological issues. In time that linkage may become more apparent.

Types of Agrarian Reform

A variety of forces have produced agrarian reform. At times it has resulted from foreign pressure or occupation; sometimes it has emanated from peasant-based revolutions; and some reform programs have been introduced by governments anxious to garner peasant support. In each case, the underlying forces that first stimulated agrarian reform influence the type of program that emerges.

Externally Imposed Reform The most successful externally imposed agrarian reforms occurred in East Asia after World War II. In Japan, the United States occupation command limited land ownership to 10 acres, transferred 41 percent of the country's farmland from landlords to tenants, and controlled rents for the remaining tenants. The number of landless was reduced from 28 percent to 10 percent of the rural population, making the countryside a bastion of stability.[43] In Taiwan and South Korea, United States pressure encouraged similar reforms designed to avert rural unrest. Ownership was limited to small parcels and about one-third of each country's farmland was transferred to tenants, some 60 percent of whom became landowners.[44] In all three nations, the transformation of rural society was tremendously successful, raising agricultural productivity, improving rural living standards, and strengthening political stability. Consequently, East Asia's agrarian reforms are widely used as benchmarks to evaluate programs elsewhere in the world.

In light of these dramatic achievements, it is noteworthy how modest have been the accomplishments of later attempts at externally imposed agrarian reform. In retrospect, it appears that three unique conditions existed in postwar East Asia that have not been replicated subsequently. First was the depth of American commitment to reform. Fearing that agrarian revolution would spread from China to other Far Eastern nations, U.S. policy makers pushed hard for land reform as the best way to contain communism. A second unique element was the substantial leverage the United States could exert on those governments at the time. The Japanese were under U.S. military occupation, while the South Korean and Taiwanese governments were deeply beholden to the United States. In later years, the United States lacked comparable influence. Although it favored land reform in South Vietnam, the Philippines, and Central America, it was unwilling or unable to exert sufficient pressure on conservative governments in those nations to insure effective programs.

This suggests East Asia's final unique factor: Its landed elite were weakened and poorly positioned to defend their interests. The situation was starkest in Japan. As an occupying power, the United States could impose its will on rural landlords. Moreover, influential Japanese political leaders working with the U.S. command were equally convinced that agrarian reform was necessary.[45] In South Korea, the landlord class had collaborated with Japan during its colonial occupation of that country. Hence, when Japanese rule ended at the close of World War II, the Korean landed elite had little legitimacy or political influence. And in Taiwan, the Nationalist Party government recognized that its prior failure to implement agrarian reform on the Chinese mainland had contributed to the Communist victory there. Prodded by the United States, it was quite ready to modernize the countryside.

In the decades that followed, United States' efforts on behalf of land reform were far less effective. In Southeast Asia and Central America landlords were powerful actors in their nations' political systems. And the United States lacked either the leverage or the will to parent reform against the determined opposition of conservative elites in countries such as South Vietnam and El Salvador.

Revolutionary Transformation From the Mexican and Chinese revolutions through more recent insurgencies in the Philippines and El Salvador, most twentieth-century insurrections were peasant-based. Consequently, a fundamental goal and rallying cry of both Marxist revolutions (China, Vietnam, Cuba, and Nicaragua) and many non-Marxist upheavals (Mexico, Bolivia, and Algeria) has been agrarian reform. In the 1930s and 1940s, for example, the Chinese Communists gained considerable peasant support by transferring land to the rural poor. Following their victory in Nicaragua, the Sandinistas also implemented radical agrarian reform.

Once in power, the Chinese Communists distributed almost half of the country's arable land to nearly 60 million peasant households (encompassing over half the nation's population at that time). Like the Japanese, South Koreans, and Taiwanese, the Chinese government initially created a rural sector dominated by peasant smallholders. But that structure did not endure. Convinced that small peasant plots would reintroduce income inequality and related class divisions in the countryside, the government pressured the peasants to join state-sponsored cooperatives. As a result, by the end of 1956, almost 90 percent of all farm families had relinquished their property rights to Agricultural Producer Cooperatives (APCs).[46]

Having vanquished the landlord class, revolutionary governments are freer than other regimes to redistribute large quantities of land. In countries such as Cuba, Nicaragua, and Vietnam, estates of the defeated rural aristocracy were converted to state farms or distributed to peasant smallholders. Similarly, following their anticolonial revolutions, Algeria and Kenya redistributed the farms of former European settlers. In Mexico, some 40 percent of peasant families benefited from agrarian reform, receiving over 40 percent of the country's agricultural and forest land. Eighty percent of Bolivia's farmland was transferred to three-fourths of its rural families.[47]

Revolutionary agrarian reform programs are more likely to feature collective (or cooperative) farming rather than the peasant smallholdings promoted in the East Asian model (though a few, like Bolivia, feature family plots). Some non-Marxist revolutions such as Mexico's have distributed land through cooperatives. But it is Marxist-Leninist (communist) regimes that have insisted most adamantly upon collective farming. A few communist revolutions, most notably Cuba's and Nicaragua's, have retained private farm sectors while still encouraging peasants to sell their plots to the state. In other nations, however, including China, Vietnam, and Ethiopia, peasant resistance to forced collectivization was harshly repressed, sometimes with considerable loss of life. Eric Wolf has noted the irony of forced collectivization. Peasants, he points out, supported and fought for radical revolutions in the hopes of getting plots of land for their families. Yet after helping to bring the revolution to power, they were often coerced into collectivizing their farms.[48]

China illustrates many of the dangers of forced collectivization. As we have seen, a brief period of family farming soon gave way to collectivized farming. The process reached its apex during the Great Leap Forward (1958 to 1961), when huge agricultural communes were created. Overcentralization of decision making and poorly informed policies by government bureaucrats led to massive famine and the deaths of some 20 million to 25 million people.[49] Though the government then backed away from the commune experiment, collective farming was reemphasized during the Cultural Revolution (1966 to 1976).

Several factors explain the Marxist-Leninist preference for collective farming, whether on state farms or on cooperatives with extensive state direction. In part, it is because collectives are more amenable to state control. State bureaucracies can more readily enforce decisions about what crops are grown and what price they sell for. Collectivization has also been seen as a tool for eradicating individualistic tendencies among the peasantry. Feeling that the ownership of private plots creates a bourgeois mentality, many revolutionary regimes have, until recently, dismissed smallholdings as capitalistic.[50] Finally, state planners have insisted that larger, centralized collective farms are more efficient than smallholdings. But such efficiencies exist only in relation to the delivery of social services. In most circumstances it is indeed somewhat easier to deliver clean water, medical care, and education to centrally housed collective farms than to provide them to scattered private farm plots. On the other hand, when one measures the efficiency of agricultural production, collectives are generally less efficient. Data from Cuba, Ethiopia, Nicaragua, and China, for example, indicate that private peasant plots have higher yields than collective farms for most crops.[51]

Private smallholders are usually more productive for the same reason that they outperform large private estates in capitalist societies. Because they gain personally from increased productivity, while state farm employees do not, peasant smallholders are more motivated to work intensively. As they came to appreciate the value of smallholding, several Marxist governments distanced themselves from their earlier collectivist leanings. In Nicaragua, for example, agrarian reform officials initially had considered state farms to be the preferred form of production. Peasant cooperatives were judged next best, and private smallholdings were ranked last. Not surprisingly, peasants ranked their preferences exactly the opposite. After a time, the Sandinista government, less dogmatic than most Marxist regimes, altered its priorities in order to accommodate peasant inclinations.[52] Moreover, with the potent military challenge from the Contras, the U.S.-backed guerrillas, the government began to favor family farm plots since they would give peasant recipients incentive to fight the guerrillas.

China, which during the 1950s and 1960s had implemented one of the world's most extensive collectivized farm programs, subsequently reversed directions dramatically. Beginning in 1979, with the introduction of its "Responsibility

System," the government returned collective farm land to family plots.[53] In what amounted to a second agrarian reform, large communal farms were broken up and distributed to the peasants living on them. The ensuing "unleashing [of] the entrepreneurial talents of China's peasants" led to striking gains in farm productivity. From 1980 to 1984 alone the value of agricultural output rose approximately 40 percent.[54] Consequently, since the early 1980s, China has experienced a spectacular improvement in rural living standards. More recently, other Marxist or reformed Marxist regimes in Asia, including Vietnam and Mongolia, have also decollectivized agriculture.

Moderate Reformism   Most agrarian reform programs result neither from foreign intervention nor from revolution, though external pressures and the threat of insurrection may play a role. Egypt, Iran, India, Bangladesh, Zimbabwe, Chile, Venezuela, and Peru have redistributed agricultural land in a variety of ways. In each case, however, circumstances convinced the government that it must elicit peasant support. For example, following the Cuban Revolution, the United States and a number of Latin American governments concluded that rural reform was needed in the region in order to contain the spread of peasant unrest. Colombia, Chile, Venezuela, and Peru all enacted moderate land reform programs in the 1960s. Twenty years later, the challenge of guerrilla insurgency prompted limited agrarian reform in El Salvador.

Elsewhere, the driving force for change has been the enfranchisement of large numbers of peasants, sometimes due to the abolition of literacy requirements for voting, at other times because of a rise in rural literacy rates. In many countries with competitive electoral systems, peasants have been transformed into an important voting constituency to be wooed by competing political parties. Thus, after calling for agrarian reform, Chile's Christian Democrats, Peru's Acción Popular, and Venezuela's Acción Democrática all won national elections with extensive peasant support. Once in office, they implemented redistributive policies of varying magnitudes.[55] Similarly, in Asia, some mix of incipient rural unrest and electoral politics contributed to land reform in the Philippines and the Indian states of Kerala and West Bengal.[56]

Moderate reformism has an obvious advantage. It is relatively free of the violence and excesses often associated with revolutionary programs. But, with rare exception, its scope has been far more limited than either externally induced redistribution or revolutionary transformation. In Latin America, for example, the most comprehensive land redistribution efforts have resulted from revolutions in Cuba, Bolivia, Nicaragua, and Mexico.[57] By comparison, most reformist packages in the region have been more modest. Similarly, reformism in Asia (Bangladesh, Thailand, the Philippines, and India) also produced meager results when compared to revolutionary land redistributions in China and Vietnam.

Reformism generally produces less sweeping agrarian transformation because it occurs in countries where the landed elite are still sufficiently strong to restrict the scope of change.[58] Often, for example, moderate reform laws require monetary compensation for landlords loosing land. Consequently, financial constraints limit the scope of land redistribution. Elsewhere, cumbersome bureaucracies and court challenges have slowed the pace of redistribution to a crawl.

One notable exception to this pattern occurred in Peru from 1968 to 1979. There a sweeping reform was implemented in the absence of either external pressure or internal revolution. A nationalist, left-leaning military regime led by General Juan Velasco expropriated most of the country's large agricultural and ranching estates, turning them over to the peasants and farm laborers who had been working on them. Approximately 40 percent of the country's farmland and 30 percent of all rural families were affected.[59] Initially most of the land was transformed into cooperatives, but in subsequent years most co-ops were subdivided and converted to peasant family plots.[60]

Ultimately, Peru's agrarian reform barely benefited most of the country's peasantry for reasons to be discussed shortly. What it did accomplish, however, was to destroy the once-considerable power of the land-owning class and thereby radically transform the political and economic structure of the countryside. This was possible because there was a powerful military regime committed to a sweeping reform and capable of pushing it through. No other military government in Latin America, however, has been equally dedicated to comprehensive rural change.[61]

Even were reformist civilian governments comparably committed, they couldn't launch such a frontal assault on the powerful landed elite. To be sure, Venezuela's elected government implemented a relatively ambitious agrarian reform program. Much of the land transferred to the peasantry, however, was uncultivated public property in the nation's jungle frontier. Agrarian reforms such as this, stressing the colonization of previously unfarmed public property, enables governments to transfer land to the peasantry without challenging powerful rural interests. Unfortunately, however, most of the land turned over is of marginal quality. Moreover, since colonization frequently takes place in forested areas, it presents serious environmental dangers.

THE LIMITS OF AGRARIAN REFORM

While Taiwan, South Korea, Cuba, and China demonstrate how agrarian reform can improve peasant living standards substantially, few programs elsewhere can match their success. Peru's experience illustrates how even sweeping change initiated by a well-intentioned government may not achieve its objectives. Land redistribution was comparable in magnitude to the revolutionary transformations in Cuba, Bolivia, Mexico, and Nicaragua. Powerful hacienda owners who had once dominated the neofeudal Andean haciendas and the coastal plantations were stripped of their land and its accompanying power. But these radical changes failed to bring about the anticipated improvements in peasant living standards.

To be sure, there was considerable progress in several important areas. Previously isolated peasants entered the mainstream of economic life. Literacy rates grew rapidly and many villagers were absorbed into the national culture. Yet three decades after the reform began, neither agricultural production nor rural living standards have improved. Indeed, in many regions they have declined. Ironically, the land recipients who benefited most—coastal sugar workers—had already lived better than most of the rural poor prior to the reform. On the other hand, the country's poorest peasants generally gained little. By the mid-1980s, large parts of the Peruvian countryside were being brutalized by the military and the Shining Path, Latin America's most fanatical guerrilla group. Thus, agrarian reform failed to achieve the degree of rural equality or the social peace it was designed to create.

There were multiple reasons for the program's failures. Because of the regime's inept administrative and political style, the military government often alienated the very peasants it wished to help. For example, it organized cooperatives and peasant federations to mobilize rural support for the agrarian reform. Both were designed to facilitate the distribution of agricultural inputs to the peasantry and to open channels of communication between the government and the countryside. Laudable as these objectives were, they faltered because the process was so poorly managed. Too often the government failed to coordinate its own goals with the peasants', while state bureaucrats acted in a heavy-handed manner. As a consequence, peasants perceived officious government bureaucrats as little better than the oppressive landlords whom they had replaced.

Peru's paucity of arable land also posed a serious problem. Although the military expropriated the nation's large estates, there still wasn't enough fertile land to satisfy the peasants' needs. Ultimately, less than one-third of rural families in need received any land, and the poorest of the poor were frequently overlooked.[62] Hence, many peasants whose expectations had been raised by the promise of reform and then dashed became politically alienated.

Furthermore even the program's beneficiaries often discovered that their grants were still insufficient to alleviate their deep poverty. While the government had narrowed the gap between rich and poor in the countryside appreciably, it had failed to bridge an equally important gulf between rural and urban living standards. As in most LDCs, Peru's economic structure had long favored the urban over the rural population. For example, in many countries the state keeps the prices of some basic food crops below the free market price in order to guarantee cheap food for the politically influential urban population. A substantial improvement in peasant living standards would require the government to shift wealth from the cities to the countryside. Because of the urban sector's substantial economic and political power, however, not even the Peruvian military was prepared to take on that challenge.

Finally, whatever initial benefits agrarian reform had brought to the rural poor were largely lost in the 1980s when Peru experienced a devastating economic collapse. The entire population was adversely affected by the country's massive inflation and rapidly falling living standards.

Revolutionary agrarian reforms also have their limitations. Mexico still suffers substantial rural poverty and landlessness despite an agrarian reform that affected half the nation's peasants and agricultural land. Beginning in the 1930s, reform beneficiaries were organized into ejidos, communal units designed to channel state aid to the peasantry and increase their productivity. Following World War II, however, government agricultural policy changed in favor of larger commercial farms, while failing to channel adequate credits, infrastructure, or technology to the ejidos. Since much of the Mexican countryside is arid, the absence of government irrigation projects was particularly devastating for poor farmers. As a consequence, peasants were less able to compete in the marketplace. Many lost their farms and poured into the nation's cities or across the border to the United States.

Since 1970 the government has developed several programs designed to bolster peasant agriculture. While they have had some positive impact, they were cut short after 1982 by the country's debt crisis and severe economic recession.[63] Current government policy encourages the privatization of the communal property of the ejidos. Ultimately this may benefit the most productive peasants who will be able to buy and sell land more readily, but it may also force less competitive peasants off their farms into Mexico's already overcrowded cities.

The shortcomings of Peru's and Mexico's efforts do not imply that agrarian reform is valueless. Rather, they indicate that redistribution of land must take place in a proper political setting and must be supported by additional government measures if it is to be effective. Thus, evidence from South Asia indicates that successful reform programs are usually accompanied by some degree of peasant mobilization.[64] Prodded by peasant organizations, the state is more likely to provide land recipients with needed technical assistance, infrastructure, education, and financial credit. It must also allow them a fair price for their crops.[65] The administrative apparatus governing reform must be simple and peasant beneficiaries must be given a strong role in the decision-making process. In countries where the landed elite maintain substantial political power, landlords losing property must receive reasonable payments if the program is to be politically viable. At the same time, peasant beneficiaries must only be asked to pay an amount they can sustain if the program is to be economically feasible for them.[66] Where possible, Third World governments must reduce the tremendous gap that typically separates urban and rural living standards.

Even the most intelligently executed reform programs, however, will not be equally successful in all countries. In nations such as Peru there simply isn't enough quality land to satisfy peasant needs fully. In such cases alternative employment for the rural poor must be created in other sectors of the economy. Ultimately, each nation's agrarian reform package must be carefully designed to meet its own specific needs.

OTHER APPROACHES AND ISSUES

Since the 1970s agrarian reform has lost much of its allure, with such notable exceptions as Nicaragua and, to a more limited extent, El Salvador. Critics on the right have long felt it undermines efficient, large-scale agribusiness. Critics on the left have found the fruits of moderate reformism disappointing, claiming that it has benefited capitalists and state bureaucracies more than it has the peasantry.[67] And powerful urban interests fear agrarian reform will curtail food production. In many ways rural pressure for reform has diminished. Increasing numbers of peasants have migrated to the cities, no longer demanding change in the countryside. Most governments now attach less importance to peasant agriculture than to large, export-oriented commercial farming that earns the nation foreign exchange. While modest land redistribution programs continue in some LDCs, for now at least efforts at rural reform have shifted to other issues and other types of programs.

Integrated Rural Development

As interest in agrarian reform has diminished, a number of Third World governments have turned to Integrated Rural Development (IRD), a potentially less conflictual means of raising agricultural productivity and improving rural living standards. The underlying purpose of IRD is to channel a consolidated package of government assistance programs to selected peasant regions. That package may include agricultural inputs (e.g., seeds, fertilizers), technical assistance, credit, public health services, education, irrigation, and other infrastructure. The objective is to transform traditional peasants and the rural unemployed into efficient producers.

During the 1970s and 1980s the World Bank, the U.S. Agency for International Development (AID), and other international donors enthusiastically supported IRD programs in countries such as India, Colombia, and Mexico. In some cases, including South Korea and Nicaragua, IRD supplemented land reform. More frequently, however, it has served as a substitute, enabling centrist governments to assist a portion of the peasantry without alienating powerful landed interests.

Critics of IRD have charged that its primary objective is not to help the rural poor, but rather to establish strong state control over the peasantry.[68] Whatever its impetus, Integrated Rural Development has had a mixed record of success. In India, for example, a large program was established aimed at giving poor peasants subsidized credits to buy dairy cows. Unfortunately, the program was undermined by corruption and poor distribution of aid.[69] Even critics of Mexico's SAM program (Mexican Food System) concede that it helped many peasants. However, many of its funds earmarked for the rural poor actually benefitted large producers, ultimately creating more competition for small farmers. Similar criticisms were leveled against Brazil's Integrated Rural Development program, Polonordeste.[70]

Colombia undertook one of Latin America's most ambitious IRD programs. Like many, it was designed to raise food production by providing infrastructure, credit, and agricultural inputs to small farms. Peasants producers were encouraged to join marketing cooperatives. While the program seemed to increase food supplies for Colombia's cities, its benefits for the rural poor were quite limited. Indeed, in its second phase it concentrated on peasants with larger plots, dropping those with the smallest holdings. In her analysis of the Colombian program, Nola Reinhardt found it to be of some benefit to the peasants it served. But, she argued, Integrated Rural Development alone cannot raise rural living standards substantially, particularly those of the very poor. To achieve that, needy peasants must be given access to more land through some type of agrarian reform.[71]

In recent years, some governments and Nongovernment Organizations (NGOs) have pursued a variant of IRD known as Micro-Enterprise Development. The goal of these projects is to help peasants develop self-sustaining forms of farming that draw upon, but preserve, the area's natural resources. Poor farmers living in or near ecologically fragile zones are particularly targeted. In one of the more well known enterprises, the World Wildlife Federation has helped peasants in Brazil's Amazonian jungle to sell the nuts they harvest to American candy and ice cream manufacturers. It is hoped that the profits yielded by the nuts will convince the peasants to preserve the local forest rather than clear it for cultivation.

Crop Pricing

While this chapter has focused on the issue of peasant access to land, it has also shown that farmers in many LDCs suffer from unfavorable government price policies. By imposing price controls on food crops, many Third World governments, most notably in Africa and the Middle East, further impoverish their farm populations and create disincentives for food production. Anxious to assure a supply of cheap food for their urban population, governments have controlled prices on basic commodities (such as bread, rice, sugar, and milk) holding their price below their free market value. These policies also are designed to promote industrialization by providing workers with cheap food, thereby moderating their wage demands.[72]

In Africa, governments commonly control the price of export crops as well as domestic foods, extracting the difference between the rate paid farmers and the world market price as a de facto tax. One early study found that farmers in that region often received less than two-thirds, and in some case less than half, of the value of their export crops.[73] While designed to furnish the urban poor and middle class with cheaper food and to generate government revenues from exports, price controls ultimately have perverse effects. They particularly damage poor agricultural producers and induce food shortages by creating disincentives to production. In Egypt, for example, when the government controlled the price of basic food grains, large landlords either evaded government controls or switched to other, uncontrolled crops. Peasants were less capable of switching crops and thus suffered declining incomes.[74]

Throughout Africa, price controls have reduced food output by driving many farmers out of business and reducing production incentives for the rest. For more than two decades, per capita food production has declined and the continent has become increasingly dependent on food imports and foreign aid. While there is no single cause of that deterioration, a recent study of African famine argues that government price controls and inefficient government bureaucracies have aggravated the problem.[75] Research comparing Zimbabwe's agricultural policies with those of Mozambique, Tanzania, and Zambia reveals that production has been healthier in the former country where farmers are paid the market price for their crops.[76]

Unfortunately once governments have embarked on the path of commodity price regulation they are soon caught in a conflict between short-term political pressures and long-term production needs. The immediate effect of price deregulation would be a sharp rise in food prices. Governments that have done this (often in response to external pressures) have frequently been faced with urban protests, including riots aimed at toppling the government. Not surprisingly, few administrations have been willing to risk such unrest, particularly since a major group adversely affected by the price hikes, the urban middle class, is usually a vital base of government support. In the long run, however, better crop prices should stimulate greater food production, ultimately leading prices to decline again (though not necessarily to their prior low).

As many developing nations are turning to neoliberal economic policies, some of the effects may benefit rural producers.[77]

CONCLUSION

For decades government development policies in most LDCs have emphasized industrial growth and urban modernization, often to the detriment of the rural sector. In many cases the consequence has been stagnant agricultural production, rising food imports, rural poverty, and heavy rural-to-urban migration. In some instances, rural poverty has led to peasant insurrection. Most notably in Latin America, pro-urban government policies, along with the forces of capitalist development, have driven many peasants into the rural or urban working class in a process known as proletarianization.[78] Pessimistic scholars have predicted the inevitable spread of large, mechanized farms to the detriment of peasant family farming.

More recently, research in countries such as Bolivia, Ecuador, and Colombia has revealed that in at least some regions innovative peasants have adapted skillfully to the forces of rural capitalism and modernization. Many have taken advantage of new commercial opportunities to compete successfully in the marketplace.[79] In Africa and Asia peasant smallholders remain an even greater component of rural society. Rather than abandoning the peasantry as a relic of history, Third World governments and international agencies should seek balanced economic and political development that gives proper weight to the rural sector and its peasant component.

DISCUSSION QUESTIONS

1. Third World peasants have frequently been described as conservative or apolitical. Yet at the same time they have been major players in revolutionary movements. How can those two images be reconciled?

2. What are the major arguments that have been raised for and against agrarian reform programs in the developing world?

3. Describe the different types of agrarian reform programs that have been introduced. Briefly discuss some of the advantages and disadvantages of each type of reform.

4. How have government crop-pricing policies often disadvantaged the rural producer and inhibited production?

NOTES

1. Roy L. Prosterman and Jeffrey M. Riedinger, *Land Reform and Democratic Development* (Baltimore, MD: Johns Hopkins University Press, 1987), p. 1.

2. Published statistics on the proportion of rural poverty in any country are usually imprecise. They often vary greatly from study to study and should be treated as educated estimates designed to serve as guideposts. Occasionally the data clash with the "common sense" observations of experts who have studied the region. In the decade since these U.N. data were collected, the populations of most of the countries studied have increased appreciably, the percentages of their populations living in the countryside have dropped (sharply in some cases), and the actual number of persons living in rural poverty (as opposed to the percentage) has risen.

3. Figures are extrapolated from earlier data in M. Riad El-Ghonemy, *The Political Economy of Rural Poverty* (London: Routledge and Kegan Paul, 1990), pp. 302–303, 17–19. The data were adapted from FAO (The United Nations Food and Agricultural Organization), *The Dynamics of Rural Poverty* (Rome: 1986).

4. Merilee S. Grindle and John W. Thomas, *Public Choices and Policy Change: The Political Economy of Reform in Developing Countries* (Baltimore, MD: Johns Hopkins University Press, 1991), p. 46.

5. Alain de Janvry, *The Agrarian Question and Reformism in Latin America* (Baltimore, MD: Johns Hopkins University Press, 1981), pp. 7–60.

6. The terms agrarian reform and land reform are often used interchangeably. Technically, land reform refers only to the redistribution of land to needy peasants or laborers. Agrarian reform is a broader term that encompasses the financial and technical aid, infrastructure, and the like that are normally need to go with land redistribution if it is to be effective.

7. Marcus Franda, "An Indian Farm Lobby: The Kisan Sammelan," in *The Politics of Agrarian Change in Asia and Latin America*, ed. Howard Handelman (Bloomington: Indiana University Press, 1981), pp. 17–34.

8. George Foster, "Introduction: What Is a Peasant?" in *Peasant Society*, ed. Jack Potter, George Foster, and May Diaz (Boston: Little, Brown, 1967); Teodor Shanin, "The Nature and Logic of the Peasant Economy," *Journal of Peasant Studies* 1, nos. 1–2 (1974).

9. Eric R. Wolf, *Peasants* (Upper Saddle River, NJ: Prentice Hall, 1966), p. 10.

10. Prosterman and Riedinger, *Land Reform and Democratic Development*, p. 41.

11. Karl Marx Capital, quoted in Teodor Shanin, "Peasantry as a Political Factor," *Sociological Review* 14 (March 1966): 6.

12. Robert Redfield, *Peasant Society and Culture: An Anthropological Approach* (Chicago: University of Chicago Press, 1965), p. 77.

13. See, for example, Oscar Lewis, *La Vida* (New York: Random House, 1966); George M. Foster, "Peasant Society and the Image of the Limited Good," *American Anthropologist* 67 (April 1965): 293–315.

14. Phyllis Arora, "Patterns of Political Response in Indian Peasant Society," *Western Political Quarterly* 20 (September 1967): 654.

15. See, for example, *New York Times*, July 4, 1993.

16. Ronald J. Herring and Charles R. Kennedy, Jr., "The Political Economy of Farm Mechanization Policy: Tractors in Pakistan," in *Food, Politics and Agricultural Development: Case Studies in the Public Policy of Rural Modernization*, ed. Raymond F. Hopkins, Donald J. Pachula, and Ross B. Talbot (Boulder, CO: Westview Press, 1979), pp. 193–226.

17. James C. Scott, *Weapons of the Week: Everyday Forms of Peasant Resistance* (New Haven, CT: Yale University Press, 1986).

18. One of the most insightful books on the role of the peasantry in twentieth-century revolutions is Eric R. Wolf, *Peasant Wars of the Twentieth Century* (New York: Harper and Row, 1969).

19. James C. Scott, *The Moral Economy of the Peasant: Rebellion and Subsistence in Southeast Asia* (New Haven, CT: Yale University Press, 1976); James C. Scott and Benedict J. Kirkvliet, *How Traditional Rural Patrons Loose Their Legitimacy* (Madison: University of Wisconsin, Land Tenure Center, 1975).

20. Wolf, *Peasant Wars*.

21. Samuel P. Huntington, *Political Order in Changing Societies* (New Haven, CT: Yale University Press, 1968), p. 375.

22. Ibid.

23. Roy L. Prosterman, Mary N. Temple, and Timothy M. Hanstad, introduction to *Agrarian Reform and Grassroots Development: Ten Case Studies*, ed. Prosterman, Temple, and Hanstad (Boulder, CO: Lynne Rienner Publishers, 1990), p. 1.

24. Hectares, rather than acres, are the standard measurement of farmland area in most of the world. One hectare is equivalent to 2.47 acres.

25. Anthony L. Hall, "Land Tenure and Land Reform in Brazil," in *Agrarian Reform and Grassroots Development*, p. 206.

26. Carrie A. Meyer, *Land Reform in Latin America: The Dominican Case* (New York: Praeger Publishers, 1989), p. 38.

27. Rupert W. Scofield, "Land Reform in Central America," in *Agrarian Reform and Grassroots Development*, pp. 154–155.

28. D. P. Chaudhri, "New Technologies and Income Distribution in Agriculture," in *Peasants, Landlords and Governments: Agrarian Reform in the Third World*, ed. David Lehmann (New York: Holmes and Meier Publishers, 1974), p. 173; Howard Handelman, introduction to *The Politics of Agrarian Change*, p. 4.

29. F. Tomasson Jannuzi and James T. Peach, "Bangladesh: A Strategy for Agrarian Reform," and Jeffrey Riedinger, "Philippine Land Reform in the 1980s," in *Agrarian Reform and Grassroots Development*, pp. 84, 19.

30. Henry Shue, *Basic Human Rights: Subsistence, Affluence and U.S. Foreign Policy* (Princeton, NJ: Princeton University Press, 1980). For a discussion of the moral issues, see Joseph S. Nye, Jr., "Ethical Dimensions of International Involvement in Land Reform," in *International Dimensions of Land Reform*, ed. John D. Montgomery (Boulder, CO: Westview Press, 1984), pp. 7–29.

31. Keith Griffin, *Land Concentration and Rural Poverty*, 2d ed. (London: Macmillan, 1981), p. 10.

32. Huntington, *Political Order*, p. 375.

33. Bruce M. Russet, "Inequality and Instability: The Relation of Land Tenure to Politics," *World Politics* 16 (April 1964): 442–454; Prosterman and Riedinger, *Land Reform*, p. 24.

34. William Thiesenhusen, introduction to *Searching for Agrarian Reform in Latin America*, ed. William Thiesenhusen (Boston: Unwin Hyman, 1989), p. 18. An advocate of agrarian reform in Latin America, Thiesenhusen does not imply that peasants in that region are ill equipped to receive land.

35. Ibid., pp. 16–20; Peter Dorner, *Latin American Land Reforms in Theory and Practice* (Madison: University of Wisconsin Press, 1992), pp. 21–29; R. Albert Berry, "Land Reform and the Adequacy of World Food Production," in *International Dimensions*, pp. 63–87.

36. William C. Thiesenhusen and Jolyne Melmed-Sanjak, "Brazil's Agrarian Structure: Changes from 1970 through 1980," *World Development* 18 (1990): 393–415.

37. Albert R. Berry and William R. Cline, eds., *Agrarian Structure and Productivity in Developing Countries* (Baltimore, MD: Johns Hopkins University Press, 1979).

38. Riedinger, "Philippine Land Reform," p. 19.

39. Dorner, *Latin American Land Reforms*, pp. 23–25; Berry, "Land Reform," p. 72; Michael R. Carter and Jon Jonakin, *The Economic Case for Land Reform: An Assessment of 'Farm Size/Productivity' Relations and Its Impact on Policy* (Madison: University of Wisconsin Department of Agricultural Economics, 1989), quoted in Dorner.

40. James Grant, "Development: The End of Trickle Down," *Foreign Policy* 12 (Fall 1973): 43–65.

41. Bruce F. Johnston and John W. Mellor, "The Role of Agriculture in Economic Development," *American Economic Review* 51 (September, 1961): 566–593.

42. Dorner, *Latin American Land Reforms*, pp. 29–31.

43. Ronald P. Dore, *Land Reform in Japan* (London: Oxford University Press, 1959); Mikiso Hande, *Modern Japan* (Boulder, CO: Westview Press, 1986), pp. 347–348.

44. Shirley W. Y. Kuo, Gustav Ranis, and John C. H. Fei, *The Taiwan Success Story: Rapid Growth with Improved Distribution in the Republic of China, 1952–1979* (Boulder, CO: Westview Press, 1981); Gregory Henderson, *Korea: Politics of the Vortex* (Cambridge, MA: Harvard University Press, 1968).

45. Dore, *Land Reform in Japan*, pp. 147–148.

46. John W. Bruce and Paula Harrell, "Land Reform in the People's Republic of China: 1978–1988," Land Tenure Center Research Paper No. 100, University of Wisconsin-Madison, 1989, pp. 3–4; Vivienne Shue, *Peasant China in Transition—The Dynamics of Development Toward Socialism, 1949–56* (Berkeley: University of California Press, 1980).

47. Thiesenhusen, *Searching for Agrarian Reform*, pp. 10–11.

48. Wolf, *Peasant Wars*.

49. Harry Harding, *China's Second Revolution* (Washington, DC: Brookings Institution, 1987), p. 12; Suzanne Ogden, *China's Unresolved Issues*, (Englewood Cliffs, NJ: Prentice Hall, 1989), pp. 46–50; Nicholas Lardy, *Agriculture in China's Modern Economic Development* (Cambridge, UK: Cambridge University Press, 1983).

50. There are exceptions to this pattern, particularly outside the Third World. Poland and Yugoslavia, for example, did not collectivize agriculture during the Communist era. Cuba, and especially Nicaragua, had private farms alongside a larger collectivized sector.

51. For a crop-by-crop analysis of state and private sector farm productivity in Cuba, see Nancy Forster, "Cuban Agricultural Productivity," in *Cuban Communism*, 7th ed., ed. Irving Louis Horowitz (New Brunswick, NJ: Transaction Publishers, 1989), pp. 235–255.

52. Forrest D. Colburn, *Post-Revolutionary Nicaragua: State, Class and the Dilemmas of Agrarian Policy* (Berkeley: University of California Press, 1986), and Laura J. Enríquez, *Harvesting Change: Labor and Agrarian Reform in Nicaragua* (Chapel Hill: University of North Carolina Press, 1991), offer contrasting analyses.

53. Nicholas Lardy, "Agricultural Reforms in China," *Journal of International Affairs* (Winter 1986): 91–104. The program was announced in 1978 but was not implemented for two years.

54. Harding, *China's Second Revolution*, p. 106.

55. David Lehmann, "Agrarian Reform in Chile, 1965–1972: An Essay in Contradictions," in *Peasants, Landlords*, pp. 71–119; Marion R. Brown, "Radical Reformism in Chile: 1964–1973," in *Searching for Agrarian Reform*, pp. 216–239.

56. Riedinger, "Philippine Land Reform," and Ronald Herring, "Explaining Anomalies in Land Reform: Lessons from South India," in *Agrarian Reform and Grassroots Development*, pp. 15–75; K. N. Raj and Michael Tharakan, "Agrarian Reform in Kerala and its Impact on the Rural Economy," and Ajit Kumar Ghose, "Agrarian Reform in West Bengal," in *Agrarian Reform in Contemporary Developing Countries* (New York: St. Martin's Press, 1983) ed. Ajit Kumar Ghose, pp. 31–137.

57. Thiesenhusen, introduction to *Searching for Agrarian Reform*, pp. 1–41; Meyer, *Land Reform in Latin America*, p. 4. Thiesenhusen and Meyer each calculate the percentage of farm land redistributed and the percentage of rural families benefiting. Although they use somewhat different time periods and Meyer analyzes a wider sample of nations, they arrive at very similar rankings.

58. de Janvry, *The Agrarian Question*.

59. Howard Handelman, "Peasants, Landlords and Bureaucrats: The Politics of Agrarian Reform in Peru," in *The Politics of Agrarian Change*, pp. 103–125; Cristóbal Kay, "The Agrarian Reform in Peru: An Assessment," in *Agrarian Reform in Contemporary Developing Countries*, pp. 185–239.

60. Michael Carter and Elena Alvarez, "Changing Paths: The Decollectivization of Agrarian Reform Agriculture in Coastal Peru," in *Searching for Agrarian Reform*, pp. 156–187.

61. Agrarian reforms enacted by the Ecuadorian and Panamanian militaries were far more modest.

62. Howard Handelman, "Peasants, Landlords and Bureaucrats," pp. 103–125; Kay, "The Agrarian Reform in Peru," pp. 185–239.

63. Merilee S. Grindle, *Searching for Rural Development: Labor Migration and Employment in Mexico* (Ithaca, NY: Cornell University Press, 1988); Grindle, "Agrarian Reform in Mexico: A Cautionary Tale," in *Agrarian Reform and Grassroots Development*, pp. 179–204; Steven E. Sanderson, *The Transformation of Mexican Agriculture* (Princeton, NJ: Princeton University Press, 1986); Frank Meissner, "The Mexican Food System (SAM)—A Strategy for Sowing Petroleum," and M. R. Redclift, "The Mexican Food System (SAM)—Sowing Subsidies, Reaping Apathy," *Food Policy* 6, no. 4 (November 1981): 219–235.

64. Ronald J. Herring, "Explaining Anomalies in Agrarian Reform: Lessons from South Asia," in *Agrarian Reform and Grassroots Development*, p. 73.

65. Thiesenhusen, "Conclusions," in *Searching for Agrarian Reform*, pp. 483–503.

66. Prosterman and Riedinger, *Land Reform and Democratic Development*, pp. 177–202.

67. de Janvry, *The Agrarian Question*; Merilee S. Grindle, *State and Countryside: Development Policy and Agrarian Politics in Latin America* (Baltimore, MD: Johns Hopkins University Press, 1986).

68. Grindle, *State and Countryside*.

69. Demetrios Christodoulou, *The Unpromised Land: Agrarian Reform and Conflict Worldwide* (London: Zed Books, 1990), pp. 204–205.

70. Grindle, *State and Countryside*, pp. 160–174.

71. Nola Reinhardt, *Our Daily Bread: The Peasant Question and Family Farming in the Colombian Andes* (Berkeley: University of California Press, 1988), pp. 219–224.

72. Charles Harvey, ed., *Agricultural Pricing Policy in Africa* (London: Macmillan, 1988), p. 2.

73. Robert H. Bates, *Markets and States in Tropical Africa: The Political Basis of Agricultural Policy* (Berkeley: University of California Press, 1981), p. 29; see also Michael J. Lofchie, *The Policy Factor: Agricultural Performance in Kenya and Tanzania* (Boulder, CO: Lynne Rienner Publishers, 1989), pp. 57–59.

74. Marvin G. Weinbaum, *Food, Development, and Politics in the Middle East* (Boulder, CO: Westview Press, 1982), p. 61.

75. Michael F. Lofchie, "Africa's Agricultural Crisis: An Overview," and Robert H. Bates, "The Regulation of Rural Markets in Africa," in *Africa's Agrarian Crisis: The Roots of Famine*, ed. Stephen K. Commins, Michael F. Lofchie, and Rhys Payne (Boulder, CO: Lynne Rienner Publishers), pp. 3–19, 37–54.

76. Harvey, *Agricultural Pricing Policy*, pp. 236–245; Lofchie, *The Policy Factor*.

77. Neoliberalism rejects much of the state intervention in the economy that was prevalent in many developing economies and instead favors free market mechanisms. For a more extensive discussion of these issues, see Chapter 9.

78. de Janvry, *The Agrarian Question*; David Goodman and Michael Redclift, *From Peasant to Proletarian: Capitalist Development and Agricultural Transitions* (Oxford, UK: Basil Blackwell, 1981).

79. This is most impressively demonstrated in Nola Reinhardt, *Our Daily Bread*. See also Lesley Gill, *Peasants, Entrepreneurs and Social Change: Frontier Development in Lowland Bolivia* (Boulder, CO: Westview Press, 1987).

6

⧜

RAPID URBANIZATION
AND THE POLITICS
OF THE URBAN POOR

E ach day in the villages of Kenya, Pakistan, Egypt, and Colombia hundreds,
even thousands, of young men and women pack up their meager belong-
ings and board buses or trains for the long trip to Nairobi, Karachi, Cairo,
and Bogotá. Often they travel alone, sometimes with family or friends. They
are a part of one of the largest and most dramatic tides of human migration in
world history. Despairing of any hope for a better life in the countryside and
seeking new opportunities for themselves and their children, millions of villagers
leave the world they have known for the uncertainties of the city. In Africa, these
legions of migrants have been augmented by millions of refugees fleeing civil
war and famine.

Most maintain close links with their rural roots long after they have
migrated. Some come intending to accumulate savings and eventually return
to their villages. "Others alternate between city and country in a permanent pen-
dular pattern."[1] Indeed, in many parts of West Africa and Southeast Asia more
than half the urban migrant population is temporary, including those who repeatedly circulate between village and city.[2] In contrast, Latin America's cityward
migrants tend to settle permanently. But whatever their initial aspirations, they
continue to crowd the urban slums and shantytowns they have come to call
home.

Swelled by both internal population growth and the influx of migrants in
recent decades, many Third World cities have mushroomed in size and will continue to do so in the coming years (see Tables 6.1 and 6.2). Since the 1960s, the

magnitude of that expansion has placed tremendous strains on the developing world's larger cities. In Latin America, national capitals like Caracas, Venezuela, and Lima, Peru, were doubling their populations in 12 to 15 years. African cities, starting from a smaller base, expanded at an even more accelerated pace. Kinshasa, Congo, grew by nearly 600 percent between 1960 and 1983; Dar es Salaam, Tanzania, by 550 percent; and Abidjan, Côte d'Ivoire, by over 800 percent.[3] In the Middle East, Baghdad's population soared by nearly 700 percent between 1950 and 1975.

In 1970, Third World cities contained 675 million people. That population reached 1.9 billion by the year 2000 and is expected to be some 4 billion in 2025.[4] There is some debate among demographers as to what proportion of that growth has been due to internal (natural) increase and what percentage has resulted from rural-to-urban migration. It appears that about half has come from each of these sources, with a higher proportion attributable to migration in Africa and a greater percentage linked to natural increase in Asia, though there is considerable variation within both continents as well as in Latin America. [5]

Latin America (consisting of South America, Central America, Mexico, and the Caribbean) is by far the most urbanized region in the developing world. By 1990 the portion of its population living in cities (72 percent) virtually equaled that of the First World and the region is expected to surpass the developed countries by the start of the twenty-first century. With some 17 million people today, Mexico City is already one of the world's largest cities (Table 6.2) and Sao Paulo, Brazil, and Buenos Aires, Argentina are not far behind. Although poorer Central American countries such as Honduras remain less than half urban, some 85 percent of Chileans currently live in cities. (Table 6.1)

African and Asian cities encompass a considerably smaller percentage of their region's total population (35–40 percent), but they have grown at a more rapid rate in recent decades. In 1960, Casablanca, Algeria, and Cairo were the

Table 6.1 Percentage of the Population in Urban Areas, 1970-2015

Country	Percentage Urban 1970	Percentage Urban 1995	Percentage Urban 2015 (estimate)
Ethiopia	9%	15%	26%
Morocco	35	42	64
Mozambique	6	34	52
Bangladesh	8	18	31
Thailand	13	20	29
Chile	75	84	87
Honduras	29	44	56
Mexico	59	73	78

Source: United Nations Development Program, *Human Development Report 1998* (New York: Oxford University Press, 1998), pp. 174–175.

Table 6.2 Population of Third World Cities 1995–2015

| | Population | |
City	1995	2015 (estimate)
Mexico City	16,562,000	19,180,000
Tegucigalpa	995,000	2,016,000
Santiago	4,891,000	6,066,000
Cairo	9,690,000	16,530,000
Casablanca	3,101,000	4,835,000
Addis Ababa	2,431,000	6,578,000
Lagos	10,287,000	24,640,000
Bangkok	6,547,000	9,844,000
Dahka	8,545,000	19,486,000

*Source:*United Nations Development Program, *Human Development Report 1998* (New York: Oxford University Press, 1998), pp. 174–175.

only cities on the African continent with populations of over one million. Twenty-three years later, nine cities exceeded that size, with four of them surpassing two million.[6] As Table 6.2 indicates, African cities like Addis Ababa, Ethiopia, are growing at an enormous rate while Lagos, Nigeria will soon have a population of almost 25 million (Table 6.2). Within Africa, the proportion of people residing in cities varies considerably from country to country. At one end of the spectrum Ethiopia is only 15 percent urban. But urbanization is far more advanced in north African countries such as Morocco with over 42 percent of its population currently living in cities (Table 6.1).

Asia still also remains predominantly rural. For example, in the early 1990s cities represented only about 30 percent of the population in Indonesia, India, and Pakistan.[7] Yet, megacities such as Jakarta (Indonesia), Karachi (Pakistan), and New Delhi, Bombay, and Calcutta (all in India) have populations well exceeding 10 million. During the second half of the past century the populations of their metropolitan areas have leap-frogged past New York, London, and Los Angeles. While Bangladesh is now only about 20–25 percent urban, its primary city, Dhaka, will see its population more than double from 1995 to 2015, reaching an expected level of nearly 20 million (Tables 6.1 and 6.2)

THE POLITICAL CONSEQUENCES OF URBAN GROWTH

When considered as a percentage of national population, the Third World's tremendous urban growth since the middle of the twentieth century is not without precedent. According to one estimate, the proportion of the population living in cities grew from 16.7 percent in 1950 to 28.0 percent in 1975. But from 1875 to 1900, the First World's urban population increased from 17.2 to 26.1 percent, a change of similar magnitude.[8] What makes the current urban explosion unique, however, is the sheer volume of people involved. Overall populations are much larger today than they were in the First World in the late nineteenth century and are growing at a more rapid rate. It is one thing for a nineteenth-century European or North American city to grow from 80,000 to 400,000 people in a 25-year period. It is quite another for Seoul, South Korea, to mushroom from 1 million to nearly 7 million or for Kinshasa, Congo, to spiral from 400,000 to over 2.5 million in the same number of years. These massive contemporary population shifts clearly pose especially daunting challenges to the management of housing, sanitation, education, transportation, and pollution.

This chapter examines two fundamental aspects of urban politics in the developing world. First, it looks at the challenge that massive urbanization poses to political leaders and planners. Specifically, it asks how poor countries can provide the jobs, housing, sanitation, and related urban services required to meet the needs of this burgeoning population. What is the government's role in meeting those needs and how does state policy interact with private sector activity and self-help efforts?

Second, we will examine the political attitudes and behavior of city dwellers in the LDCs, focusing on the politics of the urban poor. To what extent do urban shantytown and slum dwellers have political orientations that are distinct from those of the rural poor or the urban middle and upper classes? Is rapid urbanization likely to contribute to political development or does it carry the seeds of political instability?

THE STRUGGLE FOR EMPLOYMENT

Contemporary Third World urbanization differs from the developed world's earlier experience not only in magnitude but also in terms of its economic contexts. Europe and North America's nineteenth-century urban revolution transpired on the eve of an era of unprecedented industrialization and economic growth. Modern capitalism was coming of age and could accommodate, indeed needed, the wave of migrant and immigrant laborers. By contrast, the formal economies of most contemporary developing nations have failed to provide sufficient employment to their growing urban work forces.

To be sure, many do find jobs and some low-income workers achieve impressive upward mobility. For example, one study of Howrah, an industrial city in West Bengal, found that "several hundred men who started with almost nothing now own factories large enough to employ twenty five [or more] workers," placing them "among the richest people in the community."[9] Similar examples can be found in much of the developing world. But these cases are exceptional. Economic survival remains an ongoing struggle for most of the urban poor. Even during Mexico's economic boom in the 1960s and 1970s, the country's expanding modern sector was able to provide new jobs for only about half of the people seeking to enter the urban work force. The debt crisis and severe recession that gripped Africa, Latin America, and parts of Asia in the 1980s exacerbated the problem, as industrial employment in many countries plummeted. Hyperinflation in many sub-Saharan African countries has meant that even people who are regularly employed rarely have salaries or wages high enough to support their families.

For those unable to find jobs in the formal sector of the urban economy (i.e., factories, the civil service, modern commercial enterprises) and for those whose formal sector paychecks cannot feed or house their families, the answer normally has been employment in the informal sector (or informal economy). As noted in Chapter 4, that sector is defined as the part of the economy that is "unregulated by the institutions of society [most notably the state], in a legal and social environment in which similar activities are regulated" and taxed.[10] A large proportion of the workers in the informal economy are self-employed in occupations ranging from garbage recyclers to shoe shiners, street vendors, mechanics, electricians, repairmen, plumbers, construction workers, prostitutes, and taxi drivers.

Of course, informal sector activity is not limited to the developing world. In recent years, cities like New York and Los Angeles have experienced substantial expansion in the number of unlicensed street vendors, underground garment manufacturers, and other illegal activities. In the Third World, however, the informal economy represents a far greater proportion of urban employment. During the 1970s, for example, it constituted some 35 percent of the urban work force in Malaysia; 44 percent in Nairobi, Kenya; 45 percent in Jakarta, Indonesia; and 60 percent in urban Peru.[11] As a result of Africa and Latin America's economic crisis in the 1980s and Southeast and East Asia's sharp economic decline in the late 1990s, those percentages rose substantially in many cities.

In the vast garbage dumps of Cairo, hordes of entrepreneurs can be found sifting through the refuse, looking for reusable waste. At night, on the streets of Rio de Janeiro, Brazil, and Port-au-Prince, Haiti, thousands of prostitutes search for customers. On the commercial boulevards of Manila in the Philippines and in Mexico City, an army of street vendors sells food, household appliances, and tape decks. In Lagos, Nigeria, and Lahore, Pakistan, shoemakers and carpenters, working out of their homes, sell their wares to appreciative clients. All belong to the informal economy. While it was once assumed that people working in this sector were particularly impoverished, we now know that their earning power varies greatly and that some have higher incomes than factory workers.[12] To cite one admittedly atypical example, during Nicaragua's runaway inflation in the 1980s, street vendors selling Coca-Cola earned more in a few hours than government white-collar employees made in a week. A more representative study of Montevideo, Uruguay, found that laborers in the formal and informal sectors made fairly comparable incomes.[13]

The informal economy's merits and faults have been debated extensively by social scientists. Critics point out that its workers are not protected by minimum wage laws and lack access to government health and welfare programs. Its proponents respond that it not only employs vast numbers of people who need work badly, but also contributes a substantial proportion of the Third World's consumer goods and services. In a book that has been quite influential in Latin American political circles, Peruvian author Hernando de Soto argues that Third World governments should cease trying to regulate and license the informal sector and instead allow it to flourish and expand.[14]

While the informal sector represents rather concrete, small-scale efforts by the poor (and not-so-poor) to create employment, the government's involvement in the job market has usually been more indirect. Only in Marxist countries such as China and Cuba is the state the primary urban employer. Because they consider unemployment to be unacceptable, Communist governments, until recently, often created as many jobs as necessary to achieve full (or nearly full) employment, no matter how economically inefficient that might be. Often they also restrict opportunities for rural-to-urban migration, prohibiting people from moving into cities unless they have a job. Governments in capitalist LDCs, on the other hand, reject the role of "employer of last resort" and do not limit urban migration. They may occasionally institute public works projects specifically designed to create jobs, but such efforts are normally quite limited.

Instead, Third World governments primarily influence urban employment indirectly through their national macroeconomic policies.[15] In their efforts to stimulate economic growth, they hope to generate employment over the long run. Two areas of economic policy particularly influence job creation: industrialization strategy and the containment of inflation.

Starting as early as the 1940s in Latin America and subsequently in Asia and Africa, government policy makers debated the proper strategy for industrial growth. In the decades after World War II, Latin American governments often chose to foment development through Import-Substituting Industrialization (ISI).[16] The governments of Argentina, Brazil, and Mexico, for example, created tariff walls and various fiscal stimuli to nourish local industries that produced consumer items for the domestic market. Goods such as clothing, appliances, and automobiles that had previously been imported were instead manufactured locally. One of ISI's many goals was to create industrial jobs for the urban working class. Consequently, from the 1940s into the 1970s, labor unions and industrialists, despite their differences on a host of other issues, united behind state policies favoring ISI.

Many comparatively well-paid blue-collar jobs were indeed created. But the number was still rather small relative to the vast army of unskilled laborers. Domestic markets simply weren't large enough to generate a sufficient number of industrial jobs. At the same time, the region's highly protected industries, facing little external competition, had few incentives to become more efficient. As a consequence, their products couldn't compete in the international market in terms of price or quality. By the late 1970s, Latin America's industrial economies began to stagnate.

In contrast, East Asian countries such as Singapore, South Korea, Taiwan, Thailand, and Malaysia, which had started with ISI, soon subjected their manufacturers to international competition while stressing industrial exports. Though the East Asian export-led model was initially based on the exploitation of poorly paid labor, the region's labor-intensive industries eventually generated so much employment that they drove up local wage scales. More recently, Latin American countries such as Argentina, Chile, Brazil, Colombia, and Mexico have sought to emulate East Asia's export model, with some degree of success. Job creation, however, has still lagged behind.[17]

Beginning in the early 1980s, many LDCs faced the dual problems of rampant inflation and stagnant growth. Because the solutions to each of those problems conflicted, at least in the short run, governments had to decide which one to tackle first and how to confront it. Encouraged or pressured by the International Monetary Fund (IMF), the World Bank, and private lenders, many heavily indebted African and Latin America countries adopted macroeconomic policies designed to first slash inflation rates. To do so, they tried to reduce large budgetary and trade deficits by slashing government spending (and payrolls), devaluating the national currency, and privatizing state enterprises. More recently, the overextension of East and Southeast Asian economies has forced governments in those regions to devalue their currencies as well. Although stabilization and adjustment policies such as these may be salutary in the long run (experts are divided as to their value), in the short run they always drive unemployment up sharply. And while austerity programs in countries such as Argentina, Ghana, Morocco, and Peru have curtailed inflation and eventually restored GNP growth, they have been slow to reinvigorate employment. Over the last two years (1997–1999), government economic adjustment policies in Thailand, Indonesia and Malaysia (often mandated by the IMF) have brought about massive unemployment and falling living standards.

Government policy also affects the urban job market in yet another important way, by expanding or contracting state bureaucracies and semiautonomous, state-owned enterprises known as parastatals. Throughout Africa, government bureaucracies and parastatals have employed far more people than they need. They have been overstaffed for two important political reasons: to employ potentially volatile white- and blue-collar workers unable to find jobs in the weak private sector and to provide patronage to government supporters. Until recently, for example, some 40 percent of all government employees in Sierra Leone were "ghosts," individuals on the government payroll who never showed up for work. Of course, bureaucratic overemployment, pervasive throughout the Third World, primarily benefits the urban middle class, rather than the poor who lack the necessary education for these positions. Parastatals, however (including agricultural marketing operations, electric power plants, telephone companies, and other state enterprises), employ both blue- and white-collar workers, thereby benefiting working-class and middle-class constituencies.

Since the early 1980s, the IMF and other international lenders have induced debt-ridden African governments to pare their payrolls substantially. As a result, Uganda removed some 20,000 ghosts from government employment, while Ghana dropped 11,000.[18] Austerity measures in Latin America have also involved sharp cuts in government employment. Many parastatals have been sold to investors in the private sector. Privatization has often led to substantial job losses. Following the sale of Mexico's state steel industry, for instance, more than half of its workers were laid off.[19]

Thus, for the foreseeable future a shrinking state sector will offer no relief for the growing number of urban job seekers—quite the contrary. For decades, expansion of labor-intensive, export-oriented industries provided substantial private sector employment in East and Southeast Asian nations such as Indonesia, Malaysia, Thailand, and Vietnam. Since 1997, however, the region's economic crisis has resulted in extensive plant closings. Industrial exports in Latin America tend to be more capital intensive and, hence, have generated less employment. In Africa, where economic performance in the 1980s and much of the 1990s was particularly disastrous and the size of the industrial sector remains fairly limited, the informal sector will probably provide a growing proportion of urban jobs.

THE STRUGGLE FOR HOUSING AMONG THE URBAN POOR

Of all the problems facing the urban poor, particularly the wave of new immigrants, none is more serious than finding adequate housing. With many metropolitan areas doubling in size every 10 to 20 years, traditional private sector housing cannot possibly expand fast enough to meet the need. Moreover, most of the new homes and apartment houses built for sale or rental by private firms are designed for the middle and upper classes. Low-income housing is not profitable enough to attract private sector investment. Nor has public housing been of much help. With rare exception, the amount of government housing is generally rather limited and little of it reaches the truly needy.

As a consequence of the failures of the private and state sectors, a large portion of the urban poor live in shantytowns and other forms of self-help (occupant-built) housing often referred to in the literature as "spontaneous shelter."[20] Many others crowd into preexisting urban slums. The very poorest, lacking the resources to rent or build, are left homeless, residing in doorways, cartons, unused construction material, or the like.

In all, the number of shantytown and slum dwellers combined with the homeless constitute the majority of inhabitants in Third World cities. A 1990 United Nations report on "Shelter and Urbanization" estimated that 100 million people worldwide are homeless. In Cairo, several hundred thousand people live in tombs in the city's cemeteries, with no place else to go. Half the population of Ankara, Turkey, and about one-third of Manila and São Paulo live in squatter settlements and other forms of spontaneous shelter.

For many of these people, sanitary conditions are particularly problematic. A recent United Nations report calculated that over 18 percent of the Third World's urban population have no access to clean water, while over 28 percent lack sanitation facilities. Although the proportion of city dwellers without those vital services has fallen somewhat, the absolute number unserved have risen, as a result of rapid urban growth. Less than one-third of the inhabitants of Sao Paulo and New Delhi are served by sewage systems, while in Karachi it is only 20 percent. Tap water is equally hard to come by, reaching only half the population of Acapulco, Mexico, and one-third of Jakarta. Those who lack running water must either purchase it from private vendors (such as water trucks) at high prices or drink unsafe water. An estimated 100,000 inhabitants of Bangkok, Thailand, for example, obtain their drinking water from canals and other waterways that are dangerously polluted by industrial and human waste.[21] In light of these difficult conditions, LDCs have sought an appropriate state response.

Public Housing and the Role of the State

Governments throughout the developing world have constructed public housing as a means of alleviating housing shortages. In China, workers in state enterprises are assigned apartments linked to their employer. Cuba's revolutionary regime has built large apartment blocks housing 25,000 to 40,000 persons on the outskirts of its largest cities.[22] During Venezuela's petroleum boom, the government constructed as many as 34,000 urban housing units annually.[23] In the 1960s and 1970s various African governments established housing agencies with far more limited resources. One of the continent's most ambitious programs was in the Côte d'Ivoire, where some 40,000 units were constructed during the 1970s, almost all in the capital city of Abidjan. By the close of that decade the Kenyan government also was building over 3,000 units annually.[24]

In time, however, it became clear that public housing provided insufficient shelter for the poor and, indeed, sometimes made things worse. In the capitals of India, Senegal, and Nigeria, for example, state housing projects often were designed to eradicate "urban blight." Prior to their construction, "unsightly" squatter settlements or slums were demolished so that the city could be more aesthetically pleasing to the political elite, urban planners, middle-class residents, or foreign tourists. Rarely did the people who had been evicted from their homes subsequently secure residence in the newly constructed public housing projects. Even those who were given alternate housing were usually relocated on the edges of town, far removed from their work places.

Diana Patel describes how Zimbabwe's government periodically ousted the same squatters from their settlements in different parts of the nation's capital, in effect "chasing them around town." Government planners, viewing these shacks through middle-class lenses, believed that unless the squatters could afford "decent" urban housing with plumbing and multiple rooms for their families, they would be better off returning to the countryside. Absent from that calculation was an understanding that the rural housing awaiting these squatters often would be inferior to their urban hovels.[25]

Even when government housing projects do not bring about the destruction of shantytowns and slums, they still present a fundamental problem. Their cost invariably exceeds the rent or purchase price that the poor can afford to pay. Consequently, the state is faced with two options: to subsidize housing costs sufficiently so that units can be rented or purchased by the poor; or to rent or sell the dwellings to those who can better afford them, namely the middle class. Despite its initial attraction, subsidized housing has several drawbacks. It is too costly for most LDCs to sustain and it quickly becomes a political plum. Almost invariably it is allocated on the basis of political criteria rather than need and, consequently, rarely serves the poor.

Most Third World governments lack either the economic resources or the political will to house the most needy city dwellers. Studies in a wide variety of LDCs reveal that residents in state housing generally come from the middle class. They not only can better sustain the rents, thereby reducing (but not eliminating) the size of government housing subsidies, but they also have the political influence to acquire this valuable resource. Political patronage plays an important role in housing allocation, with policemen, government bureaucrats, teachers, and activists in the ruling party being the most common recipients.[26]

In Marxist regimes, where class considerations are far less relevant, public housing is more likely to serve the poor. But political connections remain important and funding remains inadequate. Following the Cuban Revolution, "early housing policies reflected Fidel Castro's belief that nothing was too good for the working class."[27] Housing projects such as Santiago's José Martí provided schools, day-care centers, theaters, clinics, and stores for its close to 40,000 inhabitants. But by lavishing excessively "luxurious" housing on early recipients, the government soon ran out of funds for the many others needing shelter. Thus, the East Havana project, planned for 100,000 dwelling units, ultimately contained only 1,500. While lacking adequate resources itself, the government discouraged or prohibited private and self-help housing (i.e., units built by the owner) until recently.[28] Not surprisingly, Cuba, like most Marxist regimes, has suffered chronic housing shortages.[29]

More successful public housing programs have been initiated in Hong Kong and Singapore, two capitalist icons. Each has housed a substantial portion of its population in large government apartment blocks. The experiences of these two very atypical city-states (Hong Kong now is part of China but retains considerable autonomy), however, can hardly be replicated elsewhere in the developing world. For one thing, both have extremely small areas and populations. Physical space is so limited that they have few alternatives to building high-rise apartment complexes. And, as a consequence of their rapid and sustained economic growth, their governments have far greater financial resources than do other LDCs; indeed their current GNP/capita is so high that they can scarcely be classified as economically underdeveloped any longer.

In the rest of the Third World, however, at best only a small fraction of the urban poor's housing needs can be satisfied by fully built public housing. Few developing nations other than the oil-rich Gulf states have the financial resources to subsidize large numbers of residences. Consequently, most analysts feel that state funds would be better spent helping a larger number of beneficiaries in less costly ways.

Spontaneous Housing

Social scientists and architects have long maintained that the most effective remedy for housing shortages in Third World cities is spontaneous (or self-help) shelter—the very shantytowns or squatter settlements that are so frequently viewed as a blight. In cities throughout the LDCs, the poor have frequently built their own homes, usually with some hired or volunteer assistance. While living in these dwellings, many proprietors also rent space to tenants, particularly in Africa. In some cases the owners are squatters, living on land that has been occupied illegally, though often with the compliance of government authorities.[30] Other residents, living in so-called "pirate settlements," have purchased their lots from land speculators but lack legal titles because their community doesn't have basic urban services (such as water) or otherwise fails to conform to government zoning requirements.[31]

Spontaneous housing may consist of a few isolated homes or a community of many thousands. For example, on the dried-out marshlands outside Mexico City, the municipality of Netzahualcóyotl began as a pirate settlement in the 1940s. Though lightly settled until the 1960s, it housed 600,000 people by 1970.[32] A tenants' strike eventually induced the government to provide badly needed urban services and grant the squatters legal recognition. Elsewhere, up to 40 percent of Nairobi's population and one-fourth to one-third of the inhabitants of Djakara (Indonesia), Karachi (Pakistan), and Lima (Peru) live in squatter settlements.[33]

These homes, argued John F. C. Turner, had erroneously been viewed as a problem, when in fact they are a major part of the solution to urban housing needs.[34] Rather than build public housing, he insisted, Third World governments can serve many more people by removing legal and political obstacles to spontaneous housing settlements and by helping residents upgrade the dwellings that they have built. Self-built homes have several important advantages over public housing.[35] First, they actually serve the poor, whereas much public housing (outside of communist countries) does not. Second, they afford occupants the opportunity to upgrade their homes continually. For example, in Lima's vast network of shantytowns one may observe many wood and straw shacks whose owners are building brick walls around them, slowly constructing a better home as funds become available. Third, precisely because they are user-built, these homes better address the needs and desires of their residents than do units built by government planners. Finally, squatter settlements have the "churches, bars and neighborhood stores that help create a sense of community" and that are too often lacking in large, impersonal public housing projects.[36] Given these advantages, argue proponents of spontaneous housing, the state's most constructive role would be to end squatter evictions and instead grant them the land titles and other assistance needed to improve their dwellings.

Sites-and-Services Programs

Many planners who favor a more active role for the state view the Turner thesis as a convenient excuse for governments that don't wish to serve the needs of the poor. Championing self-help housing, charge these critics, merely perpetuates the status quo and allows the state to direct its limited housing resources toward the middle class.[37]

By the 1970s, however, many Third World governments, the World Bank, and other foreign aid donors were pursuing a middle ground between providing fully built public housing and a policy of laissez faire (i.e., having the poor build their own shelter). In countries as diverse as Colombia, India, Malawi, and Turkey, the state has sold or rented to the poor parcels of land with basic services such as running water, sewage, and electricity. Purchasers then build their own homes on the sites as they do with spontaneous housing. In some cases governments provide credit, technical assistance, or low-cost construction materials.[38]

These "sites-and-services" programs have several obvious advantages. First, they allow the government to steer user-built housing to locations that are safer and more environmentally sound. By contrast, unregulated spontaneous shelter in Caracas, Venezuela, illustrates the dangers of unzoned squatter settlements. There, more than half a million people live on precarious hillsides in shacks that are periodically victimized during the rainy season by dangerous mudslides. Second, in contrast to many sprawling squatter settlements, residents of these locations have electricity, sanitation, and other needed services from the outset. Finally, while occupants must purchase their sites, the lots are far more affordable than are fully built state housing units. The government can further assist residents by providing cheaper credit and construction materials.

Critics of sites-and-services programs note, however, that even these relatively inexpensive lots are too costly for the poorest of the poor. While conceding that the communities developed on these sites are often healthier, safer, and more aesthetically pleasing, some scholars contend that the trade-off is fewer homes for the very poor. In addition, they charge that these programs "cream off" relatively "more affluent" and talented residents from unaided slums and shantytowns, thereby leaving the older communities bereft of leadership. Finally, they note that governments are likely to locate sites-and-services projects in more remote areas of town in order to remove the poor from downtown business areas. As a consequence, residents are far removed from their jobs and from many important urban facilities.[39]

Such criticisms notwithstanding, we have seen that sites-and-services programs have some clear advantages over unaided spontaneous shelter and are clearly more beneficial to the poor than is fully built, public housing. Unfortunately, many of these programs were not self-financing (i.e., government income from the rent or sale of lots did not cover costs). Consequently, during the Third World's 1980s economic crisis and the East Asian crisis of the late 1990s, governments often abandoned them, once again leaving the poor to fend for themselves. Finally, both sites-and-service programs and unregulated squatter settlements have faced a growing obstacle in recent years. As a consequence of increasing urban sprawl, cities have ever diminishing space available for any type of self-built housing.[40]

THE POLITICS OF THE URBAN POOR: CONFLICTING IMAGES

How do the urban poor react politically to their daily struggle for jobs and shelter? The politics of the urban poor, like those of the peasantry, have been depicted in sharply conflicting manners.[41] When social scientists first noted the sweep of cityward migration and urban growth in the developing countries, many of them viewed the sprawling slums and squatter settlements as potential hotbeds of unrest or even revolution. In one of the most influential early works on Third World politics, James Coleman warned, "There exist in most urban centers . . . elements predisposed to anomic activity."[42] Samuel Huntington maintained that urban migrants themselves were unlikely to challenge the existing order, but their children certainly might: "At some point, the slums of Rio and Lima . . . are likely to be swept by social violence, as the children of the city demand the rewards of the city."[43] And economist Barbara Ward, taking note of shantytown poverty and the rise of radical urban movements, insisted,

> unchecked . . . left to grow and fester, there is here enough explosive material to produce . . . bitter class conflict . . . erupting in guerrilla warfare, and threatening, ultimately, the security even of the comfortable West.[44]

As we will see, the urban poor have, indeed, been important participants in recent Third World revolutions. In addition, rioting over food prices and bus fares has shaken Algiers, Caracas, Santo Domingo, and other cities. But the urban conflagrations that many predicted have rarely taken place. Most of the poor have shunned violence. And voters in the slums and squatter settlements of the LDCs have been as likely to support right-wing or centrist candidates for office as radicals.

Initial expectations of a violent or radicalized urban lower class were based on a set of premises that have generally proven erroneous. To be sure, many urban migrants came to the cities with raised expectations and heightened political sensitivities. When their hopes for a better life were not satisfied, argued many scholars, they would likely erupt in fury against the system, or at the very least support the most radical political parties. But, horrendous as the slums of Cairo, Calcutta, or Karachi may appear to the Western observer, migrants usually find them preferable to their earlier conditions in the countryside. In fact, the urban poor are far more likely than their rural counterparts to enjoy electricity, sewage, access to tap water, and educational opportunities for their children. In many countries, urban migration also allows escape from rural, semi-feudal social controls or ethnic civil war.

Small wonder that surveys of migrants in Ankara, Baghdad, Bogotá, Mexico City, Rio de Janeiro, and other cities indicate that most respondents feel better off in their urban hovels than they had been in their rural villages.[45] A study of 13 low-income neighborhoods in Bogotá, Colombia; Valencia, Venezuela, and Mexico City revealed that between 64 and 76 percent of the respondents believed that their settlement was "a good place to live" while only 11 to 31 percent felt they lived in a "bad place."[46] Undoubtedly, the severe economic recession during the 1980s that sharply lowered urban living standards in Africa and Latin America and the more recent economic crisis in Asia gave slum dwellers a more jaundiced view of their condition. Yet survey research indicates that even when the urban poor do not feel their own lives have improved, they generally remain optimistic about the future and about prospects for their children.[47]

When early expectations of urban radicalism rarely materialized, some scholars reached diametrically opposite conclusions. For example, based on his studies of low-income neighborhoods in Mexico and Puerto Rico, anthropologist Oscar Lewis concluded that most of the urban poor are prisoners of a "culture of poverty." Lewis described a subproletariat that lacks class consciousness, economic and political organization, or long-term aspirations. While distrustful of government, they feel powerless and fatalistic about effecting change. The culture of poverty, he argued, is inherently apolitical and, hence, quite unlikely to generate radical or revolutionary activity.[48]

A related body of literature described the urban poor as "marginal"—outside the mainstream of the nation's political and economic life. Consequently, it was argued, there is a political vicious cycle in which the poor's exclusion leads to increased apathy on their part. They demonstrate a "lack of active participation due to the fact that . . . marginal groups make no decisions; they do not contribute to the molding of society."[49] Like the victims of Lewis's culture of poverty, marginals allegedly show little class consciousness or capacity for long-term collective action.

Just as initial predictions of radicalism and violence among the urban lower class proved to be greatly exaggerated, so too did assertions that the poor were invariably apathetic and fatalistic. To be sure, most low-income communities are not very politicized. In his study of the poor in Guatemala City, Bryan R. Roberts found that "they claim to avoid politics in their local work, and to them the term 'politician' is synonymous with deceit and corruption."[50] This is not the result of apathy or fatalism, however, but rather stems from the realistically "perceived impracticality of changing the existing order" in most Third World countries[51] or, in the case of Guatemala, a repressive political atmosphere. On the other hand, when given the opportunity to organize (i.e., when their political activity is not repressed) and when there is a realistic chance of attaining some benefits from the political system, many low-income communities, or at least an activist minority within them, have seized the opportunity. Studies of Caracas, Lima, and Rio, for example, reveal a number of poor neighborhoods with extensive political cooperation and organization. Moreover, their community leaders often have a keen sense of how to manipulate the political environment.

In time, social scientists came to question the concepts of marginality and the culture of poverty.[52] Clearly, a more nuanced view of urban politics in the LDCs requires us to ask: Under what circumstances do the urban poor organize politically? What goals do they seek and how do they pursue them? What factors determine whether their political organization is peaceful or violent, conservative or radical, reformist or revolutionary?

FORMS OF POLITICAL EXPRESSION AMONG THE URBAN POOR

Political scientists have long understood that the urban poor tend to be better informed and more active politically than their rural counterparts. Indeed, some of the leading early scholarship on Third World politics used a nation's level of urbanization as an indicator of its degree of political participation.[53] City dwellers have higher levels of literacy than peasants do, greater exposure to the mass media, and more contact with political campaigns and rallies.

This does not mean that most residents of poor urban neighborhoods are highly politicized. To the contrary, many of them are uninterested, apathetic, or even fatalistic about political events.[54] Nor does it even mean that the minority of political activists are necessarily radicalized, indignant about their economic conditions, or interested in insurrectionary activity. What it does mean is that the urban poor generally vote in higher numbers than the peasantry. And it means that many low-income neighborhoods and communities, having intelligently assessed what kinds of benefits they can reasonably hope to extract from the political system, have organized to secure them. Contrary to initial expectations that the disoriented and frustrated urban poor would riot and rebel, they have tended, instead, to be rather pragmatic and careful in their political behavior.

Individual Political Behavior

For most slum and shantytown dwellers, opportunities for individual political activity are rather limited. Voting has little meaning in most developing nations. In Africa, the Middle East, and much of Asia, contested elections, at least until recently, have been exceptional. Many African and Middle Eastern regimes engage in nonparticipatory politics designed to exclude the masses. After an authoritarian interlude, democracy has gradually returned to most of Latin America and tentatively started in parts of Africa, but its relevance to the poor remains unclear.

An alternative, often more fruitful type of individual political activity takes the form of clientelism. As Josef Gugler and others have noted, members of the urban lower class seek to advance their interests by attaching themselves to a patron within the government or a powerful political party, faction, or movement.[55] Clientelism (i.e., patron-client relationships) consists of "the dispensing of public resources as favors . . . by political power holders/seekers and their respective parties, in exchange for votes or forms of popular support." While offering concrete advantages for the less powerful partner (i.e., the client), it is at its heart "a strategy of elite controlled political participation fostering the status quo."[56] Among the urban poor, potentially frustrated or radicalized individuals and groups can be co-opted into the political system with the lure of immediate, if limited, gains.

Patron-client relations, of course, were typical of American big-city political machines in the late nineteenth and early twentieth centuries. Political parties offered needy immigrants jobs, Christmas turkeys, or bags of coal in return for their support at the polls. Today, in countries throughout Africa, the poor attain credit, employment in parastatals, and the like by volunteering support for the governing political party or local government strongman. Elsewhere, even in countries with competitive elections (such as India, Uruguay, and the Philippines), political bosses garner votes and volunteers primarily through patronage.

For most of the urban poor, however, collective rather than individual activity appears to be the most productive form of political participation. Many low-income neighborhoods have organized rather effectively to extract resources from the political system. Not surprisingly, one of their most common objectives is to secure land titles for their homes along with basic services such as sanitation, sewage, tap water, education, and paved streets.

Collective Goals: Housing and Urban Services

On the outskirts of Lima, Peru, several million people live in squatter communities known originally as barriadas and more recently as pueblos jóvenes. Typically these settlements were born out of organized invasions of unoccupied land, either publicly owned or with disputed ownership:

> Some invasions involve relatively small groups of families who join together on an informal basis shortly before the occupation of the land. Others involve hundreds of families and are planned with great care. The leaders of these invasions often organize well before the invasion occurs and meet many times to recruit members, choose a site and plan the occupation itself.[57]

Although they were obviously illegal, David Collier found that nearly half of these land seizures (involving over 60 percent of Lima's squatter population) were conducted with explicit or tacit government approval.[58] While the authorities didn't want this phenomenon to get out of hand, they understood that permitting a controlled number of invasions onto low-value land (much of it public) enabled the poor to build their own homes with little cost to the state. There were political benefits to be gained as well. By protecting the

invaders from police eviction, a political leader or governing party could garner future electoral support from the community. In many cases, squatters also
paid off local authorities prior to their invasions.

When Peru's leftist military regime seized power in 1968, it was anxious to
mobilize the urban poor but at the same time to reduce spontaneous grass-roots
political activity. The generals issued an urban reform law benefiting existing
squatter communities; they sought to mobilize, yet control, the poor through
SINAMOS, a state-controlled political organization for the rural and urban
masses; and they took a tougher stance against new land invasions. Henry Dietz's
study of six poor Lima neighborhoods shows that community leaders in several
locations were quite adept about moving from competitive electoral politics to
the new rules of enlightened authoritarianism.[59] Mobilized neighborhoods used
an impressive array of political tactics to secure assistance from the military
regime. These included working through SINAMOS, enlisting the aid of a sympathetic Catholic bishop whom the church had assigned to the shantytowns,
gaining the support of foreign Non-Governmental Organizations (NGOs), publishing letters in leading newspapers, pressuring local government bureaucrats,
and directly petitioning the president.

Lima's squatter settlements have long attracted the interest of political scientists and anthropologists because of their unusually high level of political activity. But research elsewhere in Latin America has found similar ties between poor
neighborhoods and the state.[60] For example, in her study of low-income neighborhoods in Mexico City, Susan Eckstein describes how powerful community
leaders tied to the ruling party (the PRI) are the links between the government
and the grass-roots level. Because these community organizations tend to be
short-lived and are controlled from the top down, Eckstein is skeptical about
how much benefit the poor accrue by operating through Mexico's clientelistic
system. Still, she concedes that over the years poor neighborhoods have successfully petitioned the government for water, electricity, local food markets,
schools, public transportation, and the like.[61]

The politics of low-income neighborhoods throughout the developing
world tend to resemble Peru's and Mexico's in two important respects: the scope
of their demands and their relationship to the national political system. Urban
case studies in India, Pakistan, the Philippines, and other LDCs repeatedly show
the demands of the poor to be quite limited and pragmatic.[62] At times they are
defensive, simply asking not to be evicted from illegal settlements. Frequently
their political objectives focus on housing. But, as Turner suggested, squatters
and slum dwellers rarely want the government to build homes for them, pre-
ferring instead the means to do it themselves. Some neighborhoods may ask
for a medical clinic, a market, or a preschool lunch program. None of these objectives, however, involve a fundamental challenge to the political system or a major
redistribution of economic resources.

Such limited demands are intimately related to the structure of political
organization in low-income neighborhoods. Political inputs from the poor are

filtered through patron-client linkages to the state, powerful political parties, or political bosses. Organizations may be based in neighborhoods; may be tied to ethnic, religious, or racial identities; or may simply be formed around powerful political figures. In the slums of Madras, India, where politics are closely linked to the film industry, clientelistic organizations grow out of local fan clubs for politically active movie stars.[63]

Whatever its base, patron-client politics inherently reinforces the status quo. In return for votes or other forms of political support, the state delivers some of the goods or services that residents need. In many cases a neighborhood's rewards are very paltry. Elsewhere, political systems are far more responsive to the needs of the poor. In either case, however, the state engages in "divide and rule" politics, as poor urban districts compete with each other for limited government resources.[64]

Critics of clientelistic politics point out that the benefits that accrue to slums and shantytowns are rather limited. While some communities gain water, electricity, or clinics, many others are left out. Moreover, even successful neighborhoods find it difficult to maintain pressure on the system over time because local political organizations generally atrophy after a number of years. Consequently, as Alan Gilbert and Peter Ward charge, "The main aim of community-action programs is less to improve conditions for the poor . . . than to legitimate the state . . . to help maintain existing power relations in society."[65] As an alternative to clientelism, critics favor a more independent, and perhaps more radical, form of mobilization that would raise the urban poor's political consciousness and, hopefully, lead to more sweeping redistributive policies, benefiting far more people.

Other analysts, however, take a more positive perspective toward clientelism. While recognizing its shortcomings, they insist that the limited benefits that it brings are clearly better than nothing. Viewed in the broader context of society's tremendous inequalities, paved streets or clean drinking water, a clinic or a marketplace may not seem like sufficient gains to a middle-class observer. But they are usually greatly appreciated by the low-income neighborhoods that need them badly. A radical regime might redistribute more to the poor, but that is not a viable option in most LDCs.[66]

The benefits of clientelism vary from country to country, depending on the nature of their political system and the state of the economy. In open and democratic societies such as Chile in the early 1970s and currently, or even in quasi-democratic governments such as Mexico's, the poor have broader opportunities to organize, demonstrate, petition, and vote. Clearly their capacity to demand rewards from the state are greater than under authoritarian regimes such as the Pinochet dictatorship in Chile or Ferdinand Marcos's martial law government in the Philippines. At the same time, the benefits that clientelistic systems can allocate to low-income neighborhoods are constrained by the state's economic resources. During their petroleum booms, the Mexican and Venezuelan governments could be more generous to the urban poor. Even in more difficult economic times, the Mexican government has used revenues from the sale of state enterprises to finance public works projects in urban slums. Conversely, the impoverished dictatorships of sub-Saharan Africa have neither the political will nor the economic resources to aid their slums and squatter settlements.

During the 1980s, a number of independent grass-roots organizations emerged in the poor neighborhoods of Brazil, Chile, Mexico, and several other Latin American countries. Known as new social movements, they avoided clientelistic linkages with the government or political parties, keeping independent even of leftist parties. For example, following Mexico City's immense earthquake in 1985, slum dwellers, frustrated by the ineptitude of government redevelopment efforts, formed an effective network of self-help associations. In Monterrey radicalized squatters in the community of Tierra y Libertad (Land and Liberty) hijacked several buses, forcing the public transport company to extend its routes further into their neighborhood.[67] Ultimately, however, these independent movements had limited longevity. By the early 1990s they were being overshadowed by President Carlos Salinas's public works network for poor neighborhoods known as the National Solidarity Program. Using traditional clientelistic techniques, his administration won the support of the poor by establishing new schools, clinics, and the like through government-affiliated neighborhood groups.

Whatever the merits or limits of clientelism, its scope and range refute many initial assumptions about the politics of the urban poor. On the one hand, the patron-client negotiations involved frequently show neighborhood leaders to be more politically skilled than some analysts had assumed. While many slum dwellers suffer from fatalism and excessive individualism, others are capable of sophisticated political organization and bargaining with the state. On the other hand, the poor rarely engage in the kind of revolutionary activity, violent upheavals, or radical politics that others had expected. During the 1980s when living standards declined precipitously in much of the Third World, there was some increase in protest activity.[68] But the extent of rioting and social unrest remained surprisingly limited. Similarly, the slums of Bangkok have remained politically peaceful despite Thailand's current, severe economic crisis. To be sure the sharp recent decline in Indonesia's economy produced severe urban rioting which toppled the Sukarno dictatorship in 1998. But it was university students, not the poor, who demonstrated against the government. Jakarta's slum dwellers have vented their anger, instead, against the affluent Chinese minority.

Radical Political Behavior

While most of the Third World's urban poor have favored moderate and pragmatic forms of political expression, there have been important exceptions. In some countries, such as Chile in the early 1970s and Peru in the 1980s, they have voted in substantial numbers for Marxist political candidates. And in a few cases, urban slum and shantytown dwellers have been important players in revolutionary upheavals.

In 1970, Salvador Allende, candidate of Chile's leftist Popular Unity (UP) coalition, became the developing world's first democratically elected Marxist President. Allende received considerable electoral support in the campamentos (squatter settlements) that ring the capital city of Santiago. In addition, a number of campamentos were organized by the UP or by the MIR (Leftist Revolutionary Movement), a movement to the left of the UP that periodically engaged in armed struggle.[69] In 1983, the poor of Lima played a major role in electing a Marxist mayor, Alfonso Barrantes. These examples as well as the Communist Party's electoral successes in several Indian cities indicate that the poor do support radical political parties under certain circumstances. Those parties must have a realistic chance of winning at the local or national level and, hence, the possibility of delivering benefits to their supporters. Thus, even radical voting is often based on very pragmatic calculations. Not long after supporting Barrantes for mayor, Lima's poor rejected him for the post of president, seeing even his moderate Marxism as nonviable at the national level.[70] More often the urban poor are attracted to charismatic populists (left- or right-wing) such as the recently elected President of Venezuela, Hugo Chávez.

Squatters or slum dwellers are even less like to embrace urban guerrillas or other revolutionary movements. Teodoro Petkoff, a former leader of the Venezuelan Communists' urban guerrilla wing in the early 1960s, has noted how even residents of Caracas's poor barrios who belonged to leftist unions rejected the guerrillas. Blue-collar workers often elected Communist union representatives in those days, Petkoff observed, because they felt that union militants would deliver more at the bargaining table. But when it came to voting for national office, Caracas's poor were more prone to support the two mainstream parties (Social Democratic and Christian Democratic) or even the former right-wing dictator, all of whom had a better track record of delivering rewards to their supporters.[71]

Talton Ray's study of barrio politics suggests why residents were unlikely to support the armed insurrection of the FALN:

> The FALN's urban guerrilla warfare proved to be a grave tactical error [creating a] . . . mood of revulsion . . . in the barrios. Terrorist activities struck much too close to home. . . . Almost all of the murdered policemen were barrio residents.[72]

More recently, Peru's Sendero Luminoso (Shining Path) guerrillas have had some success in the shantytowns of Lima. However, in view of Sendero's terror and intimidation tactics against both the peasantry and the urban poor, there is every reason to believe that it inspires more fear and acquiescence than support. When the popular vice-mayor of one of Peru's largest and most politically militant shantytowns, Villa El Salvador, tried to keep Shining Path out of her community, she was brutally assassinated. In any event, Sendero activists in both the countryside and urban slums have more often been students and teachers, rather than the poor themselves.

This is not to suggest that the urban poor never support revolutions. Josef Gugler notes that in four of the Third World's most recent insurrections—in Bolivia, Cuba, Iran, and Nicaragua—the cities played a central role.[73] However, in all but Nicaragua (where the urban poor's mass demonstrations were critical), social classes other than the poor took the lead in the cities: miners, blue-collar workers, artisans, the lower-middle class, and the national police in Bolivia; students and university graduates in Cuba; theological students and petroleum workers in Iran. Douglas Butterworth's study of the former inhabitants of a Havana slum, Las Yaguas, found that most were barely aware of Fidel Castro's existence during his rise to power.[74]

CONCLUSION

While the rate of urbanization has slowed somewhat in the LDCs, absolute increases in city populations will be greater than ever in the coming decades (Table 6.2). Thus, governments will have to heed urban needs, including those of the poor. Still, even with the best-intentioned public policies, developing economies will be hard pressed to provide sufficient jobs, housing, sanitation, and social services. Economic crises such as Latin America's and Africa's in the 1980s and East Asia's in the late 1990s have made the task all the more difficult. Urban crime, pollution, and AIDS will add tremendously to the burdens on the political-economic systems.

Given the current weakness of the radical left, however, and the tendency of the poor to engage in adaptive behavior, urban discontent is more likely to express itself in occasional rioting than in mass insurrection or revolution. In the Middle East, the urban poor and perhaps the middle class may turn to Islamic fundamentalism as many have already done in Iran, Algeria, and Egypt. Elsewhere, crime and drug usage are more likely than radical politics to threaten stability in the proximate future. In the long run, Third World governments may be able to cope with these problems if they can generate sustained economic growth. In the short term, however, the possibility of increased state repression persists in many countries as the military and middle class become fearful of urban crime and disorder.

DISCUSSION QUESTIONS

1. How have Third World governments been involved in providing urban housing? To what extent have such efforts benefited or hurt the urban poor?

2. Describe the advantages and limitations of spontaneous housing. In what ways are sites-and-services programs an improvement over spontaneous housing? Are there disadvantages to sites-and-services programs?

3. Discuss the political orientations of the urban poor.

4. Discuss the role of clientelism or patron-client relationships in the politics of the urban poor.

NOTES

1. Stella Lowder, *The Geography of Third World Cities* (New York: Barnes and Noble, 1986), p. 19.

2. Sally Findley, "The Third World City," in *Third World Cities*, ed. John Kasarda and Allan Parnell (Newbury Park, CA: Sage Publications, 1993), pp. 14–16.

3. R. A. Obudho, "Urbanization and Urban Development Strategies in East Africa," in *Urban Management*, ed. G. Shabbir Cheema (New York: Praeger, 1993), figures extrapolated from Table 4.2, p. 84.

4. G. Shabbir Cheema, "The Challenge of Urban Management," in *Urban Management*, p. 2.

5. David Drakakis–Smith, *Urbanization, Housing and the Development Process* (New York: St. Martin's Press, 1980), p. 6; Samuel Preston, "Urban Growth in Developing Countries," in *The Urbanization of the Third World*, ed. Josef Gugler (New York: Oxford University Press, 1988), pp. 14–15, using earlier data, indicates a higher percentage of increase due to natural growth; Findley, "The Third World City," p. 15, using more recent data, indicates a higher percentage of increase due to migration.

6. Obudho, "Urbanization and Urban Development Strategies," p. 84.

7. Alan Gilbert and Josef Gugler, *Cities, Poverty and Development*, 2nd ed. (New York: Oxford University Press, 1992).

8. John V. Graumann, "Orders of Magnitude of the World's Urban and Rural Population in History," *United Nations Population Bulletin* 8 (1977): 16–33, quoted in Preston, "Urban Growth," p. 12.

9. Raymond Owens, "Peasant Entrepreneurs in an Industrial City," in *A Reader in Urban Sociology*, ed. M. S. A. Rao, Chandrashekar Bhat, and Laxmi Narayan Kadekar. (New Delhi, India: Oriental Longman, 1991), p. 235.

10. Manuel Castells and Alejandro Portes, "World Underneath: The Origins, Dynamics and Effects of the Informal Economy," in *The Informal Economy: Studies in Advanced and Developing Economies*, ed. Alejandro Portes, Manuel Castells, and Lauren A. Benton (Baltimore, MD: Johns Hopkins University Press, 1989), p. 12.

11. Om Prakash Mathur, "Managing the Urban Informal Sector," in *Urban Management*, p. 179. The data is drawn from ILO studies.

12. Gilbert and Gugler, *Cities, Poverty and Development,* p. 98. Gugler argues that the composition of the informal economy is so diverse that he questions whether it can really be referred to as a sector.

13. Alejandro Portes et al., "The Informal Sector in Uruguay," *World Development* 14 (1986), pp. 727–741.

14. Hernando de Soto, *The Other Path* (New York: Harper and Row, 1989), translated from the Spanish edition.

15. Dennis Rondinelli and John Kasarda, "Job Creation Needs in Third World Cities," in *Third World Cities*, pp. 92–120.

16. Macroeconomic policy will be discussed in far greater detail in Chapter 10. The reader wishing to better understand the economic analysis offered briefly in this section is referred to that chapter.

17. Stephan Haggard, *Pathways from the Periphery* (Ithaca, NY: Cornell University Press, 1990).

18. Richard Sandbrook, *The Politics of African Economic Recovery* (New York: Cambridge University Press, 1993), pp. 60–61.

19. *New York Times*, October 27, 1993.

20. While squatter settlements or shantytowns can accurately be called poor neighborhoods, not everyone living in them is poor. Data from Istanbul, Rio, Caracas, and elsewhere show that some shantytown residents are white-collar workers or well-paid blue collars. Some better-off residents live there because rents elsewhere are too high. Others have enjoyed upward mobility since settling there, but stay because of attachments to friends and community.

21. Statistics in the preceding paragraphs come from Om P. Mathur, forward to Kamlesh Misra, *Housing the Poor in Third World Cities* (New Delhi, India: Concept Publishing Company, 1992), pp. 6–8; Gilbert and Gugler, *Cities, Poverty and Development*, p. 115.

22. Fred Ward, *Inside Cuba Today* (New York: Crown, 1978), pp. 36–38.

23. Howard Handelman, "The Role of the State in Sheltering the Urban Poor," in *Spontaneous Shelter*, ed. Carl V. Patton (Philadelphia: Temple University Press, 1988) pp. 332–333.

24. Richard Stern, "Urban Housing in Africa: The Changing Role of Government Policy," in *Housing Africa's Urban Poor*, ed. Philip Amis and Peter Lloyd (Manchester, England: Manchester University Press, 1990), pp. 36–39.

25. Diana Patel, "Government Policy and Squatter Settlements in Harare, Zimbabwe," in *Slum and Squatter Settlements in Sub-Saharan Africa*, ed. R. A. Obudho and Constance Mhlanga, (New York: Praeger, 1988) pp. 205–217.

26. Susan Eckstein, *The Poverty of Revolution: The State and the Urban Poor in Mexico*, 2d ed. (Princeton, NJ: Princeton University Press, 1988); Henry Dietz, *Poverty and Problem Solving Under Military Rule* (Austin: University of Texas Press, 1980), p. 41; Howard Handelman, *High-Rises and Shantytowns* (Hanover, NH: AUFS, 1979), p. 17; B. Sanyal, "A Critical Look at the Housing Subsidies in Zambia," *Development and Change* 12 (1981): 409–440.

27. Handelman, "The Role of the State," p. 339.

28. Some experts call Cuba's construction of microbrigade housing (houses built by teams of worker volunteers) self-help. But they are built by groups under state direction who don't design the homes and don't conform to much of the self-help model discussed later in the chapter.

29. Gilbert and Gugler, *Cities, Poverty and Development*, p. 139.

30. David Collier, *Squatters and Oligarchs* (Baltimore, MD: Johns Hopkins University Press, 1976).

31. Gilbert and Gugler, *Cities, Poverty and Development*, p. 123.

32. Alan Gilbert and Peter Ward, *Housing, the State, and the Poor* (New York: Cambridge University Press, 1985), pp. 86–87.

33. Diana Lee-Smith, "Squatter Landlords in Nairobi," in *Housing Africa's Urban Poor*, p. 177; Douglas Butterworth and John Chance, *Latin American Urbanization* (New York: Cambridge University Press, 1981), p. 147; Collier, *Squatters and Oligarchs*, pp. 27–28.

34. John F. C. Turner, "Barriers and Channels for Housing Development in Modernizing Countries," *Journal of the American Institute of Planners* 33 (May 1967): 167–181; John F. C. Turner and Robert Fichter, eds., *Freedom to Build* (New York: Macmillan, 1972); see also William Mangin, "Latin American Squatter Settlements: A Problem and a Solution," *Latin American Research Review* 2, no. 3 (1967): 65–98.

35. Gilbert and Gugler, *Cities, Poverty and Development*, pp. 117–130; Carl Patton, "Prospects for the Future," in *Spontaneous Shelter*, pp. 348–355.

36. Handelman, "The Role of the State," p. 328.

37. Peter Nientied and Jan van der Linden, "Approaches to Low-Income Housing in the Third World," in *The Urbanization of the Third World*, pp. 138–156; R. Burgess, "Petty Commodity Housing or Dweller Control? A Critique of John Turner's Views on Housing Policy," *World Development* 6 (1978): 1105–1133.

38. Handelman, *High-Rises and Shantytowns*; A. A. Laquian, "Whither Site and Services," *Habitat* 2 (1977): 291–301; Thomas Pennant, "The Growth of Small-Scale Renting in Low-Income Housing in Malawi," in *Housing Africa's Urban Poor*, pp. 196–200.

39. Ernest Alexander, "Informal Settlement in Latin America and its Policy Implication," in *Spontaneous Shelter*, pp. 131–133; Drakakis-Smith, *Urbanization, Housing and the Development Process*, pp. 141–142; Jorge Hardoy and David Satterthwaite, *Shelter, Need and Response* (New York: John Wiley, 1981); Lisa Peattie, "Some Second Thoughts on Sites-and-Services," *Habitat Intentional* 6 (Winter 1982): 131–139.

40. Gilbert and Ward, *Housing, the State and the Poor*.

41. Joan Nelson, *Access to Power* (Princeton, NJ: Princeton University Press, 1979), Chapter 4; Howard Handelman, "The Political Mobilization of Urban Squatter Settlements," *Latin American Research Review* 10, no. 2 (1975): 35–72; Gilbert and Gugler, *Cities, Poverty and Development*, Chapter 7.

42. James Coleman, "Conclusion: The Political Systems of Developing Nations," in *The Politics of Developing Areas*, ed. Gabriel Almond and James Coleman (Princeton, NJ: Princeton University Press, 1960), p. 537.

43. Samuel Huntington, *Political Order in Changing Societies* (New Haven, CT: Yale University Press, 1968), p. 283.

44. Barbara Ward, "Creating Man's Future Goals for a World of Plenty," *Saturday Review* 9 (August 1964): p. 192.

45. Joan Nelson, *Migrants, Urban Poverty, and Instability in Developing Nations* (Cambridge: MA: AMS Press and the Harvard University Center for International Affairs, 1969), pp. 18–20; Eckstein, *The Poverty of Revolution*, p. 41.

46. Gilbert and Ward, *Housing, the State and the Poor*, p. 215.

47. Ibid., pp. 57–61.

48. Oscar Lewis, *The Children of Sanchez* (New York: Random House, 1961), and *La Vida* (New York: Random House, 1966).

49. Jorge Giusti, "Organizational Characteristics of the Latin American Urban Marginal Settler," *International Journal of Politics* 1, no. 1 (1971): 57.

50. Bryan R. Roberts, *Organizing Strangers: Poor Families in Guatemala City* (Austin: University of Texas Press, 1973), p. 299.

51. Alejandro Portes and John Walton, *Urban Latin America* (Austin: University of Texas Press, 1976), p. 108.

52. Janice Perlman, *The Myth of Marginality* (Berkeley: University of California Press, 1976); William Mangin, "The Role of Regional Associations in the Adaptation of Rural Migrants to Cities in Peru," in *Contemporary Cultures and Societies of Latin America*, ed. Dwight Heath and Richard Adams (New York: Random House, 1974).

53. Karl Deutsch, "Social Mobilization and Political Development," *American Political Science Review* 55 (September 1961): 493–514; Daniel Lerner, *The Passing of Traditional Society* (Glencoe, IL: Free Press, 1958).

54. Of course, even in highly educated, industrial democracies such as the United States, many citizens are also apolitical. Moreover, that political apathy extends to members of the middle class.

55. Gilbert and Gugler, *Cities, Poverty and Development*, pp. 180–187; S. N. Eisenstadt and L. Roninger, *Patrons, Clients and Friends* (New York: Cambridge University Press, 1984).

56. A. Bank, "Poverty, Politics and the Shaping of Urban Space: A Brazilian Example" *International Journal of Urban and Regional Research* 10, no. 4 (1986): 523.

57. Collier, *Squatters and Oligarchs*, p. 41.

58. Ibid., p. 44.

59. Dietz, *Poverty and Problem-Solving under Military Rule.*

60. Wayne Cornelius, *Politics and the Urban Poor in Mexico* (Stanford, CA: Stanford University Press, 1975); Gilbert and Ward, *Housing, the State and the Poor*, pp. 189–196.

61. Eckstein, *The Poverty of Revolution*, Chapter 3.

62. Frans Schuurman and Ton van Naerssen, *Urban Social Movements in the Third World* (New York: Routledge, 1989).

63. Joop de Wit, "Clientelism, Competition and Poverty: The Ineffectiveness of Local Organizations in a Madras Slum," in ibid., pp. 63–90.

64. Jan van der Linden, "The Limits of Territorial Social Movements: The Case of Housing in Karachi," in *Urban Social Movements*, p. 101.

65. Gilbert and Ward, *Housing, the State and the Poor*, p. 175.

66. Marxist governments often redistribute significant resources to the poor soon after taking power. At the same time, however, with the notable exception of China, leftist regimes generally have a poor record of economic growth. In Nicaragua, for example, the urban poor benefited initially from Sandinista welfare programs but then saw their standards of living deteriorate sharply due to the U.S.-backed Contra war as well as to poor economic management by the Sandinistas. In other revolutions, such as Cuba's, China's, or Vietnam's, where counterrevolutionary activity has been less extreme, experts differ sharply regarding how the urban poor have fared in the long run.

67. Vivien Bennet, "The Evolution of Popular Movements in Mexico Between 1968 and 1988," in *The Making of Social Movements in Latin America*, ed. Arturo Escobar and Sonia Alvarez (Boulder, CO: Westview Press, 1992); Menno Vellinga, "Power and Independence: The Struggle for Identity and Integrity in Urban Social Movements," in *Urban Social Movements*, pp. 151–176.

68. Susan Eckstein, *Urbanization Revisited: Inner-City Slum of Hope and Squatter Settlement of Despair* (Storrs: University of Connecticut and Brown University Occasional Papers in Latin American Studies, 1989), p. 14.

69. Handelman, "The Political Mobilization of Urban Squatter Settlements: Santiago's Recent Experience," *Latin American Research Review* 10, no. 2 (1975): 35–72.

70. Henry Dietz, "Political Participation in the Barriadas: An Extension and Reexamination," *Comparative Political Studies* 18, no. 3 (1985): 323–355.

71. My own conversations with Petkoff 1976 and 1978. Petkoff left the Communist party to help found a democratically oriented Marxist party called MAS. He was subsequently elected to Congress on the MAS ticket and in the late 1990s held a powerful cabinet position.

72. Talton Ray, *The Politics of the Barrios of Venezuela* (Berkeley: University of California Press, 1969), pp. 132–133.

73. Josef Gugler, "The Urban Character of Contemporary Revolutions," in *The Urbanization of the Third World*, pp. 399–412.

74. Douglas Butterworth, *The People of Buena Ventura* (Urbana: University of Illinois Press, 1980), pp. 19–20.

7

❦

REVOLUTIONARY
CHANGE

*Revolutions, however one may be tempted to define them, are not mere
changes.*[1]

The opening decades of the twentieth century ushered in the Mexican and
Russian Revolutions. The closing decades witnessed the collapse of Soviet
Communism, the transformation of the Chinese and Mexican revolutions,
and the decline of Cuba's revolutionary regime.[2] No era in world history has
encompassed more revolutionary upheaval. Yet as that century came to a close,
the force that had once promised (or threatened) to transform the face of the Third
World appeared to be spent, at least for the time being.

Karl Marx, the foremost prophet of revolution, expected such insurrections
to take place in industrialized European nations where an exploited working
class would rise up against the oppressive capitalist system. Instead, modern
revolutionary movements have been a Third World phenomenon, fought primarily by the peasantry. And Europe's only important twentieth-century revolutions—in Russia and Yugoslavia—occurred in countries where capitalism and
industrialization were comparatively less developed. The remaining communist
regimes in Eastern Europe were installed by Soviet intervention, not through
indigenous upheavals.

In the Third World, the appeal of revolutionary change has been its assur-
ance of rapid and sweeping solutions to the problems of underdevelopment. It
promises to end colonial control, terminate dependency, uphold national sovereignty, eliminate gross social and economic inequalities, speed economic
development, politically mobilize the population, and transform the political
culture. Not surprisingly, many of the poor and oppressed along with numerous

intellectuals and alienated members of the middle class have found revolutionary ideologies and myths quite appealing.

Some revolutionary governments—including China, Cuba, and Mexico, for example—were able to deliver on a number of their promises, at least initially. Under Mao Zedong, China redistributed land to the peasantry, created a large industrial base, and transformed itself into a world power. Cuba introduced extensive agrarian reform, a mass adult literacy campaign, and a rural health program. Mexico reestablished national sovereignty over its natural resources, initiated an agrarian reform, and transformed itself into a Third World industrial power.

Often, however, these gains have come at great cost, including political repression and considerable human suffering. To be sure, even the sharpest critics of the Chinese revolution cannot deny that its people currently enjoy better medical care, more education, and better living conditions than ever before. At the same time, however, some 30 million or more starved to death in the 1950s due to the mistaken experiments of Mao's Great Leap Forward. Millions more suffered humiliation, imprisonment, or death (some 400,000) in the Cultural Revolution (1966 to 1976). Most Communist governments have had their gulags for real and imagined political opponents. In Vietnam, many suspected dissidents were sent to "reeducation" camps, while a smaller, but still significant, number were imprisoned in Cuba.

In some cases—Angola, Mozambique, Kampuchea (Cambodia) —huge portions of the population died as the result of civil war or the regime's brutality, with little or nothing positive to show for it.[3] In Kampuchea, the fanatical Khmer Rouge killed over a million people—including much of the country's educated class—while accomplishing nothing for its people. Over the years, even the more idealistic (if sometimes brutal) revolutionary regimes were often transformed into corrupt bureaucracies, run by a new generation of opportunistic *apparatchiks* who never had risked anything for the revolution's ideals.

After examining the meaning of revolution and classifying different types of twentieth-century revolutions, this chapter will discuss the causes of revolutionary upheavals, the principle sources of support and leadership for revolutionary movements, and the policy objectives of revolutionary governments.

DEFINING REVOLUTION

Scholars have argued endlessly about what constitutes a revolution and whether particular upheavals such as the American Revolution or Iran's Islamic Revolution were, in fact, true social revolutions.[4] Thus, Chalmers Johnson notes, "half the battle will lie in answering the question, 'What is revolution?'"[5] In its broadest and least precise usage, the term is applied to any non-legal, nondemocratic, or violent overthrow of government. Peter Calvert offers perhaps the most open definition when he maintains that revolution is "simply a form of governmental change through violence."[6] Such a definition, however, seems too loose since it encompasses military coups and other upheavals that do little more than change the formal structure of government.

Most scholars insist on a more rigorous definition, arguing that revolutions must involve fundamental political, economic, and social change.

Samuel P. Huntington has suggested:

> A revolution is a rapid, fundamental, and violent domestic change in the dominant values and myths of society, in its political institutions, social structure, leadership and government activity and policies. Revolutions are thus to be distinguished from insurrections, revolts, coups and wars of independence.[7]

Unfortunately, the distinctions Huntington proposes in the last sentence are not always easily made. For example, "wars of independence" such as Algeria's and Angola's (sometimes called "wars of national liberation") are widely considered authentic social revolutions because they ushered in fundamental societal change.[8] On the other hand, Theda Skocpol accepts Huntington's starting definition, but narrows it somewhat by claiming that "social revolutions are accompanied and in part effectuated through [massive] class upheavals."[9] She adds:

> Social revolutions are set apart from other sorts of conflicts . . . by the combination of two coincidences: the coincidence of societal structural change with class upheaval; and the coincidence of the political with social transformation.[10]

Skocpol concedes that according to her more restrictive, class-based definition, only "a handful of successful social revolutions have ever occurred." The most clear-cut cases are the three she has studied in great detail: France (1789), Russia (1917), and China (1911 to 1949). Other, less restrictive definitions of revolution encompass Mexico, Bolivia, Cuba, Nicaragua, Peru, Algeria, Ethiopia, Mozambique, Angola, Eritrea, Vietnam, Kampuchea, Turkey, Libya, Egypt, and Iran. What is common to all of these is that insurgency brought sweeping changes to the country's political, economic, and social structures.

It is because revolutions involve a fundamental transfer of political and economic power, rather than merely rearranging the chairs at the captain's table (as most military coups do), that they are invariably violent. Not surprisingly, government officials and social classes that have long held power (and perhaps oppressed the majority) and who now face uncertain futures normally fight bitterly to stay on top. Should the revolutionaries triumph, old elites will be removed from power, new ones will be installed, and, at least in some respects, there will be a broadening of political, economic, and social participation to include those further down the social ladder. This does not imply that revolutionary governments are democratic—they virtually never are. But they are almost always more broadly participatory and egalitarian than the regimes that they toppled.

I will classify as a revolution any insurgency that brings about such comprehensive political and socioeconomic changes. The upheaval may be rooted in class struggle (China and Nicaragua), as Skocpol insists, or, contrary to Huntington, it may be a war of national liberation (Algeria and Mozambique), so long as it overturns critical political and economic institutions and changes the country's underlying power structure. In fact, the borderline between nationalist and class-based revolutions is often difficult to discern. The Vietnamese revolution most clearly combined anticolonial and class struggle.[11] But even primarily class-based revolutions, such as China's, Mexico's, Cuba's, and Nicaragua's, had important, nationalist, anti-imperialist elements to them.

Revolutions may be Marxist (China, Vietnam, Kampuchea, and Cuba), partially Marxist (Nicaragua), or non-Marxist (Mexico, Bolivia, Libya, Algeria, and Iran). Marxism has been particularly appealing to many revolutionaries because it has promised the redistribution of economic resources, the ideological rigor, and the new set of political myths that they seek. But the revolutionary's vision of social justice need not be tied to Communism, it also may come from nationalism, Islam, or a number of other ideologies.

Revolutions generally come to power through mass uprisings, featuring strikes, protest marches, and street riots (Russia, Bolivia, and Iran), or through guerrilla warfare (China, Vietnam, and Cuba), or a combination of both (Nicaragua). There also have been, however, a few elite revolutions in which military officers or upper-level bureaucrats have overthrown the regime and instituted far-reaching socioeconomic changes that far transcend the objectives of mere coups.[12] Primary examples include Mustafa Kemal Ataturk's revolt in Turkey in 1919, Abdel Gamal Nasser's officer's revolt in Egypt in 1952, and Peru's "revolution from above" in 1968, all led by progressive military officers (see Chapter 8).

UNDERLYING CAUSES OF REVOLUTION

Just as experts have failed to agree on a common definition of revolution, they have also been divided as to the causes of revolutionary insurrection. Some theories focus on broad historical trends, including changes in the world order, that their proponents believe make revolution likely or even inevitable. Other explanations center on weaknesses in the ancien régime (the old political order), looking for factors that caused the prerevolutionary state to fall. And yet others focus on the major player in Third World revolutions, the peasantry, asking what factors cause them to revolt.

Inexorable Historical Forces

Karl Marx viewed revolution as an inexorable historical force growing out of class inequalities that are rooted in unequal ownership of the means of production. Those who command the economic system, he argued, control the state as well. Over time, subordinated classes will become alienated from the political-economic system and attain sufficient political skills and vision (class consciousness) to overthrow the existing order. Thus, Marx maintained, the British Revolution (or Civil War) of 1640 and the French Revolution were carried out by the ascendent bourgeoisie in order to topple the ancien régime controlled by the aristocracy and landed oligarchy. Both revolutions were part of a broader European transition from agrarian feudalism to industrial capitalism. Although Marx recognized that the new capitalist order represented a more advanced and productive stage in history, he insisted that it still depended on the exploitation of the working class. In time, he predicted, as the exploitation of the proletariat became more manifest and as workers developed sufficient class consciousness, they would overthrow capitalism and install revolutionary socialism.[13]

More than any other revolutionary theorist, Marx influenced the course of history, since most of the twentieth-century's influential revolutionary leaders—including Lenin, Mao Zedong, Ho Chi Minh, Ché Guevara, and Fidel Castro—were guided by his ideas. His writings evoked the centrality of class struggle in most revolutionary movements. But, as even sympathetic analysts have noted, "he was, first and foremost a nineteenth century man" whose ideology was closely linked to the era in which he lived.[14] "Marx's theoretical approach," wrote one contemporary Marxist sociologist, "enabled him to explain the past but failed him in his predictions."[15] Thus, no country has ever had the succession of revolutions that he predicted, first capitalist, then socialist.[16] Indeed, the major locus of twentieth-century revolution was the Third World—not advanced capitalist nations—and the major protagonists have been peasants rather than industrial workers.

Mao Zedong, the father of the Chinese Revolution, accepted Marx's view of revolution as part of a historical dialectic. Like other Third World Marxists, he continued to view capitalist exploitation and the resultant class conflict as the root cause of Communist upheavals. However, the Chinese Communists' record of failure in the 1920s convinced him that their orthodox commitment to proletariat revolution was not viable in a country in which the working class constituted such a small percentage of the population. Consequently, he reinterpreted Marxist revolutionary strategy so as to make it more applicable to China and other parts of the developing world. Mao developed a theory of peasant-based struggle and a military strategy designed to encircle and conquer China's cities following a period of protracted rural guerrilla warfare.[17] The success of his strategy in the world's most populous country and its application elsewhere in the Third World make Mao the greatest twentieth-century practitioner of revolutionary warfare.

In Vietnam and Cuba, Ho Chi Minh and Ché Guevara refined Mao's vision of "peoples' wars" to make it more compatible with conditions in Southeast Asia and Latin America. While all of them demonstrated that Communist revolutions could take place in countries that are not highly industrialized (Cuba came closest to Marx's ideal), they still adhered to Marx's theory of history and his vision of class struggle.

Regime Decay

Even before the collapse of the Soviet bloc, it had become obvious that there was no irreversible march toward revolution and that, in fact, revolutions are rather rare and unique events. Theta Skocpol, herself a Marxist, argues that neither the repression of the masses nor the skills of revolutionary leadership alone can bring about successful social revolutions. These factors may be necessary, but they are not sufficient. Rather, revolutions only succeed when the state is undermined by international pressures such as war, economic competition, or an arms race. Modernization of Britain and other European powers, she contends, created severe military and economic pressures on less developed countries within and outside of Europe. Some of those states, such as royalist France, czarist Russia, and imperial China, were less able to adjust to these challenges and, hence, were more susceptible to revolutionary challenges.[18]

In the Russian case, excessive military entanglements, foreign indebtedness, and the disastrous entry into World War I undermined the czarist state. Successive military defeats in two wars, first by the Japanese (1905) and then by the Germans (1917), did in the regime. Similarly, China's Manchu dynasty, having been fatally weakened first by European and then Japanese imperialism, was toppled easily by Guomindang (Nationalist) forces in 1911. Elsewhere, stronger regimes were able to withstand comparable challenges, but the Russian and Chinese states were too weak to marshal sufficient economic and military resources. Ultimately, peasant rebels led by "marginal elites" (university students and middle-class professionals alienated from the system) toppled the old order.[19] Ironically, much as military competition undermined the Czarist government and set the stage for the Russian Revolution, some 70 years later the Soviet-American arms race weakened the USSR and encouraged its collapse.

Thus, Skocpol and others have argued that the primary factor contributing to revolutionary transformation is not the revolutionaries' strategy, tactics, or zeal, but rather the internal rot of the decaying old regime. For example, Japan's invasion of China prior to World War II undercut the legitimacy of the Nationalist government. The Japanese occupation demonstrated that the Nationalists were too corrupt and incompetent to resist, while the People's Liberation Army (the Communist guerrillas) were far more effective. When the Chinese Revolution resumed after World War II, the areas where the Communists won their major military victories were often the same ones in which they had organized mass resistance against the Japanese.[20]

Indeed, military defeat and the resulting delegitimation of the regime in power have frequently set the stage for subsequent revolutions. The destruction of the Ottoman empire in World War I and the Japanese invasions of British, French, and Dutch colonies (Burma, Vietnam, and Indonesia) during World War II all led to revolutions of various sorts.[21] Similarly, Egypt's defeat at the hands of Israel (1948 to 1949) set the stage for Nasser's "elite revolution." War frequently has the additional effect of disrupting life for the peasantry, many of whom then seek physical protection by the revolutionary forces and a new social structure. For example, in several accounts of life in rural China during the civil war and Japanese invasion, "one is struck by the number of peasants . . . who had their routines upset through the [war-related] death of their kin before they joined revolutionary organizations."[22]

But governments may be undermined by factors other than military defeat. In Cuba and Nicaragua prolonged dictatorships became obscenely corrupt. Fulgencio Batista rose from the rank of army sergeant to become Cuba's dominant political actor in 1933. Under his administration and those of others he dominated, corruption infested all ranks of his government, with the national lottery becoming a center of graft. Batista's links to the American Mafia helped turn Havana into a playground for affluent tourists seeking gambling and prostitution. Over the years Nicaragua's Somoza dynasty seized a large portion of the national economy while their National Guard engaged in more petty graft, like the interception and sale of earthquake relief materials sent from the United States.

A further factor undermining the legitimacy of both dictatorships was their subservience to the United States and their violations of national pride. In countries that had undergone U.S. military occupation early in the twentieth century and that had remained firmly in the American sphere of influence, this was a particularly sensitive issue. Nicaragua's hated National Guard (first headed by Somoza's father) had been created during the U.S. Marine occupation. Decades later, the younger Somoza, a West Point graduate, was derisively referred to as "the last Marine." In both countries the combination of rampant corruption and blatant affronts to nationalist sensibilities united people across classes—from peasants and students to powerful businessmen—against the government. Lacking real commitment to the regime, Batista's undisciplined army offered surprisingly little resistance to Fidel Castro's small guerrilla force. In Nicaragua, Somoza's National Guardsmen—knowing that little good was in store for them if they lost—put up a stronger fight against the Sandinistas, but also fell relatively quickly.[23]

Revolutionary opportunities also may develop when the economy deteriorates, standards of living decline, and the government is unable to meet long-standing economic responsibilities to its population. For example, the position of China's Guomindang government was eroded by runaway inflation. Declining living standards also helped spark the Kenyan rebellion against British colonialism. Thus, maintains Charles Tilly, one cause of revolution is "the sudden failure of government to meet specific obligations which members of the subject population regarded as well established and crucial to their welfare."[24]

While Skocpol, Tilly, and others have focused on the decay of state authority at the national level, revolutions can also be linked to the breakdown of authority at the grass-roots level. We observed earlier (in Chapter 5) that the web of patron-client relationships linking peasants to their landlords and other local power brokers helps maintain stability in the countryside. Peasants may accept a high degree of injustice if the village political boss or the local landlord can compensate by providing the villagers with badly needed benefits. If, however, rural patrons become unwilling or unable to continue providing benefits the peasants have come to expect, then their authority will break down. At this point, the state may step in to replace traditional patrons or, if the state is also unable to provide that function, revolutionary groups may become the peasants' new political patron.

Challenge from Below

Revolutionary movements can only succeed against discredited or weakened governments, but to win they must also mount a well-organized and politically coherent challenge from below. Otherwise, the old regime—weak though it may be—will either remain in power (the Third World is full of incompetent and discredited governments that linger on) or it will collapse into semianarchy (as Somalia did after its longstanding dictator fell).

Tilly contends that three things must happen before a revolutionary movement can succeed. First, the revolutionaries must establish themselves as a competing political force offering an alternative sovereignty, that is, a viable, contending government. Second, significant portions of the population must support the revolutionary alternative. Third, the established government must be unable to suppress the revolutionary opposition.[25] Following the collapse of the czarist regime, for example, the Russian Bolsheviks established workers' Soviets (Communist political committees) to challenge the sovereignty of Alexander Karensky's provisional government. And Asia's protracted guerrilla wars illustrate this point particularly well. During the Chinese Revolution, the Red Army established extensive "liberated zones" under communist control. There, the party distributed land to the peasants and instituted other grass-roots reforms, thereby successfully presenting itself to the peasantry as an alternative government. In South Vietnam, the National Liberation Front (Viet Cong) behaved similarly.

But what causes a revolution to break out in a particular place and time? Samuel Huntington maintains that the probability of mass upheaval is measured by the balance between the capabilities of state political institutions on the one hand, and the extent of political and social mobilization on the other. Most revolutions, he notes, occur neither in highly traditional societies nor in very modern ones. Rather, they are most likely to erupt in modernizing countries—those in transition from traditional culture to modernity.[26] In such countries, as greater urbanization, education, and related social changes raise the level of political mobilization, civil society makes increased demands on the political system. Unless appropriate institutions capable of accommodating this increased political participation can be developed in a timely fashion, the system will invariably become more unstable.

Huntington then distinguishes two distinct revolutionary patterns: a "Western" model in which "the political institutions of the old regime collapse . . . followed by the mobilization of new groups into politics and then by the creation of new [revolutionary] political institutions" (i.e., regime decay precedes a full challenge from below); and an "Eastern" revolutionary model that "begins with the mobilization of new groups into politics and the creation of new [revolutionary] political institutions and ends with the violent overthrow of the political institutions of the old order." The French, Russian, and Mexican Revolutions fit the Western model, as did the fall of China's Manchu Dynasty. Communist revolutions in China and Vietnam illustrate the Eastern model.[27]

James C. Davies turns from the broad historical-social forces that make revolution possible to the question of why particular individuals choose to join an uprising, revolt, or revolution. He asserts that, contrary to what we might expect, people do not rebel when they are experiencing prolonged or permanent suffering. "Far from making people revolutionaries, enduring poverty makes for concern with one's solitary self or solitary family, at best a resignation, or mute despair at worst."[28]

To seek the source of political upheavals, Davies combines economic and psychological explanations. Drawing upon historical data for Dorr's Rebellion (an 1842 workers' uprising in Rhode Island), the Russian Revolution, and the Egyptian Revolution of 1952, he concludes that each uprising was first preceded by a period of sustained economic growth followed by a sharp downturn (Fig. 7.1). Unlike Marx, Skocpol, or Tilly, Davies lumps together small uprisings (Dorr's Rebellion), elite military "revolutions" (Egypt), and mass revolutions (Russia) in his "J-curve" theory.[29]

As a country's economy grows for a period of time, he suggests, people's expectations rise correspondingly (parallel to the long side of the J). However, those expectations continue to rise even after the economy enters its downturn. What emerges is "an intolerable gap between what people want and what they get."[30] Davies argues that the American and French revolutions, the American Civil War, the rise of German Naziism, student unrest in the United States during the 1960s, and the African-American civil rights movement can all be explained by economic J-curves as well.[31] Using twentieth-century data from 17 LDCs, Raymond Tanter and Manus Midlarsky confirmed Davies's thesis in Asia and the Middle East, but not in Latin America. Moreover, their Asian and Middle Eastern cases indicated that the higher the rate of economic growth prior to a downturn and the sharper the slide immediately preceding a revolution, the longer and more violent the subsequent upheaval.[32]

Davies's theory is one of the most influential, psychologically based explanations of revolutionary behavior. There is, however, an important limitation to his findings. His conclusions were based entirely on countries in which revolts or revolutions took place. That raises the question of whether there are countries that did not have social upheavals despite having experienced a J-curve in their economies. In fact, Davies admits that there are. He notes the absence of mass unrest in the United States during the Great Depression, a period of devastating economic downturn.

Mexico's experience over the past half-century offers a more contemporary contradiction. After nearly four decades of solid growth, Mexico's economy turned sharply downward in the 1980s, lowering popular living standards more than 30 percent. Contrary to Davies's theory, however, there was remarkably little political violence or mass unrest in the 1980s. In 1994, a rural uprising in the state of Chiapas shook the political system, but that occurred after the national economy had begun to improve. Moreover, though symbolically important, the Chiapas uprising was limited to a very small and remote area and never threatened to topple the system.

Most of the other Latin American countries also enjoyed strong economic growth from the 1950s through 1970s, followed by a severe economic crisis in the 1980s that lowered living standards substantially. Yet, once again, popular unrest was generally quite limited (with the notable exceptions of Peru and El Salvador). Thus, as Davies concedes, his theory identifies necessary but not sufficient conditions for unrest. While a J-curve often leads to revolution, it is not a reliable predictor of mass insurrection.

Ted Gurr has also developed a psychological model involving the gap between people's expectations and reality. Like Davies, he seeks to explain all types of civil violence, not just revolution. Gurr argues that "the necessary precondition for violent civil conflict is relative deprivation defined as actors' perception of the discrepancy between their value expectations [i.e., what people believe they deserve from life] and value capabilities . . . conditions that determine people's perceived chances of getting . . . what they . . . expect to attain."[33]

Unlike Davies, however, Gurr's notion of relative deprivation is not only economic. Thus, he posits that there will be civil unrest if large numbers of people are deprived of something they have come to expect or if they have suffered

Figure 7.1 Davies's psychological model showing the gap between people's expectations and economic reality.

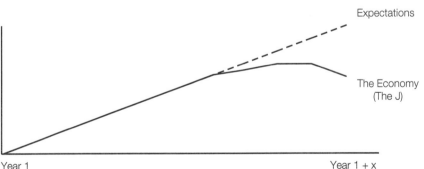

a blow to their status or their preferred social order. For example, the Shah's attempts to modernize the status and dress of Iranian women was admired in the West but it violated the worldview of the Shi'ite population. The closer people are to attaining their goals, says Gurr, the greater will be their frustration if they fail to achieve it. Note, for example, the intensified frustration of West Bank and Gaza Palestinians as PLO-Israeli talks over their future dragged on.

Finally, Gurr observes that the type of civil violence a country experiences will depend on which segments of society are experiencing relative deprivation. If the poor are the only ones frustrated, there may be political "turmoil" (spontaneous, disorganized violence) but not a revolution. Only when elites—more educated and politically experienced individuals who can provide leadership—also suffer relative deprivation can there be revolutionary upheaval (organized, instrumental violence).

Conclusion

None of the major theories of revolution offer a single "correct" explanation. For one thing, they often focus on different aspects of the issue. Thus, while Gurr and Davies ask why individuals join revolutionary movements or revolts, Skocpol focuses on the international economic and military factors that have weakened the state prior to successful revolutionary insurrections.

Clearly no revolution is inevitable and successful ones are rare. While the causes of unrest may lie in relative deprivation and the regime's loss of legitimacy, the ultimate success or failure of revolutionary movements depends on the relative capabilities of the contending forces. Only by evaluating the political-military strength of those who rebel compared to the state's capacity to defend itself can we understand why some revolutionary movements succeed while others fail.

As we have seen, major revolutions often occur after a country has been defeated in war (as in Russia, China, Bolivia, Turkey, and Egypt) or its government has been ousted temporarily (as Europe's colonial powers in East and Southeast Asia were during World War II). They may also break out when a government is particularly corrupt (as in Cuba and Nicaragua) or especially oppressive (as in Mexico and Iran).

In all of these cases the incumbent regime had lost its legitimacy (what the Chinese and Vietnamese called "the mandate of heaven"). Thus, the czarist and Guomindang governments both fell when they proved incapable of defending their people's sovereignty. Similarly, Batista lost his authority when he turned Havana into "the brothel of the Caribbean." So too did the Shah after his Westernization program offended Iran's Islamic mullahs. British, French, and Dutch colonial rule in Asia had rested, in part, on the local population's belief that Europeans were very powerful and better equipped to govern. When the Japanese ousted colonial governments in Burma, Malaysia, Vietnam, and Indonesia, they demonstrated that Asians could defeat Europeans at their own game. Consequently, restoring colonialism after World War II proved impossible.

Finally, the authoritarian nature of many Third World states also may ulti-mately undermine them. Batista, the Shah, and Somoza illustrate that point. Because their governments had never been legitimized through free and honest elections, they could not convincingly claim to represent the people. Overlook-ing that danger throughout the Cold War, the United States frequently supported authoritarian governments in such far-flung places as Paraguay, Cuba, Nicaragua, Chile, Zaire (Congo), Somalia, South Korea, Iran, and Pakistan. When criticized by human rights groups, U.S. spokespersons implicitly or explicitly responded that "if we don't support these governments, more repressive revolutionary regimes will seize power." While this was probably true in some instances, more generally democracy actually offers the best inoculation against revolution. One of the few rules about revolution that holds true universally is this: there has never been a successful revolution launched against a democratic government.

LEVELS OF POPULAR SUPPORT

Ché Guevara, the leading military strategist of Cuba's guerrilla insurrection, once commented that when one engages in revolution, one either wins or dies. Though overstating his point a bit, Guevara effectively highlighted the tremendous risk revolutionary fighters undertake, be they poor peasants or radicalized univer-sity students. Rebels almost always face superior gun power and a range of repressive state institutions (secret police, the military, etc.). Not surprisingly, in most instances the insurgents lose. One study of Latin American insurrection counted 28 guerrilla movements operating from 1956 to 1990. Of these, only 2 succeeded (Cuba's July 26 Movement and Nicaragua's Sandinistas).[34] Asia and Africa are also littered with the bodies of dead revolutionaries from failed insur-gencies. Even victorious revolutions, such as Vietnam's and China's, leave behind vast numbers of fallen fighters and supporters. Those who survive often return home to devastated villages and suffering families. Not surprisingly, then, the personal decision to engage in revolution is not taken lightly.

How much of the population must support a revolution if it is to suc-ceed? What type of people are most likely to join the movement? The answer to the first question is quite ambiguous. There is no fixed or knowable pro-portion of the population that must support an insurrection in order for it to triumph. Following World War II, a majority of Ukrainians probably favored a separatist movement fighting the Soviet government, but the uprising was still crushed by the powerful Red army. On the other hand, insurgencies have succeeded elsewhere with the active support of less than 20 percent of the civil-ian support.

To evaluate public opinion during a revolutionary upheaval, it is useful to distinguish between at least five different groups in the civilian population. First, there are those who strongly support the government and believe that their fate is linked to the regime's survival. Government officials, military officers, sol-diers, land owners, and business people with close links to the state often fall in this group. It may also include ethnic groups tied to the regime (such as the Hmong people in Laos), people ideologically committed to the system, and a variety of other people with a vested interest in preserving the status quo.

A second group in society also supports the government, but more conditionally. For example, during the 1960s, most Venezuelans backed the administration that was fighting pro-Cuban guerrillas. A plurality of them had voted for the government in democratic elections and many belonged to the governing Acción Democrática party or its affiliated labor and peasant unions. To be sure, many also shared the guerrillas' criticisms of Venezuelan society (gross inequalities, squalid urban shantytowns, and the like), but they strongly objected to the insurgents' indiscriminate use of violence.[35] Had the government mishandled the insurrection and, like other Latin American regimes, become highly repressive, its broad level of mild popular support undoubtedly would have declined.

A third, often critical, segment of the population supports neither the revolutionaries nor the government, either being apathetic or disliking both sides. Large numbers of Indian peasant communities in the highlands of Peru were brutalized in 1980s and 1990s by the Shining Path (Sendero Luminoso) guerrillas, an extremely fanatical and brutal Maoist movement. Many were victimized by the Peruvian army, whose repressive tactics were condemned by human rights observers. It appears that most peasants wished a plague on both their houses. Elsewhere, even in less harsh environments, most citizens, particularly those in the line of fire, studiously avoid taking sides for their own preservation.

A fourth group, drawn largely from peasants, workers, the urban poor, and alienated members of the middle class, sympathizes with the revolutionary cause and may lend occasional support. For example, many peasants in Cuba and Vietnam offered food and shelter to guerrilla units and warned them when the army was coming. In countries such as China and El Salvador, where the guerrillas controlled "liberated zones" for an extended period of time, such support networks grew quite large. Even after the signing of the Salvadorian peace treaty, when the FMLN guerrillas shifted to the electoral arena, peasant support for their candidates has remained high in many of their old revolutionary strongholds. In cases where the revolution is based on mass insurrection rather than a guerrilla war (such as Iran) or a mixture of the two (such as Nicaragua), urban sympathizers are critical actors in street demonstrations and rallies.

Finally, there is a relatively small minority of the population that actively involves itself in the revolutionary struggle for an extended period. In Cuba, Nicaragua, and Peru, for example, committed students, teachers, and professionals have assumed leadership positions. Many peasants (including women and teenagers) in China, Vietnam, and El Salvador have provided the revolution's foot soldiers. Some join out of desperation, because their village has been destroyed by the armed forces or because they fear being drafted into an army they despise. Others are attracted by the revolutionaries' promises of land reform, education, and a more just social order.

To succeed, revolutionary leaders must attract a core of firmly committed activists, willing to risk their lives for the cause, as well as a larger circle of secondary supporters. How large their numbers must be depends on the extent of government decay and loss of legitimacy. It also depends on how well armed government troops are, how effectively they fight, and how much foreign support the government has. Fidel Castro's rural force of only a few hundred troops (supported by some urban guerrillas) easily defeated Batista's much larger but dispirited army. But El Salvador's far larger and better-equipped guerrilla army could not unseat a government bolstered by extensive United States economic and military aid. Yet, even the commitment of great numbers of U.S. troops and massive military assistance could not save the South Vietnamese government from the Viet Cong and its North Vietnamese supporters.

An equally important target population for the revolutionary leadership are the people in the second category (mild government supporters) and the third (neutrals). In Third World countries with large urban populations (including Iran and much of Latin America), a government can maintain power in the face of considerable peasant unrest and rural guerrilla warfare so long as the regime controls the cities and retains the support of the urban middle class. It is particularly crucial that it maintains support from civil servants, businesspeople, and professionals. Although those middle-class groups are not normally very radical, they can become disenchanted with especially corrupt, repressive, and ineffectual regimes. In Iran, the tide turned in favor of the revolutionary mullahs when Tehran's bazaar shopkeepers lost confidence in the Shah's government.

The Sandinista Revolution also illustrates this point well. Because the Somoza family grabbed such a large portion of the Nicaraguan economy, their greed adversely affected not only the poor, but prosperous businesspeople as well. As the Sandinista uprising spread, and as the National Guard became more openly repressive, the business community increasingly criticized the government. Highly visible committees of business leaders demanded Somoza's resignation. Their ranks included the head of the country's Coca-Cola bottling plant, its most prominent publishing family (the Chamorros), and the largest supermarket and cooking oil magnate. These people were wary of the Sandinistas (who made no secret of their leftist ideology), but shared their objective of ousting Somoza.[36]

While flying from Panama to Miami during the height of the Nicaragua insurrection, I found myself seated next to a wealthy Nicaraguan chemical plant executive who held an engineering degree from M.I.T. "What do you think is going to happen back home?" I asked in a noncommittal manner. "Somoza has to go," he replied, "he's too damned corrupt and he's wrecking the country." "But what if you [i.e., reformist business leaders] have to share power with the Sandinistas after he goes?" I persisted.[37] "I don't like those guys," said he, "but if sharing power with them is what it takes to get rid of Somoza, then we'll have to do it." It was clear to me at that point that the Somoza government was doomed.

In short, for a revolution to take place there must be wide-scale disaffection with the government in power, disaffection that reaches beyond the ranks of the poor and the oppressed to the heart of the middle class and even the business community. It is not likely, nor is it necessary, that a huge portion of the disaffected actively support the revolution, only that some do (including a highly committed core) while many more, like that Nicaraguan executive, simply cease supporting the government.

PEASANTS AS REVOLUTIONARIES

Let us now turn our attention to the ranks of the active revolutionary supporters, particularly the last group, revolutionary activists. One of the most widely accepted observations about Third World revolutions is that they are fought largely by peasants. Iran is the exception. There the Shah was toppled as the result of urban street demonstrations and protests. Urban populations in Mexico, Bolivia, Cuba, and Nicaragua played key roles as street demonstrators, guerrillas, or revolutionary soldiers as well. But in each case peasants were of equal or greater importance. In Africa and Asia, revolutionary movements have been overwhelmingly rural in character. The Chinese Red Army and the Viet Cong, for example, were manned overwhelmingly by peasants. Consequently, it is important to ask, "What factors induce peasants to risk joining a revolution and what type of peasants join?"

Why Peasants Rebel

In our earlier discussion of Third World rural society (see Chapter 5), we noted that traditional peasant culture tends to be rather conservative. Since major economic and political changes frequently affect villagers adversely, they have good reason to cling to tradition. The intrusion of market forces into their communities, however, sometimes so unsettles their world that it radicalizes them. On the one hand, increasing numbers of subsistence farmers (i.e., peasants producing primarily for their own families) are induced, pressured, or forced by the government to enter the commercial market for the first time. Once involved in commercial agriculture, they often experience volatile price fluctuations for their crops, shifts for which they are ill prepared.

At the same time, rural landlords, whose exploitation of the peasantry in traditional society was constrained by their reciprocal obligations, come to view their tenants merely as factors of production in the new market economy. Hacienda owners who previously funded their peons' fiestas often conclude that such expenditures are no longer financially prudent in a more competitive market environment. Other landlords entering the commercial market may decide to mechanize production and evict tenant farmers from their land.

For all of these reasons, rural society's transition from neofeudal to capitalist production precipitated several Third World revolutions in the twentieth century.[38] James Scott notes that the injury that peasants suffer during that transformation is not merely economic or physical, it is also a moral hurt. To be sure, the precapitalist rural order was full of grave injustices. But those inequities were somewhat mitigated by a web of reciprocal obligations among peasants and between landlords and peasants. It is the collapse of that "moral economy," he argues, that drives many peasants to revolution.[39] Similarly, Eric Wolf insists that in countries as disparate as Cuba, Mexico, Algeria, Vietnam, and China, peasants participating in revolutions were not trying to create a new socialist order. Rather, they were seeking to restore the security of their traditional way of life.

Which Peasants Rebel

Even in a single country or region, peasants are not a homogeneous mass. Some, referred to as Kulaks, own larger plots of land and employ other peasants to work their land with them. Others are landless or own extremely small plots. And still others work as wage laborers on large estates or rent parcels of land from the landlord, paying their rent in cash, labor, or sharecropping.[40] Each group of peasants has distinct political and economic needs.

Those whose security is most threatened by economic change are the most likely to join revolutionary movements or more limited uprisings. Analyzing data collected from 70 developing nations during the period 1948 to 1970, Jeffrey M. Paige concluded that the most likely peasant candidates for revolutionary insurgencies are sharecroppers and wage laborers who work for landlords that lack financial resources outside of their land.[41] These peasants are in a very precarious economic position yet their landlords are unlikely to make economic concessions to them. Research on Latin American guerrilla movements revealed that squatters (peasants illegally occupying land) and other peasants who face eviction from the land they cultivate also are more likely to support insurrections.[42] Peasants may also feel financially insecure because of weak crop prices. In Peru's Ayacucho province, the birthplace of the Shining Path guerrilla insurrection, peasants had experienced declining terms of trade for two decades (the cost of the goods they consumed had been rising faster than the price of the crops that they raised and sold). Caught in an ongoing financial squeeze, they were more receptive to Shining Path's appeals.[43]

All of the peasants who are more prone to support revolution, then, have one element in common—they are threatened with the loss of land and/or livelihood. Conversely, the most conservative peasants are those with secure title to their landholdings and relatively stable prices for their crops. It is for this reason that many analysts have argued that the best protection against revolution is an agrarian reform that distributes land, secure titles, and support services to the peasantry.

Peasant insurrection is also more likely in certain types of rural areas. The Chinese, Vietnamese, Cuban, and Nicaraguan guerrillas all received their greatest peasant support in regions that had a prior history of peasant resistance, what one author called a "rebellious culture."[44] Castro's home province, Oriente, referred to as "the cradle of the Cuban Revolution," had a history of unrest dating back to the nineteenth-century slave revolts against the Spanish. China's Hunan province (Mao's home) and the area around León in Nicaragua had similar records. Often, a related factor is a local history of lawlessness and hostility toward the legal authorities. For example, Pancho Villa operated in a region of Mexico long known for cattle rustling and banditry. Similarly, Cuba's guerrillas based themselves in the Sierra Maestra mountains, a region with a tradition of smuggling, marijuana growing, and banditry.

REVOLUTIONARY LEADERSHIP

Although peasants furnish the foot soldiers for revolution, rarely do they provide the leaders. They may stage spontaneous uprisings or even widespread revolts on their own, but they lack the organizational and political skills needed to conduct a broader social revolution. Consequently, both the upper echelons and the middle ranks of revolutionary leadership are usually occupied by people with more education and greater political experience. There are some exceptions to that rule. Mexico's Emiliano Zapata was a horse trainer from a peasant family who only learned to read when he was an adult.[45] More recently, the FARC guerrillas in Colombia have been led largely by peasants.[46] Ultimately, however, their lack of political experience proved costly. Zapata, for example, was outmaneuvered and killed by a rival revolutionary leader, Venustiano Carranza, a wealthy land owner.

More typically, the most prominent revolutionary figures come from middle-class or even upper-class backgrounds. In Latin America, at least, "they are drawn disproportionately from the intelligentsia, not only highly educated, but also largely involved in the production of theories."[47] Trained as a librarian, Mao Zedong was the son of a rural grain merchant. Ho Chi Minh, the son of a rural Mandarin family, practiced a number of professions, including photography, after completing his education. Ché Guevara was a doctor whose mother came from an aristocratic Argentine family and whose father was an architect. Fidel Castro received a law degree at the University of Havana, where he was a leader in student politics. His father, a Spanish immigrant, had started life in Cuba as a worker but eventually became a wealthy land owner. Most of the nine comandantes who directed the Sandinista revolution also were from solid middle- or upper-class families and were well educated. President Daniel Ortega and his brother, Defense Minister Humberto Ortega, were the sons of an accountant-businessman. Luis Carrión's father was a millionaire and he had attended an American prep school. Although one comandante, Henry Ruiz, came from a poor urban family, none of them were of peasant origin.[48] And a study of nearly 2,000 leading party activists conducted by the Vietnamese Communists after the second World War revealed that 74 percent were either intellectuals or of bourgeois background, 7 percent were workers, and only 19 percent came from peasant families.[49]

Peasants are more numerous at the middle and lower ranks of revolutionary leadership. Not surprisingly, they have been more broadly represented at all leadership levels in Asian nations such as China, Vietnam, and Kampuchea where peasants account for most of the population. During their two-decade revolutionary struggle, the Chinese Communist party and Red Army provided many avenues of upward mobility to activists of peasant origin. After 1928, peasants and children of peasants received preference in admission to the party. As late as 1985, decades after the Communist victory, one-third of all Communist party members were peasants (some 10 percent were illiterate).[50] Similarly, El Salvador's and Peru's guerrilla movements had a high proportion of lower- and middle-level leaders from peasant origins, although many of them first left their villages and entered teaching or similar occupations.

The educational and social gap separating the guerrilla leadership and the peasantry whom they hope to lead can be a considerable obstacle unless the leaders have a firm understanding of local peasant culture. Although Mao became something of an urban intellectual, his rural background had given him an understanding of Hunan's village culture. Fidel Castro was no peasant either, but his upbringing in Oriente province had familiarized him with the region's rural poor. In Venezuela, several of the FALN guerrilla commanders were sons of local landlords who traded on their fathers' patron-client ties to the nearby peasants.[51]

On the other hand, aspiring revolutionary leaders who came to the countryside from urban backgrounds or from other regions, countries, or ethnic backgrounds were likely to be rejected by the peasantry. The wider the linguistic, cultural, or racial gap between city and countryside and the greater the history of rural exploitation, the harder it is for guerrilla leaders to break through the peasants' wall of distrust toward outsiders. In Cuba, where racial or ethnic divisions were not strong, Ché Guevara was accepted by the peasants of the Sierra Maestra. So when he later ventured to Bolivia to spread the revolution, he was ill prepared for the tremendous suspicion its Aymara Indian peasants harbor toward white urban outsiders. There he was killed by an antiguerrilla unit of the Bolivian armed forces, aided by local peasants who saw no reason to risk their safety for an alien agitator. Similarly, Hector Béjar, a failed Peruvian guerrilla leader, later wrote candidly in his memoirs on how he—a coastal white journalist and poet—had great difficulty winning the trust of the highland Quechua-speaking Indian peasants whom he had hoped to lead.[52]

REVOLUTIONARIES IN POWER

While many comparative studies have examined the causes of revolution, there is far less cross-national research on the policies that revolutionary regimes implement once in office. Perhaps guerrilla fighters in the hills have inspired more sympathy and romance than have revolutionary bureaucrats in the corridors of power. The record suggests, however, that major Third World social revolutions have accomplished more than their detractors admit but less than their supporters claim.

Greater social, economic, and political equality has been a primary objective of Marxist and non-Marxist revolutionary regimes alike. That quest begins in the struggle to assume power, when revolutionary leaders use egalitarian appeals to garner support from peasants and workers at the bottom of the social ladder. Recognizing the critical importance of that support, Mao Zedong declared that the peasantry are to the guerrilla army what the ocean waters are to fish. To win their loyalty, the Red Army treated China's peasants with a respect that no previous military force or government had afforded them.[53] Similarly, in Cuba, "the army's brutal treatment of the peasants" contrasted with "Castro's policy of paying for the food purchased from the peasants . . . and putting his [mostly urban] men to work in the coffee fields."[54]

Once in power, revolutionaries have continued to emphasize equality. Along with redistribution of land and other economic resources, there is a cultural and psychological dimension as well. At meetings of the Committees for the Defense of the Revolution (CDRs) in Cuba, men are pressured to share in domestic work at home. New forms of address like compañero (comrade) as well as the universal use of the "familiar" grammatical form in speaking to others are designed to reduce long-standing class barriers. Cultural and social egalitarianism has been less pronounced in non-Marxist revolutions. Still, in countries such as Bolivia and Mexico there has been limited improvement in the Indian peasantry's social status relative to whites and mestizos.

As we have seen, revolutions open up new channels of upward social mobility for peasants and workers who previously had few such opportunities. The highest positions in the government and ruling party generally continue to be held by people from middle- to upper-class origins. Below them, however, many revolutionary activists from humble backgrounds hold lower- or middle-level political positions that they could never have attained under the old order. Revolutionary parties and mass organizations such as Mexico's National Peasant Confederation or Cuba's CDRs try to give peasants and workers a greater sense of participation in the political system.

Finally, revolutions tend to improve the degree of economic equality. The Bolivian, Mexican, Nicaraguan, Cuban, Chinese, and Vietnamese governments instituted agrarian reform programs that redistributed land from the rural oligarchy to the peasantry.[55] At the national level, Marxist regimes have generally achieved greater income equality than other LDCs at a comparable stage of economic development. Economic equality has been further enhanced by government subsidies for housing, transportation, food, and medical care, all designed to make them more accessible to the poor. In Cuba, for example, free medical care and mass inoculation programs appreciably improved health standards, particularly in the countryside (though those conditions have deteriorated during the post-Soviet economic collapse). On the other hand, centrist revolutions in Bolivia and Mexico have done little to improve income distribution or otherwise relieve economic inequality. Mexico, for example, retains one of the Third World's more inegalitarian patterns of income distribution.

It would be wrong to assume, however, that any revolution ever achieves full equality. The gaps between rural and urban populations are often narrowed but never eliminated. Skilled workers and professionals continue to get higher salaries than peasants or blue-collar workers even if that gap is also narrowed. At the same time, an insidious new form of inequality frequently seeps in. Newly entrenched party and government officials begin to appropriate special perquisites for themselves. In China, the Communist party cadre are well known for their fancy lifestyles and their children are hated for their arrogance. Algeria's revolutionary government quickly lost touch with the masses. Milovan Djilas, a disillusioned former leader of the Yugoslav revolution (who was jailed for his frank criticisms), warned of the rise of a "new class," an elite of party officials.[56]

Another major revolutionary objective has been mass political mobilization. As Samuel Huntington notes, "a full-scale revolution . . . involves the rapid and violent destruction of existing political institutions, the mobilization of new groups into politics, and the creation of new political institutions."[57] Thus, in China, Vietnam, Cuba, and Nicaragua, government incentives and pressures induced a large portion of the population to join revolutionary support groups.[58] At one time close to 90 percent of the Cuban population belonged to their neighborhood CDR.

At its best, mass mobilization has increased the government's capacity to build the economy (e.g., by mobilizing volunteer labor) and has been an effective vehicle for combating sexism, racism, and criminality. In its worst sense it has been used for vigilantism against alleged counterrevolutionaries and as a means of thought control. At CDR meetings members are familiarized with the current government political line, induced to volunteer for projects such as cutting sugar cane, and imbued with greater revolutionary consciousness.[59] In China under Mao, mass mobilization often involved brutal political campaigns asking millions of citizens to root out and punish alleged enemies of the revolution. Hundreds of thousands were persecuted, jailed, or killed in the "Anti-Rightist Campaign" (1957) and the Cultural Revolution (1966 to 1976).[60]

Mass mobilization is designed to isolate and control those citizens who do not support the revolution and to activate those who do or might. The revolutionary party usually stands at the center of the mobilization process. Most revolutionary regimes have created a dominant party, such as the Chinese Communist party or Mexico's PRI, whose identity is scarcely distinguishable from the government's. Opposition parties are usually prohibited or else are allowed only in a weakened condition. Among Marxist governments, only Nicaragua's Sandinista party allowed itself to be voted out of office. Elsewhere, a number of non-Marxist revolutionary parties have lost favor over time. They may either hand over the reins of power to the opposition and become just another competing party (as in Bolivia), resort to fraud when faced with the prospect of losing (as in Mexico until recently), or cancel elections that the opposition is expected to win (as in Algeria).

In short, while revolutionary regimes claim to speak for the people and in many respects often do, they are hardly ever democratic. Because they view themselves as the only legitimate voice of the popular will and the popular good, they tend to regard opposition groups as enemies of the people that should not be tolerated. There are, however, some exceptions. The Sandinista government allowed opposition parties and interest groups to function, though they were sometimes harassed. The opposition newspaper, *La Prensa*, was frequently censored or shut down for brief periods, but it continued to attack the Sandinista government bitterly up to the time that the paper's editor, Violeta Chamorro, was elected to the nation's presidency. For the most part, however, even those Communist governments that have opened up their economies to free-market reforms (China and Vietnam) have maintained a repressive Leninist political structure, intolerant of any opposition voices.

While the first generation of revolutionary leaders often comes to office full of idealism, they or the generation that succeeds them generally succumb in some way to the corruptions of power. In Vietnam and China—where today's private sector entrepreneurs depend on the government for licenses, raw materials, and the like—bribing the right state official has become a necessity of doing business.[61] Cubans, who felt that their government had upheld a higher level of honesty, were shocked when the Ochoa affair revealed that high-ranking security and military men were involved in drug deals (government corruption has become pervasive in the last decade following the country's economic collapse). And after the Sandinistas left office, disillusioned supporters learned that party officials had kept for themselves some of the fancy mansions confiscated from the Somoza regime. It is not that revolutionary regimes are necessarily more corrupt than other Third World governments; often they are less so. It is just that their followers, many of whom made considerable sacrifices for the cause, had expected more.

CONCLUSION

Throughout most of the twentieth century, revolutionary movements had a tremendous impact on the developing world. That influence was greatest in Asia, where the Chinese Revolution transformed the lives of one-fifth of humanity and where revolutionary struggles in Vietnam, Laos, and Kampuchea involved France and the United States in major wars. Failed communist insurgencies also had a great impact on other Asian nations such as the Philippines and Malaysia. In Africa, the majority of the region's revolutions have been anticolonial wars of national liberation (in Algeria, Angola, Mozambique, and Namibia) or secessionist wars (Eritrea and southern Sudan). The more class-related revolutions on the continent (including those of Egypt, Ethiopia, and Libya) were generally elite revolutions carried out by military officers.

Latin America has had two non-Marxist insurrections (in Bolivia and Mexico), two Marxist revolutions (in Cuba and Nicaragua), and several unsuccessful guerrilla movements (in El Salvador, Guatemala, Colombia, Uruguay, Venezuela, and Peru). Both the region's revolutions and its failed insurgencies have had spillover effects in neighboring countries. Thus, the Cuban Revolution spawned various agrarian reform programs elsewhere in Latin America, designed to avert the spread of revolution. The Nicaraguan Revolution inspired both agrarian reform and greater government repression in nearby El Salvador.

But as we enter the twenty-first century, the appeal of revolution, particularly of the Marxist variety, has waned considerably. Indeed, the world seems a graveyard of failed revolutions. The Soviet Union, considered the fountainhead of Communist revolution, lies in ruins and its primary successor state, Russia, struggles to survive the errors of its Bolshevik past. Communism is equally discredited in most of Eastern and Central Europe where it recently held sway. Cuba's government (like Nicaragua's before it) has seen its impressive earlier gains in education, health care, and social equality greatly eroded by a collapsed economy. And for many other recently fallen or still surviving Marxist and neo-Marxist revolutionary regimes, the score card of successes and failures is far more disheartening. Countries such as Afghanistan, Angola, Cambodia, Ethiopia, Mozambique, and Myanmar have suffered unbelievable devastation with little or nothing to show for it.

Evaluating the quality of revolutionary change elsewhere is more difficult, for it is complicated by the analyst's ideological lenses and the difficulty of isolating the effects of revolutionary policy from a host of other intersecting factors. For example, critics of the Chinese Revolution argue that the socioeconomic gains attained under Mao were achieved in spite of his policies, not because of them. They further insist that the country's rapid economic growth under Deng Xiaoping merely demonstrates the advantages of free-market reforms. Others maintain that Cuba's substantial gains in health care and education since its revolution have been no more impressive than Costa Rica's and that they only were accomplished with the benefit of massive Soviet aid.

On the other hand, revolutionary sympathizers contend that Cuba's economic problems were caused largely by the United States' economic embargo and that the American-backed Contra war (coupled with a trade embargo) destroyed the Nicaraguan revolution's previous economic and social accomplishments. Neither side can prove that it is right nor can it demolish the other side's arguments because too much of its case is based on hypotheses about how things might have been if history were different.

It is likely that the age of revolution is drawing to an end in the Third World. The demise of Soviet and Eastern European communism exposed more clearly the deficiencies of Marxism-Leninism. So too has China's and Vietnam's acceptance of many free-market (capitalist) elements into their economic policies.[62] As communism has been discredited, even among many of its once-fervent adherents, its capacity to attract new revolutionary fighters, people willing to risk their lives fighting for the Marxist-Leninist ideal, has diminished sharply. Communist and other nondemocratic ideologies, once chic among Third

World intellectuals and political activists, have ceased being fashionable.[63] For example, in the face of armed resistance to its rule, Afghanistan's People's Democratic Party renounced its former Marxist ideology in a failed effort to maintain power. One Afghan leader tried to explain away the party's earlier communist beliefs by explaining that they had been adopted at "a time when Marxism-Leninism was quite in fashion in underdeveloped countries." In southern Africa, where Angola's governing party was making a comparable conversion, the nation's president warned that continuing to support the Marxist-Leninist model "would be rowing against the tide [of democracy]."[64] Similar transformations have occurred within Nicaragua's Sandinista party and El Salvador's FMLN, both former revolutionary movements that subsequently transformed themselves into democratic political parties.

How many revolutionary upheavals will take place in the coming years is hard to predict and the answer is partially a matter of semantics (i.e., how one chooses to define a revolution). However, now that colonialism has come to an end in Africa and Asia, and South Africa has adopted majority rule, there is little possibility of wars of national liberation as we have known them.

Class-based revolutions remain a possibility in societies that suffer from large socioeconomic inequities, sharp rural-urban divisions, and nonresponsive governments. However, as we have noted, the collapse of the Soviet bloc, the abandonment of Marxist economics in China and other Leninist states in Asia, the failure of the Nicaraguan revolutionary government, and Cuba's current economic crisis have all substantially diminished the appeal of revolutionary Marxism. For example, El Salvador's FMLN guerrillas ended their 12-year struggle, signing a peace treaty that gave them some, but not all, of the reforms they had long fought for. Similarly, the Sandinistas, who also function as a legitimate opposition party in Nicaragua, have moved somewhat toward the political center and moderated their revolutionary rhetoric.[65] Marxist guerrilla groups continue to battle in Peru (where they appear to be quite weakened) and Colombia (where, supported by cocaine and protection money, they remain quite strong), but neither there or in the other LDCs where such movements persist do their chances for success seem very promising. In the impoverished southern Mexican state of Chiapas, the Zapatista (EZLN) insurrection attracted considerable support from Mexicans of all social classes. But the EZLN has clearly expressed its preference for working within the framework of a more democratic political system and has not carried out any armed attacks to speak of since the first few days of 1994 when it burst onto Mexico's political scene. Nobody, including its supporters, believe it has the capability of mounting a revolutionary movement.

Undoubtedly, most internal war in the coming decades will be ethnically based, involving movements that seek to secede or to gain greater rights for their people. Insurgencies of this type are most likely to occur in Africa and Southeast and South Asia. They also could conceivably involve uprisings by indigenous peoples in Latin America. Whether these movements can properly be called revolutions, however, is uncertain. They satisfy neither Huntington's nor Skocpol's definition. Hence, it is probably more accurate to call them civil wars, secessionist movements, or ethnic conflicts, rather than revolutions.

DISCUSSION QUESTIONS

1. What are some of the major factors that have led to the collapse of state power and the rise of revolutions?

2. What factors account for the declining likelihood of further Third World revolutions?

3. Discuss some of the psychological theories of revolution (i.e., the theories of James C. Davies or Ted Robert Gurr).

4. What segments of the population are more likely to support revolutionary movements and how much support do such movements need in order to succeed?

5. Discuss some of the major accomplishments and failures of revolutionary governments.

NOTES

1. Hannah Arendt, *On Revolution* (New York: Viking Press, 1963), p. 13.

2. China's Leninist regime remains in place but the principles of Marxist economics and class politics have been abandoned.

3. In Angola and Mozambique most of the killing was carried out by counterrevolutionary forces. For the hundreds of thousands of innocent civilians butchered, however, it mattered little which side killed them.

4. One classical study of historical change argues that the American war of independence was not a revolution. See Barrington Moore, Jr., *The Social Origins of Dictatorship and Democracy* (Boston: Beacon Press, 1966), p. 112. For a contrary view, see J. Franklin Jameson, *The American Revolution Considered as a Social Movement* (Boston: Beacon Press, 1956), pp. 16–20, 32–35.

5. Chalmers Johnson, *Revolution and the Social System* (Stanford, CA: Hoover Institution, 1964), p. 2.

6. Peter Calvert, "Revolution: the Politics of Violence," *Political Studies* 15, no. 1, (1967): 2; and *Revolution and Counter Revolution* (Minneapolis: University of Minnesota Press, 1990).

7. Samuel P. Huntington, *Political Order in Changing Societies* (New Haven, CT: Yale University Press, 1968), p. 264. A similar definition was offered decades earlier in Sigmund Neumann, "The International Civil War," *World Politics* 1, no. 3 (April 1949): 333–334, fn. 1.

8. Norman R. Miller and Roderick R. Aya, *National Liberation: Revolution in the Third World* (New York: Free Press, 1971).

9. Theda Skocpol, "France, Russia, China: A Structural Analysis of Social Revolutions," *Comparative Studies in Society and History* 18, no. 2, (1976): 176.

10. Theda Skocpol, *States and Social Revolutions: A Comparative Analysis of France, Russia and China* (Cambridge, UK: Cambridge University Press, 1979), p. 4.

11. John Walton distinguishes between the handful of "great revolutions" that satisfy Skocpol's definition and a larger number of "national revolts" that are based on class and

nationality and that he feels are not particularly distinguishable from social revolutions. John Walton, *Reluctant Rebels* (New York: Columbia University Press, 1984), pp. 1–36.

12. Ellen Kay Trimberger, "A Theory of Elite Revolutions," *Studies in Comparative International Development* 7, no. 3 (1972): 191–207; Ellen Kay Trimberger, *Revolution from Above: Military Bureaucrats and Development in Japan, Turkey, Egypt and Peru* (New Brunswick, NJ: Transaction Books, 1978).

13. Karl Marx and Frederick Engels, *Manifesto of the Communist Party* (New York: International Publishers, 1948).

14. A. S. Cohan, *Theories of Revolution* (London: Thomas Nelson and Sons, 1975), p. 72.

15. Irving M. Zeitlin, *Marxism: A Re-examination* (Princeton, NJ: Princeton University Press, 1967), p. 142.

16. In other words, no Marxist revolution has taken place in a country where capitalism was entrenched. By the end of the twentieth century, in a complete turnabout of Marxist theory, Communist regimes in the Soviet Union and Eastern Europe were falling to capitalism. It is still too early to know what form that transition will ultimately take.

17. Stuart R. Schram, *The Political Thought of Mao Tse-tung* (New York: Praeger, 1969).

18. Skocpol, *States and Social Revolutions*.

19. Skocpol, "France, Russia, China."

20. Chalmers Johnson, *Peasant Nationalism and Communist Power* (Stanford, CA: Stanford University Press, 1962).

21. Johnson, *Revolution and the Social System*.

22. Joel Migdal, *Peasants, Politics and Revolution* (Princeton, NJ: Princeton University Press, 1974), p. 252.

23. Ramón L. Bonachea and Marta San Martín, *The Cuban Insurrection, 1952–1959* (New Brunswick, NJ: Transaction Books, 1974); Jorge L. Domínguez, *Cuba: Order and Revolution* (Cambridge, MA: Belknap Press of Harvard University Press, 1978), pp. 93–95; John A. Booth, *The End and the Beginning: The Nicaraguan Revolution* (Boulder, CO: Westview Press, 1982).

24. Charles Tilly, *From Mobilization to Revolution* (New York: Addison-Wesley, 1978), pp. 204–205.

25. Charles Tilly, "Does Modernization Breed Revolution?" *Comparative Politics* 5, no. 3 (April 1974): 425–447.

26. Huntington, *Political Order in Changing Societies*, p. 265.

27. Ibid., p. 266.

28. James C. Davies, "Toward a Theory of Revolution," *American Sociological Review* 27, no. 1 (February 1962): 7.

29. The economic pattern he describes can be graphed as the letter "J" tipped over, with the long side representing the period of economic growth and the rounded part depicting the downturn.

30. James C. Davies, "Toward a Theory of Revolution," reprinted along with other articles on the causes of revolution in James C. Davies, ed., *When Men Revolt and Why* (New York: Free Press, 1971).

31. Ibid., and James C. Davies, "Revolution and the J-Curve," in *Violence in America: Historical and Comparative Perspectives, a Report Submitted to the National Commission on the Causes and Prevention of Violence*, ed. Hugh Davis Graham and Ted Robert Gurr (New York: New American Library, 1969), Vol. 2, pp. 547– 577.

32. Raymond Tanter and Manus Midlarsky, "A Theory of Revolution," *Journal of Conflict Resolution* 11, no. 3 (1967): 264–280.

33. Ted Robert Gurr, "Psychological Factors in Civil Violence," *World Politics* 20, no. 2 (1967–1968): 252–253; see also Ted Robert Gurr, *Why Men Rebel* (Princeton, NJ: Princeton University Press, 1970).

34. Timothy P. Wickham-Crowley, *Guerrillas and Revolution in Latin America* (Princeton, NJ: Princeton University Press, 1992), p. 312. Revolutions and guerrilla wars are not synonymous, of course. In recent decades, however, virtually all revolutionary struggles have been fought by guerrillas in Latin America and other parts of the Third World.

35. A guerrilla attack on a tourist train strongly alienated public opinion. Ultimately, a number of guerrilla leaders renounced violence and, following a government amnesty, entered electoral politics. Teodoro Petkoff, a former guerrilla who has since enjoyed a distinguished career as a congressman and cabinet minister and run unsuccessfully for president, told me in a 1978 interview that the use of violence had lost the Left considerable public support and had been a major error.

36. Booth, *The End and the Beginning*.

37. At that time such an alliance was being discussed in the U.S. press and government circles. Neither Nicaraguan businessmen nor the State Department harbored any illusions that they could keep the Sandinistas out of power at that point. However, they and the Carter administration hoped that the Sandinistas were not strong enough to hold power exclusively. In fact, after the Somoza regime was ousted, the Sandinista government did initially include progressive business leaders, but they soon left.

38. Eric R. Wolf, *Peasant Wars of the Twentieth Century* (New York: Harper and Row, 1969). For a discussion of similar factors in the capitalist transformation of Europe, see Karl Polanyi, *The Great Transformation* (New York: Rinehart, 1957).

39. James C. Scott, *The Moral Economy of the Peasant: Rebellion and Subsistence in Southeast Asia* (New Haven, CT: Yale University Press, 1976); James C. Scott and Benedict J. Kirkvliet, *How Traditional Rural Patrons Lose Legitimacy* (Madison: University of Wisconsin, Land Tenure Center, 1975).

40. Sharecroppers are tenant farmers who pay their rent by giving the landlord a percentage of their crop.

41. Jeffrey M. Paige, *Agrarian Revolution: Social Movements and Export Agriculture in the Underdeveloped World* (New York: Free Press, 1975), Chapters 1–2.

42. Wickham-Crowley, *Guerrillas and Revolution*, Chapter 6.

43. Cynthia McClintock, "Sendero Luminoso: Peru's Maoist Guerrillas," *Problems of Communism* 32, no. 5 (September–October 1983): 19–34.

44. Wickham-Crowley, *Guerrillas and Revolution*, pp. 246–250; Wolf, *Peasant Wars*.

45. John Womack Jr., *Zapata and the Mexican Revolution* (New York: Vintage, 1968).

46. Wickham-Crowley, *Guerrillas and Revolution*, p. 145.

47. Ibid., p. 213; Alvin Gouldner, *The Future of Intellectuals and the Rise of the New Class* (New York: Seabury Press, 1979), pp. 53–73.

48. Dennis Gilbert, *Sandinistas: The Party and the Revolution* (New York: B. Blackwell, 1988); for detailed information on the social backgrounds and occupations of a substantial number of Latin American guerrilla leaders, see Wickham-Crowley, *Guerrillas and Revolution*, pp. 327–339.

49. Thomas H. Green, *Comparative Revolutionary Movements* (Upper Saddle River, NJ: Prentice Hall, 1974), p. 18.

50. Of course the percentages of peasants and illiterates in the party were still well below their proportions in the general population, but they were higher than in most LDCs.

51. Wickham-Crowley, *Guerrillas and Revolution*, p. 143.

52. Hector Béjar, *Peru 1965: Notes on a Guerrilla Experience* (New York: Monthly Review Press, 1970).

53. Among the many writings on Maoist ideology and strategy, see Stuart R. Schram, *The Political Thought of Mao Tse-tung* (New York: Praeger, 1963); Arthur Cohen, *The Communism of Mao Tse-Tung* (Chicago: University of Chicago Press, 1964); Cohan, *Theories of Revolution*, pp. 93–110.

54. Sebastian Balfour, *Fidel Castro* (New York: Longman, 1990), p. 49.

55. Peasants have been most pleased when they received individual family plots and far less satisfied when agrarian reform converted the old agricultural estates into cooperatives or state farms.

56. Milovan Djilas, *The New Class* (New York: Praeger, 1957).

57. Huntington, *Political Order in Changing Societies*, p. 266.

58. See, for example, William J. Duiker, *The Communist Road to Power in Vietnam*, 2d ed. (Boulder, CO: Westview Press, 1996).

59. Richard R. Fagen, *The Transformation of Political Culture in Cuba* (Stanford, CA: Stanford University Press, 1969); Domínguez, *Cuba: Order and Revolution*.

60. There is a voluminous literature on the Cultural Revolution. Liang Heng and Judith Shapiro, *Son of the Revolution* (New York: Vintage, 1983), offer a moving personal account of both the Anti-Rightist Campaign and the Cultural Revolution. See also K. S. Karol, *The Second Chinese Revolution* (New York: Hill and Wang, 1974); Jean Esmein, *The Chinese Cultural Revolution* (New York: Anchor Books, 1973); and Lowell Dittmer, *Liu Shao-ch'i and the Chinese Cultural Revolution* (Berkeley: University of California Press, 1974).

61. Liang Heng and Judith Shapiro, *After the Nightmare* (New York: Collier, 1986).

62. Nicholas Nugent, *Vietnam: The Second Revolution* (Brighton, England: In Print Publishers, 1996), Chapters 5–6.

63. On this theme, see Forrest Colburn, *The Vogue of Revolution in Poor Countries* (Princeton, NJ: Princeton University Press, 1994).

64. Both quotes come from Colburn, *The Vogue of Revolution*, p. 89.

65. Actually, a faction of the FSLN, led by former Vice-President Sergio Ramírez and other party intellectuals has broken from the party to form their own, social democratic Sandinista party. The Sandinistas' major faction, led by former president and revolutionary leader Daniel Ortega maintains a more revolutionary style and rhetoric, though still considerably more moderate than when the FSLN was in power in the 1980s. While El Salvador's FMLN has not formally split, there are also internal divisions within that party over how far it should go in renouncing earlier revolutionary ideas.

8

⚭

SOLDIERS AND POLITICS

During the years I was in the State Department, I was awakened once or twice a month by a telephone call in the middle of the night announcing a coup d'état in some distant [Third World] capital with a name like a typographical error.[1]

Even the most developed governments occasionally have been headed by men emerging from the ranks of the military. American president Dwight Eisenhower, French president Charles de Gaulle, and Israeli prime minister Ehud Barek all used distinguished military careers as stepping stones to the leadership of their nations. But each of them entered politics as a private citizen, having first retired from the armed forces. Moreover, their accession to high office was achieved through a democratic election.

What has distinguished Third World politics is the extent to which the military has intruded as an institution, either as a dominant interest group or as the governing power. Unlike their counterparts in industrial democracies, soldiers in the LDCs often reject the dividing line between military and political activity. A pronouncement by the Indonesian armed forces prior to their assumption of power illustrates that perspective well:

> The army, which was born in the cauldron of the Revolution, has never been a dead instrument of the government, concerned exclusively with security matters. The army, as a fighter for freedom, cannot remain neutral toward the course of state policy, the quality of government, and the safety of the state.[2]

To be sure, there are countries such as India, Malaysia, Kenya, Tunisia, Mexico, and Costa Rica where the military has not intruded deeply into politics for decades. But, such restraint has been exceptional. Until recently, the military's political involvement in most of the Third World has been so pervasive that it has become a defining characteristic of political underdevelopment. The wave of democratic transitions during the closing decades of the twentieth century diminished the military's political influence in many LDCs, especially in Latin America. But in Africa, the Middle East, and parts of Asia and Central America, the armed forces remain a potent political force.

Thus, George Ball's frequent experience with coups d'état as a high-ranking official in the Kennedy and Johnson administrations was not unique. One study of military intervention revealed that 59 LDCs experienced 274 attempted coups between 1946 and 1970. Twenty-three of those countries were subjected to 5 or more takeover attempts in little more than two decades. Bolivia and Venezuela led the way with 18 coups each.[3] In the three decades since that study, the roll call of attempted and successful coups in the developing world has continued, rising at times in one region, abating at other times in another. Only since the 1980s has the number of new military takeovers declined.

Starting in 1952 with North Africa's first coup d'état in Egypt, and General Mobutu's 1960 takeover in the Congo-Kinshasa, the first in sub-Saharan Africa, that continent's politics have been particularly dominated by the armed forces. From 1958 to 1984, there were over 62 coups (and 60 failed attempts) in Black Africa, affecting over 80 percent of the nations in that region.[4] In 1982 to 1983 alone, Upper Volta (now Burkina Faso) experienced three military takeovers in only nine months! On average during the 1980s, 65 percent of Africa's population was governed by the armed forces. Noting the absence of electoral change in the region, one observer argued that "coups had become the functional equivalent of elections, virtually the sole manner of ousting incumbent political leaders."[5]

In recent decades, the extent of military rule in Latin America has risen and fallen in cycles. After a period of widespread civilian governance in the region, a new wave of military intervention began in the early 1960s, most notably in Brazil. Subsequently, Chile and Uruguay, South America's most established democracies, were transformed into highly repressive military regimes. By the mid-1970s, Colombia, Costa Rica, Cuba, Mexico, and Venezuela were the only nations in Latin America still governed by civilians.[6] Since the start of the 1980s, however, another cycle of change has restored elected government throughout the region. While civilian rule seems to have taken firm root in some nations (such as Argentina and Brazil), the future of democratic government remains somewhat uncertain in countries such as Guatemala, Haiti, and Paraguay.

Although there are a number of military regimes in the Islamic nations of North Africa (Algeria, Libya, and Sudan), indirect military dominance is more common in the Middle East. Presidents Husni Mubarak of Egypt and Hafez Assad of Syria are military men, while Iraq's Saddam Hussein is a civilian who has adopted military trappings. All three, however, govern through political parties closely linked to the armed forces. Elsewhere in the region, monarchies in Morocco, Jordan, Saudi Arabia, Kuwait, and the smaller Gulf states have, at least until now, successfully controlled the military.

In Asia, the South Korean army has gradually transferred the reins of government to elected civilians but continues to exercise political influence. Thai military officers, by contrast, have been more reluctant to exit the political arena. Since entering politics in 1932, they have held the prime minister's post over 70 percent of the time. Although active military officers have been constitutionally barred from holding political office since 1983, several retired officers have continued to serve as prime minister.[7] Bangladesh and Pakistan have also alternated between army rule and military-dominated civilian regimes for decades. Myanmar's military regimes have been more enduring and more brutal, as was General Suharto's government in Indonesia until it was toppled in 1998. By contrast, India, Malaysia, and the Philippines have enjoyed uninterrupted civilian government.

Over the past few decades there has been a dramatic decline in the number of military governments among the LDCs. As we have seen, that trend has been most pronounced in Latin America where, for the first time ever, democratic government seems to be taking root firmly. A number of other military governments have given way to elected governments in Africa and Asia. Still the military continues as a powerful political force in much of Africa and the Middle East and wields considerable political influence over many civilian governments in Asia and Latin America.

Frequently the armed forces exercises veto power over decisions in particular policy areas. In some countries, military leaders protect their own budget, determine who serves as defense minister, or control military promotions. Elsewhere, the scope of their influence is far greater, including defense policy, foreign affairs, and even economic policy. Thus, even though Guatemala has had civilian governments since 1985, the president would not dare pursue a policy that threatened the army's interests. Similarly, when Corazón Aquino served as Philippine president, she regularly consulted on major issues with her military chief of staff, General Fidel Ramos, who later succeeded her as president.[8]

In order to examine military involvement in Third World politics, this chapter will explore a series of interrelated questions: What accounts for the high level of armed forces involvement? Why have countries such as India, China, Malaysia, Costa Rica, and Tanzania been able to establish greater civilian control while so many other developing nations have failed? How do the structures of military regimes differ from one another? What does the military hope to accomplish when it seizes power? How successful has it been in achieving its political and economic goals? Is military rule generally beneficial or detrimental to economic and political development? How does the record of military regimes as a whole compare with that of civilian governments in attaining economic growth and political stability? What factors induce military regimes to step down? And, what role will the armed forces play in those LDCs where it has been forced from the center of political power?

THE CAUSES OF MILITARY INTERVENTION

Two alternative perspectives have been offered to explain the frequency and nature of military intervention in developing countries. The first focuses on the internal characteristics of the armed forces itself. The second stresses the broader political environment in which the generals operate, most notably the weakness of civilian regimes.

The Nature of the Armed Forces

In the past, many political scientists maintained that Third World armies enjoy greater organizational cohesion and clarity of purpose than do civilian political institutions, hence their proclivity to intervene. As one leading analyst concluded, "The ability of officers to intervene in domestic politics and produce stable leadership is [directly] related to internal [military] social cohesion."[9] Stressing the importance of understanding the military's inner workings, scholars examined the officer corps' class origins, educational level, ideological orientations, and internal organization. These factors, they suggested, affect the probability of military involvement in politics and help determine the officers' goals.

Obviously military politics is greatly influenced by the officers' education and training. In his highly influential book *The Soldier and the State*, Samuel Huntington argued that a country wishing to keep the military out of politics must impart professional values to its officers.[10] Ideally, as military training and techniques become more sophisticated, officers develop specialized and complex military skills while becoming more politically neutral. Under those circumstances, he claimed, "a clear distinction in role and function exists between military and civilian leaders."[11] But, Huntington warned subsequently, such a division of function will only develop if military training is addressed toward external threats such as war with other nations. Should the focus of military education shift toward internal warfare—controlling guerrilla unrest or other civil insurrection—professionalization will not suffice to keep the military out of politics. [12]

Building on this theme, Alfred Stepan distinguished between "old" and "new" military professionalism. The former, typical of developed countries such as the United States, emphasizes skills appropriate to "external security." As military officers are trained to repel foreign enemies, Stepan agreed, they can be expected to remove themselves from domestic politics. In many developing nations, however, armed forces training (new professionalization) primarily prepares them for internal warfare against class- or ethnically based insurgencies.

Following the Cuban Revolution, Latin American generals and U.S. policy makers shared a common concern over leftist guerrilla movements in the region. Training of Latin American officers at home and in the United States emphasized counterinsurgency techniques as well as "civic action" programs (e.g., road and school construction) designed to "win the hearts and minds" of the local population. American policy makers claimed that such preparation would provide the military with a professional mission and thereby remove it from national politics. Invariably, however, teaching officers to deal with internal security threats involved them in the study of domestic political and economic issues, thereby drawing them into the political arena.[13]

Nowhere was this more evident than in Brazil's Superior War College (ESG) and Peru's Center for Higher Military Studies (CAEM). Offering each country's most capable officers sophisticated courses on domestic political, economic, and social issues, the two academies could not help but politicize their students. As severe inflation and political polarization worsened in Brazil, and as peasant unrest surged in Peru's neofeudal countryside, officers in both armies came to feel that they were more qualified than civilian politicians to solve their country's problems. After seizing power in the 1960s, the generals dramatically restructured the political-economic order in both nations, though their ideologies and programs were diametrically different.

The Nature of Civil Society

While research into the internal structure and dynamics of the armed forces has been very valuable, it has its limits. Increasingly, scholars have come to understand that the likelihood and nature of armed forces political intervention cannot be ascertained merely by evaluating factors such as military cohesion, size, or ideological orientation. There is, for example, surprisingly little correlation between the military's size or firepower and its propensity to topple civilian governments. West Africa's first coup was carried out in Togo by an army of 250 men and a small number of retirees from the former French colonial force. "In Dahomey, General Sogol, who had come to power [himself] by a coup d'état, was overthrown by sixty paratroopers."[14] Several other takeovers in the region were also executed by small and poorly armed units. By way of contrast, the armed forces of Israel, Sweden, and the United States have never attempted coups despite their large size, strong internal cohesion, and considerable military prowess.

Ultimately, then, the military's propensity to intervene in politics is less a function of its own might than of the weaknesses of civilian political institutions. As Samuel Huntington has insisted, "the most important causes of military intervention in politics are not military, but political and reflect not the social and organizational characteristics of the military establishment but the political and institutional structure of society."[15] Hence, it is in the fabric of civil society that the second body of explanatory theories focuses its attention.

If a civilian government enjoys widespread support, maintains stability, and presides over a healthy economy, it is relatively immune to coups. Conversely, "in times of uncertainty and the breakdown of [civilian political] institutions, soldiers come into their own; when there is no other effective organization of society, even a small, weak army may take command over a large, unorganized mass."[16]

In his classic study of civil-military relations, *The Man on Horseback,* Samuel E. Finer maintained that national political cultures could be ranked according to the following three criteria: [17]

1. The extent of public support for the procedures used to transfer political power and for the corresponding belief that only those procedures are legitimate.
2. The degree of public awareness regarding the individuals and institutions holding sovereign authority, and the degree to which the population believes that no other person or group can legitimately hold that power.
3. The strength of civil society. That is, the extent to which the populace is organized into groups such as political parties, labor unions, business associations, or churches that act independently of the government.

The higher a nation's political culture ranks on each of these three dimensions, argued Finer, the lower the likelihood of military interventionism. In short, countries are most capable of maintaining civilian rule when there is wide consensus on the legitimacy of civilian government along with independent interest groups capable of defending that principle—taking to the streets if need be.

When the government retains widespread citizen loyalty, even if coups are tried they will usually fail. A recent "Second World" example demonstrates well what can happen when the civilian government enjoys greater legitimacy than its military opponents. In 1991, when Soviet generals and hard-line Communist civilian officials staged a coup aimed at ousting Mikhail Gorbachev, thousands of civilians joined Russian President Boris Yeltsin in defending the Russian parliament with their bodies. At the same time, key commanders of troops sent to take Moscow and St. Petersburg refused to support the rebellion. Thus, the coup d'état failed badly because Yeltsin and Gorbachev had sufficient legitimacy to survive.

In contrast, the legitimacy of civilian regimes in many developing nations is low. Disgruntled military elements are therefore more inclined to overthrow them, while loyalist troops and civilians are less likely to risk their lives defending them.

A variety of factors may either strengthen or undermine a government's legitimacy. From an institutional perspective, civilian regimes stand most firmly when they are supported by broadly based political parties. Where party systems are deeply entrenched in the fabric of society and elicit widespread support, the likelihood of military intervention is greatly diminished.[18] Indeed, a country's susceptibility to coups is less influenced by its level of democracy than by the degree to which its party system penetrates and organizes society. Thus, authoritarian systems in Mexico, Cuba, and China (all dominated by a single party) have controlled the military as effectively as democratic party systems in Venezuela and India.

Put under sufficient stress, however, not even a strong party system can fully immunize a political system from military interference. For much of the twentieth century, vibrant, competitive parties in Uruguay and Chile shielded those countries from the pattern of military takeovers that plagued most of Latin America. By 1973, however, increased class conflict and political polarization had undermined the political order in both countries, ushering in authoritarian military regimes.

Civilian governments are most vulnerable during periods of economic decay (particularly runaway inflation), when they are unable to maintain political stability, or when they are widely perceived as being corrupt. All of these circumstances undermine their legitimacy and increase popular expectations that military rule can improve the situation. In nations such as Nigeria, Thailand, and Pakistan, soon after seizing power coup leaders declared their intention of rooting out widespread corruption. Following severe economic and political crises in Argentina, Brazil, Chile, and Uruguay, the new military authoritarian regimes set out to crush Leftist movements, restore social order, and reinvigorate the economy.

All of this indicates that a nation's propensity for military intervention correlates strongly with the nature of its political institutions and political culture. Yet a nation's socioeconomic and cultural conditions alone do not fully account for the variation in civil-military relations. Elite values and behavior also play an important role. For example, India and Venezuela, with political-economic circumstances quite comparable to those of their neighbors, have far less military intervention. The explanation may lie in the values of their political elites: elected officials and government bureaucrats, along with political party, business, and labor leaders.

India illustrates this point well. Adjoining several countries with histories of military intervention (Pakistan, Bangladesh, Myanmar, Thailand), it has been governed exclusively by civilians since independence. There is little to suggest that the Indian public, largely rural and illiterate, has a political culture substantially different from that of its neighbors. Socioeconomic indicators are lower than Thailand's. It appears, however, that India's political elite subscribes more strongly than its neighbors to the principle of civilian control.

At the same time, a rapid change in elite values can impact civil-military relations significantly. For example, Venezuela was governed by the military for much of the first half of the twentieth century. Since 1959, however, over 40 years of elected government transformed the country into one of Latin America's more stable democracies.[19] While a number of factors contributed to this dramatic turnabout, one critical element was a change in elite attitudes during the dictatorship that followed Venezuela's first experiment with democracy (1945 to 1948). Recognizing that political polarization had precipitated the 1948 coup, leaders of the major political parties agreed to moderate political conflict. In 1958, the principal democratically oriented political parties signed the Pact of Punto Fijo, increasing interparty cooperation and setting the basis for civilian political dominance.[20] By 1992, however, Venezuela's severe economic crisis had so eroded civilian support for elected government that two unsuccessful coup attempts drew broad, popular support and democracy is currently shaky.

PROGRESSIVE SOLDIERS AND MILITARY CONSERVATIVES

Given the disorder and conflict that characterize so many Third World civilian governments, the question arises whether military involvement might bring greater stability and national development, at least in the short run. Once in office, are the generals and colonels likely to be a force for progressive change or defenders of the status quo? Some of the leading early modernization theorists felt strongly that the armed forces could contribute to development. Marion J. Levy was impressed by the military's alleged rationality, disciplined organization, and commitment to modern values. Taking its critics to task, he maintained that the armed forces might be "the most efficient type of organization for combining maximum rates of modernization with maximum levels of stability and control."[21] Lucian W. Pye also saw the military as one of the best-organized major institutions in otherwise "disorganized transitional societies." It was, said Pye, at the forefront of technical training and a leader in imparting the values of citizenship.[22] For Manfred Halpern, the Middle Eastern military was "the vanguard of nationalism and social change."[23]

Positive evaluations such as these predominated in the early modernization literature.[24] They were based to some extent on an idealized vision of the professional soldier: trained in modern organizational techniques; nationalistic; above narrow tribal, class, and regional interests. At times these writings reflected the authors' strong preference for order and stability, coupled with the assumption that the military could bring order out of chaos. Occasionally, they drew on a few military success stories and projected them on a larger screen. One early model was the Turkish military revolt led by Mustafa Kemal (Ataturk) in 1922. During the next two decades Ataturk and his followers modernized the country before eventually turning it over to civilian rule.[25] Another frequently cited military reformer was Egypt's Colonel Abdel Gamal Nasser, who rose to power in the 1950s seeking to reform his country's social institutions while strengthening its military. Subsequent reformist militaries elsewhere have often been labeled "young Turks" or "Nasserites."

Over the years an array of soldiers have seized power, promising to modernize their country through industrialization, greater labor discipline, expanded education, agrarian reform, or other fundamental changes. Those on the left, in countries such as Upper Volta, Libya, and Peru, have promoted economic redistribution, greater state intervention in the economy, mass mobilization, and a struggle against imperialism. Conversely, conservative generals in Brazil, Chile, Indonesia, and South Korea repressed mass political participation while encouraging investment by domestic and multinational corporations.

Why then do some military regimes champion the poor while others support wealthy corporate and land-owning interests? To find the answer we must examine the class origins of the officer corps, the nation's level of socioeconomic development, and the class alliances that emerge in the political system. Research in various parts of the developing world frequently has shown that officers tend to come from middle-class backgrounds, at least in Asia and Latin America. Typically, their fathers were either officers, storekeepers, merchants, mid-sized landowners, teachers, or civil servants.[26] Not surprisingly, then, military regimes commonly identify with the goals and aspirations of their nation's middle class.

But what are those goals and what political ideologies and government programs emerge from them? In the least developed Third World countries, officers often view economic elites, including powerful land owners and multinational corporations, as the source of their country's backwardness. The middle class itself frequently resents those same elites for obstructing its own rise to political and social prominence. In such a setting, both groups may perceive the relatively unmobilized lower class as a potential ally in the battle against the oligarchy. For example, soon after taking power Peruvian General Juan Velasco denounced the traditional land-owning class and the country's economic dependency as the sources of Peru's underdevelopment. In the following years, the military's ambitious land redistribution, shantytown reform, expropriations of property belonging to multinational corporations, expansion of the state economic sector, and mass mobilization greatly altered the country's political and economic landscape. Elsewhere, "General Omar Torrijos of Panama railed against oligarchical control and encouraged the lower class to participate in politics."[27] Muammar Qadhafi's government in Libya and a number of Marxist military regimes in Africa were also cut from similar cloth.

As a country modernizes, however, and as lower-class mobilization intensifies, the military confronts a changing political panorama. Urbanization, the spread of secondary and university education, and the development of a more complex economy all enlarge and strengthen the middle class, enabling it to wrest a share of political power from the economic elites. At the same time, industrialization increases the size of the working class and strengthens the trade union movement. Urbanization also creates a growing and sometimes militant shantytown population. And the commercialization of agriculture often triggers unrest in the countryside (see Chapter 5). Not surprisingly, the middle class (having achieved a share of political power) and its military partners now come to see the more activated and politicized lower classes as a threat rather than a useful ally.

If the Left has considerable mass support and there is growing political unrest, the military is even more likely to ally with the economic elite and to repress mass mobilization. In Chile, the election of Salvador Allende's Marxist government and the accompanying mobilization of workers, peasants, and urban poor polarized the country along class lines. In nearby Uruguay, the Left's electoral appeal was not as strong, but labor-industrial conflict was intense and the Tupamaros, a potent urban guerrilla force, were engaged in a campaign of political kidnappings and other forms of violence. In both countries, the perceived threat of mass mobilization and an ascendent Left caused the military to topple long-standing democracies.

In short, then, the more underdeveloped a country is and the weaker its middle class, the greater its likelihood of having a progressive military.[28] But, notes Eric Nordlinger, "the soldiers who have power in countries with an established middle class . . . act as more or less ardent defenders of the status quo."[29] Similarly, Samuel Huntington observes:

> In the world of the oligarchy, the soldier is a radical; in the middle class world, he is a participant and arbitrator; as mass society looms on the horizon he becomes the guardian of the existing order. . . . The more advanced a society becomes, the more conservative and reactionary becomes the role of the military.[30]

THE GOALS OF MILITARY REGIMES

Having observed the range of ideological orientations among military governments, we will now examine these regimes' varying structures and the primary political-economic goals associated with each.

Personalist Regimes

In the world's most underdeveloped nations, with low levels of military professionalization, limited citizen participation, extensive political corruption, and little semblance of representative government, military officers frequently seize power for their own personal enrichment and aggrandizement. Their administrations tend to be highly personalistic, that is, they are led by a single charismatic officer with a strong personal following. In order to bolster his support, however, the leader allows some government plunder to pass on to the military or civilian clique surrounding him. "Legitimacy is secured through patronage, clientelistic alliances, [and] systemic intimidation."[31]

In Latin America, personalist dictatorships have been most common in the less developed political systems of Central America and the Caribbean. One of the most prominent examples was the Somoza dynasty in Nicaragua. As leader of the country's National Guard, General Anastasio Somoza seized power in 1937, primarily seeking his own enrichment. Governing a small and impoverished nation, he amassed several hundred million dollars by using state resources to purchase construction firms, urban real estate, electrical power plants, air and shipping lines, cement factories, and much of the nation's best farm land. Following his assassination in 1956, his political and financial empire passed to his two sons, who ruled the country in succession until the 1979 Sandinista Revolution.[32]

Other personalist regimes in the Americas included the Batista government in Cuba (which eventually fell victim to Fidel Castro's revolutionary army) and Alfredo Stroessner's dictatorship in Paraguay. Batista had links to the Mafia's gambling and prostitution operations in Havana. Stroessner and his associates enriched themselves by collaborating with international smugglers and drug dealers. More recently, corruption continues to permeate the Haitian armed forces and police. Reaping the profits of drug dealing and other illegal activities, General Raoul Cédras and his military colleagues were naturally reluctant to yield power to the elected president, Jean-Bertrand Aristide.[33]

Personalist military regimes have also been common in sub-Saharan Africa, sometimes led by upwardly mobile junior officers or even enlisted men such as Ghana's Flight Sergeant Jerry Rawlings and Liberia's Sergeant-Major Samuel Doe. While some, like Rawlings, were well intentioned, they have done little to develop their countries. The most infamous personalist dictators in the continent have been Uganda's Idi Amin Dada and the Central African Republic's Jean-Bédél Bokassa. Enamored as much of power as of wealth, Amin played upon and exacerbated Uganda's ethnic divisions during his brutal eight-year reign (1971 to 1979). He not only expelled the country's sizable Asian population but also murdered many thousands of his countrymen, most notably members of the previously influential Langi and Acholi tribes. Seeing enemies at every turn, he even executed one of his wives and had another tortured. In an attempt to maintain absolute control over the armed forces, he purged or executed much of the officer corps, eventually creating an army largely composed of foreign troops (principally Sudanese and Zairian).[34]

Equally megalomaniac, the Central African Republic's Marshal Bokassa unleashed a reign of death and terror on his country following his seizure of power in 1965. Having plundered the treasury of one of the world's more impoverished nations, he concluded that the presidency was not a sufficiently exalted position. So he lavished millions on his own coronation as the country's new emperor. Ultimately, Amin and Bokassa so outraged the world community that they were ousted through external intervention. Amin fell to a Tanzanian invasion, while Bokassa was toppled by a French-sponsored coup.[35]

Because personalist dictators lack a meaningful ideology or policy program to legitimize their regime, they commonly must share some of the spoils of state plunder with their military and civilian supporters in order to maintain themselves in power. For example, Zaire's President Mobutu, until recently Africa's most enduring military dictator, made himself one of the richest men on earth while opening up the floodgates of corruption to his military and civil service. In this manner, he kept himself in power for three decades while bankrupting the national government and destroying a once-dynamic economy. By the late 1990s, however, as the Zairian economy collapsed, his government unraveled, falling rapidly to a rebel force.[36] The Somoza dynasty maintained the critical support of Nicaragua's National Guard by allowing its officers to share in the regime's plunder. In the most egregious example, following an earthquake that devastated the nation's capital, Guard officers appropriated relief supplies sent from the United States and sold them for a profit.[37]

Institutional Military Regimes

As the political and economic systems of many Third World nations modernize, corresponding changes take place in military attitudes and institutions. Selected officers attend advanced military academies at home or abroad. Sometimes they enroll in specialized seminars with civilian leaders, establishing links with politicians, businessmen, or academics. Through these programs they become more deeply exposed to their country's political and economic problems.

When these "new soldiers" seize power, they are more likely to govern collectively than to vest total authority in the hands of a single leader. To be sure, some institutional military regimes have been dominated by a single figure such as Libya's Muammar Qadhafi, Indonesia's Suharto, Syria's Hafez Assad, and Chile's Augusto Pinochet. As with purely personalist dictators, these men may be motivated by "covert ambition, fear, greed and vanity."[38] Still, even in such cases, many officers hold influential government positions and there is a degree of institutional decision making. Moreover, regime goals are broader than any single leader's ambitions. In Indonesia, for example, active and retired military officers at one time held nearly half the positions in the national bureaucracy and some two-thirds of provincial governorships.[39] In a like manner, the Argentine military dominated top positions in almost all government ministries during its most recent period in office.

Institutional military governments are generally headed by collegial bodies such as Niger's Supreme Military Council or Myanmar's Revolutionary Council. Comparable councils or juntas have governed Algeria, Argentina, Brazil, Ethiopia, Thailand, Uruguay, and a host of other countries.[40] Typically, one active or retired officer serves as president and wields the most power. Often, however, his term of office is limited. For example, presidents of recent military governments in Argentina and Brazil were restricted by their colleagues to a single term. In some countries, including South Korea, Brazil, and Indonesia, the armed forces tried to legitimize their rule by forming political parties that offered candidates in tightly controlled elections. Commonly, military candidates retire from active duty before standing for office. And in Egypt, Iraq, and Syria, military and civilian elites have joined together to form a ruling political party.[41]

Institutional military regimes can be as repressive and brutal as personalist dictatorships, sometimes more so. Their day-to-day governing style, however, is more bureaucratic and sophisticated, commonly drawing on the talents of highly trained civilian technocrats.[42] Moreover, unlike purely self-aggrandizing personalist leaders, they are more likely to support the aspirations of the middle class (from which most offices have sprung), more prone to espouse a coherent political ideology, and more likely to champion nationalistic causes.

Most institutional military governments pursue four broad objectives, or at least profess to do so.

First, whatever their real motivations, they usually justify their seizure of power by denouncing the alleged corruption of the government they have ousted. Thus, when Bangladesh's Lt. General Husain Muhammad Ershad led a 1982 army coup, he charged that the outgoing administration had "failed totally because of [its] petty selfishness . . . and unbounded corruption."[43] Parallel proclamations have been made by incoming military leaders in Uruguay, Pakistan, Thailand, and much of Africa. All have promised to clean up the mess.

A second goal—one rarely publicly articulated or acknowledged—is the advancement of military corporate interests. As Ruth First observed in Africa, while coup leaders may claim to have seized power for the good of the nation or other broad political purpose, "when the army acts, it generally acts for army reasons."[44] When officers are unhappy with their salaries, defense budgets, or the level of arms purchases, they will usually respond. They also react negatively to civilian government "interference" in military affairs (such as deviating from normal officer promotion practices) or other diminutions of armed forces autonomy.

Ever since coups in Togo, Ghana, Mali, Congo-Brazzaville, and Algeria in the 1960s, African armies have frequently seized power to protect themselves against competing military units (presidential guards and the like), to increase their troop strength, to raise their salaries, or to augment their budgets.[45] Repeated coups in Bangladesh have been motivated by similar desires for greater military spending and by resentment against civilian interference in military promotions.[46] In Southeast Asia, on the other hand, "neglect of [military] corporate interests" by civilian governments "is often a background factor contributing to a general sense of alienation [by the armed forces] rather than an immediate cause of intervention."[47] Still, army dissatisfaction with defense expenditures contributed to coups in Burma, Thailand, and pre-Communist Cambodia, Laos, and South Vietnam. In the last three cases, officers believed their takeovers would increase United States military aid.[48]

A third common goal is the maintenance or restoration of order and stability. Institutional coups oftentimes occur when the country has experienced or anticipates civil unrest, guerrilla activity, or civil war. For example, the military first entered politics in South Korea when the administrations of Syngman Rhee and Chang Myon were challenged by student and labor unrest (though other factors also played a role). Thailand's many coups have frequently followed strikes and street demonstrations in Bangkok.

Officers are particularly troubled by radical challenges to the political and economic order and by threats to the safety and integrity of the armed forces. During the early 1960s, Indonesian civilian president Sukarno moved his regime leftward and became increasingly dependent on the country's large Communist party, much to the discomfort of his conservative military command. In 1965, leftist military officers assassinated Lt. General Achmad Yani and five other officers, claiming they had been plotting a coup against Sukarno. The armed forces responded with a massive attack against the Communists, eventually killing some half a million suspected party supporters. (The ethnic Chinese minority was particularly targeted.) Two years later, army leader General Suharto ousted

Sukarno and assumed the presidency, a post he held until 1998.[49] Similarly, in Argentina, Brazil, and Uruguay, military dictatorships in recent decades were partially inspired by the generals' fear of Leftist unions, guerrillas, and political parties.[50] In 1992, the Algerian armed forces terminated parliamentary elections that seemed sure to bring victory to the FIS, a group of militant Islamic fundamentalists.

Finally, most institutional military regimes hope to stimulate their nation's economy. As we have noted, coups frequently follow a period of rampant inflation, work stoppages, and economic stagnation. For example, a statistical analysis of military intervention in 38 Black African governments over a two-decade period revealed that coups are most likely to occur after an economic downturn.[51] Similar patterns exist in Asia and Latin America.

Third World militaries are particularly committed to industrialization. From a purely logistical perspective, industrial growth promises to provide them with arms and supplies that now must be imported from abroad. In the least developed countries, such production may be limited to food, uniforms, or rifles. On the other hand, in countries such as Brazil, Indonesia, and South Korea, a highly advanced arms industry produces planes, tanks, and sophisticated weaponry for domestic consumption and export. Even when it has no direct military applicability, industrialization is a source of national pride and international prestige. Small wonder, then, that in Latin America and parts of Asia there has long been a political alliance between industrialists and the armed forces.[52]

Having reviewed the goals of institutional military governments in general, we will now focus on two distinct regime types that have received considerable attention in recent years: the Bureaucratic Authoritarian regime and the revolutionary military regime.

Bureaucratic Authoritarian Regimes Beginning with the Brazilian coup d'état of 1964, through the Argentine military takeovers of 1966 and 1976, to the 1973 coups in Uruguay and Chile, four of the most socioeconomically developed countries in South America succumbed to authoritarian rule. Chile and Uruguay had also been the most long-standing democracies in the region, free of military domination for decades. Thus, the coups contradicted the widely held assumption at that time that both socioeconomic development and the creation of a strong party system would prevent military intervention.

Once in power, these regimes endured longer than did typical military governments in the region, lasting between 12 years (Uruguay) and 21 (Brazil).[53] By South American standards, they were also far more repressive. Political party activity was suspended for extended periods, labor unions and other grass-roots organizations were crushed, strikes were prohibited, and many suspected political dissidents were jailed and often tortured. In Argentina and Chile thousands of people were murdered, many of them taken from their homes never to be seen again.

In a series of provocative writings, Argentine political scientist Guillermo O'Donnell referred to these military governments as Bureaucratic Authoritarian (BA) regimes. Compared to previous military dictatorships, they had a more extensive bureaucratic structure, included in that structure like-minded civilian technocrats, penetrated more deeply into the spheres of civil society, were especially closely linked to Multinational Corporations (MNCs), and were highly repressive.[54]

O'Donnell focused on closely related economic and political factors that explained the rise of these BA regimes in the most developed area of Latin America. First, he argued, economic growth in these countries had come to a relative standstill because they had developed as far as they could with their available capital and technology. Further growth would require heavy investment in capital goods industries and new technologies, both of which could only be provided by multinational corporations. But MNCs (as well as domestic companies) had been reluctant to invest because of frequent labor conflicts in these countries, civil unrest, and Leftist electoral strength. All of these, in turn, primarily resulted from economic stagnation, high inflation, and declining living standards for workers.

The military looked very dimly at the growing radicalism and political polarization of society. In Argentina, Chile, and Uruguay, urban guerrillas added to the perceived threat. The goal of the new BA regimes, then, was to crush leftist unions, political parties, and guerrilla movements; limit wages; create a "stable environment for investment"; and work closely with MNCs and domestic big business to control inflation and reinvigorate the economy. Beyond repressing the Left, the armed forces sought to depoliticize society and exclude the population from political participation for a prolonged period. At the same time, the military wished to extend the role of the private sector and hopefully roll back state economic intervention such as welfare programs, minimum wage guarantees, and state ownership. Many of these objectives, of course, are consistent with the goals of other institutional military regimes articulated earlier. These involve, however, a more precise and elaborate "game plan" and a far more fundamental restructuring of society.

Revolutionary Military Regimes In a number of developing nations, the military has pursued goals diametrically different from the BA regimes' conservative agenda. Rather than excluding much of the population from the political system, they have extended political and economic participation to formerly excluded groups. Virtually always, however, that participation has been tightly controlled by an authoritarian political structure.[55]

In Africa, various "military marxist regimes" have laid out a program of cultural nationalism, anti-imperialism, mobilization of the peasantry and working class, nationalization of parts of the private sector, expansion of the state's economic role, and redistribution of the nation's economic resources to the poor. Revolutionary soldiers have usually been led by radicalized officers from the junior ranks. In a speech outlining the goals of Upper Volta's military government, Captain Thomas Sankara articulated the Marxist rhetoric typical of such regimes:

> The triumph of the Revolution . . . is the crowning moment of the struggle of the Volta People against its internal enemies. It is a victory against international imperialism and its internal allies. . . . These enemies of the people have been identified by the people in the forge of revolutionary action. They are: the bourgeoisie of Volta [and] . . . reactionary forces whose strength derives from the traditional feudal structures of our society. . . . The People in our revolution comprises: The working class . . . the petty bourgeoisie . . . the peasantry . . . [and] the lumpen proletariat.[56]

Similarly radical declarations have been made by military regimes in Ethiopia, the Sudan, Somalia, Congo-Brazzaville, Benin (formerly Dahomey), and Madagascar. Like other African military regimes, however, these governments have been led by men lacking extensive political experience or social sciences training (though they tend to be more educated than the officers who preceded them). Consequently, their Marxist ideals were "self-taught, ideologically immature and crude, and riddled with inconsistencies."[57] For some, Marxism simply expressed their strong nationalism and distaste for the European powers that had colonized the continent. For others, revolutionary rhetoric came almost as an afterthought, a means of justifying their seizure of power and authoritarian control. Thus, the government of Colonel Mengistu in Ethiopia, perhaps Africa's most prominent radical military regime, did not embrace Marxism-Leninism until it had been in office for three years. In Dahomey, General Mathieu Kerekou declared his government Marxist and created "revolution committees" simply as a pretext for spying on the civil service.[58]

Outside of sub-Saharan Africa, Leftist, but non-Marxist, military regimes have arisen in places as disparate as Libya, Iraq, Myanmar, Panama, and Peru. Peru's military seized power in 1968, seeking to curtail the power of the traditional rural oligarchy and incorporate the peasantry, working class, and urban poor into the political system.[59] Comparable, though far more modest, reform programs were introduced by military regimes in Panama and Ecuador.

THE ACCOMPLISHMENTS AND FAILURES OF MILITARY REGIMES

How successfully have military governments achieved the goals just articulated and how well have they served their country? Little needs to be said about personalist military dictatorships. With a few notable exceptions, they rarely make much serious pretext of serving the country. Even when they have some broader goals, their primary objectives tend to be patently self-serving. In short, it would be hard to argue seriously that dictators such as Batista (Cuba), Somoza (Nicaragua), Stroessner (Paraguay), Amin (Uganda), or Bokassa (Central African

Republic) contributed to the long-term political or economic growth of their nation. Consequently, the analysis that follows focuses on the record of institutional military governments.

Combating Corruption

Let us look first at the most commonly professed objective of institutional regimes, eliminating government corruption. Because government malfeasance is so pervasive in much of the Third World, denouncing it is a convenient means of legitimizing an extraconstitutional seizure of power. Yet most soldiers in power prove every bit as corrupt as their predecessors, or more so. To be sure, a few military regimes have been quite honest, but they are the exceptions. As one leading scholar has observed:

> Every Nigerian and Ghanaian coup . . . has had as its prime goal the elimination of deeply ingrained corruption from society. Yet, not one military administration has made truly consistent efforts in that direction . . . or for that matter remained immune to it itself. . . . [Elsewhere in Africa] in two . . . military regimes—Guinea and Burkina Faso—nepotism and accumulation of wealth commenced the very day the officer hierarchy took office.[60]

Ironically, Africa's constant military intervention tends to increase corruption in the civilian governments that are ousted. "The fear that [civilian] power may not last encourages the incoming politicians to grab what is grabbable."[61] In Asian nations such as Thailand and Indonesia the military's record has been equally disappointing. Speaking of Southeast Asia, Harold Crouch has noted that "often military officers have already become entangled in this web [of corruption] even before the coup takes place."[62] Even within those military governments that avoid gross corruption, the lure of contraband automobiles and tax-supported vacation homes proves irresistible to many officers. In short, even those military governments that take office with noble intentions soon become corrupted.

Defending Corporate Interests

When it comes to pursuing their second major objective, that of advancing their own corporate interests, not surprisingly military governments have been more successful. But their increased budgetary allocations have come at the cost of badly needed social and economic expenditures. Moreover, even from the armed forces' perspective, seizing power has been a mixed blessing.

Military rule normally leads to increased defense outlays. Typically, there are more armaments purchases, higher military salaries, better military housing, and more luxurious officers' clubs. Sometimes the size of the armed forces increases. In Asia, military officers have benefited from "lucrative public sector employment, foreign postings, and preferential treatment in the dispersal of governmental contracts."[63]

After seizing power in Libya, Colonel Qadhafi sought to insure the military's loyalty by doubling their salaries, making them the highest paid army in the Third World. In their first five years in power, Uruguay's generals raised the military and security share of the national budget from 26.2 percent to over 40 percent.[64] A parallel "bias in favor of army, police and civil-service salaries and benefits can be observed in practically every military regime in Africa."[65] And an analysis of government expenditures in Southeast Asia from 1970 through the early 1980s reveals that military-dominated regimes spent a somewhat higher percentage of the national budget and of GNP on defense than civilian governments did.[66]

Even when soldiers are not actually in control of the government, the mere specter of military intervention often leads civilian governments to bestow salary hikes and expensive weapons systems on the armed forces. For example, it would be very imprudent of the civilian governments in the Philippines, Pakistan, or Thailand to shortchange military expenditures. Even Malaysia and Singapore, with no histories of coups d'état, pay their officers generously to keep them out of politics.[67] Similarly, Colombia and Venezuela, two of Latin America's most long-lived civilian governments have supported healthy defense budgets aimed at keeping the military at bay. Only where the military has been placed under firm civilian control (Mexico) or essentially has been eliminated (Costa Rica) do defense outlays fall substantially.

Of course, the armed forces' gains in expenditures are usually the country's loss. Third World military outlays are frequently far higher than the country needs or the society can afford. As a consequence, they reduce badly needed social and economic investment. Countries in South America that have not fought an international war in decades waste fortunes on naval vessels and state-of-the-art jets. In the Middle East, the percentage of GNP allocated to defense is among the highest in the world. And in Africa, home to many of the world's poorest countries, military expenditures are especially out of proportion to economic capacities. Thus, despite having a per capita GNP less than half of Latin America's, African governments spent a third more per soldier in the 1980s.[68]

Ironically, even for the military, ruling the nation is not without its risks. Although power may enlarge defense budgets, it also tends to affect institutional cohesion adversely. Generals (or admirals) squabble over the allocation of resources and over broader policy issues. Even military governments that came to power with considerable popular support usually lose legitimacy over time as they confront difficult economic and social problems. As politically divisive issues arise, they generate splits within the high command of the armed forces.[69] In some regions, most notably sub-Saharan Africa, internal coups (one faction ousting another) have produced a series of unstable military governments. Elsewhere, the armed forces commonly return to the barracks, ceding power to civilians, to avoid further internal divisions. Eric Nordlinger's study of military governments found that they tended to dissolve in five to seven years.[70] Karen Remmer's more recent work on 12 South America military regimes between 1960 and 1990 showed 4 to be quite durable (12 to 35 years). The remaining 8, however, averaged under 7 years in office. [71]

Establishing Stability

Military officers almost universally react negatively to popular unrest and political instability. For one thing, disorder violates their hierarchical view of society. In some cases it threatens the interests of groups, such as the middle class or industrialists, closely allied to the armed forces. In other instances it poses a threat to the military itself. Military men in Latin America, for example, are keenly aware that Marxist revolutions in Cuba and Nicaragua destroyed the old military establishment. Some of Batista's officers in Cuba faced the firing squad, while many Nicaraguan National Guardsmen were imprisoned or fled the country. In Chile and Brazil, Leftist movements threatened the officers' hierarchical control of the armed forces. Similarly the generals in Algeria felt threatened by the growing strength of Islamic fundamentalism. Even "revolutionary soldiers" in Ethiopia, Libya, and Peru favor discipline and socioeconomic change controlled from the top.

In many respects military governments are particularly well suited for controlling civil unrest. They can use force with impunity to combat guerrilla insurrections, disperse street demonstrations, and ban strikes. In a few countries, extensive and sophisticated intelligence agencies like South Korea's KCIA and Chile's DINA have enabled the regime to penetrate deeply into society and control dissent. The Argentine and Uruguayan armies used repressive tactics to crush potent urban guerrilla movements. In Indonesia, the military destroyed one of the world's largest Communist parties and decimated a separatist movement in East Timor.

But these mass movements could only be defeated at a tremendous cost in human suffering. Some 3,000 people died in the Argentine army's "dirty war" against the Left, while many more were imprisoned and tortured. Students and other young people were the primary victims, many of them incorrectly identified as part of the radical opposition. In Chile, thousands of intellectuals and professionals fled the country, devastating one of the Third World's most advanced university systems and artistic communities. More than 3,000 Chileans died; many others were the victims of torture.[72] During Indonesia's "year of living dangerously" perhaps 500,000 Communists and ethnic Chinese were massacred, while some 150,000 other people died subsequently (many through starvation) in the army's victory over East Timorian separatists.[73]

In all, the military's record of providing long-term stability is mixed. In several Asian and Latin American countries, state repression, coupled with technocratic development policies, has either co-opted or decimated opposition groups. In South Korea, sharply improved living standards and gradual political change have opened the way for stable, elected government, though the military remains an important force in the background. In Argentina, Chile, and Uruguay, the BA regimes' brutality against radical movements ultimately convinced political leaders on both sides of the ideological spectrum (but especially the Left) to moderate their positions so as to not provoke further armed forces intervention. But these "successes" are the exception. Despite its brute strength, the armed forces' tenure in office has been surprisingly short lived. One early study of Third World military regimes showed that nearly half of them lasted less than two years.[74] While their longevity has increased since that time, they continue to have a detrimental effect on political development. Military rule, no matter what its accomplishments, only impedes the maturation of political parties and other civilian institutions necessary for long-term stability.

In Africa, more often than not, coups have only led to further coups with no real stability. The brutal regime of Sergeant Samuel Doe opened up Liberia to a devastating civil war that continues to rage. Armed forces rule in Ethiopia and the Sudan only exacerbated ethnically based civil wars. In the Middle East and Asia, extended suppression of dissident groups in countries such as Iraq and Burma will likely lead to greater upheavals after those regimes fall.[75]

Economic Development

Earlier we noted that coup d'états often follow economic downturns or severe inflation. Consequently, newly installed military governments commonly hope to impose fiscal discipline and thereby revitalize the economy. In South Korea, Indonesia, Brazil, and Chile, for example, conservative military regimes curtailed union activity in order to suppress wage demands. Reduced strike activity and weaker unions were expected both to lower inflation and to attract multinational investment.

Proponents of military dictatorships also assert that they can more freely make economic decisions consistent with the broad national interest because they need not pander to special interest groups. Critics counter that soldiers are not trained to manage an economy. Even when well intentioned, they tend to allocate excessive funds to defense and to wasteful, chauvinistic projects.

Examining the economic performance of military governments provides some evidence to support both sides of this debate. South Korea demonstrates that a military government can oversee a very successful economic development program. Following General Park Chung Hee's seizure of power in 1961, the military governed the country for over 25 years. During that period the Republic of Korea was transformed from an underdeveloped nation into one of the world's most dynamic industrial economies.[76] Moveover, sustained economic growth was accompanied by very equitable distribution of income. Consequently, South

Korea is now cited, along with Taiwan, Hong Kong, and Singapore, as a model of well-executed economic development.

Elsewhere in Asia, Indonesia's military also presided over rapid economic growth from the mid-1960s to late 1990s. During the 1970s and early 1980s, some of the country's extensive petroleum revenues were plowed back into labor-intensive export industries. At the same time, rural development programs and mass education improved income distribution and, coupled with economic growth, substantially reduced the number of Indonesians living in poverty. Thailand, governed by the military for much of the last decades, also participated in East and Southeast Asia's economic boom.[77] However, excessive borrowing, "crony capitalism" (plentiful government loans and contracts to politically connected businesspeople), and corruption brought on a severe financial crisis in East and Southeast Asia beginning in 1998. Sharp declines in production, plant closings, currency devaluations, and inflation all eradicated some of the gains which the population had enjoyed in the preceding decades.

Two of Latin America's major Bureaucratic Authoritarian regimes, Chile and Brazil, had more ambiguous economic records. After several false starts, Chile's probusiness, export-oriented policies ushered in a period of strong economic expansion with low inflation. Pinochet's achievements, however, followed a period of severe economic hardship, with the poor being forced to bear a disproportionate share of the sacrifice. Under Chile's military government, as with the other BA regimes, income distribution deteriorated. After the restoration of democracy in 1990, the civilian governments of Patricio Aylwin and Eduardo Frei maintained high growth rates while using targeted programs to reduce the number of Chileans living in poverty.

Brazil's BA regime achieved dramatic economic growth during the late 1960s and 1970s, turning the country into an important industrial power. The benefits of that growth, however, were very poorly distributed, leaving many of the nation's poor worse off. Moreover, Brazil's "economic miracle" was built on excessive foreign borrowing, making the nation the Third World's largest external debtor. Unlike Chile, civilian rule has not improved the economy since the military stepped down in 1985. Initially, continued deficit spending and poor planning brought back the hyperinflation that the generals had vowed to eradicate. Current President Fernando Henrique Cardoso brought inflation under control in the 1990s, but economic growth since has been weak and the country's financial structure unstable.

Other Latin American military governments, including the BA regimes in Argentina and Uruguay, generally performed poorly in the economic sphere. They spent excessively on defense, borrowed too much, suffered from corruption, and, even when well intentioned, lacked a grasp of development economics. In Africa, the armed forces' economic record has generally ranged from poor to disastrous.

But if only a few military governments have outstanding records of economic achievement, it is not clear that they have performed significantly worse than civilian administrations. Efforts at systematically comparing the economic performances of military and civilian governments throughout the developing world face a number of methodological problems. Most important, it is virtually impossible to control for the myriad of other factors that might explain why one type of government has performed better than another.[78] When statistical analyses have been made, they tend to find little difference between the economic growth rates of the two types of regimes. Karen Remmer's analysis of Latin America, however, indicates that economies frequently decline right after the military has stepped down, suggesting that they, rather than their civilian successors, are responsible.[79] It is worth noting that the military rulers with the best economic performances—South Korea, Indonesia, and Chile—recognizing the limits of their own skills, pursued the policy recommendations of civilian advisors.[80]

MILITARY WITHDRAWAL FROM POLITICS

Once the armed forces have become entrenched in the political system, dislodging them is no easy task. Military withdrawal is sometimes induced by domestic unrest, revolution, or external powers. More often, however, the armed forces voluntarily returns to the barracks for one or more of the following reasons: They had limited objectives from the outset and, having accomplished their major objectives, decide to withdraw; difficult economic conditions make further governance unpalatable; extended rule threatens internal military cohesion; or the government has become so unpopular that staying in power would undermine the armed forces' legitimacy as an institution.

Many military governments see themselves as caretakers whose task it is to restore stability or solve a particular problem and then return power to the civilians. In Ecuador, for example, the armed forces frequently ousted elected leaders whom they considered too demagogic, too populist, or too incompetent. After ruling relatively briefly, they then voluntarily returned to the barracks.

Since the authors of institutional coups come to office with expectations of augmented military budgets and accelerated economic growth, their interest in power, not surprisingly, wanes when the economy turns sour. In countries such as Peru, Uruguay, Pakistan, and Thailand, economic downturns have convinced military governments to step down. Economic declines may also aggravate internal divisions within the armed forces.

In sub-Saharan Africa, governing may also exacerbate ethnic divisions within the army, particularly when officers from one tribe or religion dominate top government positions. For example, in Nigeria, the armed forces' entrance into the political arena unleashed four internal coups in a ten-year span, with ethnic tensions playing a role. Two heads of government and several other senior officers were killed in the military's internal struggles. Fearing a deterioration in military cohesiveness, some governments may prefer to step down, leaving the county's problems to civilians.

Finally, just as coups d'états are most likely when civilian governments lack legitimacy, the army is most likely to return to the barracks when its own legitimacy declines. This happens most dramatically when the soldiers are defeated in war. For example, following its humiliating defeat by Britain in the Falklands (or Malvinas) war, the Argentine military regime was forced to return power to an elected civilian government. Similarly, in Pakistan, the military had to hand power over to its leading civilian critic, Zulfiqar Ali Bhutto, after it lost East Pakistan (now Bangladesh) in a war with India.

Of course, there are other ways military regimes lose legitimacy. In Uruguay, economic decay and public revulsion against government repression so weakened the regime that it unexpectedly lost a popular referendum that it was sure it could tightly control.[81] Eventually, popular discontent induced the generals to negotiate a return of civilian government. More recently, in Thailand, massive student-led, prodemocracy demonstrations convinced the armed forces to withdraw.

While some combination of these factors accounts for the withdrawal of most military regimes, they do not guarantee that the armed forces will stay in the barracks. Quite the contrary, the soldiers are likely to return. Talukder Maniruzzaman examined 71 instances of military withdrawal from power in the Third World from 1946 to 1984.[82] In 65 percent of these cases the armed forces was back in power within five years.[83]

Since the early 1980s, however, those military regimes that have stepped down from power have been more prone to remain in the barracks. For example, as of 1999, the Latin American nations of Argentina, Peru, Ecuador, Brazil, Uruguay, Guatemala, and El Salvador, all with long histories of armed forces intervention, had enjoyed anywhere from 10 to 20 years without military rule. In South Korea decades of military dominance came to an end in 1993.[84] In Africa, military rulers in Bénin and Congo handed power to democratically elected civilian governments.[85] Indeed, during the past decade, many military regimes throughout the developing world have been replaced by elected civilian governments. While some of those democratic transitions have already been reversed, many are likely to endure.

In some cases the military's legitimacy has been undermined by years of repressive or corrupt rule. Thus, Argentina's democratic governments since the mid 1980s have been able to reduce the country's formidable armed forces to one-third its previous size. Elsewhere, as in Mozambique, El Salvador, and Nicaragua, peace treaties ending long civil wars have stipulated sharp reductions in the size of the military. In countries such as Pakistan, however, the military has maintained its share of the government budget.

Ultimately, if the armed forces is to acquiesce to its removal from the center of national politics, it will generally need to find new roles to justify its existence. This is particularly true in countries where there is little external military threat (as in Africa and Latin America where wars between nation-states, as opposed to civil conflict, has been quite rare).

NEW ROLES FOR THE ARMED FORCES

Many of the proposed "new roles" for the military are not really entirely new. They include control of drug trafficking (in parts of Latin America, the Caribbean, and Asia), antiterrorism activity, emergency relief efforts (following earthquakes, typhoons, hurricanes, and the like), and construction of infrastructure such as roads. With the expansion of the cocaine trade in recent decades, antidrug activity has become particularly important in countries such as Bolivia, Colombia, and Mexico.

Unfortunately, in the past some of these activities have brought as many new problems as solutions to old ones. In Mexico, Colombia, the Caribbean, and Central America, antidrug efforts have often corrupted the armed forces as officers change from enforcers to well-paid protectors of the drug cartels. In Mexico, for example, there have even been gun fights between antidrug units and other military units that have been paid off to protect drug bosses. At the same time, the armed forces in many LDCs have often used their mandates to combat terrorism and other forms of internal subversion as carte blanche to violate human rights and crush peaceful and legitimate political opposition groups.

With the end of the cold war, the United States has begun to exert its tremendous influence abroad, seeking to reorient the political outlook of Third World militaries. During the mid-1990s, for example, the U.S. government directed its military commanders stationed overseas to encourage foreign armed forces "to consider roles... that are supportive of civilian control and respectful of human rights and the role of law."[86] In other words, it is critical that the military's new roles be pursued in a manner that reinforces, rather than subverts, civilian control over the armed forces as well as military respect for human rights and civil liberties. This is a task easier said than done.

Finally, one last, new role for Third World militaries needs mention. In recent years countries such as India, Pakistan, Argentina, and Uruguay have supplied United Nations peace-keeping forces in trouble spots such as Bosnia, Cambodia, and Central America. This represents a very different military activity and holds great promise for supporting international peace efforts. In west Africa, regional peace-keeping forces have been sent to Liberia and Sierra Leon. Here there is some potential for mischief as regional powers such as Nigeria may use such efforts as a means of extending their own power and pursuing their foreign policy agendas.

CONCLUSION

Not long ago, a leading expert on African politics noted that "military regimes [in that region] cannot easily be distinguished from civilian regimes by their economic and social policies or abilities."[87] So too it might be argued in much of the Third World that soldiers have ruled no better and no worse than civilian governments. At times both have been guilty of corruption and human rights abuses.

Both, on occasion, have performed well. As we have seen, some military governments have achieved stability and economic growth, many others have not.

Even the most successful military regimes, however, ultimately inhibit political development. They do so because their very rationale for seizing power is "the politics of antipolitics."[88] With their hierarchical perspective and their distaste for disorder, soldiers believe in a managed society. Most reject the give and take of political competition and the compromises inherent in politics. Consequently, they

> . . . fail to see the functional aspects of the great game of politics: They severely restrict the free flow of the political process and force would-be politicians into a long period of hibernation. . . . The opportunity for gaining political skills by a people once under a military regime is likely to be continually postponed with the arrival of every new military regime.[89]

In light of that fundamental failing, what are the prospects of disengaging the armed forces from politics? The answer varies considerably from country to country and is greatly influenced by each nation's level of socioeconomic development. That is not to suggest that there is an invariable correlation between economic development and civilian political dominance. As we have noted, Bureaucratic Authoritarian regimes arose in some of Latin America's most developed nations. And two of Africa's more affluent nations, Libya and Nigeria, have been dominated by the armed forces. It appears, however, that countries must generally reach a certain floor of economic development (as measured in GNP per capita) in order to have a reasonable chance at democratic rule.[90] Once a nation has reached that floor, as its population becomes more literate, as independent secondary groups (churches, unions, and so on) develop, as the working class's ability to defend its rights grows, and as the middle class expands, eventually it is more prone to achieve democratic, civilian rule.

Socioeconomic development contributed to the transition to democratic government in South Korea and to the mass demonstrations in Thailand that toppled its most recent military government (here middle-class student leaders coordinated their street protests with cellular phones). In spite of its recent depression, Latin America's earlier, long-term economic growth has likely contributed to the maintenance of civilian government throughout the area since 1980. For the first time in recent memory the region is free of military rule and many of its countries' prospects for sustained civilian government are increasingly encouraging. History suggests that the longer countries can sustain civilian government, the lower the probability of future military intervention.[91]

In the least socioeconomically developed countries, such as Haiti, Guatemala, Myanmar, and much of sub-Saharan Africa, there is reason to anticipate continued military political involvement. These countries suffer from strong social and political polarization (based on class, ethnicity, or both), intense poverty, low levels of mass education, weak political institutionalization, and poor leadership. As a consequence, political actors, including the military, frequently resort to extralegal and violent behavior. In short, theirs is what Samuel Huntington and Amos Perlmutter have called praetorian politics, where "the wealthy bribe; students riot; workers strike; mobs demonstrate; and the military coup."[92]

DISCUSSION QUESTIONS

1. What factors influence the likelihood of military intervention in Third World politics?

2. What are the major types of military regimes and what are their goals?

3. What are the major strengths and weakness of military governments?

4. What factors induce the armed forces to withdraw from politics?

NOTES

1. George W. Ball, *The Discipline of Power* (Boston: Little, Brown, 1968).

2. Harold Crouch, *The Army and Politics in Indonesia* (Ithaca, NY: Cornell University Press, 1978), p. 345. In 1998 massive protest demonstrations, particularly by Indonesian students, forced President Suharto (a former general) from office after more than three decades in power. The political influence of the armed forces has declined since that time but is still formidable.

3. William Thompson, "Explanations of the Military Coup," Ph. D. dissertation, University of Washington, Seattle, 1972, p. 11. Quoted in Amos Perlmutter, *The Military and Politics in Modern Times* (New Haven, CT: Yale University Press, 1977), p. 115.

4. Claude E. Welch, "Military Disengagements from Politics?: Incentives and Obstacles in Political Change," in *Military Power and Politics in Black Africa*, ed. Simon Baynham (New York: St. Martin's Press, 1986), pp. 89–90; Steven Thomas Seitz, "The Military in Black African Politics," in *Civil-Military Interaction in Asia and Africa*, ed. Charles H. Kennedy and David J. Louscher (Leiden, The Netherlands: E. J. Brill, 1991), pp. 65, 67.

5. Samuel Decalo, *Coups and Army Rule in Africa* (New Haven, CT: Yale University Press, 1990), p. 2.

6. Since its 1959 revolution, Cuba's civil-military relations have been somewhat unique. While the government is essentially controlled by civilians, there is a close linkage between the ruling Communist party and the armed forces, with many military officers holding high party ranks and the party very involved in military policy. Consequently, there is considerable debate among Cuba scholars as to the military's strength relative to the Communist party.

7. Chai-Anan Samudavanija and Suchit Bunbongkarn, "Thailand," in *Military-Civilian Relations in South-East Asia*, ed. Zakaria Haji Ahmad and Harold Crouch (Singapore: Oxford University Press, 1985), p. 78; Suchit Bunbongkarn, "The Thai Military and Its Role in Society in the 1990s," in *The Military, the State, and Development in Asia and the Pacific*, ed. Viberto Selochan (Boulder, CO: Westview Press, 1991), p. 68.

8. When Aquino's term ended, Ramos was elected as her successor. During his term in office he increased the military's political role. See Jeffrey Riedinger, "Caciques and Coups:

The Challenge of Democratic Consolidation in the Philippines," in *Democracy and Its Limits*, ed. Howard Handelman and Mark Tessler (Notre Dame, IN: Notre Dame University Press, 1999).

9. Morris Janowitz, *Military Institutions and Coercion in the Developing Nations: Expanded Edition of the Military in the Political Development of New Nations* (Chicago: University of Chicago Press, 1977), p. 105.

10. Samuel P. Huntington, *The Soldier and the State: The Theory and Politics of Civil-Military Relations* (New York: Vintage Books, 1964).

11. Samuel P. Huntington, "Civilian Control of the Military: A Theoretical Statement," in *Political Behavior: A Read in Theory and Research*, ed. Heinz Eulau, Samuel Eldersveld, and Morris Janowitz (New York: Free Press, 1956), pp. 380–381.

12. Samuel P. Huntington, "Patterns of Violence in World Politics," in *Changing Patterns of Military Politics*, ed. Samuel P. Huntington (New York: Free Press, 1962), pp. 19–22.

13. Alfred Stepan, "The New Professionalism of Internal Warfare and Military Role Expansion," in *Armies and Politics in Latin America*, rev. ed., ed. Abraham Lowenthal and J. Samuel Fitch (New York: Holmes and Meier, 1986), pp. 134–150. See also Jose Nun, "The Middle-Class Military Coup Revisited," in ibid., pp. 59–95, for similar arguments.

14. Ruth First, *The Barrel of a Gun: Political Power in Africa and the Coup D'état* (London: Allen Lane/Penguin Press, 1970), pp. 208, 4.

15. Samuel P. Huntington, *Political Order in Changing Societies* (New Haven, CT: Yale University Press, 1968), p. 194.

16. Robert Wesson, preface to *New Military Politics in Latin America*, ed. Robert Wesson (New York: Praeger, 1982), p. v.

17. Samuel E. Finer, *The Man on Horseback: The Role of the Military in Politics*, 2d ed. (London: Penguin Books, 1976), pp. 78ff.

18. Huntington, *Political Order in Changing Societies*.

19. In the early 1990s, the country was shocked by two unsuccessful military coup attempts, but civilian rule survived.

20. Terry Karl, "Petroleum and Political Pacts: The Transition to Democracy in Venezuela," in *Transitions from Authoritarian Rule*, ed. Guillermo O'Donnell, Philippe C. Schmitter, and Laurence Whitehead (Baltimore, MD: Johns Hopkins University Press, 1986), pp. 196–219. See also Felipe Aguero, "The Military and Democracy in Venezuela," in *The Military and Democracy*, ed. Louis W. Goodman, Johanna S. R. Mendelson, and Juan Rial (Lexington, MA: Lexington Books, 1990), pp.257–276.

21. Marion J. Levy Jr., *Modernization and the Structure of Societies* (Princeton, NJ: Princeton University Press, 1966), vol. 2, p. 603.

22. Lucian W. Pye, "Armies in the Process of Political Modernization," in *The Role of the Military in Underdeveloped Countries*, ed. John J. Johnson (Princeton, NJ: Princeton University Press, 1962), pp. 69–89.

23. Manfred Halpern, *The Politics of Social Change in the Middle East and North Africa* (Princeton, NJ: Princeton University Press, 1963), pp. 75, 253.

24. One of the most influential was Morris Janowitz, *Military Institutions and Coercion in Developing Nations* (Chicago: University of Chicago, 1977). For a summary of those writings and further references, see Henry Bienen, "The Background to Contemporary Study of Militaries and Modernization," in *The Military and Modernization*, ed. Henry Bienen (Chicago: Atherton, 1971), pp. 1–33; First, *The Barrel of a Gun*, pp. 13–20.

25. Daniel Lerner and Richard D. Robinson, "Swords and Plowshares: The Turkish Army as a Modernizing Force," in *The Military and Modernization*, pp. 117–148.

26. Eric A. Nordlinger, *Soldiers in Politics: Military Coups and Governments* (Englewood Cliffs, NJ: Prentice Hall, 1977), pp. 32–37.

27. Karen L. Remmer, *Military Rule in Latin America* (Boston: Unwin Hyman, 1989), p. 3.

28. It is not invariably the case that the armed forces in the least developed nations are reform oriented. While the military has often been progressive in the less developed nations of South America, Africa, and the Middle East, it has been quite reactionary in Central America and the Caribbean, where it has been co-opted by the upper class.

29. Eric Nordlinger, *Soldiers in Politics*, p. 173; also Huntington, *Political Order*, Chapter 4.

30. Huntington, *Political Order*, p. 221.

31. Decalo, *Coups and Army Rule in Africa*, pp. 133.

32. John Booth, *The End and the Beginning: The Nicaraguan Revolution*, 2d ed. (Boulder, CO: Westview Press, 1985).

33. Some personalist dictators, like Argentina's Juan Perón, have broader social programs. Peronism sought to industrialize the country and benefit the working class. Even personalist regimes such as his, however, still suffer from extensive corruption and over-concentration of power in the hands of one person.

34. Decalo, *Coups and Army Rule in Africa*, pp. 139–198.

35. On personal dictatorships in Africa, military and civilian, see Robert Jackson and Carl Rosberg, *Personal Rule in Africa* (Berkeley: University of California Press, 1982).

36. David J. Gould, *Bureaucratic Corruption and Underdevelopment in the Third World* (New York: Pergammon Press, 1980), p. xiv; Michael J. Schatzberg, *The Politics of Oppression in Zaire* (Bloomington: Indiana University Press, 1988). Mobutu changed the name of his country from the Congo to Zaire. After he was overthrown, the name was changed back to the Congo.

37. Richard Millet, *Guardians of the Dynasty* (Maryknoll, NY: Orbis, 1977).

38. Decalo, *Coups and Army Rule in Africa*, p. 11. Decalo argues that in Africa personalities, more so than broad socioeconomic or political variables, explain military intervention. See also his *Psychoses of Power: African Personal Dictatorships* (Boulder, CO: Westview Press, 1989).

39. Edward A. Olsen and Stephen Jurika Jr., "Introduction," and Harold W. Maynard, "The Role of the Indonesian Armed Forces," in *The Armed Forces in Contemporary Asian Society*, ed. Edward A. Olsen and Stephen Jurika, Jr. (Boulder CO: Westview Press, 1986), pp. 18, 207–208.

40. In some cases—Liberia, for example—such councils have been mere facades, with one person really in power. Thus, it is not always easy to distinguish between personalist and institutional military regimes. Ultimately, the determining factor is where real power resides rather than the formal structures.

41. Amos Perlmutter, *Political Roles and Military Rulers* (London: Frank Cass, 1981).

42. Guillermo O'Donnell, *Modernization and Bureaucratic-Authoritarianism: Studies in South American Politics* (Berkeley: University of California Press, 1973).

43. Jeffrey Lunstead, "The Armed Forces in Bangladesh Society," in *The Armed Forces in Contemporary Asian Society*, p. 316.

44. Ruth First, *Power in Africa* (New York: Pantheon Books, 1970), p. 20.

45. First, *The Barrel of a Gun*, p. 429.

46. Craig Baxter and Syedur Rahman, "Bangladesh Military: Political Institutionalization and Economic Development," in *Civil Military Interaction*, pp. 43–60.

47. Harold Crouch, "The Military and Politics in South-East Asia," in *Military-Civilian Relations*, p. 291.

48. Ibid.

49. Crouch, *The Army and Politics in Indonesia*.

50. Remmer, *Military Rule in Latin America*, pp. 3–31.

51. Seitz, "The Military in Black African Politics," in *Civil-Military Interaction*, pp. 61–75.

52. John J. Johnson, *The Military and Society in Latin America* (Stanford, CA: Stanford University Press, 1964); O'Donnell, *Modernization and Bureaucratic-Authoritarianism*.

53. Argentina's two military regimes lasted seven years each (1966 to 1973 and 1976 to 1983), with a three-year hiatus of unstable civilian government. The Pinochet government in Chile lasted from 1973 to 1990. While the Chilean dictatorship was not as long-lived as Brazil's, Pinochet himself ruled far longer than any of the generals in those four countries.

54. Guillermo O'Donnell, "Corporatism and the Question of the State," in *Authoritarianism and Corporatism in Latin America*, ed. James Malloy (Pittsburgh: University of Pittsburgh Press, 1977). The most complete analysis of O'Donnell's rather difficult theories is contained in David Collier, ed., *The New Authoritarianism in Latin America* (Princeton, NJ: Princeton University Press, 1979), and an excellent critique is found in Karen L. Remmer and Gilbert W. Merkx, "Bureaucratic-Authoritarianism Revisited," *Latin American Research Review* 17, no. 2 (1982): 3–40.

55. For a discussion of the difference between inclusionary and exclusionary regimes and their relationship to democracy and authoritarianism, see Remmer, *Military Rule in Latin America*, pp. 6–17.

56. "The Political Orientation Speech Delivered by Captain Thomas Sankara in Ouagadougou, Upper Volta on 2 October, 1983," in *Military Marxists in Africa*, ed. John Markakis and Michael Waller (London: Frank Cass, 1986), pp. 145–153 (selected portions).

57. Samuel Decalo, "The Morphology of Radical Military Rule in Africa," in *Military Marxist Regimes*, p. 123.

58. Thomas S. Cox, *Civil-Military Relations in Sierra Leone* (Cambridge, MA: Harvard University Press, 1976), p. 14.

59. Kevin Middlebrook and David Scott Palmer, *Military Governments and Political Development: Lessons from Peru* (Beverly Hills, CA: Sage Publications, 1975).

60. Samuel Decalo, "Military Rule in Africa: Etiology and Morphology," in *Military Power and Politics in Black Africa*, pp. 56, 58.

61. J. Bayo Adekanye, "The Post-Military State in Africa," in *The Political Dilemma of Military Regimes*, ed. Christopher Clapham and George Philip (London: Croom Helm, 1985), p. 87.

62. Crouch, "The Military and Politics in South-East Asia," in *Military-Civilian Relations*, pp. 292–293.

63. Charles H. Kennedy and David J. Louscher, "Civil-Military Interaction: Data in Search of a Theory," in *Civil-Military Interaction*, p. 5.

64. Howard Handelman "Uruguay," in *Military Government and the Movement Towards Democracy in South America*, ed. Howard Handelman and Thomas Sanders (Bloomington: Indiana University Press, 1981), p. 218.

65. Decalo, *Coups and Army Rule in Africa*, p. 20.

66. Crouch, "The Military and Politics in South-East Asia," p. 306.

67. Harold Crouch, "The Military in Malaysia," in *The Military, the State*, pp. 130–131.

68. Claude E. Welch Jr., "From 'Armies of Africans' to 'African Armies': The Evolution of Military Forces in Africa," in *African Armies: Evolution and Capabilities*, ed. Bruce E. Arlinghaus and Pauline H. Baker (Boulder, Co: Westview Press, 1986), p. 25.

69. On the problems soldiers face when trying to govern, see Clapham and Philip, eds., *The Political Dilemma of Military Regimes*, especially Chapter 1.

70. Nordlinger, *Soldiers in Politics*, p. 139.

71. Remmer, *Military Rule*, p. 40.

72. Pamela Constable and Arturo Valenzuela, *A Nation of Enemies: Chile under Pinochet* (New York: W. W. Norton, 1991).

73. Of course, many military regimes are not particularly repressive. However, it is precisely those that seize power to restore order in highly polarized societies that normally are the most brutal.

74. R. D. McKinlay and A. S. Cohan, "Performance and Instability in Military and Non-military Regime Systems," *American Political Science Review* 70 (September 1976): 850–864.

75. Both countries have experienced extensive ethnic unrest under semimilitary (Iraq) or military rule. Iraq's Kurdish secession movement was revitalized by the country's defeat in the Gulf War.

76. Jueng-en Woo, *Race to the Swift* (New York: Columbia University Press, 1991).

77. For a somewhat more critical view, particularly of income distribution and welfare in Indonesia, see "Military Regimes and Social Justice in Indonesia and Thailand," in *Civil-Military Interaction*, pp. 96–113; see also the chapters on South Korea, Indonesia, and Thailand in James W. Morely, ed., *Driven by Growth* (New York: M. E. Sharpe, 1992).

78. For a discussion of the problems involved in evaluating the economic performance of Latin America's military governments, see Karen L. Remmer, "Evaluating the Policy Impact of Military Regimes in Latin America," in *Armies and Politics*, pp. 367–385; Remmer, *Military Rule*, Chapter 4.

79. Remmer, *Military Rule*, pp. 197–200; Robert W. Jackman, "Politicians in Uniform: Military Governments and Social Change in the Third World," *American Political Science Review* 72, no. 4 (1978): 1262–1275; Seitz, "The Military in Black African Politics."

80. Edward A. Olsen, "The Societal Role of the ROK Armed Forces," in *The Armed Forces in Contemporary Asian Society*, pp. 95–96.

81. Howard Handelman, "Prelude to the 1984 Uruguayan Election: The Military Regime's Legitimacy Crisis and the 1980 Constitutional Plebiscite", in *Critical Elections in the Americas*, ed. Paul Drake and Eduardo Silva (San Diego: University of California Press, 1986).

82. In all of these cases military rulers were succeeded by civilians. There are, of course, also many instances of military governments giving way to other ones as the result of internal coups or other intramilitary conflict.

83. Talukder Maniruzzaman, *Military Withdrawal from Politics: A Comparative Study* (Cambridge, MA: Ballinger Publishing, 1987), pp. 21, 24–25.

84. South Korea's first democratic presidential election had been held in 1987 but the victor, Roe Tae Woo, had been a former military strong-man. Thus, full civilian government did not come until Kim Young Sam assumed the presidency in 1993. On Korea's transition, see Byung-Kook Kim, "Korea's Crisis of Success," in *Democracy in East Asia*, ed. Larry Diamond and Marc F. Plattner (Baltimore, MD: Johns Hopkins University Press, 1998), pp. 113–132.

85. Michael Bratton and Nicolas van de Walle, *Democratic Experiments in Africa* (New York: Cambridge University Press, 1997), pp. 197–203.

86. Quoted in Louis W. Goodman, "Military Roles Past and Present," in *Civil-Military Relations and Democracy*, ed. Larry Diamond and Marc F. Plattner (Baltimore, MD: Johns Hopkins University Press, 1996), p. 32. The discussion of "new roles" for the military that follows draws on Goodman's chapter.

87. Henry S. Bienen, "African Militaries as Foreign Policy Actors," in *Arms and the African*, ed. William J. Foltz and Henry Bienen (New Haven, CT: Yale University Press, 1985), p. 154.

88. Brian Loveman and Thomas M. Davies Jr., eds., *The Politics of Antipolitics: The Military in Latin America*, 2d ed. (Lincoln: University of Nebraska Press, 1989).

89. Ibid., p. 6.

90. James Malloy and Mitchell Seligson, eds., *Authoritarians and Democrats* (Pittsburgh: University of Pittsburgh Press, 1988).

91. The reader should note that all of these associations are probabilities, not certainties. No single factor, be it high literacy, a large middle class, strong political parties, or a history of civilian government, is guaranteed to inhibit military intervention.

92. Huntington, *Political Order*, p. 196.

9

❧

THE POLITICAL
ECONOMY OF THIRD
WORLD DEVELOPMENT

Most Third World governments, except for the most corrupt and ineffective, wish to promote economic growth and modernization. Growth coupled with a reasonably equitable distribution of income offers the promise of improved living standards and, presumably, increased popular support for the ruling regime.[1] It also provides added tax revenues, thereby augmenting government capacity. And economic development can enhance a nation's military strength, diplomatic influence, and international prestige.

But the substantial potential benefits of growth should not obscure the difficult questions that surround economic development: How is growth to be attained and how can the sometimes conflicting goals of economic development be reconciled? How can economic growth be achieved without doing irreparable harm to the environment? The optimism expressed by early modernization theorists regarding Third World economic development turned to pessimism during the 1980s in the face of economic crises in Africa and Latin America.[2] On the other hand, dependency theorists' pervasive pessimism concerning the limits of development in "the periphery" seemed to have been belied by East Asia's spectacular growth from the 1970s through the late 1990s (that region's deep economic crisis in the closing years of the century revived some pessimism; but, as discussed later in this chapter, it is unlikely to wipe out the region's extensive previous progress).

In recent years, scholarship on the Third World has increasingly turned to "political economy." Martin Staniland defines this field as the study of "how politics determines aspects of the economy, and how economic institutions determine the political process," as well as "the dynamic interaction between the two forces."[3] As such, it covers a wide area of inquiry. Staniland notes, for example, that as of the early 1980s his university's library catalog contained 117 books whose title began with "The political economy of . . . ." Since that time, the number has increased substantially.

This chapter will focus on several central issues: the desired role of the state in the stimulation of Third World economic growth (most notably industrialization), alternative strategies for economic development, problems relating to the distribution of wealth and income, and the dilemma of balancing economic growth with protection of the environment.

THE ROLE OF THE STATE

The question of the state's proper role in the economy has been at the center of political and economic debates for hundreds of years. As such, it is relevant to advanced industrial economies as well as less developed countries. During the sixteenth and seventeenth centuries, major European powers were guided by the philosophy of mercantilism, which viewed a nation's economic activity as a means of enhancing the political power of the state and its monarch. Government, consequently, was viewed as "both source and beneficiary of economic growth."[4] That perspective was sharply challenged by the eighteenth-century Scottish political economist Adam Smith, who favored a minimalist state that would allow market forces a rather free hand. The following century, Karl Marx, reacting to the exploitative nature of early capitalism, assigned the state a dominant position in the ownership of the means of production and the regulation of the market. Finally, in the twentieth century, Sir John Maynard Keynes advocated a substantial degree of government intervention in the economy but rejected Marxist prescriptions for state ownership and centralized planning.

Today, the collapse of the Soviet "command economy" and the poor economic performance of the few remaining Communist nations (with the exception of those like China and Vietnam that have largely abandoned Marxist economics) have fairly well discredited the advocates of state-dominated economies. But no government fully embraces laissez faire either (i.e., allowing market forces a totally free reign with no government intervention). All countries, for example, no matter how committed to unrestricted capitalism, have laws regulating banking, domestic commerce, and international trade. Most have some degree of environmental regulation. Even in societies with limited state economic intervention, government fiscal policies (taxation and expenditure) and monetary policies (money supply and interest rates) influence the market. Ultimately, then, any government must decide where to position itself between the extreme poles of a command economy and laissez faire.

For a number of reasons that debate is particularly relevant in the LDCs. The fragile nature of many Third World economies, their high level of poverty, poor distribution of resources, great dependence on world market forces, and endangered ecology have frequently encouraged governments to assume an active economic role. Many LDCs also lack a strong entrepreneurial class or a private sector with substantial capital to invest. In such situations, governments have built the steel mills and sugar refineries that the private sector could or would not (especially when nationalist sentiments limit foreign investment). More recently, governments have been called upon to protect the environment against the ravages of economic development. Not surprisingly, then, state economic intervention traditionally has been more pronounced in Africa, Latin America, and South Asia than in the world's industrial democracies. As we will see, however, these interventionist tendencies have begun to subside in the past two decades.

The pages that follow will lay out a number of models for the role of the state in Third World economies, ranging from command economies such as Cuba's to very limited state economic intervention in Hong Kong. In considering these alternatives, the reader should keep in mind that these are ideal types. Few countries perfectly fit any of these models (Cuba's Marxist government, for example, has always permitted private farming) and countries have often adopted some mix of approaches. Other patterns are also possible and the options discussed below are by no means exhaustive.

The Command Economy

Marxism began as a critique of capitalism in the Western world during the early stages of industrial development. Hence, it is not surprising that the ideology initially appealed to many Third World leaders and would-be leaders who saw comparable injustices in their own economic systems. A fundamental Marxist criticism of capitalism is that it produces an inequitable distribution of wealth and income because those who control the means of production (industrialists, landlords, and the like) exploit those who work them (the working class, peasants).

That argument is particularly persuasive in Latin America and much of Africa, where there are broad disparities between rich and poor. Concern over these inequities is magnified by the fact that as countries move from the lowest to the middle level of development the gaps between rich and poor often widens.[5] This suggests that inequalities in wealth and income may worsen before they diminish in the poorer nations of Africa and Asia.[6] Consequently, one attraction Marxism has for its supporters is its claim to more equitable income distribution.

A second assertion made by Third World Marxist regimes is that only they can free LDCs from the yoke of dependency. Since dependency theorists tend to view an exploitative relationship between core industrial nations and peripheral LDCs as the inevitable outcome of capitalist trade and investment patterns, they often advocate revolutionary change and a Marxist economy as the only means of achieving economic independence and development. It is in that spirit that Havana's José Martí airport displays an intriguing sign reading "Welcome to Cuba, the only free territory in the Americas."

Finally, a major appeal of Communism to many Third World leaders has been its centralized, state control over the economy. A command economy, first developed in the Soviet Union, has two central features. First, most of the means of production are owned and managed by the state. That includes factories, banks, major trade and commercial institutions, retail establishments, and, frequently, farms. All Communist countries have allowed a certain amount of private economic activity, but the private sector is very secondary, except in countries such as China that have largely abandoned Marxist economics in recent years. Second, prices and decisions on what to produce are determined by state planners. Their centralized control over the allocation of resources and the labor market is as important as state ownership itself.

Marxists view market (capitalist) economies as anarchistic because the most fundamental decisions over the allocation of resources and the determination of prices are left to the whims of supply and demand. They reject Adam Smith's notion of the "invisible hand," whereby the good of society is advanced most effectively when individual actors (business people, workers) seek to maximize their own economic advantage. Adam Przeworski notes an intriguing organizational aspect of capitalism: People get up in the morning and find their newspaper or milk carton sitting outside their door without even knowing who delivered it. Marxists, he notes cynically, continue to insist that the paper or carton couldn't possibly be there without a central planner guaranteeing its arrival.[7]

With the collapse of Eastern European Communism and the development of "market socialism" in China and Vietnam, the failures of command economies have become more evident. As Przeworski, himself a democratic socialist, argues, under a centrally planned economy not only would milk delivery deteriorate, but there also would be constant shortages of both cartons and milk. Indeed, the flaws of Communist economies are now so obvious as to hide their earlier accomplishments.

By being able to dictate the movement of people and resources from one sector of the economy to another, Communist countries such as the Soviet Union and China were able to jump-start their industrial development. During the 1920s and 1930s, "entire industries were created [in the USSR], along with millions of jobs that drew peasants away from the countryside and into higher-paying jobs and higher living standards."[8] Western estimates of Soviet economic performance during its industrialization phase indicate that between 1928 and 1955 GNP grew at an impressive average annual rate of roughly 5 percent.[9] During the early decades of its revolution, China also moved quickly from a backward agrarian economy to a far more industrialized society. According to one leading authority, between 1952 and 1975 its economy grew at an average annual rate of 8.2 percent, while industry surged at 11.5 percent.[10] These rates far exceed the norm in other developing nations as well as in industrial democracies.[11] Other analysts believe that China's growth rates could not be quite that high because of the setbacks of the Great Leap Forward and the Cultural Revolution. Still, compared to India, Pakistan, and other LDCs during that period, China's growth, just like the Soviet Union's decades earlier, was impressive. Small wonder that the Soviet and Chinese models (though in many ways different from each other after 1966) were attractive to many Third World leaders.

Command economies have also performed impressively in terms of income distribution. Indeed, it is here that Communist LDCs most clearly outperform their capitalist counterparts. In Cuba, for example, the revolution brought a substantial redistribution of income from the richest 20 percent of the population to the poorest 40 percent.[12] The poor also benefited from an extensive land reform program and more equitable distribution of health care (though some gains were largely undermined in the 1990s following the loss of Soviet economic assistance). Equality was further enhanced by mass adult literacy programs and the expansion of education. Nor was Cuba unique in this respect. Cross-national, statistical comparisons indicate that Communist countries as a whole have more equal income distribution than do capitalist nations.[13]

In time, however, the weaknesses of command economies have outweighed their accomplishments.[14] In the absence of consumer signals, state planners have little basis for deciding what and how much to produce. Factory managers in a centrally controlled economy are rewarded for meeting their output quotas, with little concern for product quality. Even in the best of circumstances, a centralized, command economy needs a highly skilled and honest bureaucracy equipped with sophisticated technology (such as advanced computers). None of these qualities are normally present in Third World bureaucracies. Instead, inefficient state bureaucracies are given inordinate power and, as Lord Acton warned, "power tends to corrupt and absolute power tends to corrupt absolutely." Analysts of Chinese politics, for example, have observed that the price of doing business for local entrepreneurs is bribing government officials (cadres) or their adult children.[15] More generally, command economies are known for their large, privileged class of state and party bureaucrats (apparatchiks), who enjoy perquisites unavailable to the rest of the population.

While the Soviet Union and China enjoyed impressive bursts of growth in the early decades of their revolutions, each eventually ran out of steam as their economies became larger and harder to control centrally. Moreover, command economies are more adept at building heavy industries (steel, tractors) than in developing sophisticated, high-tech production or the distribution of consumer goods. The Soviets, for example, were more proficient at building large numbers of crude tractors and massive amounts of steel than in providing an automobile or home washing machine that worked well. By the late 1970s and 1980s, with both countries' economies deteriorating, their leaders, Deng Xiaoping and Mikhail Gorbachev, recognized the need to decentralize their economies and reduce state control. China's transition to "market socialism" (a mixture of free market economics; private, cooperative and state economic sectors; and reduced but ongoing state controls) has been tremendously successful, producing one of the world's fastest growing economies. However, in the Soviet Union and its primary successor state, Russia, weaker economic reforms under Gorbachev (perestroika) and Boris Yeltsin have failed to arrest the country's downward slide.

The collapse of Soviet and Eastern European Communism and China's remarkable economic transformation have inspired market-oriented reforms in other state-dominated economies. Vietnam, for example, has transferred state farm land to the peasantry and freed prices from state controls. Mongolia, like China, has opened up a stock exchange for aspiring entrepreneurs. Elsewhere in Asia and Africa, governments such as Myanmar and the Congolese Republic have privatized much of the state sector and reduced government economic controls. In Cuba, the withdrawal of Soviet bloc aid has halted many of that country's impressive earlier gains in health care, nutrition, and education. Stripped of his primary benefactor, even Fidel Castro, one of the last true believers in Marxist economics, has been forced to accept certain free market innovations.

For both Eastern European and Third World nations that have abandoned or reformed their command economies, the transition has frequently been very difficult. Often the economic order previously imposed by government authorities is removed without adequate free market incentives to replace it. In a sense, the "stick" driving the economy forward has disappeared before workable "carrots" have been developed. Workers who accepted spartan living conditions in return for guaranteed income and social services (what the Chinese call the "iron rice bowl") find themselves stripped of these guarantees with no improvement in living standards. In Eastern Europe, the collapse of command economies has led, at least temporarily, to declining living standards. In Asia, however, that transition, under the guidance of Communist authoritarian regimes that are still firmly in place, has been far smoother and, at least in China, living standards have risen sharply.

Latin America Statism

Even in capitalist Third World countries, the state has often played a leading economic role, seeking to function as an engine of industrial growth. In the period between the two world wars, many Latin American nations pursued state-led industrialization. That process was accelerated during the Great Depression when countries in the region had difficulty finding markets for their primary exports (food and raw materials) and, consequently, lacked foreign exchange for industrial imports. Argentina, Brazil, Chile, Uruguay, and Mexico were among the early leaders in the push toward industrialization.

With the exceptions of revolutionary Cuba and, briefly, Nicaragua, Latin American countries have left most productive capacity in the hands of the private sector. The state, however, has often owned or nationalized strategically important enterprises or those that have failed to attract sufficient private capital. Thus, until the region's recent spate of privatizations, railroads, electric power plants, petroleum extraction, mines, steel mills, telephone companies, armaments factories, and airlines were frequently state owned.

Two aspects of state ownership contradict popular stereotypes. First, government takeovers in the Third World did not necessarily create tensions with the domestic private sectors. The most important nationalizations—including Mexican and Venezuelan petroleum, Chilean and Peruvian mining, and Argentine railroads—affected companies that had been owned by multinational corporations, not local capitalists. More important, the state used its ownership of telephone companies, electric power, railroads, petroleum, and the like to provide private-sector industries with subsidized communication, transportation, and power. Second, until the 1980s, some otherwise conservative governments in Latin America were as likely to enlarge government ownership in the economy as were left-of-center or populist regimes. Thus, for example, during the 1960s and 1970s, Brazil's right-wing military dictatorship substantially increased state ownership within the economy.

More important, however, than government ownership itself in Latin America (always encompassing a small, though critical, portion of the economy) was the state's dominant role in fomenting private-sector industrial growth. Starting early in the twentieth century in Argentina and Brazil, and subsequently spreading to most of South America and Mexico, Latin American governments initiated programs of Import-Substituting Industrialization (ISI). Discussed more extensively below, ISI was designed to develop national economies by manufacturing consumer goods domestically that had previously been imported.[16] While industrialization was implemented by private firms (both national and multinational), government policies were important in stimulating development. Protective tariffs, import quotas, favorable currency exchange rates, and controlled interest rates were all used to promote industrial development.

In many ways, ISI was successful, most notably in Argentina, Brazil, Colombia, and Mexico. Throughout the region there was a vast population movement from countryside to city (see Chapter 6). From 1945 to 1970, Latin America's rate of investment was higher than in the industrial world and from 1960 to 1980 its manufacturing grew faster as well.[17] Virtually every country in the region began to manufacture basic consumer goods such as textiles, apparel, packaged food, furniture, and home appliances. Larger Latin American countries developed steel mills, automobile plants, and other heavy industries. A substantial number of blue-collar jobs were created, and the size of the middle class expanded. Although the biggest manufacturing plants (such as automobiles) were foreign owned, local entrepreneurs also played an important role in the region's industrial expansion.

Despite its many successes, however, state-sponsored industrialization created inefficiencies and inequalities. Inefficient domestic industries received excessive protection, traditional agricultural exports were affected adversely, and the income gap widened between urban and rural populations as well as between skilled and unskilled workers.

While state promotion of industrialization was useful, perhaps even necessary in the early stages of economic growth, it went too far and too long. Rather than becoming a finely calibrated tool for economic stimulation, it became a politically based juggernaut. Mexico illustrates both the accomplishments and subsequent weaknesses of statism in the region. Between the mid-1930s and 1970, the national government contributed between 35 and 40 percent of the country's total investment.[18] At the same time, the state-owned petroleum and railroad industries provided private industry with subsidized energy and transport (i.e., priced below the free market value).[19] Government trade and labor policies protected Mexican companies from foreign competition and held down wages as a means of stimulating further investment.

As a consequence, between 1935 and 1970, industrial output grew at an average annual rate close to 10 percent, one of the strongest performances in the world.[20] Overall economic growth, averaging about 6 percent annually, was also among the world's highest. During the 1970s and early 1980s, however, the role of the state in the economy and the number of parastatals (state-owned enterprises) increased enormously.[21] By the mid-1980s, the government operated nearly 1,200 state enterprises (though many of these were quite small). The sharp increase in Mexico's petroleum export earnings during the 1970s, coupled with the nation's great income inequalities and extensive poverty, created political pressures on the government to subsidize consumer prices and to create jobs in state enterprises. These spiraling government expenditures contributed to fiscal deficits and growing foreign indebtedness in spite of rising petroleum revenues. Elsewhere in Latin America a similar process occurred, though usually on a more reduced scale.

Two glaring areas of inefficiency, relevant not only to Mexico but also to many developing countries, should be noted. First, while it is certainly possible to run state enterprises efficiently (for example, many of the companies nationalized by France's socialist government in the 1980s were well operated), it rarely happens in Latin America or other LDCs. Because of high unemployment and underemployment, government enterprises are under great political pressure to hire excess labor. Consequently, almost all parastatals are overstaffed.[22] In addition, these companies are usually under irresistible political pressure to sell basic consumer goods and services (as well as some intermediate goods) at highly discounted prices. For example, prior to 1991 Argentineans rode the state railroads for a nominal fee and received highly subsidized electricity. Not long ago, gas was selling in Venezuela for 22 cents per gallon.[23] Ultimately, the combination of money-loosing parastatals, consumer subsidies and subsidies to private sector producers helped bankrupt many Latin American governments. By 1982 virtually every government in the region was deeply in debt and experiencing severe fiscal problems.

Another important flaw in Latin America's development model was the inefficiency it encouraged in the private sector. A wall of high tariffs and import quotas largely shielded manufacturers of domestic consumer goods from foreign competition. To be sure, governments throughout the world (including the United States) have effectively employed protectionist measures to help infant industries get off the ground during the early stages of industrialization. In Latin America, however, rather than being a temporary stimulus, protectionist measures became permanently embedded, thereby giving local companies little incentive to increase their productivity.

Since the 1980s, most Latin American nations have sharply reversed their earlier statist orientations, moved by the region's severe debt crisis and economic depression. In Mexico, the de la Madrid and Salines administrations (1982 to 1994) shut down or privatized over 80 percent of the country's 1,155 state enterprises, including the national airline, telephone complex, and banking system.[24] Argentina's president, Carlos Menem, leader of the very Peronist party that had vastly expanded state economic activities in the 1940s, reversed his party's policies by privatizing large portions of the state sector. In Chile, the move toward a slimmed-down state was begun by the right-wing military dictatorship of General Augusto Pinochet (1973 to 1990). But when democracy was finally restored, the new governing coalition (including the Socialist party) accepted much of the Pinochet economic model that they had once criticized so strongly.

While these reductions in state-sector activities may have been necessary, they were usually undertaken at great human cost. Throughout Latin America, hundreds of thousands of workers lost their jobs as parastatals were closed down or had their labor force substantially reduced through privatization. In Mexico alone an estimated 400,000 jobs were eliminated in the course of the government's economic liberalization program (as the policy of reducing state economic activity is called). For example, more than half the workers formerly employed in state steel mills lost their jobs when those companies were privatized.[25] Similar layoffs have taken place in Argentina, Chile, Peru, and Venezuela as well. At the same time, reduced protectionism in much of the region has opened the door to a surge of imported consumer goods, thereby reducing sales (and employment) by local firms that failed to compete. Finally, the elimination or reduction of government consumer subsidies sharply increased the cost of many basic necessities including a variety of foods, gasoline, public transportation, and electricity.

The debt crisis and related economic recession, coupled with the elimination of consumer subsides, all contributed to a sharp decline in Latin American living standards during the 1980s. In Peru and Venezuela, for example, real incomes fell by nearly 40 percent.[26] Since the early 1990s, however, Latin America's "lost decade" has drawn to an end and many of the region's economies have begun to grow after years of contraction (though there have been major bumps in the road for countries such as Brazil and Mexico).[27] In Mexico, just as in Argentina and Chile, populist and leftist parties that had once been the most staunch advocates of government economic intervention now reluctantly concede that the state sector had grown too unwieldy and had to be cut back.[28] Extensive state spending coupled with government inability or refusal to tax the more affluent strata of society had resulted in massive fiscal deficits and runaway inflation. Only by substantially cutting budgetary deficits have Latin America's governments been able to control inflation that during the 1980s had reached annual rates of 1,000 to 15,000 percent in Brazil, Argentina, Peru, and Nicaragua.

East Asia's Developmental State

While Latin America's economies were stagnant or shrinking after 1982, a number of East and Southeast Asian nations grew at phenomenal rates until the close of the 1990s. East Asia's NICS Newly Industrializing Countries—South Korea, Taiwan, Hong Kong, and Singapore (known as the "little tigers")—and China, now the world's third largest economy, have received the most attention. To begin with, their impact on world trade is now enormous. In recent years, China has secured the second largest trade surplus with the United States (after Japan) of any country in the world. Taiwan, Korea, and even tiny Hong Kong have each exported more manufactured goods annually than all of Latin America combined.[29] Right behind China and the little tigers, Southeast Asian economies such as Thailand's, Malaysia's, and Indonesia's also grew impressively. Not surprisingly, then, East and Southeast Asia's current economic downturn has negatively impacted U.S. farmers and manufacturers who have come to rely on exports to that region.

From the mid-1960s until the region's recent economic slide, Taiwan, South Korea, Singapore, Hong Kong, Thailand, Malaysia, Indonesia, and China all grew at annual rates of 4 to 10 percent (China has sometimes exceeded 10 percent).[30] Equally impressive, the benefits of rapid growth were relatively equitably distributed, with a far narrower gap between rich and poor than in Latin America or Africa.

With the exception of Communist China (which has also introduced many free market aspects into its economy), these countries have based their growth in large part on free market principles. To a greater extent than elsewhere in the Third World, production has been primarily privately owned, with a relatively limited state sector.[31] Not surprisingly, this has led conservative economists to hail the East Asian economic miracle as a triumph of unfettered capitalism, a testimony to keeping government out of the economy.[32]

But many scholars specializing in East Asian economies argue that, to the contrary, governments in that region have actively stimulated economic growth.[33] Examining the reasons for Japan's spectacular postwar economic resurgence, Chalmers Johnson first formulated the notion of the developmental state.[34] The meaning of that term is best understood by comparing the role of government in industrialized, East Asian capitalist nations (Japan, South Korea, and Taiwan) to that in Western industrial nations whose economies developed in the early stages of capitalism (e.g., Britain and the United States). The early developers established regulatory states in which "government refrains from interfering in the marketplace, except to insure certain limited goals (e.g., antitrust regulations, protection of consumer rights)" while the East Asian developmental states "intervene actively in the economy in order to guide or promote particular substantive goals (e.g., full employment, export competitiveness, energy self-sufficiency)."[35]

Japan's powerful Ministry of International Trade and Industry (MITI), Johnson notes, guided and directed that country's postwar industrial resurgence. Subsequently, many aspects of Japan's state-guided, capitalist development model were adopted in varying manners by South Korea, Taiwan, Singapore, Indonesia, and other industrializing nations in East and Southeast Asia.[36] Each country typically has a powerful government ministry or agency "charged with the task of planning, guiding and coordinating industrial policies."[37] These include South Korea's Economic Planning Board, Taiwan's Council for Economic Planning and Development, and Singapore's Economic Development Board, all somewhat modeled after MITI. Government intervention is far more extensive and direct than in the West, influencing economic sectors (such as agriculture and industry), whole industries (such as computers, automobiles, and electronics), and particular companies (such as Hundai).[38]

Not all development states are the same. For example, the bonds between government and big business are tighter in South Korea than in Taiwan, while state enterprises are more important in Taiwan than in Korea. In Singapore government control over labor is more extensive than in the other two countries.[39] But in all of them the state plays an important role, guiding the private sector toward targeted economic activities and stimulating growth in areas that the government wishes to expand. Sometimes government planners will even pressure particular industries or companies to specialize in certain products and abandon others.

State influence in East Asia has been more indirect than it was during Latin American industrialization, but it is significant nonetheless. Government tools used to sway private sector activity include tax policy, control over credit, and influence over the price of raw materials. For example, when the South Korean and Taiwanese governments wished to develop the electronics, computer software, and automobile industries, they intervened aggressively, rather than leaving it to the marketplace. They established related research institutes; granted preferential access to credit for companies in targeted industries; temporarily required local companies that had been importing targeted parts for their products to switch to domestic producers so as to stimulate production; and offered trade protection to new industries for limited periods of time (for example, South Korea temporarily banned all imports of computers; Taiwan did the same for textiles).[40]

While the East Asian development model's tremendous success has won it widespread admiration, some observers are cautious about its applicability elsewhere. One concern is the model's political prerequisites. Chalmers Johnson notes that most developmental states have been authoritarian or what he calls "soft authoritarian" during their major industrialization push.[41] Since its return to Chinese rule, Hong Kong, a former British colony, has limited its brief experiment with democracy. The governments of Malaysia, Singapore, and Indonesia all have repressed democratic expression to varying degrees. Taiwan and South

Korea industrialized under authoritarian governments, though both have subsequently become democracies. Of course, Japan, the original developmental state, is a democracy. But until 1993 its political system had been dominated by a single party for some 40 years. Many analysts feel that authoritarian or semi-authoritarian rule (including the ability to direct management and control labor) was required for the East Asia's rapid economic growth, at least at the earlier stages. Thus, one must wonder how the developmental state would perform under the pressures for democracy now spreading across the Third World.

A second important concern is the transferability of East Asian political and economic practices to other parts of the Third World.[42] The developmental state seems to require two qualities that are in short supply in the developing world: a highly skilled government bureaucracy and close cooperation between leading economic sectors, most notably business, labor, and agriculture. In Indonesia, for example, a team of skilled government economists known as "the Berkeley Boys" (most of them with graduate degrees from the University of California at Berkeley) have overseen that country's economic development. Similarly, South Korea's highly trained state technocrats work closely with the country's dominant business conglomerates (chaebols), such as Hundai and Samsung.[43] Similar cooperation between sophisticated government planners and big business (unchallenged by a relatively docile working class) has contributed to the economic surges elsewhere in East Asia.

Some have argued that East Asian Confucian culture—featuring nationalism, cooperation, and a strong work ethic—has been a critical ingredient in rapid economic growth.[44] If that is true, then development models that work in that region may not transfer well to other cultures. Of course, similar cultural explanations have previously been offered for the rise of capitalism in Western Europe. Max Weber long ago associated the birth of capitalism with the Protestant work ethic and attitude toward wealth.

But explanations such as these have always provoked considerable controversy. Critics point out, for example, that although China, Taiwan, Japan, Singapore, Hong Kong, and South Korea all do have Confucian cultures, rapidly developing Malaysia and Indonesia are predominantly Muslim. Defenders of the cultural thesis counter that most wealthy businessmen in Malaysia and Indonesia and many powerful state planners come from those countries' Chinese (Confucian) minority populations. A different, more telling, criticism of the cultural thesis notes that Confucian culture has been around for centuries while the East Asian miracle is only a few decades old.[45] Ironically, before the region's takeoff, some Western scholars attributed its poverty, in part, to Confucian culture.

Ultimately, it is implausible that there is something so uniquely Asian about the developmental state that it cannot be reproduced elsewhere. But few African, Middle Eastern, or Latin American nations currently offer hospitable conditions for its spread. Most still lack the highly professional, merit-based bureaucracies and the tradition of cooperation between key economic actors that would permit them to replicate the East Asian model at this time. And, as we shall see, even in Asian countries such as Indonesia, a form of "crony capitalism" developed in which the government provided well-connected investors with special opportunities. Such distortions, in turn, contributed heavily to the recent economic crisis in the region.

The Neoclassical Ideal

Unlike the preceding models, the neoclassical perspective assigns government a very restricted economic role.[46] The state, it argues, should provide certain "public goods" including defense, a legal system, education, and environmental protection; supply physical infrastructure such as railways, sewers, and harbors when it is infeasible for private capital to do so; and redistribute enough income to the poorest strata of society to meet their basic needs.[47] But, say neoclassical critics, Third World governments have injured their economies, even when motivated by the best of intentions, by moving far beyond that limited role. Thus, neoclassicists attribute many of Africa's and Latin America's past economic development problems to excessive state intervention, while they credit East Asia's success to government's allegedly limited role in that region.

Neoclassical economists insist that free market forces should be allowed to determine supply and set prices without government interference. As a consequence, they have criticized government policies introduced over the years in Africa, Latin America, and South Asia for the purpose of stimulating industrial growth. These include tariffs, import quotas, and other forms of protectionism that interfere with free trade and drive up consumer prices; artificial currency exchange rates that distort the prices of exports and imports; state subsidies to producers and consumers; and various price controls on products and interest rates. All of these measures, argue the neoclassicists, distort the market and the choices made by companies, consumers, and governments. Only when they are removed can the economy "get prices right" (i.e., let them be determined by the free market).

To some degree, the neoclassicists have won the debate against advocates of extensive state intervention. As we have observed, governments throughout Africa and Latin America have begun the process of liberalizing their economies in recent years, deregulating the private sector and freeing prices. Protectionist barriers are being dismantled in favor of free trade. Government subsidies to industry and to consumers have been reduced, often out of financial necessity. And many state enterprises have been privatized. In part, these changes are the consequence of pressures that international lending agencies such as the World Bank and the International Monetary Fund (IMF) have exerted on Third World governments. But they also spring from the widespread conviction within the LDCs themselves that earlier statist models have failed, while East Asia's more market-oriented policies have succeeded. A Mexican economist self-deprecatingly described to me how he and his colleagues had abandoned their earlier radical ideas for a more mainstream ideology. "We've taken our old photos of

Zapata (hero of the Mexican Revolution) off our office walls," he joked, "and put up Adam Smith."

Still, it is one thing to recognize that the neoclassicist had a good point when they charged that government intervention had gotten out of hand. It is quite another to concede that the neoclassical model has triumphed. To begin with, there is a problem of classification. Conservative economists like Nobel Prize winner Milton Friedman see East Asia as the neoclassical model in action, proof positive of what free enterprise can do if government leaves it alone. But, as we have seen, most specialists on East Asia insist that government intervention has been a fundamental ingredient of industrial growth in that region.[48] Far from "following the market," the state has actively "governed the market."[49] So, while the neoclassicist's criticisms of statist policies ring true, they take their case too far in prescribing an abstentionist state.

In fact, the only East Asian economy that has nearly conformed to the neoclassical model has been Hong Kong's and the city's recent absorption into communist China does not seem to have altered this pattern. As the least regulated economy in the area, it has seemingly been a success story for unrestricted capitalism. But Hong Kong is such a unique case that it may not offer many lessons for other countries. For one thing, its economic boom began when it was a British colony, not an independent country. Unrestricted until the last years of British colonialism by elections or other democratic inputs, government technocrats have been allowed to make decisions without much concern regarding popular reaction (a situation that has been somewhat restored since China's takeover). More important, Hong Kong consists mostly of a single city with no rural population to speak of. Like Singapore, it hasn't had to deal with rural poverty or the related problems that are so daunting in most Third World countries.

Some of the strongest criticisms of neoclassical economics have come from environmentalists. From their perspective, even a modified policy of laissez faire, acknowledging some state responsibility for the environment, is totally inadequate. As Richard Albin notes:

> The idea that private interest, operating within unfettered markets, will tend to produce a close approximation of the socially optimal allocation of resources, was close to the truth when output (population, too) was so much smaller.[50]

But, he argues, as world population and pollution reach dangerous levels, society can no longer afford to let free market mechanisms allocate penalties for pollution. Such remedies would come far too late (further discussion of economic growth and the environment follows later in this chapter).

Conclusions

Political scientists and economists will long continue to debate the state's proper role in Third World economies. As time goes on, new models will undoubtedly emerge. Still an emerging consensus has evolved in recent decades. On the one hand, the level of government intervention in both the command economies and Latin American statism was undoubtedly excessive. At the same time, the extremely limited government role advocated by the neoclassicist is unrealistic and inadequate. East Asia's developmental state model has been the most successful. But it is unclear whether it can be replicated elsewhere.

Finally, two additional problems further cloud the debate. First, periodic changes in world politics and the international economy, often unforseen, constantly alter the equations of economic development. Recent examples include the oil price shocks of the 1970s, transformations in the international division of labor, and the collapse of communism as a viable model. Second, a model that succeeds in one country will not necessarily work in another. Countries vary greatly in size, human capital, natural resources, and the like. Thus, cookbook formulas will likely prove inadequate.

INDUSTRIALIZATION STRATEGIES

The debate over the desired level of state economic intervention raises a second question. What type of development strategy should the state and the private sector pursue? Since the time of Britain's Industrial Revolution, governments have equated industrialization with progress, economic independence, national sovereignty, and military strength. Latin America's largest countries launched their major industrialization drive in the 1930s. Following World War II, a host of newly independent Asian and African countries expanded their industrial capacities. Steel mills and auto plants became symbols of national prestige.

Neoclassical economists criticized many of these efforts, arguing that each country should specialize in those economic activities for which it has a "comparative advantage." That is, it should produce and export those goods it can provide most efficiently and cheaply relative to other nations. Based on that logic, neoclassicists maintained that most Third World nations should abandon grandiose plans for industrialization and concentrate, instead, on the production and export of raw materials or agricultural products.[51] It made more sense, they pointed out, for Sri Lanka to be exporting tea (where it has a comparative advantage) so as to use those earnings to import, say, cars or washing machines, rather than manufacture those products itself.

Neoclassical analysis demonstrated why Ghana shouldn't have built steel mills or Uruguay manufactured refrigerators. Still, many LDCs have been reluctant to depend fully on revenues from primary exports, in part because agricultural and raw-material prices are so volatile. Consequently, economists often advocate balanced growth whereby some manufacturing is developed (i.e., those in which the country is relatively efficient) while traditional primary goods production and export are still emphasized.

Industrializing nations have generally pursued two alternative strategies: Import-Substituting Industrialization (ISI) and Export-Oriented Industrialization (EOI). In the first case, LDCs reduce their dependency on manufactured imports by producing more of them at home. Although ISI has been pursued in many parts of the Third World, including East Asia during its early industrial development, it has been most closely identified with Latin America. And while most Latin American countries now aspire to some form of EOI, that strategy is generally associated with East Asia. In addition, Latin American ISI has been closely linked with statism, while East Asian EOI has been associated with the developmental state. Still the two factors (degree of state intervention and type of industrialization strategy) are distinct, and for example, a developmental state might easily foment ISI. It is for this reason that we will analyze the two issues separately.

Import-Substituting Industrialization (ISI)

National economic policies are partly the product of deliberate choice, partly the result of political and socioeconomic opportunities and constraints. Thus, ISI emerged as a development strategy in Latin America during the 1930s as the worldwide depression sharply reduced international trade.[52] Because the industrialized nations of North America and Europe curtailed their consumption of Third World primary goods, Latin America was deprived of the foreign exchange needed to import manufactured consumer goods. As long as the First World could not afford as much Chilean copper, Argentine beef, or Brazilian coffee, those countries would lack the revenues needed to import apparel, furniture, and appliances.

Initiated as an immediate response to the international economic crisis, ISI was subsequently transformed into a long-term strategy for industrial development. With substantial unemployment at home and their urban populations pressing for economic growth, government leaders also had a political imperative to industrialize. Nationalist presidents such as Argentina's Juan Perón and Brazil's Getúlio Vargas forged populist coalitions of manufacturers, blue-collar workers, and the urban middle class, all of them committed to industrialization. The always-powerful armed forces, though wary of the populists' reformist rhetoric, shared their commitment to industrialization because of its obvious military benefits.

In order to protect embryonic domestic industries from foreign competition, numerous consumer-goods imports (ranging from electrical appliances to automobiles) were subjected to quotas and high tariffs. At the same time, however, planners also wanted to facilitate other types of imports, namely capital equipment (machinery and so on) and raw materials needed to manufacture consumer goods locally, as well as some goods desired by urban consumers but not produced domestically. To reduce the cost of those imports, governments overvalued their own currencies.[53] Eventually most Latin American countries established multiple currency exchange rates, with differing rates for transactions tied to imports, exports, and other financial activities. To further encourage industrial development, governments offered domestic manufacturers tax incentives, low interest credit, and direct subsidies.[54]

For several decades, the ISI strategy produced impressive results. From the 1940s to the early 1970s, Latin America (most notably Argentina, Brazil, Colombia, and Mexico) enjoyed high investment rates, strong economic growth, and even higher rates of industrialization. Not surprisingly the strategy was emulated in many parts of Africa and Asia, sometimes, though surely not always, with comparable success. Turkey, for example, enjoyed strong ISI before shifting to EOI during the 1980s.[55] Even East Asia's highly admired industrial export miracle was preceded by a period of ISI.

Ultimately, however, the ISI strategy as implemented in Latin America seriously undermined that region's economies. As John Sheahan notes, "it fostered production methods adverse for employment, hurt the poor, blocked the possible growth of industrial exports [and] encouraged high-cost consumer goods industries."[56] While some initial protection for infant industries was necessary, Latin American protectionism was continued far too long at levels that were too high, thereby offering domestic industries little incentive to become more efficient. As a consequence, consumers paid excessive prices while the region's manufacturers failed to become competitive in the world market.

To understand how poorly Latin America's NICs fared in international trade relative to their East Asia counterparts, it is useful to compare Mexico (one of the region's major industrial powers) with East Asia's little tigers (South Korea, Taiwan, Hong Kong, and Singapore). Mexico has a larger population than the other four combined. It also has a considerable geographic advantage over them, being located thousands of miles closer to the United States, the world's largest importer. Yet as of the mid-1980s (prior to NAFTA), the combined manufactured exports of the little tigers was 20 times as high as Mexico's.[57]

Unfavorable currency exchange rates and export taxes put traditional primary goods exporters at a competitive disadvantage, thereby depriving the country of needed foreign exchange revenues. At the same time, because local consumer-goods manufacturers were allowed to import capital goods cheaply, the region never developed its own capital-goods industry and, instead, imported manufacturing technologies that were inappropriate to local needs. Subsidized imports of machinery and heavy equipment encouraged capital-intensive production (i.e., using relatively advanced technologies and machinery while employing fewer workers) rather than the labor-intensive techniques common to Asia. The ISI model of industrialization benefited a small, relatively well paid, "labor elite" (i.e., skilled, unionized workers employed in highly mechanized factories). But it failed to provide enough jobs for the region's unemployed and underemployed.

Ironically, although ISI was originally designed to make Latin America more economically independent, in the end it merely replaced dependence on consumer-goods imports with dependence on imported capital goods, foreign technologies, and overseas bank credit. Traditional primary exports were allowed to languish while little was done to develop new manufactured exports.

Increased balance of trade deficits contributed to Latin America's spiraling foreign debt, leading eventually to a major debt crisis and an economic depression
in the 1980s.[58]

The crisis, standing in stark contrast to East Asia's prosperity at that time,
induced Latin American governments to abandon their inwardly oriented economic policies as they seek to emulate East Asia's export-driven model. The
North American Free Trade Agreement (NAFTA) between Mexico, Canada, and
the United States is the most dramatic manifestation of that region's move toward
EOI.[59] Chile and Argentina, once among the most inward-looking economies in
the hemisphere, have been at the forefront of export manufacturing and free
trade.

Export-Oriented Industrialization (EOI)

East Asia's NICs initiated their industrialization drive through import substitution, just as their Latin American counterparts had done years earlier. Soon,
however, they diversified into manufacturing for export. Early protectionist
measures were phased out, thereby forcing local companies to become more
competitive. State agencies shaped the market, pressuring manufacturers and
offering them incentives to export. By 1980, manufactured goods constituted
over 90 percent of all South Korean and Taiwanese exports, while representing
only 15 percent in Mexico and 39 percent in Brazil.[60] Fueled by their dynamic
industrial export sectors, East Asia's booming economies became the envy of
the developing world.

There are a number of explanations for East Asia's turn to manufactured
exports and for Latin America's initial failure to do the same. For one thing, the
East Asian industrialization drive began in the 1960s, a period of unprecedented
expansion in world trade (inspired by the GATT, the General Agreement on Trade
and Tariffs, and the West's economic boom). The opportunities offered by out-
wardly oriented growth were more obvious to government policy makers at that
time. Conversely, the expansion of Latin American industrialization began during the Great Depression, a period of greatly restricted world trade. Indeed, it
was their very inability to export traditional products at that time that inspired
Latin American nations to turn to ISI. In retrospect, Latin America should have
moved on to EOI after World War II, but ISI seemed to be working so well until
the mid-1970s that there was little incentive to change.

Ironically, another reason why East and Southeast Asian countries chose
EOI is that their economic opportunities seemed more limited than Latin America's. Because of their smaller populations, Hong Kong, Singapore, and Taiwan
(though not South Korea) saw ISI (which relied upon the domestic market) as
less feasible for them than for larger countries like Mexico, Argentina, Brazil, and
Colombia.[61] In addition, with fewer agricultural goods or raw materials to export,
East Asians turned a weakness into a strength by emphasizing manufactured
exports.

A final factor that distinguished East Asia from Latin America was the influence of U.S. advisors and the differing training and economic orientation of government technocrats. During the decades after World War II, Latin American government planners shaping industrial policy were strongly influenced by the United Nations Economic Commission for Latin America (ECLA), a vigorous advocate of ISI. Until the 1980s, Latin American intellectuals remained very committed to economic nationalism and the need to limit U.S. influence. On the other hand, because of Taiwanese and South Korean military and political dependency on the United States during the postwar decades, their leaders were far more receptive to American policy advisors advocating EOI. East Asian economic planners often received their graduate training at American universities where they were inculcated with the values of free trade. It was not until the 1970s and 1980s that the so-called "Chicago and Berkeley boys" as well as other U.S.-trained economists favoring free trade began to direct economic policy in Latin America.[62]

EAST AND SOUTHEAST ASIA'S ECONOMIC CRISIS

The Onset of the Crisis

On July 2, 1997, the Thai government announced that the exchange rate for their national currency, the baht, which had previously been fixed (i.e., the Thai government had guaranteed that its value relative to the dollar remained constant) would henceforth be allowed to float (its value would now fluctuate based on market forces).

> To the casual observer this was. . . hardly worth [much] attention. . . . But to individuals controlling huge pools of investment resources in Southeast Asia [including foreign investors], this was a flashing red light signaling danger for the entire region.[63]

As the value of the baht fell, investments on the Thai stock exchange and bank accounts held in bahts also lost value. For both the Thai government and private companies that had secured extensive loans (in dollars) from international banks, this meant that the cost (in bahts) of repaying those loans climbed precipitously.[64] International banks, in turn, curtailed further (dollar) loans to Thailand knowing that it would be difficult for debtors to repay, while the Thai private sector reduced its demand for foreign loans for the same reason.

Panic soon an set in. Thai and foreign investors began to unload their stocks on the Bangkok stock market and to sell other liquid securities. As confidence in the baht declined, Thais holding baht bank accounts rushed to convert their holdings into dollars or other hard currencies, thereby further undermining the value of the national currency. Rather than basing their decisions on a reasoned analysis of Thailand's economic capabilities, investors increasingly chose "the pure psychology of escape. All controllers of liquid capital . . . began behaving like spooked wildebeests on the Serengeti."[65]

At the same time, for the many Thai businesses with overextended foreign debts, the costs of repayment were becoming overwhelming. Companies that imported consumer goods or manufacturing inputs (machinery, raw materials, technology licenses) found the price of doing business rising sharply as the value of the baht declined. Before long, many companies were closing down and laying off workers.

Had the 1997 economic crisis been limited to Thailand, it would have been tragic for the Thai people but would have had little consequence for the world economy. Not surprisingly, however, foreign and domestic investors in other Southeast and East Asian boom economies began to fear that those countries might also be overheated and plagued by the same fragilities (including overly extended external debts) that had undermined Thailand's economy. Indonesia, Malaysia, and later South Korea all were forced to devalue their currencies and were plunged into deep recessions. During the following year, the economic crisis threatened to spread to Hong Kong and sent chills down the spines of the region's two economic giants, Japan and China. At the same time, however, countries with relatively smaller foreign debts (Taiwan, Singapore, the Philippines, Vietnam and China) were less vulnerable to capital flight and, at least until this point, have survived the crisis relatively well.

Causes of the Asian Crisis

What was perhaps most shocking about Asia's sharp economic plunge was how utterly unexpected it had been. Virtually up to the day that Thailand announced its intention to float the baht (beginning the crisis) respected financial analysts had portrayed Southeast and East Asian economies as vibrant and growing. Why were the world's investment specialists so taken by surprise? What caused the initial virus in Thailand and why did it spread so rapidly and insidiously to neighboring countries?

Several previously unnoticed weaknesses in the region's economies set the stage. Precisely because economic performance had been so spectacular for years, both investors and lending agencies had come to see rapid growth as virtually inevitable. Consequently, they threw caution to the wind. Businesses in Thailand, Indonesia, Malaysia, and South Korea had borrowed and invested excessively. From 1992 to 1997 alone, Asian companies (excluding Japan) had borrowed over $700 billion from the rest of the world. The result was questionable investments, manufacturing overcapacity, and overconstruction of new real estate. The downtown business centers of Bangkok, Jakarta (Indonesia), and Seoul (South Korea) were dotted with new, half-occupied office buildings. Not surprisingly, Southeast and East Asia's external debts eventually exceeded their capacity to readily repay. In truth, economic growth is invariably cyclical and no country or region can maintain high growth rates indefinitely. In particular, annual growth of the magnitude of 7–12 percent is only possible when economies are first taking off and such rates cannot be sustained once these countries become more developed.

A second problem was that credit in some countries was often not directed to firms or industries that could most effectively invest it. In Indonesia, "crony capitalism" saw the Suharto dictatorship steering government aid and bank credits to political insiders, most notably the president's children who became billionaires. Corruption was not as pervasive in South Korea but the country's major industrial conglomerates enjoyed a cozy relationship with the government that allowed them ready access to state credit and other forms of government assistance.

These underlying, long-term weaknesses were then aggravated by additional, short-term problems. For a period of time several Southeast Asian countries had pegged their currencies to the dollar, meaning that their governments had guaranteed to keep their value fixed relative to the dollar. The purpose of that arrangement was to assure foreign investors that the value of their investment in the region would not be undermined by devaluation as it had been in many Latin American countries.[66] But, in the mid-1990s, when the dollar strengthened, the region's pegged currencies automatically gained value with it (relative to currencies such as the Japanese Yen). As a consequence, the price of Southeast Asia's exports increased while the cost of its imports declined, contributing to a growing trade deficit. This compounded the adverse effects of China's 1994 currency devaluation that had lowered the price of its exports and enabled it to undersell Southeast Asian products (especially electronics) on the international market.

Consequences of the 1997 Crash

While Thailand's decision to devalue the baht was an unavoidable reaction to the country's growing trade deficit, it prompted panic among major portfolio investors elsewhere in Southeast Asia. Before long, as investors pulled out of Indonesia and unloaded its currency, that government was forced to devalue the rupiah. The crisis next spread to Malaysia and South Korea. Ultimately, its implications were even broader, as international financial institutions watched events in Asia and became increasingly concerned about their investments in other LDCs. Asia's sharp currency and stock market declines spread to Russia and caused steep drops in the Argentine, Brazilian, and Chilean stock markets as well. Many experts feared a serious recession in China and a renewed economic crisis in Latin America. So far, both have stood firm, though Latin America remains vulnerable.

As Asia's financial crisis intensified, the region sunk into a deep economic recession, inflicting enormous pain on the population. Unable to pay their debts, many companies were forced into bankruptcy, throwing their employees out of work; inflation heated up dangerously; and domestic banks, faced with extensive defaults on their loans, declared bankruptcy themselves.

> Along the way, billions of dollars in production and hundreds of millions of jobs [were] lost. . . . Since the crisis began [through October, 1998], $1 trillion in loans

[went] bad, $2 trillion in equity capitalization for the Asian stock markets . . . vaporized, and $3 trillion in GDP growth [was] lost.[67]

Implications for Asia's Growth Model

What does the recent economic crisis imply about the viability of East and Southeast Asia's developmentalist state and its export-led growth model? Is that model now no longer attractive? Conservative critics argue that the crisis shows the dangers of "too much government control."[68] Because investment decisions in the area were so influenced by government planners rather than by market forces, these analysts contend, bank loans and government aid too often went to well-connected industries and industrial sectors, rather than to those who could make best use of the assistance.

There is certainly some truth to this charge, particularly where crony capitalism prevailed as in Indonesia and South Korea. However, it is unlikely that state planning per se was the major cause of the crisis. After all, China and Vietnam—the countries with the highest degree of state planning in the region—suffered no financial crisis. Nor did Taiwan's and Singapore's developmentalist states. Rather, the key causal factor seems to have been external indebtedness. Countries such as Thailand, Indonesia, and South Korea (or, outside the region, Mexico and Brazil) that had borrowed abroad excessively fell into trouble. Those that had either exercised restraint (Taiwan and China) or had been unable to secure extensive foreign credit (the Philippines and Vietnam) were not badly hurt.

The most important elements of East and Southeast Asia's development model—widespread public education aimed at developing a skilled work force, agrarian reform, equitable income distribution, emphasis on manufactured exports—did not contribute to the crisis and remain the region's strengths. The time has probably come to reduce the role of the developmentalist state, and most countries in the region have already begun to do so. But the model seems to have served its purpose well in getting those economies off the ground and running.

In the future, Asian governments would do well to let their currencies float freely (to continually appreciate or decline in value according to market forces) rather than allow a pegged currency to become seriously overvalued, thereby forcing the government to devalue it sharply. Borrowers and lenders also need to be more careful about seeking and extending credit. At the same time, the World Bank and IMF, both of which failed to anticipate the Asian crisis (as they had failed earlier with the 1994 Mexican peso crisis), must better monitor the financial health of LDCs and must offer the financial community better advance warning about serious imbalances in currency values. So too must private rating services, such as Standard and Poor's and Moody's, which also failed to alert investors of the problem by lowering Asia's credit ratings.

None of these flaws, however, calls into question Asia's underlying development model.[69] Indeed, experts such as Joseph Stiglitz, chief economist of the World Bank, and Jeffrey Winters argue that bad private-sector decisions, not the developmentalist state, caused the crisis. Further, they insist that East and Southeast Asia's economies remain fundamentally strong.[70] In fact, by the end of 1998, the financial crisis seemed to be easing and many economists predicted that the region would resume modest economic growth by the year 2000. In the meantime, however, millions of Asians have sunk into poverty and virtually none of the governments in the region has a social safety net to protect the newly unemployed, homeless, and hungry.

GROWTH WITH EQUITY

Until this point, our discussion of economic development has focused on measurements of production. Indeed, this is often the primary or sole measure of development used in popular or scholarly analysis of economic performance. We read periodically that the economies of, say, Chile, Thailand, or China have been doing well of late, as evidenced by annual GNP growth of 6 to 9 percent. Far less attention has been focused on how that growth is distributed. It is to that important dimension that we should now turn.

Early debate on Third World development often pitted conservative social scientists against progressives, with the former group primarily interested in the prerequisites of growth and the latter more concerned with problems of equity. For example, while mainstream economists were impressed with Brazil's rapid economic expansion in the late 1960s and early 1970s, left-of-center critics pointed out that extremely unequal income distribution prevented the benefits of the country's "economic miracle" from reaching the poorest half of the population. At the same time, while left-leaning economists were favorably impressed by Cuba's far-reaching income redistribution and social welfare programs from the 1960s to the early 1980s, conservative critics noted its record of erratic economic growth.

Market-oriented economists generally believed that increased inequality was actually necessary in the early stages of economic development because it concentrated capital in the hands of entrepreneurs who could invest it in productive activities. Critics countered that development of that sort would do little to help the majority of Third World people. In the near future, they argued, the bottom half of the population would benefit more from meaningful redistribution of wealth and income, even with zero growth, than from steady economic growth without redistribution.[71]

In time, however, analysts of varying persuasions have concluded that there is no intrinsic contradiction between these two goals. In fact, a proper development strategy entails growth with equity.[72] Recent research suggests that since the 1960s, countries with higher levels of income equality have grown faster than those with highly concentrated patterns. East Asia's economic takeoff since the 1970s and 1980s demonstrates that point. Thus, Taiwan and South Korea have coupled spectacular economic growth rates with income distributions that are among the world's most equitable.[73] Indeed, broadly based purchasing power in both those countries has helped further stimulate their economic growth. In South Korea, for example, almost all peasant families have acquired television sets over the years (and many are now switching to color), a feat barely conceivable in Africa or Latin America. During the takeoff of Korean television manufacturing, these domestic purchases supplemented exports in stimulating that industry's growth.

What explains the higher level of economic equality in East Asia as compared to Africa or Latin America? What explains variations within each region, such as greater equality in Argentina and Uruguay than in Brazil and Venezuela? One important explanatory factor is the pattern of land distribution in the countryside. For a variety of reasons, farm land is generally far more equitably distributed in Asia than in Latin America.[74] While the size of Latin America's largest landholdings has declined in recent decades, estates of several thousand acres were common in the recent past and many remain today in countries such as Brazil. On the other hand, the largest holdings in Asia (where there is much heavier population pressure) are rarely over one or two hundred acres.

Land holding patterns reflect both historical legacies and contemporary government policies. Spanish colonialism established an agrarian structure in Latin America and the Philippines dominated by large latifundia. In contrast, Japanese colonial authorities in Korea and Taiwan encouraged smallholder farming. Although European colonial regimes established large, export-oriented plantations in Southeast Asia, land ownership was still never as concentrated in that area as in Latin America. It is surely not coincidental that the nation with one of the most concentrated land and income distributions in East Asia, the Philippines, is also the region's only country that shares Latin America's Spanish colonial heritage. In the postcolonial period, South Korean and Taiwanese agrarian reform led to more egalitarian land distribution in those countries (just as American-imposed reform had done in Japan after the war). By reducing rural poverty, land reform contributed to higher overall levels of income equality in the region.

A second major determinant of national income distribution is the relationship between rural and urban living standards. Although city dwellers enjoy higher incomes and greater social services throughout the Third World, the urban-rural gap is particularly marked in Africa and Latin America. Residents of Mexico City, for example, have incomes averaging four to five times higher than in the countryside. There are many reasons for such discrepancies, but government policy often plays an important role. In Chapter 5 we saw that until recently African and Latin American governments kept the price of basic food crops below their market value so as to satisfy urban political constituencies.[75] By contrast, East Asian farmers generally receive the free market price for their crops or even subsidized prices above market value.

Industrial policy also affects income distribution. Latin America's ISI strategy encouraged the importation of capital equipment for domestic industries. Such capital-intensive development created a limited number of relatively well-paid, skilled industrial jobs but left behind many poorly paid, "unskilled" urban workers and rural peasants. Conversely, East Asia's EOI strategy took advantage of that region's large, disciplined, but poorly paid, labor force.

Initially employing labor-intensive methods that utilized their pool of cheap labor, both Taiwan and South Korea successfully exported "low-tech" goods such as textiles and footwear. As increased numbers of workers were employed, two changes took place over time. First, greater demand for labor in export manufacturing caused factory wages to rise; second, rural-to-urban migration (due to the lure of factory jobs) reduced the supply of rural labor, thereby driving up income levels in the countryside. What had begun as a policy exploiting cheap labor eventually promoted economic growth, higher wages, and greater income equality.[76] As wage levels rose substantially in the four little tigers, those countries shifted from low-tech products to more sophisticated exports such as electronics, commercial services (most notably Singapore), computer software, computers, and automobiles (South Korea). Production of apparel and other low-wage items was passed on to poorer (low-wage) Asian nations such as Malaysia, Thailand, Indonesia, and Sri Lanka.

A final factor distinguishing East Asia from the rest of the Third World is its comparatively high educational level.[77] Table 9.1 offers educational data from four East Asian, four Latin American, and two African nations. The first column indicates primary school enrollment as a percentage of all children at primary school age. While data are unavailable here for three countries, other evidence indicates that Malaysia and Hong Kong have fairly high primary school enrollment ratios, while Nigeria's is considerably lower. Over all, primary

Table 9.1 Comparative National Educational Levels

Country	Primary Enrollment	Primary Completion	Secondary Enrollment	Post-Secondary Enrollment
Hong Kong[a]	—	97%	73%	13%
Singapore	100%	98	69	—
South Korea	100	99	88	41
Malaysia	—	96	56	7
Cuba	95	89	89	21
Mexico	98	72	53	14
Colombia	73	57	52	14
Brazil	88	20	39	12
Nigeria	—	84	20	3
Togo	72	46	22	3

[a]Formerly a British colony; now part of China.
Source: UNDP, *Human Development Report 1993* (New York: Oxford University Press, 1993), pp. 162–163.

enrollments are highest in Asia, somewhat lower in Latin America, and lowest in Africa.

The second column indicates the percentage of beginning students who eventually complete elementary school. Here the gap between East Asia and the other regions is quite notable. In all four Asian cases the completion ratio is over 95 percent. By contrast, only Cuba and Nigeria have ratios over 72 percent in Africa and Latin America, and the Nigerian figures are based on a smaller starting rate.

The third and fourth columns indicate the percentage of students who enroll in secondary school (junior high school and high school) and in postsecondary education. At the secondary level, East Asian nations once again perform most strongly, though Cuba has the best individual record. Only in postsecondary enrollment, with the strong exception of South Korea, is East Asia's record somewhat weaker than Latin America's. This reflects a conscious decision by East Asian governments to emphasize university education less strongly than Latin America has and, instead, to concentrate educational resources in the primary and secondary levels.

Because increased education opens up greater opportunities for upward mobility, national educational levels tend to correspond with income equality.[78] Thus, the most educated populations in Latin America (Cuba, Argentina, Uruguay, Costa Rica) also have the most equitable income distributions in the region. Conversely, Brazil, with a very poor educational record, has one of the region's poorest income distributions. Cultural norms limiting female education have impaired East Asia's performance beyond the secondary level (again, with the notable exception of South Korea). However, the widespread availability of primary and secondary education has contributed to greater income equity.

ECONOMIC DEVELOPMENT AND THE ENVIRONMENT

Throughout the world, in developing countries as well as developed ones, economic growth inevitably involves a degree of environmental degradation. For example, prior to European settlement, the east coast of the United States was covered with thick forest. Since then, population growth, urban sprawl, and farming have destroyed most of it. Today, acid rain (produced by coal usage in the American Midwest) continues to take its environmental toll. Massive dams in China flood valuable farmland and natural habitat. Industrial plants in Germany's Ruhr Valley pollute rivers and the air. Only in recent decades have environmental groups, organized primarily in industrialized nations, begun to question the trade-offs between growth and the conservation of our natural resource heritage. Some of the more radical environmentalists in the United States and Europe have proposed zero growth strategies in highly industrialized nations. These would include efforts to contain population growth as well as the creation of a less consumer-oriented society.

The Costs of Growth

But the option of zero growth or even of reduced economic growth is not really viable in the Third World. In countries such as India, Indonesia, Egypt, Nigeria, and Brazil, where substantial portions of the population live in poverty, it would be politically suicidal and ethically questionable for government leaders to propose limiting economic growth. The "green (ecology) movement" arrived much later in the LDCs than in the industrialized West and its strength and objectives remain more limited. Today, the world's industrialized nations continue to be the major consumers of natural resources, the leading polluters of air and water, and the major contributors to global warming, ozone-layer depletion, and other looming ecological disasters. For example, in recent years, developed nations consumed some 80 percent of the world's paper, 80 percent of its iron and steel and over 85 percent of its chemicals. Per capita consumption of cars in the developed world is more than 25 times as high as in the LDCs, cement consumption is 3.5 times as high, and iron, and steel consumption is 13 times as high.[79]

Yet, ironically, it is those same developed countries which now insist that the LDCs become better environmental citizens. In response, Third World leaders complain that the United States, with only some 4 percent of the world's population, consumes over 25 percent of the planet's resources.[80] Hence, the LDCs feel put upon when asked by industrialized nations to limit their share of environmental destruction.[81]

To be sure, many of today's most pressing environmental challenges are to be found in the developing world. Peasants hungry for firewood in Rwanda, Nepal, India, and Paraguay deplete nearby forests. In African countries such as Sudan, Nigeria, and Burkina Faso, 75 percent or more of all energy is supplied by burning wood. In Indonesia, wood provides 50 percent of the nation's energy, while in Nepal it contributes 90 percent. Giant cattle ranchers and armies of migrant peasants in Brazil burn vast areas of the Amazonian jungle each year to clear the land for cultivation. In Malaysia and Indonesia, Japanese-owned logging firms cut down large tracts of rain forest for furniture manufacturing. Since 1950 alone, over 20 percent of the earth's tropical rain forests have been destroyed. As a consequence, rains and waterways wash off topsoil, rainfall patterns shift, and both droughts and floods occur more frequently. For example, the devastating, hurricane-caused floods that destroyed much of Honduras and Nicaragua (along with other parts of Central America) in 1998 were exacerbated by deforestation. The same is true of many of Africa's recent droughts. Excessive farming on unforested lands adds to the problem. In short, in many parts of the Third World, the arable land area is declining and deserts are growing.

Third World cities such as Shanghai, Cairo, New Delhi, and Sao Paulo have grown at an alarming rate in recent decades (Chapter 6), producing enormous quantities of raw sewage, auto emissions, and industrial waste. As they become choked with cars and buses (few of which have adequate emission control devices), air quality rapidly deteriorates. Mexico City, now the world's largest city, has had some of the world's most polluted air (though it has introduced important environmental protection measures since the 1980s). Operating with few environmental safeguards, many mines, oil fields, chemical plants, and industrial sites pollute their surroundings. In many LDCs misuse of insecticides and industrial accidents have led to a substantial number of deaths and birth defects. Some of these ecological tragedies adversely affect only the people living in the developing world. Others have broader impacts which influence the industrialized world as well, partly accounting for the concern of Western environmental activists.

While many environmental problems are unrelated to economic growth or industrialization, and while some of the world's least developed nations face severe ecological difficulties such as deforestation, it remains true that economic growth, urbanization, and industrialization present particular challenges. Population growth, rapid in some parts of the developing world, moderating in others, puts further strains on the world's resources. Some of the environmental damage currently taking place in the LDCs is confined to their own borders. Other problems spill over to their neighbors or have consequences for the entire world.

Environmental Decay as a Third World Problem

Nowhere is the difficult trade-off between economic growth and environmental conservation more starkly illustrated than in China, home to more than one-fifth of the world's population. Since the government introduced free-market economic reforms in the 1980s, the country has enjoyed the world's highest rate of economic growth, averaging perhaps 8–10 percent annually. Living standards have tripled and millions of Chinese citizens have moved out of poverty. The number of people who have been spared from hunger, disease and early death is undoubtedly staggering. Balanced against those gains, however, is an enormous degree of air and water pollution, and extensive destruction of the country's farm land, raising the prospect of future famine just when China has finally managed to feed its population adequately. By 1990, China consumed 10 percent of global energy and was responsible for 11 percent of carbon dioxide emissions, a figure that continues to rise as the economy leaps forward.[82]

Attracted by higher urban living standards, millions of peasants have migrated to the cities, often abandoning farms in productive agricultural regions. In addition, substantial amounts of farm land has been paved over for highways, factories, and urban sprawl. Since the late 1950s, China's total arable land has decreased by somewhere between 15 and 55 percent (depending on what estimate one accepts), while population has grown by some 80 percent. Though China's annual rate of population growth is currently relatively low (1 percent or lower), loss of farm land because of economic development continues to accelerate at an alarming rate. From 1992 to 1993 alone, arable land area fell by 5.5 percent. So far, the country has averted hunger by farming the remaining land more intensively, and some recent grain harvests have reached record or near-record levels. But this intensive use of fertilizers and pesticides eventually depletes the soil, and a food crunch likely looms in the coming decades.

Environmental Decay in the LDCs as a Global Problem

The debate over Third World environmental policy is further complicated by the fact that many LDCs are stewards to natural resources that are critical to the entire world. For example, the massive, purposeful burning of the Amazonian rain forest contributes significantly to global warming. Destruction of rain forests there as well as in Africa and Asia deprives the world of many animal species and plant forms that are potentially key ingredients in life-saving medicines of the future.[83] Population growth and the destruction of natural habitat threaten the existence of the world's remaining pandas in China and the low-land gorillas in Rwanda.

Unfortunately, the very economic development that Third World people rightfully aspire to poses potentially disastrous threats to the environment. It would be unthinkable to tell the average Indian or Egyptian that they should not yearn for a significantly higher standard of living. But, barring major technological and political breakthroughs, achieving a level of affluence worldwide would overtax the planet's resources. Invariably, economic development includes greatly increased usage of fossil fuels (coal, petroleum, and natural gas) and a corresponding rise in pollution. Brazil, China, and India already rank third through fifth in the world (behind the United States and the former Soviet Union) in greenhouse gas emissions (carbon dioxide and other emissions from fossil-fuel usage that trap the earth's heat and produce global warming). As China's economy continues its rapid growth and as India industrializes further, these two Asian giants will surely use more fossil fuels for their factories and vehicles, thereby accelerating the greenhouse effect on global warming.

The Search for Sustainable Development

Discussion of the environmental consequences of economic growth often centers on the concept of "sustainable development" defined as economic development that "consumes resources to meet [this generation's] needs and aspirations in a way that does not compromise the ability of future generations to meet their needs."[84] Whenever feasible, this involves the use of "renewable resources" (such as wind and water power for generating electricity) in place of resources that cannot be replaced (coal, petroleum) or which are currently being consumed at a faster rate than they can be replaced (tropical rain forests, ocean fish such as salmon). It also requires consumption of resources in a way that least pollutes the environment: limiting auto and industrial emissions, finding sustainable substitutes for pesticides and other agricultural chemicals that pollute the soil and water system, reducing the use of chemicals that destroy the world's ozone layer.[85]

In theory these are goals to which all nations, rich and poor alike, can aspire. During the 1990s a number of international conferences (both regional and global) were held and agreements signed designed to protect the world's environment. The most important of these was the 1992 United Nations Conference on Environment and Development (UNCED, or the Earth Summit as it came to be known) in Rio de Janeiro, Brazil. It produced a "Framework Convention on Climate Change," a nonbinding commitment to reduce and limit greenhouse emissions by the year 2,000; the "Convention on Biological Diversity," designed to protect species and ecosystems; "Agenda 21," an action plan for sustainable development into the twenty-first century; and the "Rio Declaration" which lists 27 guiding principles on the environment and development, including the LDCs' right to economic development and the alleviation of poverty.

While the Rio Earth Summit and subsequent international conferences, such as the 1995 UN Summit on Climate Change in Berlin, have achieved potentially useful accords and have had great symbolic importance, many critics question their actual impact on the environment.[86] Frequently they produce little more than admirable aspirations and unenforceable regulations. Few would challenge the lofty goal of continued economic growth in the context of environmental conservation. But it is far from clear how those two-pronged objectives can and should be achieved and what trade-offs are appropriate. From the perspective of the developing countries, which are most in need of economic growth, the question is how much of that cost they can and should sustain.

> At the Rio Summit, the conflicts between the rich and poor became evident. The Northern [industrialized] countries, which felt vulnerable to global environment problems such as climate change and biodiversity loss, attempted to extract commitments on environmental conservation from the South. However, the South, which felt more vulnerable to perceived underdevelopment was concerned with extracting [economic] transfers from the North.[87]

It is well and good, say Third World leaders, for already-industrialized nations to ask China and Mexico to reduce smokestack emissions or to ask Thailand and Brazil to sustain their rain forests, but First World nations, which have historically wreaked the most havoc on the environment, should defray much of the cost.

The difficult trade-off between growth and environmental protection was vividly brought home to me at a meeting in Jamaica with local social scientists. After one U.S. scholar noted the importance of preserving the island's ecology, a Jamaican economist sarcastically replied, "You Americans raped your environment in order to develop your country and raise your standard of living. Now we Jamaicans reserve the right to do the same."

A number of years ago, journalists in northern Brazil interviewed the mayor of a poor fishing village whose local waters had been contaminated by industrial mercury pollution. Knowing that the fish they ate would eventually probably cause horrible illness or death, the villagers continued to eat it. "For us it is a choice," said the mayor, "we can either starve to death now or face the prospect of mercury poisoning later." Similarly, developing nations face hard choices between short- and long-term consequences. For example, however much Indonesia's political leaders may wish to conserve their country's rain forests, they know that wood-product exports are an important component of the country's industrial development. Furthermore, such exports are also needed to help repay the country's external debt. Similarly, pollution from India's new factories (many of which can't afford adequate emission controls) may eventually contribute to increased cancer rates and pulmonary diseases. For now, however, they create badly needed jobs.

Some Signs of Progress

While environmental problems still loom large, there are some hopeful signs of progress. Both the governments of developing countries and international development agencies have become more conscious of the growth-ecology trade-off. Together they are looking for ways to achieve sustainable development that minimizes harm to the environment. Many LDCs that previously saw the "green movement" as a Western conspiracy to keep them underdeveloped have come to realize that sustainable growth is also in their own interest.

One of the most important means of improving living standards and preserving the environment is population control. Other solutions can also help: the use of renewable fuels such as solar energy and water power (nuclear energy remains far more controversial); organic farming that replenishes, rather than depletes, the soil; government rules and regulations that discourage, rather than encourage, irrational use of rain forest areas (until recently, for example, Brazilian tax laws encouraged ranchers to cut down Amazonian forests); and stricter antipollution controls. For example, Mexico City has improved its air quality by closing down some cement plants and oil refineries and moving others out of the city, by requiring private cars to be off the road one day per week, and by replacing city taxis and buses with newer vehicles which have better emission controls.

Ultimately, however, even if all of the most sophisticated environmental measures were to be implemented, they still would not be likely to reconcile fully the tension between growth and environmental conservation. Furthermore, most of these measures either require substantial financial outlays or result in foregone income opportunities. If the world's industrial powers want the LDCs to make such sacrifices, they will probably have to underwrite much of the cost. This might involve debt forgiveness, subsidized technology transfers, and even outright grants.[88]

Which of the economic models discussed earlier in this chapter is best equipped to handle the environmental challenge? The answer is not clear. It seems certain that preserving the environment requires active state intervention. Since factory owners cannot be counted on to monitor and limit their own pollution nor citizens to voluntarily limit their use of automobiles, state regulation of some kind is needed. Consequently, the neoclassical model of government noninterference seems inappropriate in this area.

In theory, command economies have substantial capability to defend the environment since the state controls the means of production. In fact, however, communist governments from Russia and Poland to China and North Korea have had miserable environmental records. On the one hand, directives to managers of state enterprises usually demand that they maximize production, with little thought given to environmental consequences. On the other hand, absent a free society and a free mass media, citizens are unable to organize green pressure groups or even to know the extent of ecological destruction.

Thus, it appears that if developing nations are to have any chance at sustainable development, they must combine an honest, effective, and responsible state with a free, democratic society where environmental activists can mobilize popular support.

CONCLUSION

Often it has been easier to recognize what has not worked in the Third World than to identify what has. The dependency theorists' assumption that economic liberation lay in reducing or severing ties to the capitalist core has not held up to the light of careful scrutiny. Similarly, extensive state intervention has failed to provide economic salvation. At the same time, the neoclassical, minimal state can hardly address the deep inequities, societal cleavages, and looming ecological nightmares plaguing the LDCs.

To be sure, East Asia's developmental state, actively guiding development without interfering excessively, seems to have struck the proper balance. Many Third Word countries have also rushed to embrace East Asia's export-oriented industrial model. Beyond the previously mentioned problem of transferability, however, there are at least two other fundamental concerns about universalizing the East Asian experience.

The first concerns the degree to which the world economy can absorb industrial exports. East Asia launched its EOI strategy during a period of unparalleled economic growth in the First World. International trade was expanding rapidly and the developed world could absorb a rising tide of industrial exports. Since the 1970s, however, First World economic growth has slowed down, due first to rising energy costs and more recently to the transfer of industrial jobs to the NICs. Even should Japanese and Western economic growth recover their former dynamism, some doubters question whether the international market can absorb an ever-enlarging flow of industrial exports (most notably from a looming economic giant, China) or whether protectionist measures in the First World might place a cap on imports.[89] Supporters of EOI counter that there is no sign of a looming cap on industrial imports, particularly since the larger NICs have become major importers themselves.[90]

But if economic growth models are successfully applied in Africa, Latin America, and South Asia, a further concern will arise. Rapid economic development has already taken a tremendous ecological toll in Asia and other parts of the Third World. Tropical rain forests in Brazil, Peru and Indonesia are rapidly being depleted. Since the late 1950s, China's economic expansion has contributed to the removal of up to one-third of the country's farm land from agricultural production. Huge amounts of crop land have been converted to housing (much of it for poor peasants), freeways, factories, shopping malls, or the like. Hunger has been averted by increasing crop yields per acre, but such intensive farming further erodes the soil.[91] In addition, ever-growing Chinese energy consumption will likely put a strain on world petroleum supplies in the coming decades and will contribute to global warming. As India begins a more modest but still significant economic takeoff, such problems are certain to be compounded. New models of ecologically sustainable development will have to be formulated.

Finally, the recent Asian financial crisis demonstrates that even the most sophisticated and apparently successful development models can encounter serious difficulties.

DISCUSSION QUESTIONS

1. What have the been the major accomplishments and failures of command economies?

2. Compare the nature of state economic intervention in Latin America to East Asia's developmental state.

3. What are the major arguments presented in the neoclassical development model?

4. What were the major causes of East and Southeast Asia's recent economic crisis? What implications did the crisis have for evaluating the region's economic model?

5. In what ways does economic growth in the Third World contribute to environmental degradation?

NOTES

1. Of course, we have seen that in the short to medium run, economic growth can be politically destabilizing. But if growth can be combined with equitable distribution, the chances of unrest are greatly diminished. In any event, all other factors being equal, in the long run rising living standards should rebound to the regime's political advantage. The potentially destabilizing effects of unequal economic growth are treated elsewhere in this book and will not be discussed in this chapter.

2. Joan M. Nelson, ed., *Economic Crisis and Policy Choice: The Politics of Adjustment in the Third World* (Princeton, NJ: Princeton University Press, 1990); Dharam Ghai, ed., *The IMF and the South: The Social Impact of Crisis and Adjustment* (London: Zed Books, 1991).

3. Martin Staniland, *What Is Political Economy?* (New Haven, CT: Yale University Press, 1985), p. 6.

4. Ibid., p. 12.

5. Simon Kuznets, *Modern Economic Growth: Rate, Structure and Spread*, 7th ed. (New Haven, CT: Yale University Press, 1976); Hollis Chenery and Moises Syrquin, *Patterns of Development, 1950–1970* (London: Oxford University Press, 1975).

6. Of course, these are general tendencies or trends, not inviolable rules. Thus, East and Southeast Asian countries such as Taiwan, South Korea, and Malaysia have entered or passed through the intermediate stage of development without an appreciable worsening of income distribution.

7. Adapted from Adam Przeworski, *Democracy and the Market* (New York: Cambridge University Press, 1991), p. 105, fn. 10. A number of the insights in this section come from Przeworski.

8. Ed A. Hewett, *Reforming the Soviet Economy: Equality versus Efficiency* (Washington, DC: Brookings Institute, 1988), p. 38.

9. Abraham Bergson, *The Real National Income of Soviet Russia since 1928* (Cambridge, MA: Harvard University Press, 1961), p. 261.

10. Harry Harding, *China's Second Revolution* (Washington, DC: Brookings Institution, 1987), pp. 30–31.

11. Stephen White, John Gardener, and George Schopflin, *Communist and Postcommunist Political Systems* (New York: St. Martin's Press, 1990), p. 322; Harding, *China's Second Revolution*, p. 30.

12. Claes Brundenius, *Revolutionary Cuba: The Challenge of Economic Growth with Equity* (Boulder, CO: Westview Press, 1984); Carmelo Mesa-Lago, *The Economy of Socialist Cuba: A Two-Decade Appraisal* (Albuquerque: University of New Mexico Press, 1981).

13. Erich Wede and Horst Tiefenbach, "Some Recent Explanations of Income Inequality," *International Studies Quarterly* 25 (June 1981): 255–282.

14. An obvious moral and political weakness, not discussed here, is that command economies require government repression. I am taking that very serious flaw as a given and am limiting my discussion in this chapter to the system's economic strengths and weaknesses.

15. Liang Heng and Judith Shapiro, *After the Nightmare* (New York: Collier, 1986).

16. John Sheahan, *Patterns of Development in Latin America* (Princeton, NJ: Princeton University Press, 1987).

17. Ibid., p. 85.

18. Dale Story, *Industry, the State and Public Policy in Mexico* (Austin: University of Texas Press, 1986), p. 68.

19. Both those industries were nationalized in the 1930s. Subsequently, the state also took over electricity and telecommunications.

20. Dale Story, *Industry, the State and Public Policy in Mexico* (Austin: University of Texas Press, 1986), p. 21. My statistic is extrapolated from Story's data.

21. Samuel Schmidt, *The Deterioration of the Mexican Presidency: The Years of Luis Echeverría* (Tucson: University of Arizona Press, 1991), pp. 162-164; Elia Marún Espinosa, "Intervencionismo estatal y transformaciones del sector empresa pública en México," in *El Nuevo Estado Mexicano: Estado y Economía*, ed. Jorge Alonso et al. (Mexico City: Nueva Imagen, 1992), pp. 193–240.

22. For startling data on overstaffing and "ghost workers" in Africa, see Richard Sandbrook, *The Politics of Africa's Economic Recovery* (New York: Cambridge University Press, 1993), pp. 43, 61.

23. *New York Times*, December 7, 1993.

24. *New York Times*, November 2, 1993.

25. Ibid.

26. Howard Handelman and Werner Baer, eds., *Paying the Costs of Austerity in Latin America* (Bolder, CO.: Westview Press, 1989); Stephan Haggard and Robert R. Kaufman, eds., *The Politics of Economic Adjustment* (Princeton, NJ: Princeton University Press, 1992).

27. Economic growth, though obviously beneficial, does not necessarily translate immediately into higher living standards for much of the population. For example, in 1991 and 1992 Venezuela's economy grew at a rate of some 9 percent, the fastest rise in Latin America. Yet living standards continued to decline for many workers whose wages failed to keep up with steep inflation. As a consequence, during a period of rapid growth Venezuela suffered substantial popular unrest and two failed military coups.

28. During Mexico's 1994 presidential campaign, I interviewed a major spokesperson for the PRD, the country's principal Left opposition party. Though he had once been a Marxist congressman, he readily conceded that President Salinas' economic liberalization program, involving massive layoffs of state workers, had been necessary. That interview took place a week after the peasant uprising in Chiapas that many analysts believed had shifted the Mexican political spectrum to the left.

29. Robert Wade, *Governing the Market: Economic Theory and the Role of Government in East Asian Industrialization* (Princeton, NJ: Princeton University Press, 1990), p. 34.

30. Extrapolated from Sinichi Ichimura and James W. Morley, "The Varieties of Asia-Pacific Experience," in *Driven by Growth*, ed. James W. Morley (Armonk, NY: M. E. Sharpe, 1992), p. 6, and Steven Chan, *East Asian Dynamism* (Boulder, CO: Westview Press, 1990), p. 8; UNDP, *Human Development Report, 1997* (New York: Oxford University Press, 1997), pp. 21–22.

31. Again, China does not fit that model. A large, though rapidly falling, share of its economy continues to be state owned, while another substantial portion is run by cooperatives. State regulation, though reduced, is still formidable. Thus, despite its many changes since the early 1980s, Communist China remains distinct from the other Asian economies described in this section and will be excluded from the discussion that follows.

32. Milton and Rose Friedman, *Freedom to Choose* (New York: Harcourt Brace Jovanovich, 1980), p. 57; David Felix, "Review of Economic Structure and Performance: Essays in Honor of Hollis B. Chenery," *Economic Development and Cultural Change* 36, no. 1 (1987): 188–194; Ian Little, "An Economic Reconnaissance," in *Economic Growth and Structural Change in Taiwan*, ed. Walter. Galenson (Ithaca, NY: Cornell University Press).

33. Wade, *Governing the Market*; Gary Gereffi and Donald L. Wyman, eds., *Manufacturing Miracles* (Princeton, NJ: Princeton University Press, 1990); Stephan Haggard, *Pathways from the Periphery* (Ithaca, NY: Cornell University Press, 1990); Chalmers Johnson, "Political Institutions and Economic Performance: The Government-Business Relationship in Japan, South Korea and Taiwan," in *The Political Economy of the New Asian Industrialism*, ed. Frederic C. Deyo (Ithaca, NY: Cornell University Press, 1987).

34. Chalmers Johnson, *MITI and the Japanese Miracle* (Stanford, CA: Stanford University Press, 1982).

35. Chan, *East Asian Dynamism*, pp. 47–48.

36. Chalmers Johnson, "Political Institutions and Economic Performance," in *The Political Economy of the New Asian Industrialism*, ed. Frederic C. Deyo.

37. Chan, *East Asian Dynamism*, p. 49.

38. Johnson, "Political Institutions," p. 159.

39. Haggard, *Pathways from the Periphery*.

40. Robert Wade, "Industrial Policy in Asia: Does it Lead or Follow the Market?" in *Manufacturing Miracles*, pp. 231–266; Wade, *Governing the Market*.

41. Johnson, "Political Institutions."

42. For a criticism of the developmental state concept and its alleged benefits, see Cheng-tian Kuo, *International Competitiveness and Industrial Growth in Taiwan and the Philippines* (Pittsburgh, PA: University of Pittsburgh Press, forthcoming).

43. These conglomerates dominate the economy. By the mid-1980s, Korea's ten largest chaebols produced two-thirds of the nation's GNP. See Wade, *Governing the Market*, p. 309.

44. Herman Kahn, "The Confucian Ethic and Economic Growth," in *The Gap between Rich and Poor*, ed. Mitchell A. Seligson (Boulder, CO: Westview Press, 1984).

45. Christopher Ellison and Gary Gereffi, "Explaining Strategies and Patterns of Industrial Development," in *Manufacturing Miracles*, pp. 395–396.

46. Neoclassical economics (or the neoclassical approach) is a revised formulation of Adam Smith's classical economic approach.

47. Wade, *Governing the Market*, p. 11.

48. Alice H. Amsden, *Asia's Next Giant: South Korea and Late Industrialization* (New York: Oxford University Press, 1989); see also the works by Haggard, Wade, and Johnson cited earlier in this chapter.

49. Wade, *Governing the Market*.

50. Richard Albin, "Saving the Environment: The Shrinking Realm of Laissez-Faire," in *International Political Economy*, 2d ed., ed. Jeffrey A. Frieden and David A. Lake (New York: St. Martin's, 1991), p. 454.

51. Bela Balassa, *The Newly Industrializing Countries in the World Economy* (New York: Pergamon Press, 1981).

52. This section draws heavily on Sheahan, *Patterns of Development in Latin America*, pp. 82–98.

53. For example, if a nation's currency was worth 10 pesos to the dollar in the free market, governments might impose official rates of 5 pesos to the dollar for trade purposes. This would artificially double the value of the peso, thereby halving the number of dollars needed to import a forklift or machine lathe. At the same time, consumer goods produced domestically with the imported machinery would still be protected against import competition by tariffs and quotas.

54. Ibid., p. 84; Werner Baer, "Import Substitution and Industrialization in Latin America: Experiences and Interpretations," *Latin American Research Review* 7, no. 1 (1972): 95–122.

55. Helen Shapiro and Lance Taylor, "The State and Industrial Strategy," in *The Political Economy of Development and Underdevelopment*, ed. Charles K. Wilber and Kenneth P. Jameson, 5th ed. (New York: McGraw-Hill, 1992).

56. Sheahan, *Patterns of Development*, pp. 86–87.

57. Wade, *Governing the Market*, pp. 34, 36.

58. Barbara Stallings and Robert Kaufman, eds., *Debt and Democracy in Latin America* (Boulder, CO: Westview Press, 1989); Handelman and Baer, *Paying the Costs of Austerity*; Haggard and Kaufman, *The Politics of Economic Adjustment*.

59. Haggard, *Pathways from the Periphery*.

60. Gary Gereffi, "Paths of Industrialization: An Overview," in *Manufacturing Miracles*, p. 15. Brazil's proportion grew steadily from 8 percent in 1965 to 45 percent in 1987. Mexico's manufacturing ratio, on the other hand, was quite volatile, falling from 31 percent of exports in 1975 to 15 percent in 1980, only to jump back to 47 percent in 1987. In large part this reflected the shifting price and significance of petroleum exports.

61. Gary Gereffi and Donald Wyman, "Determinants of Development Strategies in Latin America and Asia," in *Pacific Dynamics*, ed. Stephan Haggard and Ching-in Moon (Boulder, CO: Westview Press, 1989), p. 37. Gereffi and Wyman, however, cite Bela Balassa's research warning against overstating the importance of size.

62. Robert Dore, "Reflections on Culture and Social Change," in *Manufacturing Miracles*, pp. 353–367.

63. Jeffrey A. Winters, "Asia and the 'Magic' of the Marketplace," *Current History* 97 (December 1998): 420. Winters offers a clear analysis of the nature and causes of the Asian crisis and his ideas permeate this section.

64. In other words, if the baht had previously been worth $0.10 then a Thai business borrowing $1 million from a U.S. bank would convert that loan into 10 million bahts. But if the decision to float the value of the baht caused its value to fall to $0.05, then the loan of $1 million would cost 20 million bahts to pay back.

65. Ibid. The Serengeti is the African plain famed for its wild life.

66. In other words, a floating exchange rate presents the possibility that a foreign investor could invest, say, $1 million in the Thai economy (converting it into bahts at, say, 10 bahts per dollar) and the find out the following week that the baht had been devalued to 20 per dollar, thereby reducing the dollar value of the investment by 50 percent.

67. Winters, "Asia and the 'Magic' of the Marketplace," p. 419.

68. Charles Wolf Jr., "Too Much Government Control," *Wall Street Journal*, February 4, 1998.

69. Meredith Woo-Cumings, "All in the Family: Reforming Corporate Governance in East Asia," *Current History* 97 (December 1998): 426–430.

70. Joseph Stiglitz, "Bad Private-Sector Decisions," *Wall Street Journal* (February 4, 1998).

71. Irma Adelman and Cynthia Taft Morris, *Economic Growth and Social Equity in Developing Countries* (Stanford, CA: Stanford University Press, 1973). A similar argument has been made in research by Keith Griffin.

72. Perhaps the most important seminal work in this area was Hollis Chenery et al., *Redistribution with Growth* (London: Oxford University Press, with World Bank and University of Sussex, 1974). There have been large numbers of World Bank studies supporting this strategy.

73. Richard E. Barrett and Soomi Chin, "Export-Oriented Industrializing States in the Capitalist World System: Similarities and Differences," in *The Political Economy of the New Asian Industrialism*, pp. 28–31; Ward, *Governing the Market*, p. 38.

74. Howard Handelman, ed., *The Politics of Rural Change in Asia and Latin America* (Bloomington: Indiana University Press, 1981).

75. Robert H. Bates, "Governments and Agricultural Markets in Africa," in *Toward a Political Economy of Development*, ed. Robert H. Bates (Berkeley: University of California Press, 1988); see also Michael J. Lofchie, *The Policy Factor: Agricultural Performance in Kenya and Tanzania* (Boulder, CO: Lynne Rienner Publishers, 1989), pp. 57–59; Charles Harvey, ed., *Agricultural Pricing Policy in Africa* (London: Macmillan, 1988), p. 2.

76. Sheahan, *Patterns of Development*; Haggard, *Pathways from the Periphery*, Chapter 1.

77. I have previously discussed two other influences on distribution that need not be repeated here. First, as Simon Kuznets has demonstrated, countries in the intermediate stage of economic growth tend to have more unequal income distribution than either poor or industrialized nations. Second, all other factors being held equal, socialist or Marxist regimes have more equal distribution than capitalist ones.

78. Haggard, *Pathways from the Periphery*, pp. 239–240. Haggard notes, however, that some research has challenged the widely assumed correlation between education and income

equality. See Frederick Harbison, "The Education-Income Connection," *Income Distribution and Growth in Less-Developed Countries*, ed. Charles R. Frank and Richard C. Webb (Washington, DC: Brookings Institute, 1977).

79. Gareth Porter and Janet Welsh Brown, *Global Environmental Politics* (Boulder, Co: Westview Press, 1996), p. 113.

80. Bhaskar Nath and Ilkden Talay. "Man, Science, Technology and Sustainable Development," in *Sustainable Development*, ed. Bhaskar Nath, Luc Hens, Dimitri Devuyst (Brussels, Belgium: VUB University Press, 1996), p. 37.

81. For a general discussion of international environmental debates, see Jacqueline Vaughn Switzer and Gary Bryner, *Environmental Politics: Domestic and Global Dimensions* (New York: St. Martin's Press, 1998), pp. 200–234.

82. Marian A. L. Miller, *The Third World in Global Environmental Politics* (Boulder, Co: Lynne Rienner Publishers, 1995), pp. 43–44.

83. A surprisingly high proportion of advanced, modern medications use ingredients drawn from tropical rain forests.

84. Nath and Talay, "Man, Science," p. 36.

85. For information on the debate over sustainable development, see Ken Conca, Michael Alberty and Geoffrey D. Dabelko (ed.), *Green Planet Blues: Environmental Politics from Stockholm to Rio* (Boulder, Co: Westview Press, 1995), pp. 205–238.

86. Colin Sage, "The Scope for North-South Co-operation," in *Environmental Policy in an International Context: Prospects*, ed. Andrew Blowers and Pieter Glasbergen (New York: John Wiley & Sons, 1996), pp. 188–89. For strong criticism of what the Rio Earth Summit failed to accomplish, see p. 190 of that chapter.

87. Andrew Blowers and Pieter Leroy, "Environment and Society: Shaping the Future," in *Environmental Policy*, ed. Blowers and Glasbergen, p. 262.

88. Some environmental experts believe that it will be impossible to maintain sustainable development and that the world faces certain ecological disaster. See Joseph Wayne Smith, Graham Lyons and Gary Sauer-Thompson, *Healing a Wounded World* (Westport, CT: Praeger Publishers, 1997).

89. Robin Broad and John Cavanagh, "No More NICs," *Foreign Policy* 72 (Fall 1988): 81–103.

90. Communication with Stephan Haggard, April 6, 1994.

91. *New York Times*, March 27, 1994.

10

DEMOCRATIC CHANGE
AND THE CHANGE
TO DEMOCRACY

I n early 1990, Nelson Mandela, the world's most renowned political prisoner, left his cell in Pollsmoor prison and was transported triumphantly to South Africa's capital, Pretoria, (ending 27 years of incarceration). There, he and other freed black leaders from his recently legalized political party, the African National Congress, eventually negotiated an end to white-minority rule. When, four years later, South Africa's newly enfranchised black majority chose a new national parliament which then elected Mandela to the presidency and chose a new national parliament, the country completed its dramatic yet peaceful transition to democracy, a change that few could have anticipated even a few years earlier. President Mandela's triumph accelerated Africa's "second independence," a swell of political liberalization (easing of repression) in much of the continent that has sometimes culminated in the birth of electoral democracy.[1] Though progress toward democracy in that region was modest at best, and in many cases was subsequently reversed, significant democratic breakthroughs were achieved in countries such as Benin, Madagascar, Mali and Namibia.

In Asia, Corazon (Cory) Aquino became the leader of Filipino "people's power"—mass, peaceful demonstrations for democracy staged by students, shopkeepers, professionals, businesspeople and even Catholic nuns. Aquino's husband, Benigno, had been the Philippines's leading opponent of President Ferdinand Marcos's corrupt dictatorship. When Aquino was assassinated by government agents, Cory assumed the leadership of her country's democracy movement. Backed by the Catholic clergy, her supporters took to the streets day after day, peacefully challenging government troops. Ultimately, when Marcos tried to deny Ms. Aquino her apparent victory in a hastily called "snap presidential election" (1986), the commander of the armed forces, General Fidel Ramos, and Defense Minister Juan Ponce Enrile joined the opposition, forcing Marcos to step down.

In the years that followed, student-led demonstrations against South Korea's military regime (inspired, in part, by events in the Philippines) accelerated that country's transition to democracy. And, more recently (1998), "people's power" demonstrations in Indonesia toppled the 30-year dictatorship of President Suharto, though it is not yet clear how democratic that country's new government will be. Of course, not all of the region's pro-democracy movements have been successful. In China, massive student demonstrations were crushed by army tanks in Tiananmen Square, while Myanmar's military squashed democratic protests, at least for now, by killing thousands. But these setbacks notwithstanding, much of Asia has made significant progress toward democracy in the past two decades.

The most sweeping democratic changes, however, took place in Latin America (1978–1990), affecting almost every country in the region. Unlike Asia and Africa, Latin America's democratization generally lacked charismatic heroes in the mold of Mandela, Aquino, or Burmese opposition leader and Nobel Peace Prize winner Daw Aung San Suu Kyi. Nor was it typically precipitated by mass demonstrations. Instead democratic transitions often followed extended negotiations between the outgoing authoritarian government and its opponents, with change coming in stages. Yet Latin America enjoyed two important advantages over Africa and Asia. To begin with, prior to its earlier wave of military takeovers in the 1960s and 1970s, the region had enjoyed the developing world's strongest democratic tradition, most notably in Chile, Costa Rica, Uruguay, and Venezuela. Second, Latin American nations were among the first LDCs to achieve the levels of literacy and economic development that are usually needed for stable democratic government. Not surprisingly, then, the region's current transition or return to democracy has been more sweeping and more successful than elsewhere in the Third World, ultimately affecting virtually every country in the hemisphere except Cuba.

In all, since the 1970s the upsurge of political freedom in the developing world coupled with the collapse of Soviet and Eastern European communism has produced history's greatest advance toward democracy. If these changes can be maintained they promise to influence virtually every aspect of Third World politics discussed in this book.[2]

DEMOCRACY DEFINED

Discussions of democratic transformations frequently have been complicated by disagreements over the precise meaning of democracy itself. Currently, most political scientists define democracy procedurally. That is, democracy is explained in terms of necessary *procedures* governing the election and behavior of government officials. The least demanding, minimalist, definition focuses almost exclusively on elections. It simply defines democracy as a political system that holds relatively fair, contested elections on a regular basis.[3] I will refer to countries that meet that minimal standard as "electoral democracies." While this bare-bones definition seems reasonable (after all, most Americans define democracy in terms of free elections), it allows a number of rather questionable governments to be included in the "democratic club." For example, the current governments in Colombia, Peru, Turkey, and Sri Lanka meet this standard, yet they massively violate human rights while battling armed insurgencies.[4] In all of those countries, government troops routinely massacre villagers and torture prisoners. Guatemala and Pakistan also meet the standards of electoral democracy yet their armed forces regularly intervene in politics, often overriding decisions made by elected officials.

As the norm of open elections has become more universally accepted in recent decades, the number of electoral democracies worldwide has more than doubled. But many of these governments still manipulate the mass media and violate their citizens' civil liberties. In this chapter I will use the term "semi-democracies" to refer to those "electoral democracies" whose governments repress civil liberties and otherwise breach the principles of a free society. Their elections may be relatively free, but their societies are not. Currently, semi-democracies include Guatemala, Mexico, Peru, Pakistan and Singapore.

A more stringent definition of democracy, the one used in this chapter, demands more than just fair elections. Instead it defines full democracy (sometimes called "liberal democracy") as a political system in which most of the country's leading government officials are elected;[5] there is nearly universal suffrage;[6] elections are largely free of fraud and outside manipulation; opposition-party candidates have a real chance of being elected to important national offices; and minority rights as well as civil liberties generally are respected (including free speech and free "press"). All of these conditions help guarantee that democratic governments are accountable to their citizens in a way that authoritarian regimes are not.[7] Thus, full democracies (or simply "democracies" without adjectives or hyphens) encompass not only freely contested elections, but also respect for civil liberties, support for pluralism in civil society,[8] respect for the rule of law, accountability of elected officials, and civilian control over the armed forces.

This suggests that competitive elections have limited value if unelected individuals or groups who are not accountable to the public (such as the heads of the armed forces, organized crime bosses, business elites or foreign powers) control elected officials from behind the scenes. And free elections don't establish true democracy if elected officials then arbitrarily arrest opposition leaders or widely violate civil liberties.

Finally, some scholars offer an even higher standard for democracy (raising the bar further, so to speak). They argue that *any* purely procedural definition of democracy, no matter how exacting, is incomplete. Instead, they insist, real democracy requires not only fair elections and proper government *procedures* (as just outlined) but also fair and just government *policy outcomes* ("substantive democracy"). For example, such democracy requires that citizens have equal access to public schooling and health care regardless of their social class or ethnicity. Consequently, they argue that any procedural democracy—such as India, El Salvador, or Bangladesh—that tolerates gross economic inequalities, ethnic prejudices, or other major social injustices is not truly democratic.

These critics make an important point. Procedural democracy alone does not guarantee a just society; it is just a step in the right direction. But, it is a more important step than these critics acknowledge. Because governments in procedural democracies are accountable to the people, they are less vulnerable to revolution and other forms of civil unrest; they are also extremely unlikely to make war against other democracies (indeed, war between two democracies is essentially unknown); prodded by a free press and public opinion, they also are more responsive to domestic crises such as famines (consequently, there has never been an extended famine in any procedural democracy); and, the many previously cited exceptions notwithstanding, democracies are generally more respectful of civil liberties.[9]

So, mindful of the fact that democratic societies never correct all social injustices (the United States, for example, has long tolerated racial discrimination), I will define democracy strictly procedurally. Issues of substantive democracy (eradicating poverty, racism, sexism and the like) are obviously important, but they are a separate matter.

DEMOCRATIC TRANSITION AND CONSOLIDATION

In the discussion that follows the term *democratic transition* (or "transition to democracy") means the process of moving from an authoritarian regime to a democratic one. The transition period begins when authoritarian governments show the first significant signs of collapsing or of negotiating an exit from power. It ends when the first freely elected government takes office. Thus, for example, in South Africa the democratic transition began in 1990 when the white-minority government of President Frederik de Klerk decided to free Nelson Mandela and open negotiations with the African National Congress party. It concluded four years later when Mandela was inaugurated as the nation's elected president. Even after a transition is completed, however, new democracies often remain fragile, with the distinct possibility that they will falter.

Only when democratic institutions, practices, and values have become deeply entrenched in society can we say that a country has experienced *democratic consolidation*. Consolidation is a process through which democratic norms (democratic "rules of the game") become accepted by all powerful groups in society, including labor, business, rural landlords, the church, and the military. And no important political actor contemplates a return to dictatorship. Or, as Juan Linz and Alfred Stepan put it, democracy is consolidated when it "becomes the only game in town" even in the face of severe economic or political adversity.[10] Consolidation may begin when the democratic transition ends and it is only completed when democracy is securely entrenched.

Unfortunately, however, not all transitions to democracy are subsequently consolidated. Many countries revert to dictatorship or remain mired in political disorder. For example, between 1958 and 1975, 22 countries that had democratized during the "postwar" era (1943–1962) slipped back to authoritarianism. Similarly, some of the most recently installed democracies have already collapsed, while democratic values and practices in other countries—such as Russia, Guatemala, Mali, and Mozambique—are anything but secure. It is worth noting, for example, that Russia's parliament is dominated by antidemocratic parties (especially the Communists and Liberal Democrats) and that President Boris Yeltsin has frequently violated the Russian constitution and democratic norms in his battles with the parliament.

On the other hand, in successfully consolidated (or reconsolidated) democracies such as South Korea, Chile, and Uruguay, democratic values predominate, previously antidemocratic political parties and groups (such as the Communist party and former Tupamaru guerrillas in Uruguay) have accepted democracy as "the only game in town," and the once-dominant armed forces now seemingly accepts civilian control. That does not mean that consolidated democracies can *never* collapse. "Never" is a long time, and in the past seemingly consolidated Third World democracies such as the Philippines, Chile, and Uruguay were toppled by authoritarian forces. But, at the least, consolidated democracies are secure for the foreseeable future. And they will continue to endure unless some deep societal divide emerges to tear them apart.

AUTHORITARIAN BEGINNINGS

With the disintegration of Soviet bloc communism and the expansion of democracy in the developing world, a growing worldwide consensus has come to favor democracy as the best form of government. But that has not always been so. In the decades after World War II, as a legion of African, Asian, and Middle Eastern countries achieved independence, many Third World leaders and foreign observers believed that these emerging nations were not ready for democratic government and, perhaps, that democracy was not even desirable at that stage of their socioeconomic development. To be sure, a number of newly independent countries, particularly former British colonies in Africa, Asia, and the Caribbean, established parliamentary government and other democratic political institutions modeled after their former colonial masters, just as Latin American countries more than a century earlier had patterned their political institutions after the United States'. But only in a small number of cases (including India,

Malaysia, Jamaica, and other small, island nations in the Caribbean) did democracy take hold.

Since that time, Middle Eastern nations have been ruled by monarchs (Saudi Arabia, Kuwait, Morocco, and Jordan), all-powerful single parties (Egypt, Sudan), or personalistic military and civil-military dictators (Iraq, Syria). In sub-Saharan Africa single-party systems were established in many new nations (including Tanzania, Senegal, Guinea), often to be followed by military dictatorships (Nigeria, Liberia) or absolute, one-man rule (Uganda, Central Africa Republic). Democracy fared somewhat better in Asia but was frequently cut short by the military (Thailand, South Korea, Myanmar). Corrupt and inept postwar governments in China, Vietnam, Cambodia, and Laos were overthrown and replaced by communist revolutionary regimes. Latin America, benefiting from more than a century of self-rule and from greater socioeconomic development, had the most success. Indeed, during the 1950s relatively democratic governments was pervasive in the region. But political intervention by the armed forces persisted and in the 1960s and early 1970s a new wave of military takeovers swept the region. It was not until the 1980s that democracy once again became the norm.

JUSTIFYING AUTHORITARIAN RULE

In the midst of democracy's current worldwide advance, it seems hard to believe that not long ago, freely elected governments and flourishing civil societies were often seen as unattainable or even undesirable in many LDCs. Modernization theorists frequently claimed the newly emerging states of Africa and Asia were not sufficiently developed, economically or socially, to sustain political democracy.[11] And dependency theorists declared that democracy was unlikely to emerge in the LDCs because powerful industrialized nations were allied with local political and economic elites to bolster unrepresentative governments.

Some scholars worried that levels of mass political participation were outstripping government's capacity to accommodate society's political demands. Unless Third World political institutions could be strengthened, they warned, political unrest threatened to derail economic and political development.[12] Given the dangers of social disorder, some analysts and Third World leaders used this argument to justify authoritarian rule as a necessary stopgap.

Only with socioeconomic modernization, it seemed, could LDCs produce citizens capable of effective political participation. Increased education and literacy were seen as necessary to expand society's political knowledge and develop effective political participation. We now know that countries are unlikely to establish stable, democratic government unless they have risen above the bottom ranks of poverty (as expressed by GNP per capita) and have reached a literacy rate of at least 50 percent.[13] In addition to raising literacy, modernization also enlarges the size of the middle class and the organized (unionized) working class, both of whom are essential for a more stable and inclusive democracy.[14]

But an obvious chicken-and-egg quandary presented itself. If socioeconomic modernization is necessary to establish democracy, how can a democratic government be the agent of modernization? Some answered that it couldn't; only a strong and stable authoritarian government—such as General Augusto Pinochet's dictatorship in Chile or South Korea's various military governments—could jump-start modernization. Only later, when the country was "ready," could dictatorship give way to democracy.[15] Other scholars noted yet another obstacle to democratic government in the developing world. They argued that many LDCs, held back by authoritarian traditional values, lacked a democratic political culture and that democracy would have to be preceded by modernization of social values.[16]

Not long ago, many Third World leaders insisted that not only would it be difficult to establish democracy in their countries, but that it was not even desirable at that stage of their development. In Africa, many first-generation, post-colonial leaders created single-party systems, banning or restricting opposition political parties. They often argued that ethnic (tribal) tensions in their country made competitive elections too risky since they would prompt different political parties to represent contending tribes, further polarizing the country. Other new national leaders were influenced by Marxist-Leninist beliefs that they had acquired during their university days in Europe. They maintained that poverty, tribalism, and dependency at home were so severe that an all-powerful state linked to a "vanguard party" (one that always knows what is in the best interests of the people) was needed to lead the country forward. Later, as many of these governments failed miserably, military dictators took their place, claiming that civilian rulers were too corrupt or too weak to govern effectively. In the Middle East similar justifications were used for one-party or military rule. More recently, Islamic fundamentalist governments in Iran, Sudan, and Afghanistan have prohibited political opposition groups whom they regard as infidels.

While democratic or semidemocratic governments were common in Latin America in the 1950s, during the two decades that followed, a series of military coups installed repressive governments in most of the region. These new authoritarian leaders typically justified their rule by pointing to perceived leftist threats and the need to reinvigorate industrial growth. Meanwhile in East Asian nations such as South Korea, Taiwan, and Singapore, authoritarian rulers clung to power long after their countries had passed the thresholds of economic and social modernization normally associated with democratic transitions. They insisted that their dictatorships were necessary to ward off external threats (from China or North Korea) and claimed that their society's Confucian culture was not receptive to political opposition groups, seeing them as disrupting social harmony.

According to one respected count, in the mid-1970s only 39 of the world's nations were functioning democracies. Virtually all of those were industrialized, economically prosperous countries in North America, Europe, and Australia-New Zealand. Meanwhile democracy seemed to be in retreat in the Third World as countries such as Argentina, Chile, Nigeria, and the Philippines succumbed to dictatorships. Thus Larry Diamond notes:

> Indeed, the mid-to-late 1970s seemed a low-water mark for democracy . . . and the empirical trends were reified by intellectual fashions dismissing democracy as an artifice, a cultural construct of the West, or a "luxury" that poor states could not afford.[17]

THE THIRD WAVE AND ITS EFFECT ON THE THIRD WORLD

Since that time, however, developing countries have enjoyed the most sweeping transition ever from authoritarianism to democracy or semidemocracy. Writing shortly before the fall of the Soviet Union, Samuel Huntington counted 29 countries throughout the world that had democratized in the previous 15 years alone (1974–1989). Of these, 20 were LDCs.[18] While some of the countries on that list had questionable democratic credentials (Romania, Peru, and Pakistan, for example) and others quickly slid back to authoritarian rule (Nigeria, Sudan), there can be no denying that the worldwide trend toward democracy since the mid-1970s has been palpable.

Huntington noted that the current surge of democratic expansion is, in fact, the third such wave that the modern world has experienced since the early 1800s. In each wave, major political forces and intellectual trends in key countries had a contagious impact on other nations. At the same time, however, the first two waves were followed by periods of backsliding in which some countries reverted to authoritarian rule. That process has already begun in some third-wave nations.[19]

The first democratic wave (1828–1926), by far the longest, began under the influence of the American and French Revolutions (as well as the Industrial Revolution) and ended not long after World War I. Change was largely confined to Europe and to former British colonies with populations primarily of European descent (the United States, Canada, New Zealand, and Australia). The second, much shorter, wave (1943–1962) was precipitated by the struggle against fascism during World War II and the subsequent collapse of European colonialism in Africa and Asia. In this period, democracy was introduced to a number of LDCs, but in most cases the new governments at best only met the standards of electoral democracy (competitive elections).

It is the recent "third wave" (1974–) that most draws our attention here because of its pervasive and seemingly lasting reverberations in the LDCs. Of course, third-wave transitions were most dramatic in the former Soviet Union and its Eastern European communist allies. Pictures of young Germans chopping at the Berlin Wall and of Boris Yeltsin facing down a military coup against Mikhail Gorbachev's reforms were among the most powerful political images of the late twentieth century. But in developing nations as diverse as South Africa, Mali, the Philippines, South Korea, Argentina, and Chile, years of authoritarian or semi-authoritarian rule were ending as well.

This wave of democratization, continued into the 1990s. Between 1988 and 1994 the number of electoral democracies in Africa rose from only 3 to 18.[20] In 1997, Mexico's PRI, the world's longest-ruling political party (after the fall of the Soviet Communist party), lost control of the principal house of Congress. And, the following year student demonstrators in Indonesia, the world's fourth most populous nation, toppled Asia's most enduring military dictator. The spread of electoral democracy has been impressive. As of 1974, only 27.5 percent of the world's nations allowed free and fair elections for national office. By 1996, however, that proportion had risen to 61 percent.[21]

INTERNATIONAL CAUSES AND CONSEQUENCES OF THE THIRD WAVE

Invariably, worldwide political changes of this magnitude are inspired and influenced by broad currents that transcend national boundaries. A number of factors contributed to the most recent democratic revolutions. For one thing, the economic crisis that devastated so many Third World countries in the 1980s revealed that authoritarian governments are no more effective and no less corrupt than the elected governments that they had earlier so contemptuously swept aside. Furthermore, because dictatorships lack the legitimacy that free elections bestow on democratic governments, their support depends much more heavily on satisfactory job performance. So when dictators in countries such as Argentina, Nigeria, and Peru dragged their country into war or economic decay, their support rapidly eroded. In Africa, the gross mismanagement and corruption of both military and single-party regimes caused their countries' economies to implode, as the continent's per capita GNP declined by some 2 percent annually in the 1980s. In Latin America, military rulers had a relatively good economic record in Chile and, for a period, in Brazil, but performed poorly elsewhere. In time, almost all of the region's authoritarian regimes were undermined by the 1980s debt crisis.

By contrast, many East Asian dictatorships—most notably South Korea's, Taiwan's, Indonesia's and Singapore's—enjoyed spectacular economic success until the continent's 1997 financial crisis. Ironically, however, rather than generate wider support for those governments, rapid economic growth and modernization generated a burgeoning middle class possessed of democratic aspirations and the political skills to pursue them. As in Africa and Latin America, this growing number of informed citizens were often incensed by the lack of opportunities for meaningful political participation, the scope of government repression, and the extent of state corruption.

Throughout the world, no sooner had democratic upheavals occurred in one nation than they then spread quickly to neighboring countries. In Eastern Europe, Poland's Solidarity movement inspired democratic efforts in Hungary, East Germany and what was then Czechoslovakia. They, in turn, prompted antigovernment protests in Bulgaria, Albania, and Romania. Students in South

Korea watched evening news stories on pro-Aquino demonstrations in the Philippines and took the lessons of people's power to heart. And in Latin America democratization in Brazil or Argentina had a contageous affect elsewhere.

As the democratic tidal wave swept forward, some authoritarian leaders began to get the message. Generals in Ecuador and Paraguay watched neighboring military dictatorships fall and decided to abdicate while the going was still good. After more than 40 years of political domination by the Chinese-mainland minority and authoritarian rule by the Guomindang party, Taiwan's government opened up the political system to authentic electoral competition and political freedom. In Africa, a number of single-party states liberalized their political systems—allowing more freedom and greater political space for opposition groups—while a few actually established electoral democracy.

As we have noted earlier, the demise of Soviet and Eastern European communism exposed more clearly the deficiencies of Marxism-Leninism. As communism was discredited, even among many of its once-fervent adherents, democracy assumed greater worldwide legitimacy. The end of the Cold War also permitted the United States to be more consistent in its defense of democracy. Thus the United States now has less reason to coddle friendly, Third World dictators whose support it had previously desired in the struggle against Soviet communism. For example, the United States had supported corrupt and repressive dictators such as Mobutu Sese Seko (Zaire), Ferdinand Marcos (the Philippines), Anastasio Somoza (Nicaragua), and the Shah of Iran because they were considered necessary allies in the Cold War. With the collapse of the Soviet Union there was no longer reason to stand by such rulers.

To be sure, the United States and Western Europe had already begun more actively championing Third World democratic reform in the years preceding the Soviet Union's fall. The Reagan administration, for example, reversed its initial support for Chile's military dictatorship and encouraged the reform-minded U.S. ambassador there to work closely with the democratic opposition. But the end of the Cold War allowed Washington to pursue its democratic agenda more aggressively. In the Caribbean—where the United States was once known for supporting notorious dictators such as Fulgencio Batista (Cuba), Rafael Trujillo (Dominican Republic), and "Papa Doc" Duvalier (Haiti)—President Bill Clinton threatened U.S. military intervention unless Haiti's generals allowed the country's ousted elected president, Jean Bertrand Aristide, to return to office.[22]

THE PREREQUISITES OF DEMOCRACY IN INDIVIDUAL COUNTRIES

While the international trends just discussed served as catalysts, providing developing countries with incentives and opportunities to democratize, they cannot explain important differences *between* Third World nations. At the close of the twentieth century (and 25 years after the start of the third wave), some LDCs—such as the Congo, Vietnam, and Myanmar—remain mired in dictatorship, with little or no opening in the political system to date. Others—such as El Salvador, Mozambique, and Thailand—are in some stage of democratic transition. And, finally, some fortunate countries (including Chile, Costa Rica, Botswana, Mauritius, South Korea, and Taiwan) seem to have consolidated their democracies.[23]

What accounts for these differences? What determines whether or not a specific country embarks on the road toward democracy, whether it completes that voyage successfully, and whether it eventually consolidates democratic values, practices, and institutions? For example, how do we know if democracy eventually will take root and survive in Brazil or Russia? Why is it that democratization has advanced further in Latin America than in Africa or the Middle East?

As with most fundamental questions about politics, there are no simple answers. Scholars have debated these issues for decades and have identified a number of historical, structural, and cultural variables that help account for democracy's presence in, say, India and Uruguay, and its absence in countries such as Syria and Laos. But these analysts still disagree about the relative importance of specific variables and about the minimum level for each which a country must attain in order to achieve democracy. In the discussion that follows, I will examine a number of factors that have been widely identified as prerequisites for democracy.

Social and Economic Modernization

Some 40 years ago, Seymour Martin Lipset observed that democracy was far more prevalent in industrialized countries, such as the Unites States and Sweden, than in poorer nations—a finding congruent with modernization theory (Chapter 1).[24] Subsequent research by a wide range of political scientists has supported that claim. The reasoning behind this relationship was that

> industrialization leads to increases in wealth, education, communication and equality; these developments are associated with a more moderate lower and upper class and a larger middle class, which is by nature moderate; and this in turn increases the probability of stable democratic forms of politics.[25]

Over the years, quantitative research has identified more precisely the particular aspects of modernization that promote democracy. Philips Cutright determined that when other factors are held constant, there is a strong correlation between a country's level of mass communications and its degree of democracy, stronger even than the correlation between economic development and democracy.[26] A free and active mass media and opportunities for citizens to exchange ideas, he reasoned, promote a free society. More recently Axel Hadenius, examining the influence of dozens of independent variables, found that democracy correlates most strongly with higher levels of literacy and education.[27] An educated population, it appears, is more likely to follow politics and to participate. It is also more capable of defending its own interests. One hopeful sign for the future of democracy in the Third World is the substantial growth of literacy in recent decades. For example, from 1965 to 1995, adult illiteracy in developing countries fell by half (with Third World literacy levels reaching nearly 70 percent).[28]

As we have noted, countries whose populations are over half literate are far more likely to sustain democracy than those that fall below that mark. Similarly, Mitchell Seligson found an income threshold for sustaining democracy. While that dollar amount has varied over the years (because of inflation and changing exchange rates), the point at which democracy became likely at the close of the 1990s was a per capita GNP of roughly $2,000.[29]

That does not mean that countries inevitably become more democratic as their economies develop. In fact, there is evidence that middle-income countries are frequently less stable and more prone to dictatorship.[30] For example, in the 1960s and 1970s, although South America's most industrialized countries (Argentina, Brazil, Chile, Uruguay) were ranked as upper-middle-income nations by the World Bank, their democratic governments were toppled by military dictatorships. These exceptions are quite important, but the global evidence still shows a correlation between economic development and democracy. In recent decades, for example, East Asia's rapid economic growth, higher literacy, and expanding middle classes promoted democratic transitions in South Korea, Thailand, and Taiwan. In Latin America, where levels of modernization are relatively high by Third World standards, democracy has been widely established since the close of the 1970s. Conversely, Africa, which is home to most of the world's poorest nations, has had far less democratic success.

Class Structure

Some scholars maintain that it is not economic growth per se that induces democracy but rather the way in which that growth affects a country's social structure. Consequently, they reason, economic development supports stable democracy only if it induces appropriate changes in the country's class structure.

Since the time of Aristotle, political theorists have linked democracy and political stability to the presence of a large and vibrant middle class. The middle class, they suggest, tends to be politically moderate and serves as a political bridge between the upper and lower classes. Its members also have the political and organizational skills necessary to create political parties and other important democratic institutions. So, in those countries where economic growth fails to create a politically independent and influential middle class, modernization does not necessarily buttress democracy and may even weaken it.

In fact, the independence and power of the emerging middle class have varied greatly between regions of the world that industrialized in different historical eras. For example, industrialization and urbanization produced a larger and more powerful middle class in Northern Europe than it did one century later in Latin America, where wealth and income were far more concentrated and the middle class correspondingly weaker and more dependent. Predictably, democracy did not take hold as readily in Latin America as it had in Northern Europe.

Barrington Moore, Jr., in his widely acclaimed study of economic and political change, *The Social Origins of Dictatorship and Democracy*, identified three discrete paths to modernization, each of them shaped by the relative power of the state (the national government apparatus) and the strength of significant social classes. In one path, typified by nineteenth- and early-twentieth-century Germany, modernization was led by a strong state allied with powerful (and antidemocratic) agricultural landowners and a bourgeoisie (business class) that was dependent on the state. For Germany and for Third World countries with a similar political configuration, that combination ultimately resulted in the rise of fascism (or other ultra-rightist, authoritarian regimes). A second path to modernization, found in countries such as China, featured a highly centralized state, a repressive landowning class, a weak bourgeoisie and, eventually, a rebellious peasantry. The end result of that alignment was a communist revolution fought by the peasantry.

Finally, Moore's third path, identified most closely with Britain, was distinguished by an internally divided state and a strong bourgeoisie that was at odds with the rural, landowning elite. Only this final alignment of forces, distinguished by the urban business class's (the bourgeoisie's) powerful and independent political role, has led to liberal democracy. "No bourgeoisie," Moore noted, "no democracy."[31] Similarly, in developing nations today, a vibrant middle class, including an influential bourgeoisie, is a necessary ingredient for establishing and consolidating democracy. It should come as no surprise, then, that in countries as diverse as Chile, the Philippines, and South Korea, middle-class citizens, including university students (often the children of the bourgeoisie), have been on the front lines in recent struggles for democracy. During the 1992 pro-democracy, street demonstrations that brought down Thailand's military government, student leaders could be seen using their cell phones to coordinate their protests (a far cry from Southeast Asia's peasant revolutions decades earlier).

Very poor countries such as Afghanistan, Haiti, Kenya, or Myanmar, whose middle classes are small and dependent on the state or on rural landlords, are far less likely to attain or maintain democracy. But it is also important to remember that even though a strong middle class and bourgeoisie are *necessary* for democracy, those groups are not always democratically oriented. For example, in pre-Nazi (Weimar) Germany, and in Argentina and Chile during the 1970s, as the middle class felt threatened by social unrest from below, it threw its support to fascist or other right-wing extremist dictatorships.

More recently, Rueschemeyer, Huber Stephens, and Stephens have focused attention on the importance of *organized labor* in building democracy. They argue that while the bourgeoisie, and the middle class generally, fostered democracy in Western Europe, Latin America, and the Caribbean, they usually favored a restricted form of democracy that enhanced their own political strength (vis-à-vis the upper class and the state) but also limited the political influence of the lower class. Consequently, countries have only achieved comprehensive democracy when, in addition to a large bourgeoisie, they also had a politically potent working class (organized into strong unions) pushing for broader political representation and increased social justice.

In summary, democracy tends to flourish best where economic modernization produces a politically influential and independent bourgeoisie/middle class and where labor unions effectively defend the interests of the working class. When those classes are small, weak, or politically dependent on authoritarian elements in society (such as large, rural landowners), democratic development is less likely.

Political Culture

In the final analysis, however, neither a country's level of socioeconomic development nor its class structure can fully explain successful or failed democratization. For example, during the early decades of the twentieth century Argentina was one of the most affluent nations on earth (far wealthier than Italy or Japan) with substantial middle and working classes. Yet, rather than develop into a liberal democracy, by the 1930s the country embarked on a half-century of recurring coups and military dictatorships. More recently, Singapore, South Korea, and Taiwan retained authoritarian governments for many years after their considerable socioeconomic development.[32] And, Middle-Eastern petroleum states such as Kuwait and Saudi Arabia have made little progress toward democracy despite their considerable economic wealth. On the other hand, India has sustained democracy for most of its fifty years despite its extensive poverty and low literacy rate.

Aside from its economic level, a nation's democratic potential is also influenced by its political culture—that is, its cultural norms and values relating to politics. A country's constitution may require contested elections, a free press, and the separation of powers. But, unless the people, especially elites and political activists, value these objectives, those constitutional protections are unlikely to hold up. Some of the most important values needed to sustain democracy include the conviction that voting and other forms of individual political participation are important and potentially productive; tolerance of dissenting political opinions and beliefs, even when those views are very unpopular; accepting the outcomes of fair elections as definitive, regardless of who wins; viewing politics as a process that requires compromise; commitment to democracy as the best form of government regardless of how well or poorly a particular democratic administration performs.

The recent wave of successful and failed democratic transitions has renewed interest in how a country's political culture affects it potential for consolidating democracy. Survey research now allows us to measure more precisely the nature of a nation's political beliefs. For example, surveys conducted after the collapse of the Soviet Union revealed that Russia had yet to develop a broadly based democratic political culture. Only one in eight Russians expressed confidence in

President Boris Yeltsin's postcommunist government. A substantial minority, distressed by Russia's economic decline, yearned for the security and stability of the communist era. And many respondents cared little for protecting civil liberties and minority rights. For example, almost one in three favored the death penalty for homosexuals and for prostitutes. A smaller, but still significant, number actually supported the execution of physically handicapped people.[33] Ordinary Russians have also been highly intolerant of ethnic minorities such as central Asians in their midst. And the country's political elite has manifested little spirit of compromise. One cause for optimism, however, is that younger Russians are more likely to endorse democratic values than are older ones.

To date, in spite of such authoritarian sentiment, Russian democracy has survived the test of severe economic hardship. But it remains on shaky ground. For example, in the 1995 parliamentary election, the two strongest political parties were the Communists and Liberal Democrats (contrary to its name, the latter is a racist, neofascist party). Both of them are contemptuous of democracy.

Robert Dahl, a renowned democratic theorist, observes that all political systems eventually confront a serious crisis (such as U.S. racial unrest in the 1960s, Russia's recent economic crisis, tribal violence in Nigeria). At those times, political leaders in unconsolidated democracies are often tempted to seek authoritarian solutions such as limiting civil liberties or imposing martial law. But, if a broad segment of the population, including political elites, share democratic values—that is, if a democratic political culture has begun to take root in society—democracy can survive the crisis in tact. Dahl stresses two particularly important democratic values: First, the armed forces and police must willingly submit to the control of democratically elected civilian authorities; second, government and society must tolerate and legally protect dissident political beliefs. The first belief (civilian control of the military) is taken for granted in industrialized democracies, but not in countries such as Argentina, Guatemala, Nigeria, and Thailand, where the armed forces have long exercised veto power over the policy decisions of elected officials. Even in a relatively consolidated democracy such as contemporary Chile, the military still insists on substantial autonomy. Dahl's second cultural standard (tolerance of dissent) also presents a challenge to many developing countries where even freely elected governments often silence critics and muzzle opposition leaders.

The crucial question then, says Dahl, is: "How can robust democratic cultures be created in countries where they previously have been largely absent?"[34] He responds that there is no easy answer—developing a democratic culture is a gradual process in which socioeconomic modernization and political development need to mutually reinforce each other.

Sometimes, external actors may promote or even impose a democratic political culture on another country, as U.S. occupation forces did in Japan after World War II. Many African and Asian countries were first introduced to modern politics by the colonial powers that controlled them. Statistical analysis of developing countries reveals that one of the variables most closely associated with democratic government is having once been a British colony.[35] Of course, not all former British colonies are democracies (in fact, most of those in Africa are not). But, in general, countries that experienced British rule were far more likely to maintain democracy after independence than were those nations previously colonized by France, Belgium, Spain, or Portugal. This suggests that Britain more successfully inculcated its colonies with democratic values than did other European powers.

It seems obvious that a country's political culture influences its political system in some manner. For example, communities with high levels of mutual tolerance and those whose citizens actively follow politics are more hospitable to democracy than are less tolerant or knowledgeable societies. But how fixed in a nation's psyche are such values? Is there something inherently more democratic or more authoritarian about Norwegian, French, or Chinese cultures? Are some religions, such as Christianity, more conducive to democracy than, say, Hinduism? Here we find scholars disagreeing strongly.

Cultural stereotypes are inherently controversial and are sometimes prejudiced. But, is it not possible that careful and objective analysis might show that countries with certain religions or cultural traditions are more likely to support democratic values while others are more prone to authoritarianism? In fact we do find that predominantly Christian nations, particularly Protestant ones, are more likely to be democratic than are countries with other dominant religions, even when other possible causal factors (such as economic development or literacy) are held constant. "Protestantism is said to foster individual responsibility and is . . . thereby also more skeptical and less fundamentalist in character."[36]

More recently, observers have noted democracy's poor track record in Islamic countries, especially in the Middle East. Some maintain that Islam does not readily support democratic institutions because it fails to separate religion and politics, church, and state. Similarly, when impressive economic growth and increased educational levels during the 1970s and early 1980s failed to bring democracy to China, Singapore, South Korea and Taiwan, some experts concluded that cultural constraints must be overriding the positive influences of economic modernization. They argued that Confucian culture promotes rigidly hierarchical societies and encourages excessive obedience to authority, both of which are antithetical to democracy.[37]

Not surprisingly, cultural explanations such as these are very controversial. They are very difficult to prove and often smack of ethnocentrism and prejudice. Thus, Catholics naturally feel uneasy with theories that contrast the traditional strength of democracy in the United States, Canada, and the English-speaking Caribbean with Latin America's authoritarian tradition and suggest that Catholic values are inherently more authoritarian than Protestant norms.[38] Similarly, most Muslims and Confucianists reject theories that depict their religions as authoritarian. But do the facts support these hypotheses, however unpleasant some people may find them?

As we have noted, there is no question that Protestant nations are more likely to be democratic than are countries with other religions. Similarly, democracy certainly has not fared well in most Islamic nations. But it is difficult to ascertain how much of these disparities reflect different religious values rather than a myriad of other historical, economic, and cultural factors that are not easily controlled for. We know that some Islamic cultures *have* sustained democracy. Malaysia, for example, is among Asia's most stable democracies. And, in democracies with multiple religions, Muslims are no less democratic that their fellow citizens who belong to other religions. Thus, the Muslims of India and Trinidad-Tobago are apparently as committed to democratic values as are their Hindu and Christian counterparts (just as American Catholics are as democratically inclined as Protestants are). And, Bosnia's Muslim population clearly has shown more respect for basic civil liberties and democratic institutions than their Serbian Christian adversaries.

Even if it could be established that certain religions tend to predispose a population toward democracy or authoritarianism, there is so much variation within particular world religions (for example, Unitarians and Southern Baptists or the Shi'ia, Sunni, and Sufi branches of Islam), each with a distinct political culture, that it sheds little light to depict Protestant, Muslim, or Buddhist cultures as uniform.

Finally, and most importantly, religions and national cultures are capable of change and do not permanently mire a country or region in a particular political culture. During World War II it was widely believed that Japanese and German cultures were inherently war-like and authoritarian. Today these countries are highly consolidated democracies whose citizens are more likely to support disarmament or pacifism than are Americans. Not long ago many analysts felt that Confucian values blocked democratic transitions in East Asia. Yet, Confucianism has not impeded South Korea's and Taiwan's democratization. The fact that Catholic societies were less hospitable to democracy in the past does not mean that their political values haven't changed. Indeed, from Portugal and Spain to Argentina, Brazil and Uruguay, democracy has recently taken root in Catholic nations that not long ago were depicted as culturally authoritarian. Moreover, in recent decades the Church hierarchy itself has been a pivotal voice for democratic change in Poland, the Philippines, Chile, Brazil, and other Catholic countries.

In short, political cultures appear to be far more malleable than previously recognized. And, as Larry Diamond notes, often "democratic culture is as much the product as the cause of effectively functioning democracy."[39] Just as a democratic political culture helps to consolidate democracy, sustained democratic behavior helps society absorb democratic values.

So, while it may be difficult for some countries to develop a democratic political culture initially, the longer they continue democratic practices, the better are their chances of absorbing democratic values. Indeed, Robert Dahl's examination of 52 countries in which democracy had collapsed identified only two

(Chile and Uruguay) that had enjoyed democracy for more than 20 years prior to that collapse.[40] And even those two exceptions have since more successfully reinstituted democracy than have countries such as Bolivia and Peru that lack comparable democratic traditions. Similarly, the Czech Republic has enjoyed the same advantage over its Eastern European neighbors.

CONCLUSION: DEMOCRATIC CONSOLIDATION

What makes democracy endure? Now that a substantial number of developing countries have become democratic, which ones have the qualities to maintain and consolidate democracy? To answer that question, Adam Przeworski and his associates analyzed statistics covering a 40-year period (1950–1990) from 135 different countries.[41] Democracy, they found, is most fragile in poor countries (with per capita incomes of under $1,000) and becomes more stable as national income rises. "Above $6,000 [per capita income], democracies are impregnable and can be expected to live forever; no democratic system has ever fallen in a country where per-capita income exceeds $6,055 (Argentina's level in 1976)."[42] Several factors explain why richer democracies are more stable. For one thing, they have a crucial foundation for democratic government, higher educational levels. For another, interclass conflicts over the distribution of economic rewards are less intense in more affluent societies.

Przeworski and colleagues found that other economic indicators are also important. Contrary to the beliefs of many political scientists, the faster a nation's economy grows, the more likely it is to sustain democracy. Conversely, democracies suffering economic declines, high inflation rates, or other forms of economic crisis (such as the Russian ruble's collapse in 1998) are the most likely to become derailed from democratic consolidation.

Finally, the authors found that, surprisingly, international conditions exert a more powerful influence over a country's chances for democratic survival than do domestic economic factors. Specifically, the more prevalent and fashionable democratic government becomes worldwide, the more likely any particular Third World country is to sustain democracy, regardless of its per capita income, literacy level, or economic growth rate. In other words, as many scholars have suspected, democracy is contagious.

Other analysts have noted that developing and maintaining effective political institutions—representative and responsible political parties, a broad array of interest groups, a representative and influential legislature, a strong but controlled executive branch, an honest and independent court system—are absolutely critical for stable and effective democracy. Too often Third World judicial systems are insufficiently independent from the executive branch, have inadequate legal training, and are excessively corrupt. Consolidating democracies need to strengthen the judiciary so that it can stand up to a power-hungry president or prime minister and so that its decisions are respected by citizens.

Similarly, the legislative branch in many new democracies is too dependent on an overly powerful executive. Even democratically elected leaders often appropriate excessive power upon taking office, assuming that the voters had, in effect, delegated to them absolute authority to govern the country. For example, although elected democratically, upon assuming office presidents Carlos Menem (Argentina) and Alberto Fujimori (Peru) ran roughshod over their nation's congress and court system. Partly for that reason, Juan Linz has found that democracy is more likely to collapse in presidential systems than in countries with parliamentary forms of government.[43]

Finally, emerging democracies need to address serious social and economic injustices that threaten democratic consolidation. Without improved social conditions, democratic government may be unable to continue commanding the support of society's less fortunate. In Latin America, where income inequality is high by world standards, the gap between "haves" and "have nots" has generally widened since that region's recent transition to democracy (with the notable exception of Uruguay). Similarly, the divide between rich and poor has widened greatly in the newly democratizing countries of Eastern Europe and the former Soviet Union. In that region, much of the deterioration has been caused by an economic transition from communism to a very corrupt form of "crony capitalism." Watching the corrupt and powerful, new business tycoons use their government ties to accumulate vast wealth, some 30 percent of Russians apparently yearn for the greater economic security and equality of the old communist regime, no matter how repressive that political system was and no matter how shoddy the quality of consumer goods.

From the Philippines to Pakistan, from Colombia to Peru, the urban and rural poor suffer from highly unequal land and income distribution, pervasive poverty and crime, deficient public health systems, and corrupt and repressive local police. Until such injustices are addressed, democracy will remain incomplete and precarious.

DISCUSSION QUESTIONS

1. Discuss the differences between electoral democracy, liberal democracy, and substantive democracy. Which definition seems most useful to you.

2. What is the "third wave" of democracy and what accounts for its emergence?

3. Which social classes have historically been most supportive of democracy and which have been most antagonistic? What kind of class structure is most likely to support democratic consolidation?

4. What is the evidence that some religions are more supportive of democracy than are others? What are the strengths and weaknesses of the argument that there is a link between a country's religion and its potential for democracy?

5. What is the relationship between social and economic development, on the one hand, and political democracy, on the other?

NOTES

1. Richard Joseph, "Africa: The Rebirth of Political Freedom," in *The Global Resurgence of Democracy*, ed. Larry Diamond and Marc F. Plattner (Baltimore, MD: Johns Hopkins University Press, 1993), pp. 307–320. In retrospect, Joseph's chapter was overly optimistic about Africa's progress toward democracy.

2. By definition, consolidation of democracy reduces military rule. It also lowers the likelihood of revolutionary movements. And, greater democracy should eventually contribute to better conditions for women, the urban poor, and peasants, though those efforts are not always apparent.

3. For example, Samuel P. Huntington, *The Third Wave: Democratization in the Late Twentieth Century* (Norman: University of Oklahoma Press, 1991).

4. Colombia is one of Latin America's more enduring electoral democracies, but its government is currently viewed as perhaps the region's worst human rights violator. See *New York Times* (April 26, 1994).

5. Of course, in all democracies some major officials are appointed, such as the justices of the U.S. Supreme Court and members of the American president's cabinet. But those people are appointed by a popularly elected official (the president) and are subject to confirmation by the Congress.

6. If this standard is rigorously applied, the United States could not be considered a full democracy prior to the 1960s because large numbers of southern Blacks were barred from voting.

7. There has been a long, ongoing debate over what conditions, and how many of those conditions, a country must meet in order to be called a democracy. The definition offered here represents the current consensus and is drawn from the following sources: Philippe C. Schmitter and Terry Lynn Karl, "What Democracy Is . . . and Is Not," *Journal of Democracy* 2, no. 2 (Summer 1991): p. 75–88; Scott Mainwaring, "Transitions to Democracy and Democratic Consolidation," in *Issues in Democratic Consolidation: The New South American Democracies in Comparative Perspective*, ed. Scott Mainwaring, Guillermo O'Donnell, and Samuel Valenzuela (Notre Dame, IN: University of Notre Dame Press, 1992), pp. 297–298; Robert A. Dahl, *Polyarchy: Participation and Opposition* (New Haven, CT: Yale University Press, 1971); Robert A. Dahl, *Democracy and Its Critics* (New Haven, CT: Yale University Press, 1989); Samuel P. Huntington, *The Third Wave*.

8. Civil society is essentially the array of societal organizations—such as churches, unions, business groups, farmers' organizations, women's groups, and the like—that influence the political system but operate *independently* of government control. Typically, authoritarian governments attempt to weaken civil society (trying to place these groups under government control). So, rebuilding and strengthening civil society becomes an essential task for establishing and consolidating democratic government.

9. Huntington, *The Third Wave*, pp. 28–30.

10. Juan Linz and Alfred Stepan, "Toward Consolidated Democracies," in *Consolidating the Third Wave Democracies*, ed. Larry Diamond, Marc F. Plattner, Yun-han Chu, and Hung-mao Tien (Baltimore, MD: Johns Hopkins University Press, 1997), p. 15.

11. Seymour Martin Lipset, *Political Man: The Social Basis of Politics*, new ed. (Baltimore, MD: Johns Hopkins University Press, 1980); For a review of such research see Dietrich Rueschemeyer, Evelyne Huber Stephens, and John D. Stephens, *Capitalist Development and Democracy* (Chicago: University of Chicago Press, 1992), Chapter 2.

12. Samuel P. Huntington, *Political Order in Changing Societies* (New Haven, CT: Yale University Press, 1968).

13. Mitchell A. Seligson, "Democratization in Latin America: The Current Cycle" in *Authoritarians and Democrats: Regime Transition in Latin America*, ed. James M. Malloy and Mitchell A. Seligson (Pittsburgh, PA: University of Pittsburgh Press, 1987), pp. 7–9.

14. It is generally agreed that the emergence of the middle class and business class (bourgeoisie) in Western Europe was associated with the growth of modern democracy. See, for example, Barrington Moore, Jr., *The Social Origins of Dictatorship and Democracy* (Boston: Beacon Press, 1966); More recently, political scientists such as Rueschemeyer, Stephens, and Stephens, *Capitalist Development* have emphasized the contributions of organized labor.

15. Of course even defenders of authoritarian governments had to concede that most dictatorships are not efficient modernizers, far from it. The developing world has had more than its share of corrupt dictators (Mobutu in Zaire, Somoza in Nicaragua, Marcos in the Philippines) who have stolen millions, run their country's economy into the ground, and wrecked the nation's infrastructure and educational system. What these scholars did claim, however, was that *efficient* dictatorships such as Taiwan's or Singapore's offered the best hope for modernization. Communists, of course, saw revolutionary dictatorships such as Cuba's or China's as necessary for greater social equality, improved literacy, better health care systems, and related indicators of modernization.

16. For example, Glen Caudill Dealy, *The Latin Americans, Spirit and Ethos* (Boulder, CO: Westview Press, 1992);. The ground breaking study of political culture was Gabriel A. Almond and Sidney Verba, *The Civic Culture: Political Attitudes and Democracy in Five Nations* (Boston: Little Brown and Company, 1965) which examined political culture in the United States, Britain, Germany, Italy and Mexico.

17. Larry Diamond, "Introduction: In Search of Consolidation," in *Consolidating the Third Wave Democracies*, p. xv. The earlier figure as well as most other tallies of democracies found in this chapter come from surveys published annually by Freedom House in their report *Freedom in the World*. While Diamond suggests there were 39 democracies, Samuel Huntington counted only 30 at that time. Huntington's lower total partially reflects the fact that he did not consider countries with a population of under 1 million.

18. Huntington, *The Third Wave*, p. 271. That figure includes Turkey which I have characterized as a less developed country.

19. Huntington, *The Third Wave*.

20. Larry Diamond, *Prospects for Democratic Development in Africa* (Stanford, CA: Hoover Institution Press, 1997), Appendix. Here again, democracy was rarely fully implemented or deeply entrenched and a number of these electoral democracies have since collapsed.

21. Larry Diamond, "Introduction: In Search of Consolidation," *Consolidating the Third Wave Democracies*, p. xvi.

22. For a broader discussion on international influences favoring democratization, see Laurence Whitehead, ed., *The International Dimensions of Democratization: Europe and the Americas* (New York: Oxford University Press, 1996); Abraham F. Lowenthal, ed., *Exporting Democracy: The United States and Latin America* (Baltimore, MD: Johns Hopkins University Press, 1991).

23. Determining whether democracy has been consolidated (has become "the only game in town") in any particular country is a judgment call, over which experts may disagree. Only the test of time ultimately determines whether or not a democratic government endures.

24. Seymour Martin Lipset, *Political Man*, 1st ed. (Garden City, NY: Anchor Books, 1960).

25. Rueschemeyer, Huber Stephens, and Stephens, *Capitalist Development and Democracy*, p. 14.

26. Philips Cutright, "National Political Development: Measurement and Analysis," *American Sociological Review* 28 (April 1963).

27. Axel Hadenius, *Democracy and Development* (New York: Cambridge University Press, 1992).

28. UNDP, *Human Development Report 1997* (New York: Oxford University Press, 1997), pp. 24–26.

29. Seligson, "Democratization in Latin America: The Current Cycle."

30. Huntington, *Political Order in Changing Societies.* On the rise of repressive, authoritarian regimes in Latin America's most industrialized nations, see Guillermo O'Donnell, *Modernization and Bureaucratic Authoritarianism* (Berkeley, CA: Institute of International Studies, 1973).

31. Barrington Moore, *The Social Origins*, p. 418.

32. South Korea and Taiwan have subsequently democratized but Singapore still has not.

33. Stephen White, "Russia's Experiment with Democracy," *Current History* 91 (October 1992): 313.

34. Robert Dahl, "Development and Democratic Culture," in *Consolidating the Third Wave Democracies*, p. 34.

35. Kenneth A. Bollen and Robert Jackman, "Economic and Non-economic Determinants of Political Democracy in the 1960s," in *Research in Political Sociology,* ed. R.G. Braungart (Greenwich, CT: Jai Press, 1985).

36. Hadenius, *Democracy and Development*, pp. 118–119.

37. Samuel P. Huntington, "Will More Countries be Democratic?" *Political Science Quarterly* 99 (1984): 193–218; Huntington, *The Clash of Civilizations and the Remaking of World Order* (New York: Simon & Schuster, 1996).

38. For an argument along those lines see Dealy, *The Latin Americans.*

39. Larry Diamond, "Three Paradoxes of Democracy," in *The Global Resurgence of Democracy*, p. 104.

40. Robert A. Dahl, "The Newer Democracies: From the Time of Triumph to the Time of Troubles," in Daniel N. Nelson, ed., *After Authoritarianism: Democracy or Disorder?* (Westport, CT: Greenwood Press, 1995), p. 7.

41. Adam Przeworski et al., "What Makes Democracies Endure," in Larry Diamond et al., eds., *Consolidating Third Wave Democracies*, pp. 295–311.

42. Ibid., p. 297.

43. Juan Linz and Arturo Valenzuela, eds., *The Failure of Presidential Democracy.* (Baltimore, MD: Johns Hopkins University Press, 1994).

GLOSSARY

Agrarian reform Distribution of land to needy peasants as well as government support programs that are needed to make beneficiaries economically viable.

Ancien régime The old political order. The term is often used to describe a decaying regime threatened or ousted by a revolutionary movement.

Apparatchik A career bureaucrat in the Soviet government. Often used more broadly to refer to a bureaucrat whose primary interest is in protecting his/her authority and perquisites.

Authoritarian system A political system which limits or prohibits opposition groups and otherwise restricts political activity and expression.

Baht The Thai national currency.

Barrio A poor urban neighborhood in Latin America or the Philippines.

Bourgeoisie A Marxist term (also used by non-Marxist scholars) for those who own society's productive resources, most notably businessmen.

Bureaucratic-authoritarian regimes Military dictatorships, found most often in Latin American's more developed countries, that were based on an alliance between the military, government bureaucrats, local business elites, and multinational corporations.

Capital goods (or equipment) Goods, such as machinery, that are used for further production rather than for consumption.

Capital-intensive production Industrial or agricultural production that relies heavily on machinery and technology rather than on human labor.

Caretaker government An interim government (sometimes military) which steps in to restore order but plans to retire relatively quickly.

Caste system A rigid social hierarchy in which individuals are born with a status which they retain regardless of their education or achievement.

Chaebols The powerful industrial conglomerates that dominate the South Korean economy.

Christian (or Ecclesial) Base Communities (CEBs) Small, Catholic, neighborhood groups in Latin America that discuss religious questions and community problems. Commonly located in poor neighborhoods, many CEBs were politicized and radicalized in the 1960s and 1970s.

Civic action programs Development programs (such as road or school construction) carried out by the military.

Civil society The network of organized groups that are relatively independent of state control.

Class consciousness A measure of how much a social class (such as workers, peasants, or the middle class) view themselves as having common goals that are distinct from, and often opposed to, the needs of other classes.

Clientelism The dispensing of public resources by political power holders or seekers who offer them as favors in exchange for votes or other forms of support.

Collective farming (collectivization) Joint farming activity by a peasant community, state farm, or cooperative of some sort. In communist countries, the government often collectivized farming against the wishes of the rural population.

Colonization Asserting control over a previously independent region. Also used to describe the settlement of tropical forests or other previously uninhabited areas by migrating farmers or large agricultural operations.

Coloureds A South African term coined during the period of White rule to describe people of mixed racial background.

Command economy An economy in which most of the means of production are owned and managed by the state and in which prices and production decisions are determined by state planners.

Commercialization of agriculture The process whereby subsistence farmers (i.e., those raising largely for their own family consumption) convert, sometimes unwillingly, to farming for the commercial market.

Communal Politics (Communalism) Politics that have a strong ethnic base and often involve conflict between ethnicities.

Comparative advantage Those economic activities that a country can engage in most efficiently and cheaply relative to other nations.

Consociationalism A division of political power between formerly antagonistic groups (such as ethnicities) based on power sharing, limited autonomy, and mutual vetoes.

Consumer subsidies Payments made by the state that allow consumers to purchase goods at prices below their free market value.

Core nations The richer, industrial nations of the world.

Correlation A tendency of two or more factors (variables) to change in the same direction. For example, higher income correlates with greater education. Negative correlations move in opposite directions (e.g., alcoholism and education).

Coup d'etat (coup) A seizure of political power by the military.

Crony capitalism A corrupt form of capitalist development in which powerful, well-connected businessmen use their government ties to accumulate vast wealth.

Cultural pluralism A diversity of ethnic groups.

Culture of poverty A sense of powerless and fatalism allegedly commonly found among the urban poor.

Currency exchange rates The value of a nation's currency relative to major currencies such as the dollar or yen.

Democratic consolidation The process through which democratic norms (democratic "rules of the game") become accepted by all powerful groups in society, including labor, business, rural landlords, the church, and the military.

Democratic transition The process of moving from an authoritarian regime to a democratic one.

Devaluation (of a nation's currency) Allowing a currency which was previously overvalued [relative to the dollar and other "hard" (stable) currencies] to decline in value. This is normally done to correct a negative trade balance in which the value of imports exceeds exports.

Developmental state A state that intervenes actively in the economy in order to guide or promote particular economic development goals such as full employment.

Dirty war The military's mass violation of human rights during their fight against subversive groups in countries such as Argentina and Peru.

Double day The burden facing working women who continue to carry out most of the family's domestic responsibilities (cooking, child care, etc.) while also working outside the home.

Economic disincentives Economic policies or practices that discourage desired outcomes such as government-enforced, low food prices that discourage agricultural production.

Economies of scale Economic efficiencies achieved through large-scale operations.

Ejido Communal farms in Mexico that were given special status under the country's agrarian reform programs.

Employer of last resort An employer (normally the state) that hires people who can find no other employment.

EOI *See* export-oriented industrialization.

Ethnicity or ethnic group A group that feels it has common traditions, beliefs, values, and history which unite it and distinguish it from other cultures.

Export-Oriented Industrialization (EOI) An industrialization model heavily tied to exporting manufactured goods.

Federalism A government form that divides power between the national government and smaller governing units.

Fundamentalism A theological doctrine that seeks to preserve a religion's traditional world-view and to resist any efforts by religious liberals to reform it. It also frequently seeks to revive the role of religion in private and public life, including dress, lifestyle, and politics.

GDP *See* gross domestic product.

Gender Development Index (GDI) An index measuring a country's key social indicators (literacy, income, life expectancy) for women as compared to men.

Gender Empowerment Measure (GEM) An index of women's political empowerment based on the proportion of women holding national political offices.

Gender gap A systematic difference in social status or achievement between men and women (e.g. income).

GNP *See* gross national product

Great Leap Forward China's effort (1958—1961) to accelerate economic development rapidly by extracting tremendous sacrifices from the population.

Green movement The political movement seeking to preserve the environment.

Green revolution Dramatic increases in grain production due to improved seeds and other technological breakthroughs in the Third World (most notably in Asia).

Greenhouse effect (greenhouse gases) Carbon gases produced by burning fossil fuels. They threaten to warm the world's climate dangerously by limiting the dispersion of heat from the atmosphere.

Gross Domestic Product (GDP) A measure of a nation's production that excludes certain financial transfers normally included in GNP.

Gross National Product (GNP) A measure of a nation's total production (see gross domestic product).

Gross Real Domestic Product Gross domestic product as measured by purchasing power rather than currency exchange.

Gulags Internment camps for political prisoners. Originating in the Soviet Union, the term is also used to describe other repressive systems.

Hacienda A Latin America agricultural estate which, until recently, often included precapitalist labor relations.

HDI *See* Human Development Index.

Historical dialectic A marxist term used to describe the ongoing tension between particular forces in history.

Human Development Index (HDI) A composite measure of educational level, life expectancy, per capita GDP, and income distribution.

Import-Substituting Industrialization (ISI) A policy of industrial development designed to manufacture goods domestically that were previously imported.

Informal sector The part of the economy that is unregulated by the government or society while similar activities are regulated and taxed.

Infrastructure The underlying structures—such as transportation, communication, and agricultural irrigation—that are needed for effective production.

Internal warfare Military action aimed at controlling guerrilla unrest or other civil insurrection rather than against an external enemy.

Invisible hand The capitalist notion that the good of society is advanced most effectively when individual actors (e.g., business people, workers) seeks to maximize their own economic advantage.

Iron Rice Bowl The Chinese government's policy of guaranteeing employment and a basic living standard to its population.

ISI *See* Import-Substituting Industrialization.

Jihad An Islamic holy war.

Khemer Rouge The communist movement in Kampuchea (Cambodia).

Kulaks Wealthier peasants. Originally a term used in Russia, but later applied more broadly.

Labor-intensive industry Industries that make extensive use of human labor as opposed to machinery and technology.

Laissez faire A policy of minimal state intervention in the economy.

Latifundia Large agricultural estates.

Liberalization of the economy Reducing the degree of state intervention in the economy (referring to the eighteenth-century classical liberalism of Adam Smith).

Liberated zones Areas (most notably in the countryside) controlled by the revolutionary army. Used commonly in China and Vietnam.

Liberation theology A reformist interpretation of Catholic doctrine that stresses the emancipation of the poor.

Lost decade The decade of the 1980s during which Africa and Latin America suffered severe economic declines.

Machismo Male chauvinism (used particularly in Latin America).

Macroeconomic policy Economic policies that affect society as a whole.

Maquiladoras Mexican assembly plants that import parts from the United States and export assembled goods.

Marginal population Those excluded from the mainstream of the nation's political and economic life.

Market socialism A hybrid of Marxist economics and free enterprise that has been adopted by countries such as China.

Mass mobilization The process whereby large segments of the population become activated politically. Governments or revolutionary movements may choose to mobilize the population.

Mestizos Persons of mixed Indian and European cultural heritage (Latin America).

MNC *See* Multinational Corporations.

Moral economy The web of economic and moral obligations that bind a social unit together. Often used in reference to peasant-landlord relations in the countryside.

Mujahadeen Islamic freedom fighters or guerrillas.

Multinational corporations Corporations with holdings and operations in a number of countries. Overwhelmingly based in the developed world, many of them exercise considerable economic power in the Third World.

Nationality A population with its own language, cultural traditions, and historical aspirations that frequently claims sovereignty over a particular territory.

Neocolonialism Economic and cultural dominance of one sovereign nation over another.

Neoclassical economics Economic theory that supports a free market and very limited state economic intervention.

New social movements Grass-roots reformist movements that are free of traditional political party ties or class-based ideologies.

New world order A vision of world order under U.S. direction that many had expected to follow the collapse of the Soviet bloc and the end of the Cold War.

NIC (Newly-Industrialized Country) Countries in East Asia and Latin America (e.g., Taiwan, Mexico) that have developed a substantial industrial base in recent decades.

Nurturing professions Occupations such as teaching and nursing that are commonly filled by women and that involve roles commonly associated with motherhood.

Parastatals Semi-autonomous, state-run enterprises.

Patron-client relations Relations between more powerful figures (patrons) and less powerful ones (clients) involving a series of reciprocal obligations that benefit both sides, but are more advantageous to the patron.

People's war The term used by Chinese leader Mao Zedong and others to describe mass-based guerrilla struggles.

Perestroika The restructuring of Soviet society (most notably its economy) by President Mikhail Gorbachev.

Periphery Third World countries. They are commonly seen by dependency theorists as occupying a lesser rank in the international economy.

Pirate settlement Low-income urban settlements whose members have purchased their lots but lack legal title.

Pluralist democracy A form of government that allows a wide variety of groups and viewpoints to flourish independent of government control.

Political culture The set of political beliefs and values that underlie a society's political system.

Populism A multiclass, reformist political movement which promises increased welfare programs for the poor and middle class but rejects a basic restructuring of the economic order. Third World populist movements are often led by a charismatic (and sometimes demagogic) political leader.

Praetorian politics Politics lacking in legitimate authority, leaving competing groups in society to use whatever resources they have at their disposal (including violence, bribery etc.).

Private sector The sector of the economy that is owned by individuals or private companies.

Privatization The process of transferring to the private sector portions of the economy formerly owned by the state.

Procedural democracy Standards of democracy based on political procedures (such as free elections) rather than outcomes (such as social justice).

Professionalized military A military whose officers receive a high degree of professional training.

Progressive church The reformist and radical wings of the Catholic Church (primarily in Latin America).

Proletariat The working class (blue-collar workers).

Public sector The sector of the economy belonging to the state.

Reconciliation approach A more contemporary perspective of modernization theory which holds that it is possible for LDCs to simultaneously attain some development goals that were previously considered incompatible, at least in the short run (such as early economic growth and equitable income distribution).

Relative deprivation The gap between an individual or group's expectations or desires and their actual achievement.

Responsibility system China's policy of transferring collective farm land to peasant owners.

Revivalism Attempts to restore traditional religious practices and, sometimes, to revive the role of religion in politics.

Rupiah The Indonesian national currency.

Secularization The separation of Church and state and, more generally, the removal of religion from politics.

Shantytown A community of poor homes or shacks built by the inhabitants. Unlike slums, they are generally in outlying urban areas rather than the central city.

Sites and services Housing arrangements in which the state sells or gives each inhabitant a legal plot with basic services (such as electricity and water), leaving the recipients to build their own home.

Smallholder Peasants owning small plots of land.

Social Mobility The ability to move from one rank or social class in society to another.

Spontaneous shelter Urban housing built by the occupant.

Squatter settlement Communities built by the poor who illegally or semilegally occupy unused land.

Stabilization programs Government programs, often imposed by the International Monetary Fund (IMF), seeking to cut deeply budget and trade deficits. The purpose is to reduce inflation and stabilize the currency.

Sub-Saharan Africa Countries in Africa below the northern tier of Arab nations. Also called Black Africa.

Subsidized housing Housing provided by the state at prices below their market value.

Substantive democracy Standards of democracy that measure government policy outcomes, such as literacy and health levels or socioeconomic equality, not just democratic procedures (as distinguished from procedural democracy).

Sustainable development Economic development that "consumes resources to meet [this generation's] needs and aspirations in a way that does not compromise the ability of future generations to meet their needs."

Technocrat A government bureaucrat with a substantial degree of technical training.

Theocracy (theocratic state) A state run by religious clergy or their allies. Church and state are joined tightly.

Third Wave The widespread transition from authoritarian to democratic government that has taken place in the Third World and Eastern Europe since the mid-1970s.

Third World Countries Less developed countries in Africa, Asia, Latin America, and the Middle East.

Traditional Societies Societies that adhere to longstanding values and customs which have not been extensively transformed by modernization.

Tribe Subnational groups which share a collective identity and language and who believe themselves to hold a common lineage.

War of national liberation Wars of independence fought against colonial powers.

INDEX